A Farm Family on
Long Island's North Fork

A Farm Family on Long Island's North Fork

The Lost World of the Hallocks and Their Sound Avenue Community

RICHARD A. WINES

SUNY
PRESS

Cover photo by Bessie Hallock showing the "kitchen end" of the Hallock Homestead in 1924 with her parents Emilie and Halsey Hallock (seated), her cousin Minnie Hallock (with washing machine planter), and her sister Ella Hallock (standing in doorway). Courtesy of Hallockville Museum Farm.

Published by State University of New York Press, Albany

© 2024 State University of New York

All rights reserved

Printed in the United States of America

No part of this book may be used or reproduced in any manner whatsoever without written permission. No part of this book may be stored in a retrieval system or transmitted in any form or by any means including electronic, electrostatic, magnetic tape, mechanical, photocopying, recording, or otherwise without the prior permission in writing of the publisher.

Links to third-party websites are provided as a convenience and for informational purposes only. They do not constitute an endorsement or an approval of any of the products, services, or opinions of the organization, companies, or individuals. SUNY Press bears no responsibility for the accuracy, legality, or content of a URL, the external website, or for that of subsequent websites.

For information, contact State University of New York Press, Albany, NY
www.sunypress.edu

Library of Congress Cataloging-in-Publication Data

Name: Wines, Richard A., author.
Title: A farm family on Long Island's North Fork : The lost lorld of the Hallocks and their sound avenue community / Richard A. Wines.
Description: Albany : State University of New York Press, [2024] | Includes bibliographical references and index.
Identifiers: ISBN 9781438499833 (hardcover : alk. paper) | ISBN 9781438499840 (ebook) | ISBN 9781438499826 (pbk. : alk. paper)
Further information is available at the Library of Congress.

*To my Mother,
who started me on this journey
with a seventh-grade research paper.*

Contents

List of Illustrations	ix
List of Abbreviations	xiii
Acknowledgments	xv
Introduction	1
1. The Family Attic	9
2. The Young Halsey Hallock	29
3. Love, War, and Death: Daniel, Halsey, and the Civil War	53
4. Last Family in the Homestead: 1866–1885	67
5. Scandals in the Church	83
6. Life in the Homestead: 1885–1920	105
7. The Hallock Farm	129
8. Sound Avenue Prosperity	151
9. Love, Courtship, and Marriage on Sound Avenue	185
10. Holidays and Entertainment	201

11. What Did the Hallocks Eat? 221

12. Retirement and Old Age 239

13. Last Decades in the Homestead: 1939–1979 257

14. Epilogue: Hallockville Museum Farm, Keyspan Project, Hallock State Park 273

Appendix: Guide to the Hallocks 281

Notes 289

Bibliography 315

Index 319

Illustrations

Figure I.1.	Bessie Hallock's photograph of Sound Avenue, approx. 1930, in front of the Hallock Homestead.	2
Figure I.2.	Map of the Village of Sound Avenue, 1920–1929.	3
Figure I.3.	Bessie's photograph of the Hallock farmstead as it appeared in the 1920s.	6
Figure 1.1.	The Hallocks's pightle in front of the barn.	12
Figure 1.2.	Ella in front the shoemaker shop of her great-great-grandfather, Capt. Zachariah Hallock.	21
Figure 1.3.	Map of Hallock Farm and Hallockville Neighborhood, 1820.	22
Figure 1.4.	Herman (A) and Arminda (B) Hallock.	25
Figure 1.5.	Original 1831 Northville Church on Sound Avenue.	27
Figure 2.1.	Halsey Hallock (A) and Marietta Terry (B).	46
Figure 3.1.	Drawing by Sarah E. Luce (1838–1908) of the liberty pole, second Northville Church, and Northville Academy.	56
Figure 3.2.	Daniel Y. Hallock (c. 1864) with his wife and two sons (A) and then in uniform (B).	60
Figure 4.1.	David Halsey Hallock (A) and Emilie J. Wells (B) around the time of their marriage, 1866.	71
Figure 4.2.	Halsey Winfield "Hal" Hallock (1869–1957).	74

Figure 4.3.	Eula Hallock (1871–1968) (A) and Georgia Irene Hallock (1875–1916) (B).	74
Figure 4.4.	Bessie Leona Hallock (1880–1966) (A) and Ella Arminda Hallock (1885–1985) (B).	75
Figure 4.5.	Hannah Jemima Hallock.	79
Figure 6.1.	The District 11 school in Northville (Sound Avenue).	106
Figure 6.2.	Picnic at Hallock Pond with Eula (Hallock) Wells and Ella Hallock; their mother, Emilie Hallock; and Eula's daughters, Irene and Lois, on July 4, 1924.	108
Figure 6.3.	Halsey Hallock in 1918 with his grandson Halsey Corwin.	109
Figure 6.4.	Hallock siblings at their last reunion in 1898 in York, Pennsylvania.	110
Figure 6.5.	Hallock family portrait, 1910.	111
Figure 6.6.	The only surviving photo of the Homestead before 1903, when the Hallocks detached the 1860 west wing and moved it across the street.	114
Figure 6.7.	The former west wing after it was moved across the street in 1903.	115
Figure 6.8.	The Hallock's Model T Ford.	117
Figure 6.9.	Ella with her violin on the Homestead's front porch.	121
Figure 6.10.	Bessie (A) and Ella Hallock (B) as young women.	126
Figure 7.1.	Hallock Farm and Hallockville Neighborhood, late 19th century.	135
Figure 7.2.	Halsey Hallock driving his reaper-binder on his 80th birthday, July 4, 1918.	137
Figure 7.3.	Hal Hallock watching a newborn calf west of the Homestead Barn, 1932.	139
Figure 7.4.	Hal in 1926 bringing in a load of wood to the Homestead with a mule cart.	145

Figure 7.5.	Bessie's 1923 photo of three structures behind the Homestead Barn.	146
Figure 7.6.	Map of Hallock farmstead in 1910.	146
Figure 8.1.	Doodle by Addison J. Wells, a schoolteacher brother-in-law of Halsey Hallock, dated 1878.	152
Figure 8.2.	House built by Daniel Y. Downs.	153
Figure 8.3.	Interior of the new church erected in 1881.	160
Figure 8.4.	The first Union School built by the combined Northville school districts in 1911.	163
Figure 8.5.	Meeting of the Farmers Club in the kitchen of the Grange Hall, 1933.	165
Figure 8.6.	Number 7 passing the Sound Avenue house of John Horace Wells in a 1909 race.	170
Figure 9.1.	Sherwood Tuthill in 1891 courting future wife Nelly Brown.	190
Figure 9.2.	Henrietta (Terry) Wells wearing the plum colored dress from her wedding.	194
Figure 10.1.	Farmhouse of Melinda and Jabez Corwin.	204
Figure 10.2.	Barn raising meal at the Sound Avenue farm of Halsey's nephew Herman W. Hallock in 1915.	214
Figure 10.3.	1920s photo of a Sound Avenue Grange meeting.	217
Figure 11.1.	Family smokehouse.	227
Figure 11.2.	Halsey Hallock feeding his chickens.	228
Figure 12.1.	Halsey W. "Hal" Hallock, about 1925, driving his last load of corn to market.	239
Figure 12.2.	Bessie in the Homestead dining room in 1923 playing her piano.	243
Figure 12.3.	Ella, Georgia, and Eula with Old Nell, 1912.	244

Figure 12.4. Bessie's August 1925 photo showing her brother and sister atop the hay wagon by the barn. 245

Figure 12.5. Photograph of Emilie and Halsey by the sitting room window in their favorite rocking chairs, 1923. 247

Figure 12.6. Photo taken from *USS Shenandoah* showing Carey Camp, Hallock Pond, and Hallock farm fields. 248

Figure 12.7. Halsey Hallock's 100th birthday, July 4, 1938. 254

Figure 13.1. Genealogy chart prepared by Bessie Hallock. 259

Figure 13.2. The Riverhead Harbor Industrial Park. 263

Figure 13.3. News article featuring interview with Ella Hallock, *Suffolk Times*, January 16, 1975. 266

Figure 14.1. The Hudson-Sydlowski House enroute to the Hallockville Museum. 276

Abbreviations

BLH, "Old House": Bessie L. Hallock, "Autobiography of an Old House."

DHH, *My Memories*: David Halsey Hallock, *My Memories*, ed. Lois Young Hallockville Museum Farm: 2001.

DHH Diary: David Halsey Hallock, Diaries, 1855–1890.

HMF: Hallockville Museum Farm.

LHH, *Hallock Genealogy:* Lucius H. Hallock, *A Hallock Genealogy*, 1926.

SCHS: Suffolk County Historical Society.

ST Diary: Samuel Tuthill, Diary (1863–1890). Typescript in VW *Album XII*.

VW *Album*: Virginia Wines, *Albums I–XXXIII*.

Acknowledgments

We are lucky that the Hallock family were themselves historians. Halsey Hallock wrote copious recollections. His older sister Adelia Hallock Benjamin wrote "A Short Paper on Looking Backward" in 1917. His daughter Bessie wrote an "Autobiography of an Old House" about the history of the Homestead. Bessie, and another daughter, Ella, seemed to remember everything and told most of what she remembered to the author's mother, who took careful notes.

Moreover, the Hallocks saved everything. Not only their house but also their great-great grandfather's account book, his son's fishing records, and all manner of deeds, wills, testaments, and letters. On top of that, they collected local history. Bessie and Ella spent many long days documenting cemeteries and figuring out the connections of all the inhabitants. The Hallocks didn't save just old papers. When one of Halsey's great-nieces visited in the 1960s and happened to mention her husband's grandmother's spinning wheel in Michigan, Ella disappeared up in the attic and returned with a hank of flax grown on the Hallock farm well over a century earlier, before the family stopped growing that crop in the 1840s.

This book would not be possible without the years the author's mother, Virginia Wines, spent collecting documents and writing about local history. A great-niece of Halsey and Emilie Hallock, Virginia borrowed every local diary she could get her hands on and produced typescripts. She interviewed older members of the community. She repeatedly sat down with Ella Hallock and filled many notebooks with information from those conversations. She made copies of old photos.

She assembled the material she collected into twenty-three massive albums that she spent her final years arranging and rearranging. She organized it as only a person who lived their entire life immersed in the Sound

Avenue community could—geographically according to where each person lived on the road. The albums start on the west end of Sound Avenue and continue to the east, each one including families that lived in a small area along the street. It took fourteen fat binders to cover the whole length of Sound Avenue. Another similarly organized series runs along Main Road from east to west, starting in Mattituck and Laurel and ending in downtown Riverhead.

The geographic organization made perfect sense to her but makes little sense to anyone who did not grow up on Sound Avenue. The ultimate example of this intensely local mindset is the main table of contents. It is not found in *Album I* but rather in *Album VII*, which covers the section of Sound Avenue on which she lived.

When material did not fit into her geographic concept, she made it fit. For instance, information about a famous Hallock farm in Orient, 23 miles to the east, is included in *Album XVII*, which covers Laurel where that branch of the family originated. Similarly, a series of articles written by Henry Young, who left Sound Avenue to become a newspaper editor in Kansas, shows up in the album that includes the section of Sound Avenue where he grew up.

She repeatedly counted the pages. Her final tally—in October 1993, less than two months before her death—was 1,664 pages. But these are not actual pages, rather plastic sleeves with items on both sides and sometimes many more items stuffed inside. The actual count amounts to well over 5,000 pages. She even weighed each album, calculating the whole collection at 181 pounds![1]

Two other women also helped lay the groundwork for this project. Lois Young, a granddaughter of Halsey and Emilie Hallock, carefully preserved and curated family artifacts and papers after her aunt, Ella Hallock, moved out of the Homestead in 1979. She transcribed many of the family documents and collected them into a black binder. She assembled and identified all of the family photographs, including a spectacular collection of images Bessie Hallock took of the farmstead in the 1920s with her little Kodak Brownie camera. Young also edited her grandfather's writings into a booklet titled *My Memories*, published by the Hallockville Museum.[2] For many years she also served as collections curator at the museum.

The other remarkable woman was Estelle Evans, also a great-niece of Halsey and Emilie. Like Young and the author's mother, Evans was among the founders of the Hallockville Museum Farm. Evans also kept the family's culinary traditions alive in the Homestead kitchen and collected the old recipes from the family and community, published by the museum as *Receipts and Reminiscenses*.³

Sections of this book had their genesis in a series of special exhibits at the Hallockville Museum Farm over the last two decades. Fellow board members Paul Hoffman, Connie Klos, and Mary Anne Huntington, as well as longtime executive director Herb Strobel, all contributed significantly to that work. Deborah Remer, Amy Folk, Mary Laura Lamont, Natalie Naylor, Wendy Polhemus-Annibell, and the author's daughter, Abby Wines, helped by reading some or all of the text. Mary Anne Huntington helped in preparation of the images. Matt Kania of Map Hero, Inc., prepared the maps. Richard Carlin at SUNY Press was generous with advice and patience. Carly Miller has been a great copy editor. The author's wife, Nancy Gilbert, herself a trained historian, not only endured the writing of this book but contributed many sharp insights.

Introduction

A Special Place Called Sound Avenue

For the Hallock family, who lived for five generations in the Hallockville Museum Farm's old Homestead on the North Fork of Long Island, Sound Avenue was more than just the road that ran past their house. It was also both the name of their unique farming community and a special state of mind.

Today, Sound Avenue remains a mostly rural road, running through the heart of the North Fork's wine country. Although not far from the glitzy Hamptons on the South Fork, Sound Avenue is still a world apart. Wineries, "agritainment" operations, and sod farming have replaced most of the potato farms, but the road is still lined with working farms and old farmhouses. The avenue—and especially the area around the Hallockville Museum Farm—is a look back into what all of Long Island once was: largely rural, open fields studded with picturesque farmsteads, far removed from the suburbanization and Levittowns that have encroached much of the island.

The road itself, which today runs 16 miles from downtown Mattituck (where it is now called Old Sound Avenue) to its intersection with Route 25A in Wading River, has not always been called Sound Avenue. The very first mention in 1683 was to the "Highway that leadeth to Sataucutt." At that time, Setauket, about 30 miles away, was the next settlement west of Mattituck. By the 1730s it became "New North Road," then "Kings Highway called the North Road," then "North Country Road," and finally for most of the 19th century simply "North Road." This distinguished it from South Road, what we now call Main Road. Not until 1899, when under a new United States Post Office Department program it became part of the first rural free delivery (RFD) route on Long Island, did the road become Sound Avenue—to avoid confusion with the many other North Roads. (See fig. I.1.)

Figure I.1. Sound Avenue, approx. 1930, in front of the Hallock Homestead, visible on left. Bessie Hallock photo. *Source:* Hallockville Museum Farm. Used with permission.

Like the roadway, the unique linear community, with almost all of its houses strung along a five-mile stretch from roughly the line dividing Riverhead and Southold towns westward to Doctors Path (see fig. I.2), did not always have the Sound Avenue name. In the 17th and 18th centuries, it was simply the northern part of a large area called Aquebogue, basically the western reaches of Southold Town, which included Riverhead until 1792. In the early 19th century, the community along North Road gradually took on the name Northville. From the beginning, that name was problematic, as another Northville existed in upstate New York. When the increasingly prosperous community wanted its own post office in 1838, to avoid confusion with the upstate village of the same name, residents chose the name Success. After the road became Sound Avenue to accommodate the new RFD route in 1899, both the church and the community soon followed along.

When the inhabitants decided to incorporate as a village in 1920, they became the Village of Sound Avenue—probably the only village in the state ever named after a road. However, in a typically contradictory move, voters formally changed its name back to Northville shortly before becoming the only village to unincorporate in 1929. The school kept the Northville name

Figure I.2. Map showing the northeast corner of Riverhead Town, which became the Village of Sound Avenue in 1920. The Sound Avenue community, also known as Northville, stretched from the Riverhead-Southold town line on the east to about Doctors Path on the west, encompassing school districts 10 and 11 until they were merged into one district in 1911. Older names of surrounding communities, such as Lower Aquebogue for Jamesport, are shown in parentheses. *Source:* Map Hero, Inc.

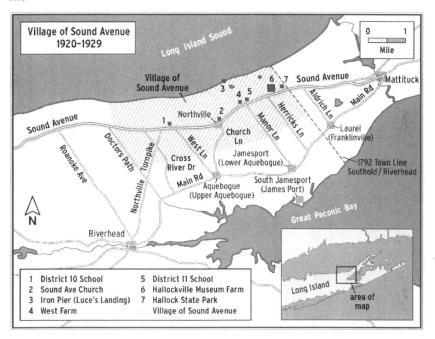

until it closed in the 1960s, but the Sound Avenue Grange, Sound Avenue Cemetery, and Sound Avenue Church stuck with that usage, and community news always appeared in the Sound Avenue columns of the local paper. For convenience of the reader, we will generally use the term Sound Avenue to describe the community, even in the years before the name was adopted, unless the Northville label is quoted or attached to a particular institution such as the Northville Academy.

Whatever its name, Sound Avenue was always more than just a 350-year-old road. It was a unique community and special world. In 1985, Steve Wick, then a reporter for Long Island *Newsday*, wrote:

> My favorite road on the East End is Sound Avenue. I love it like no other strip of asphalt I have been on. I pass along it four or five times a week and almost every time I see something I did not see before. It amazes me how much I haven't seen when I think I've seen everything. . . . Sound Avenue is the last genuinely rural road left on Long Island, nothing else comes close; the traveler sees farmers working fields on old, red tractors, migrants cutting cauliflower, and at dusk, deer along the edges of woods, gingerly moving towards an apple orchard.[4]

Barbara Shea, another *Newsday* reporter, in 2001 described Sound Avenue as "A popular route into Long Island's down-to-earth heartland . . . which weaves back and forth through time as it meanders for about 20 miles."[5] A year later, yet another *Newsday* reporter, Bill Bleyer, called Sound Avenue "A glorious time warp."[6] In 1998, A *Riverhead News-Review* editor wrote:

> If I were to take you to the ideal place that would typify Long Island—that is, the Long Island before outlet malls and traffic jams—I would not take you to the ocean, the Montauk Lighthouse or the Fire Island seashore, not even to the Hamptons. No, instead I would take you to a stretch of winding road known as Sound Avenue—a strip of pavement that meanders eastward along the North Fork for approximately 20 miles, hugging the Sound, providing a spectacular and timeless landscape of the real Long Island I love.[7]

Sound Avenue seemed always full of contradictions. In some ways it was marked by amazing stability, with many families living there for multiple generations. Occupants of the Hallock Homestead traced their ancestry back to the first settlers of the North Fork in the 1640s, as did most of their neighbors in the 19th century. Sound Avenue remains home to two farms that have been in the same family for over 350 years. On the other hand, considerable movement always occurred—both in and out. One Hallock relative moved 18 times in his life. It was a homogenous community, yet one racked by divisions. It was a community centered on its church, a somewhat "sanctimonious" place, as one Hallock descendant told the author, where even playing cards was considered sinful. Yet the community was also full of scandals and of young men who loved horse racing.

Why Read About the Hallocks?

The Hallocks were not famous, nor were they rich. Their Sound Avenue community was small and obscure—and something of a cultural backwater. Moreover, it has essentially ceased to exist today. No family member ever made it into the history books or had much impact beyond their immediate Sound Avenue world. So why read (or write) a book about this single family's story?

First, this micro view allows insights that history written from the macro level does not. This is history from the ground up, observed with a microscope, not a telescope. We can see life from an individual's perspective. Indeed, the big issues of political, intellectual, and cultural history seem to fade away. Because so many in this small community kept diaries or left memories, we often have multiple perspectives on every conflict. Individual concerns and the importance of personal relationships come into focus in a way not seen from ten thousand feet. Moreover, this intimate view allows us to see not only what they wanted us to see but also the things about which they preferred to remain silent—often the most interesting things.

Second, the Sound Avenue community is especially interesting because it remained so homogenous for so long. For well over two centuries, they were almost all descendants of the same small group of 17th-century Puritan founders. They shared the same language, the same religion, the same world view. They were mostly interrelated by marriage or cousinship. They all shared the same occupation, namely farming. Economic differences remained relatively narrow. Yet despite that long-term homogeneity, family members and the community divided bitterly on issue after issue, ranging from allowing a melodeon into the church to supporting abolitionism. Cultural wars raged, even in that little place where everyone knew each other, were interrelated, and shared a common heritage.

Third, this family has left a physical legacy, the historic buildings and rural landscape of the Hallockville Museum Farm—a place that represents what most of Long Island once looked like before being paved over for highways and subdivisions. Interpreting, understanding, and enjoying the museum requires knowing the people who lived there and bringing them alive. In this we are especially lucky the Hallock family treasured their history, saved their documents, took early pictures of the farm (see fig. I.3), and preserved their Homestead until the late 20th century when it could become a museum.

Figure I.3. Bessie Hallock's photograph of the Hallock farmstead as it appeared in the 1920s. *Source:* Hallockville Museum Farm. Used with permission.

Fourth, although the Hallock family and their community were special in many ways, in the 19th century they were typical of farming families and communities on all of Long Island, especially on the island's North Fork with its history of Puritan settlement.

A fifth and final reason is that you, the reader, will find this story interesting. It is full of good tales. We will see how a vocal supporter of abolitionism, proud that his first vote was for Abraham Lincoln, avoided the Civil War draft—and avoided the fate of the substitute hired in his place. We will see how the extended Hallock family divided bitterly over a new minister who ultimately burned down their church—and then tried to pretend that nothing had happened. We will see how this family adapted rapidly to the forces of modernity in the 19th century and then became living anachronisms in the 20th century. We will see how the community adapted to a changing world around them, including the wave of Polish immigrants that began arriving in the late 19th century. We will see how the last two generations to live in the Homestead witnessed both the arrival of the railroad on Long Island and plans for a string of nuclear power plants on the north end of their farm. Sometimes these deep dives into one community's history dig up stories about racism, prejudice, and other subjects many have chosen to forget. Other times they bring up stories of compassion or human tragedy we want to remember.

A Sound Avenue Boy

The author has a special connection to this story: he was a Sound Avenue boy. He grew up in the old farmhouse of the deacon who played a leading role in two of Sound Avenue's worst scandals. His boyhood encompassed the final years when Sound Avenue remained a world of its own. He attended the Northville elementary school in the last years before it was consolidated into a central school district. He called the last Hallock to live in the Homestead "Cousin Ella" because she was his grandmother's first cousin. As a boy and young man he was a frequent visitor in the Hallock Homestead.

He remembers all three of the unmarried Hallock siblings sitting in their "sitting room." Cousin Hal on a sort-of sofa over under the windows, Cousin Bessie on one side of the stove—which they kept running even though the heat was also on—and Cousin Ella on the other side. Then it was just Cousin Bessie and Cousin Ella, and then, for her last two decades, just Cousin Ella. He even brought his firstborn daughter to visit her. Cousin Ella was also a frequent mealtime guest at the author's home. The conversation was always lively and interesting. However, despite all those visits, he never saw any part of the Homestead besides the sitting room until it became a museum after Cousin Ella moved out in 1979.

The author wrote the first history of Northville in 1958, as a 12-year-old in seventh grade. Approximately 2,000 words long, it boasted an impressive 16 sources, including 9 interviews. Naturally the first on the list was Cousin Ella. The local chapter of the Daughters of the Revolution invited him to present the paper at one of their meetings, held in Vera Fanning's Sound Avenue farmhouse. Today, that paper remains remarkably accurate, if little more than a somewhat pedantic listing of facts and incidents.[8] Hopefully, the author's intimate knowledge of the community, combined with his subsequent training as a professional historian, can bring understanding and insights not otherwise possible, while risking the danger of being too close to his subject.

Names

Because this is an intimate history mostly about members of the Hallock family, we will generally use just first names. Where individuals were known by either their middle name or a nickname, we will use that. Although the given name of the central protagonist of this book was David Halsey Hallock, friends and family always called him Halsey. More formally he was known as D. Halsey Hallock, never by his first name. We will follow the lead of the family and refer to him as Halsey. Similarly, we will follow their lead in referring to their son Halsey W. Hallock as "Hal." Halsey's uncle, Zachariah Hallock III, will become Uncle Riah. Their cousin Samuel Tuthill will generally be Sammy, and the orphan boy Thomas Pope who came to live with the family in the 1850s will be Tommy. For those unable to remember all of the family names and nicknames, a genealogical guide to the Homestead Hallocks appears as an appendix of this book.

Additional Material

Additional material and images for which there was not room in this book can be found on the Hallockville Museum Farm website, https://hallockville.org/hallocksbook/.

Chapter 1

The Family Attic

> When the ship came to the shore in Southold the passengers didn't dare to land for fear of the Indians: but Peter Hallock was a strong man, and a bold man, and he stepped on shore first; so the place was called "Hallock's Neck."
>
> —"Hallock Ancestry"[1]

17th-Century Puritan Roots

Ancestors of the Sound Avenue Hallocks came to America as part of the great Puritan migration that brought about 21,000 of them to New England between 1629 and 1640 to escape religious persecution at home. While the main focus of this book will be the Hallocks and their Sound Avenue farming community during the lifetimes of Halsey Hallock (1838–1939) and his wife Emilie, the last couple to raise a family in the Hallock Homestead, it is impossible to understand them or their community without briefly exploring their cultural roots.

The Hallock family, like many of these Puritan immigrants, originated from East Anglia and other counties in the east of England. Most landed in Boston or nearby Massachusetts ports and initially settled in the Boston area, but within a few years they began spreading throughout New England and the Twin Forks of Long Island's East End, easily reachable by water.[2] One band of Puritans settled Southold, which initially encompassed the entire North Fork, in 1640. Other groups landed on the South Fork and founded Southampton about the same time and East Hampton a few years later.[3]

Because of this original settlement pattern from New England and because of the close proximity to Connecticut less than 20 miles away across Long Island Sound, the East End developed culturally more as a part of New England than of New York. As such, it escaped the Dutch influence found on the other end of Long Island. Architectural and cultural forms, folkways, foodways, and even dialect remained closely tied to New England and the Puritan settlers' East Anglican roots. However, due to its relative isolation on the periphery of New England, archaic cultural practices sometimes continued much longer on eastern Long Island than in the New England heartland. This was especially true of the relatively self-sufficient and isolated Sound Avenue farming community.

The cultural impact of these East Anglican Puritan roots remained evident on the North Fork well into the 20th century. The most obvious legacies are the names of the town of Southold and the county of Suffolk in which it is located. John Youngs, leader and minister of the band of settlers that arrived on the North Fork in 1640 and a direct ancestor of the Homestead Hallocks, was born in Southwold, England (where his father served as the Puritan vicar)—located in the county of Suffolk, on the shore of the North Sea in the heart of East Anglia.

The North Fork is still dotted with Presbyterian and Congregational churches directly descended from the original Puritan church founded by John Youngs in Southold in 1640. Although the theological beliefs gradually shifted away from rigorous Puritanism over the centuries, their impact continued manifest. For instance, the celebration of Christmas, originally banned by the Puritans in New England, came quite late to the Hallocks and their neighbors. As long as the Sound Avenue Church existed, the congregants still sang some of the old Puritan hymns and began every service with the "Doxology" from John Calvin's 1551 *Genevan Psalter*.

The East Anglican influence also persisted locally in the design of barns. So-called English-style barns with doors on their broad sides (as opposed to Dutch-style barns with doors on their gable ends) echoed structures common in East Anglia when the Puritans left in the 1600s.[4] The 18th-century core of the Hallockville Museum's Homestead Barn is an English-style structure. Long after more efficient barn designs became common elsewhere in the Northeast, the English-style structure persisted on eastern Long Island—well into the 20th century, including the Hallockville Museum's Naugles barn built in 1937 by Polish-Lithuanian immigrant farmers.

The early Puritan settlers also brought the "Cape Cod" story-and-a-half house configuration with them. That style developed in eastern England during the late 16th century as inhabitants there "chambered over" their single-story cottages by adding bedrooms (then called chambers) above, tucked under the eaves.[5] This became the style of almost all the earliest homes on both Cape Cod and the North Fork. With its square footprint and upstairs rooms tucked under the roofline, the "Cape Cod" was the most economical way to maximize living space with minimal exterior area. The oldest parts of the Hallock Homestead dating to the mid-1700s, as well as the museum's Bethuel Hallock house, built in 1837, are excellent examples of this design from when it was the typical starter home on the North Fork. Ironically, the style largely disappeared in England but was revived in 20th-century America by the real estate industry, which churned out large numbers of "Capes" in places like Levittown.

Another area where those Puritan roots persisted well into the 20th century—in language—is well-documented by James Evans in his monograph "Nawth Fawk Tawk."[6] Evans, a great-great-great nephew of Halsey and Emilie Hallock, grew up on Sound Avenue in the 1950s listening carefully to the accents and vocabulary he heard around him. Not surprisingly, the local speech of the Hallocks and their neighbors was related to the classic New England accent, with *r*'s added to words such as "eye-DEE-er" for idea and "SORE-it" for saw it. Equally common, according to Evans, was the penchant for dropping *r*'s where they should be, such as pronouncing "here" as "HEE-ah" and "there" as "THEY-ah." Similarly, cars became "kahs," the poor became "POO-uh," and a horse became a "HAWS" with the plural said as "HAW-us-is."

The Hallocks and their neighbors used the word "pightle" (locally pronounced PIE-kel) to describe the grassy yard in front of the barn through which their driveway looped (see fig. 1.1). "Pightle," an archaic word brought from East Anglia by the area's 17th-century Puritan settlers and not found in modern dictionaries, originally described a small meadow or enclosure. The author's grandmother had a tear-shaped lawn encircled by her driveway that she called her "pightle," as did her father (a brother of Emilie Hallock), who called a backyard surrounded by a driveway his "pightle."

The Hallock family and their Sound Avenue neighbors embraced Puritan customs well into the 20th century. For instance, inheritance never followed primogeniture, something the Puritans abolished. Instead, male children tended to get a relatively even distributions of land regardless of birth order (females received goods or money). Similarly, the youngest son often remained in and inherited the family home—something that happened repeatedly in the Hallock family over the generations, including

Figure 1.1. The Hallocks called this grassy area around which the driveway looped in front of the barn their "pightle" (PIE-kel), using the archaic term still used in the Sound Avenue community. Bessie Hallock photo, 1923. *Source:* Hallockville Museum Farm. Used with permission.

in the case of Halsey Hallock, the last to raise a family in the museum's Hallock Homestead.

The Hallock family generally followed the Puritan approach to naming children, with most, but not all, of the given names coming from the Bible—such as Zachariah, Zerubabel, Peter, and Bethuel for boys and Elizabeth, Sarah, Mary, and Hannah for girls. However, there were exceptions, such as Anglo-Saxon William and Richard, that also appear repeatedly in the Hallock genealogy. The Hallocks also followed the well-established Puritan practice of reusing names from parents or grandparents but never named a child after godparents, something considered too "popish."[7]

Puritan culture and attitudes persisted in many other ways in the Sound Avenue community. In "Nawth Fawk Tawk," Evans says that "to outsiders, many families might have seemed almost Amish until after WWII."[8] They were conservative in their cultural practices, often eschewing dancing and popular music. They neither drank alcohol nor smoked. They didn't gamble or play card games. Even coffee was suspect. While they may not have been quite as strict in their religious observances as their Puritan forebearers, they still worshipped in remarkably similar ways. However, as Evans points out, in one way they were very different from the Amish: "They were quick to adopt new technology" and modern agricultural practices.

Hallock Family Roots

The origins of the Hallock family are steeped in myth. The name is undoubtedly English, often spelled Holyoke or some variant. Early Southold records use a variety of alternative spellings: Halliock, Hallick, Hallyoake, and Holyoke. Later, some family members used Harlock, Halleck, or Hallack, but the spelling Hallock gradually became the accepted preference.[9]

The family has long been interested in its history. "Obsessed" might be a better word. The first genealogy, "A Brief Sketch of the Hallock Ancestry in the United States," was published in 1866 by the American Tract Society, a nonsectarian organization based in New York City and founded in 1825 for the purpose of publishing and disseminating Christian literature.[10] The author, Rev. William A. Hallock, was senior secretary of the society and saw the family history as closely intertwined with the protestant Christian mission of the Tract Society. The pamphlet overflowed with comments about the family's "moral character," "conscientious regard to duty," and "unpretending piety."

A 1906 update to the "Hallock Ancestry" by the original author's nephew Charles Hallock makes even clearer the purpose of this family heliography.[11] On the page following the title appears this quote about the "value of pedigree": "The knowledge that one is descended from a line of ancestors who have ascended to their God eminent for their intelligence, integrity, and piety, can but lead a person to respect himself, and to determine not to dishonor in his own life the unspotted succession to which he belongs of men great in their *goodness*." According to "Hallock Ancestry," the pioneer Hallock in America was Peter (born about 1600, death date unknown), who was the first to land among 13 "pilgrims" who left England in 1640 and landed at Southold. The pamphlet attributes the "facts" of this story to a Mrs. Elizabeth Hallock Corwin (1731–1831), who lived in the area now called Jamesport. The pamphlet goes on to attribute the "high minded piety" and "moral character" of the Hallock family to their descent from the "pilgrim" Peter Hallock. The back cover of the original edition contains a hymn, "The Pilgrim's Song," that includes the words "Aye, call it holy ground / The spot where first they trod" and ends with the claim that these "pilgrims" brought to our shores "freedom to worship God."[12] Neither the hymn nor the pamphlet mention that this freedom to worship was limited to only Puritans and did not apply to Quakers or other non-Puritan sects, or even to the established Church of England—and certainly not to "pagan" Native Americans and African-born slaves.

The story about Peter Hallock is likely entirely myth. Although the much more comprehensive 1926 *Hallock Genealogy* prepared by Lucius H. Hallock calls it a "a well authenticated legend," that work admits that the Rev. Epher Whitaker, who wrote a comprehensive history of Southold in 1881, decided after much research that "there is not a particle of evidence to be found that Peter Hallock was ever here." Similarly, Charles Craven, an early historian of Mattituck, states that "there is no valid reason for believing that [Peter] ever dwelt in Southold Town, for his name does not appear in the early records."[13] However, while no evidence exists that Peter ever set foot on the North Fork, some evidence exists that he was the brother-in-law of Rev. Christopher Youngs, vicar of Southwold England and the father of Rev. John Youngs, the first minister in Southold, New York. Nevertheless, a plaque at Founder's Landing in Southold marks the landing spot where Peter Hallock almost certainly did not land in 1640.

William Hallock, Son of Peter

Although the story about Peter Hallock in the new Southold colony in the 1640s is likely entirely myth, the presence of his son William (c. 1610–1684) is well-documented. We don't know when he arrived. Early records of the town of Southold are missing or incomplete. The first documented reference to William is not until 1652 when his name appears in the town records as the north boundary of a piece of woodland at Tom's Creek.[14] He next appears in 1661 on the list of recipients of allotments in the First Aquebogue Dividend. Then in 1666 he sells his share of Plum Island. Several other references appear over the next two decades.[15]

Significantly, on both the Plum Island deed and a 1678 land exchange, instead of signing his name he placed his "H" mark on the document. William Hallock, the storied progenitor of all the Hallocks in America, was illiterate, not even able to sign his name! He was not alone. Of the 67 names on the two documents (with some overlap), roughly a quarter of the men could only place their mark and all six of the women were similarly illiterate. The rate of illiteracy in 17th-century Southold was typical of that in Puritan New England, where historians estimate that up to one-third of the male settlers were unable to read or write.[16]

The Puritans, because of their focus on reading the Bible directly rather than relying on clergy, placed a high value on literacy. William Hallock's lack of literacy is a sign of his middling social status. Had he come from higher-status origins, he likely would have been able to read and write like Rev. John Youngs, William Wells, and the new settlement's other leading citizens.

Land Dividend

In 1661, the Southold settlement divided up its common holdings in a series of "dividends" covering the outlying parts of the town, including Orient, Cutchogue, Mattituck, and much of what is now the town of Riverhead. In the First Aquebogue Dividend, which included what is today western Mattituck and the eastern third of the town of Riverhead, William Hallock received a double allotment a half mile east of today's Hallockville Museum, a long, narrow strip that encompassed about 540 acres stretching 3.5 miles from Long Island Sound on the north to Peconic Bay on the south, but only about 1,500 feet wide (the northern end of this parcel can be seen on the map in fig 1.3). Its western boundary is today the dividing line between Riverhead and Southold towns. Aldrich Lane follows part of the eastern boundary. This land division not only brought the Hallock family to the Hallockville neighborhood but also established the distinctive pattern long narrow farms that characterize the area.

William soon built a house on the north end of those allotments, becoming the first pioneer in what is today the Sound Avenue community (no. 6 in fig. 1.3). The house and land passed down to his son Thomas Hallock (c. 1660–1719), his grandson Zerubabel Hallock I (1696–1761), his great-grandson Zerubabel Hallock II (1722–1800), and on for subsequent generations until the mid-19th century when Benjamin Laruens Hallock (1812–1895) tore down the old house and replaced it with the fine house standing today on Hallock Lane, well north of Sound Avenue.

In 1675, William Hallock gave to his stepbrother Richard Howell (1628–1709), who was also both his son-in-law and brother-in-law (see table A.2 in the appendix for Hallock family generations), a 20-rod-wide strip on the west edge of his two allotments, running from Sound to Bay, about 140 acres. The north end of this Howell parcel now constitutes the eastern-most part Hallock State Park. Richard Howell built a house on that property in 1678 (no. 5 in fig. 1.3). Howell's house stood about 1,500 feet north of Sound Avenue and only about 600 feet from his father-in-law's house to the east. In the early nineteenth century the Howells moved this house to Sound Avenue to become the west wing of a new house that is still standing today (images of B. L. Hallock and Howell houses at https://hallockville.org/hallocksbook/). The Howells and the Hallocks remained neighbors into the mid-20th century, with at least seven marital unions between the two families over the generations.

William died in 1684. His will illustrates the ways that Puritan fathers used land to control their sons. Not only did he withhold from his four sons the title to properties on which they were living during his lifetime—thus severely curtailing their freedom—he attempted in his will to control their religious life after he died by basically disinheriting a son who had become a Quaker and threatening the same fate to the other three sons if they espoused "such wicked practices" or married a Quaker.[17]

New Meeting Houses and the Great Awakening

As the number of settlers grew in the western reaches of Southold town, it became burdensome to travel many miles to the village of Southold on barely existent roads. Consequently, Zerubabel Hallock I (1696–1761), along with some of William's other grandsons, joined their pioneer neighbors in 1715 to build the first meeting house (church) in Mattituck. Similarly, settlers even further west, in the area that later became Riverhead, came together to form their own church in the late 1720s and built a new meeting house in 1731 that still stands in Jamesport, confusingly then known as Aquebogue. The Mattituck church was a little closer, so Zerubabel I and his wife, Esther, stayed with that congregation—although he did not become an actual member until January 1761, when he realized he was about to meet his maker, which occurred just four months later.[18]

Both buildings were primitive structures, typical Puritan meeting houses with narrow balconies on three sides, a high pulpit on one end, and walls plastered only below the balconies. The ceilings were open to the rafters. Neither building had any heat. The pews were straight-backed and without cushions. Services were long—at least a couple of hours in the morning and, after an hour's break for lunch, a similar length in the afternoon.[19] Following Puritan customs, men and women sat separately.

Just a few decades later, in the 1750s, the Hallocks and their neighbors became caught up in the First Great Awakening. In the century following the great Puritan migration to New England in the 1630s, like establishment churches everywhere the spirit and enthusiasm of its members gradually deadened. A revival movement began in the mid-1730s in Massachusetts and soon spread across New England to Long Island, with its close cultural connections. In various manifestations the Great Awakening tore apart churches everywhere with feuds between the Old Lights, who wanted to maintain the status quo, and New Lights, who wanted more enthusiasm in their religion.

Rev. Charles E. Craven, in his 1906 *History of Mattituck*, calls this a "religious earthquake [that] caused the foundations to tremble" and led to "most men [becoming] extremists." The conservative Old Lights viewed New Lights as "going beyond reasonable bounds in a zeal for religious excitement and emotional irregularities." The Old Lights even accused the New Lights of "fanatical extravagancies and zeal without knowledge."[20]

Inevitably, as the bickering got more intense, a schism occurred.[21] Zerubabel II (1722–1800) and his wife Elizabeth joined a group of New Light "Separates," who split off from the Mattituck and Jamesport congregations and began worshiping separately a few miles further west in Upper Aquebogue (now Aquebogue) before 1758. They soon organized as a Strict Congregational Church, with sharp distinctions between themselves and their former Presbyterian brethren at the old meeting houses in Jamesport and Mattituck. This breakaway group in Aquebogue, now worshiping in its third meeting house, built in 1862, is known today as Old Steeple Church and became the "mother church" of the many other Congregational parishes that came to dot eastern Long Island.

Schisms like this inevitably split families and neighbors. Elizabeth's father (and their next-door neighbor) Richard Sweezy, her brother Richard Sweezy Jr., and their neighbor and cousin Richard Howell all joined the new Separates church in Aquebogue.[22] However, Zerubabel's father, Zerubabel I, stayed with the Mattituck church. The senior Zerubabel's brother, James Hallock, and his second cousin, Peter Hallock, also stayed with the Mattituck church, as both names are among the signatures on a deed selling the Mattituck parsonage in 1769.[23]

For the next several generations, Zerubabel II and his progeny remained tied to the Aquebogue meeting house even though it was twice as far away as the ones in Mattituck and Jamesport. In the next generation, making the connection to the Aquebogue church even tighter, Zerubabel and Elizabeth's son, Zachariah I (1749–1820), married Hannah Youngs, the daughter of Rev. Daniel Youngs (c. 1744–1814), the much-revered minister of that church from 1782 until his death. Their son, Zachariah II, and their grandson, Herman, also stayed with the Aquebogue church for their entire lives, even though by that time a newer Congregational church existed in the Sound Avenue community.[24]

Slavery in the Family

Like the rest of Long Island, slavery had deep roots on the North Fork.[25] The first slaves likely arrived in the 1650s. By the time New York fully abolished slavery in 1827, about 550 enslaved had lived in what are today the towns of Southold and Riverhead. At its peak in 1776, according to a census that year, enslaved persons constituted 7.4 percent of the area's population. The pattern was different than in the South, where slavery was characterized by practices on its large plantations. On the North Fork, with no significant estates and a relatively egalitarian distribution of land, most enslavers held only one or two slaves, often just a single child or laborer. More than four was uncommon.

Slavery came early to the Hallock family. William II (1667–1736), one of the sons of the first William, was an enslaver. He owned slaves named Jack and Brister, whom he left to two of his sons in his will.[26] Altogether, at least 18 members of the extended Hallock family were enslavers during the nearly two centuries that slavery remained legal on Long Island. Both Zerubabel I and Zeurbabel II were enslavers, like many of their neighbors.[27] Zerubabel I's bequest to his wife Esther included "cows, a riding chair, and a horse, and all household goods (except a feather bed), and a negro slave, and £50"—hard to read without noticing how casually the "negro slave" is not even named and gets tucked into the will with household goods, a feather bed, and farm animals.[28]

Similarly, Zerubabel II, in his will written 15 years before his death in 1785, after dividing most of his land and liquid assets among his sons, bequeathed his wife Elizabeth "two cows and horse & my riding Chases and my Negro winch Ginna and Six sheep."[29] Again, one is struck by casual listing of the "Negro winch Ginna" among his worldly possessions. The first federal census, in 1790, shows him as the owner of three slaves. The second census, in 1800, the year Zerubabel died, shows his Elizabeth still owning a slave, presumably Ginna. The 1810 census shows their son Ezra, the younger brother of Zachariah, owing one slave, probably his father's "winch" Ginna that he inherited after his mother's death in 1806.

Zachariah's father-in-law, Rev. Daniel Youngs (1744–1814)—the long-time minister in the Aquebogue church where Zachariah attended—owned two slaves, according to the 1790 census. Zachariah's brother-in-law Deacon Daniel Youngs also owned a slave in 1790 and still owned one in 1820. Daniel's daughter, Arminda Youngs (1811–1882), who married Zachariah's grandson Herman Hallock and came to live in the Hallock Homestead, grew up with the slave her father still owned in 1820 and living near one of her grandfather's former slaves, listed in the censuses from 1800 through 1830 as a free Black man named Buster, Brister, Brewster Youngs, or Buster Youngs, in a household of up to eight individuals.

Slavery was no stranger to the Hallocks's community. In addition to Zachariah's maternal grandfather Richard Swezey, Jacob Aldrich and Micha Howell, other near neighbors, were also enslavers. Samuel Hudson, about a mile west of the Hallocks, owned two slaves in 1776. Eleazer Luce, Rev. Abraham Luce, Richard Brown, and James Young also became slaveowners. Rev. Luce, who still owned two slaves at the time of the 1820 census, 14 years later, donated the land for what became the Sound Avenue Church and briefly served as its minister. Certainly some of Zachariah's cobbler customers also owned slaves, and it is likely that he made shoes for their slaves and that those slaves visited his shop. Despite all of this history, Halsey and Emilie Hallock—only a generation or two removed from the institution of slavery and proud of their support for Lincoln and the abolitionist cause—conveniently never mentioned slavery as something that happened in their family or their neighborhood.

The Revolution and British Occupation

By the time Zachariah I and Hannah married in 1771, events were already underway that would soon lead to the American Revolution. As Revolutionary fervor spread, Zachariah and his neighbors Jonathan Howell, Richard Swezey, and Reuben Brown—who then lived in the Homestead—became caught up in these events. Like most of the men in Suffolk County they signed the Articles of Association in the summer of 1775.[30] Along with Brown and Howell, Zachariah served in the First Regiment of Suffolk County Militia

Men. Zachariah is listed as the second sergeant in one of the rosters in March of that year, with Reuben Brown as the fourth sergeant.[31] At least five of Zachariah's six brothers also served as minutemen.

After Washington's defeat in the Battle of Long Island on August 27, 1776, British forces quickly occupied the whole island. The British did not make conditions easy for ardent patriots, forcing thousands of them—including Brown and Howell—to flee across Long Island Sound to Connecticut, where they lived as impoverished refugees for seven long years.

While two of his more patriotic brothers served in the Continental Army and neighbors Reuben Brown and Richard Howell were forced to become refugees in Connecticut, Zachariah sat out the war, taking care of his farm and making shoes—and supposedly signing an oath of loyalty to King George.[32] With three young children, Zachariah took the path of least resistance: he did not go into exile. He did not become a spy for the Americans or see any other service for the cause subsequent to his minutemen enrollment in 1775. Again, like their amnesia about slavery, later generations of Homestead Hallocks never talked about their ancestor's lack of visible support for the Revolution—while using his service as a minuteman before the war as a justification to join the Daughters of the Revolution.

Zachariah's Land Purchases

Over the generations, William's original 540 acres was subdivided many times. Zerubabel II had seven sons. This, combined with difficult economic times around the Revolution, left him unable to carry out the Puritan imperative to provide farms for all his sons. It must have been clear to Zachariah and his brothers that they would have to provide for themselves. While Zachariah's oldest brother, Zerubabel III, stayed on his father's remaining land, the next oldest, Caleb, eventually moved to Bridgewater in Oneida County and the third-oldest, Deacon Richard, moved to Baiting Hollow in 1781.[33] Zachariah's next youngest brother, John, moved to Orange County during the Revolution, and his younger brother Daniel also lived there for a while, although he ultimately moved back to the area now known as Laurel. Only the youngest, Ezra, in another common inheritance practice in the community, ultimately received a house in his father's will.

So it is not surprising that Zachariah, after he married Hannah Youngs in 1771, began looking for more land. He was hardworking and ambitious—both a farmer and a shoemaker (see fig. 1.2). Zachariah bought his first land in 1775, a small parcel on the south side of the King's Highway

Figure 1.2. Bessie Hallock carefully posed her sister Ella in front of the shoemaker shop of their great-great-grandfather, Capt. Zachariah Hallock, which the Hallocks had moved next to the Homestead after manufactured shoes became available in the 1840s. Bessie Hallock photo, 1923. *Source:* Hallockville Museum Farm. Used with permission.

(now Main Road) in Laurel.[34] Then, in 1780, before the American victory at Yorktown, he acquired a half interest in a 150-acre parcel just west of the original William Hallock allotment. Located north of the current Hallockville Museum, this property was most of what is now Hallock State Park and the farmland immediately to the south. He bought the other half interest in the same property in 1783, before the Treaty of Paris formally ended the Revolution and the British finally ended their occupation of Long Island later that year.[35] Zachariah eventually acquired over 500 acres to the west of the original Hallock allotment—essentially the area surrounding the Hallockville Museum Farm. One of his last major purchases, in 1801, was the Reuben Brown farm with what is now the museum's old Homestead, likely built by the Brown family in two stages in the mid-18th century.

Following the imperative for good Puritan fathers, "Captain" Zachariah, as he was called after his commission in the state militia in the 1790s, needed to provide homes and farms for his three sons. After his firstborn son, Zachariah II, married 16-year-old Mary Aldrich in 1801, Capt. Zachariah settled the young couple in the old Brown house, which became the Hallock's Homestead for the next century and three quarters. Capt. Zachariah soon built a house a little further west for his second son, John, around the time of the latter's marriage in 1806. Then, when his third son, Bethuel, married in 1813, the father built the couple a new house next to his own home just to the east of the Homestead, near where the Hallock State Park visitor center sits today. Of course, also following Puritan precedents that allowed fathers to keep more control over their offspring, Zachariah did not give his sons the deeds to any of these farms until his death in 1820. The map in fig. 1.3 shows the extent of Capt. Zachariah's

Figure 1.3. Between 1780 and 1801 Capt. Zachariah Hallock purchased approximately 500 acres to the west of the original William Hallock allotment. In his will, he divided this property among his three sons, Zachariah II, John, and Bethuel, for whom he had already provided houses. As they in turn built houses for their sons and grandsons, the neighborhood became known as Hallockville. *Source:* Matt Kania, Map Hero, Inc.

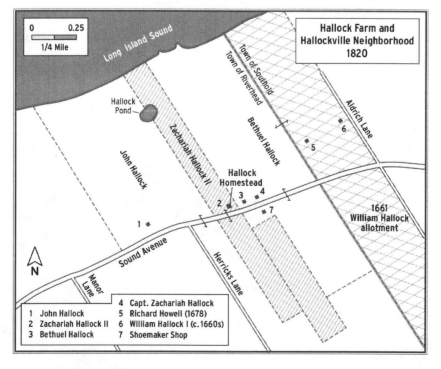

land and how it was divided after his death. Subsequently, the three sons all provided homes for their sons, and so on into the next generation. By the late 19th century, there were 11 Hallock farms, all owned by descendants of Capt. Zachariah, in this section of Sound Avenue, causing the area to be nicknamed Hallockville.

Zachariah II and the War of 1812

Zachariah II, the first Hallock to live in the Homestead, followed in his father's footsteps both as a shoemaker and a farmer—and as someone active in town affairs. When Mary, his first wife, suddenly died eight years after their marriage, leaving him with four young children, within four months he married Christiana Howell, the 25-year-old daughter of a neighbor whom he had known all her life. Although bringing a stepmother into the family so quickly may have caused interfamily strife later, it was common practice in the community. Out of the 19 marriages among Capt. Zachariah's children and grandchildren, 10 ended with the death of a wife. In each case, the husband remarried, usually quickly.

Late in the War of 1812, Zachariah II, along with his father Capt. Zachariah and his oldest son Herman, found themselves thrust into in a multiday engagement between three British warships and the local militia on the north end of the Hallock farm.[36] For some years, local farmers organized themselves into companies of 12 to 18 men to catch menhaden, which they used as fertilizer to restore their depleted soils. The morning of October 11, Zachariah II, his son Herman, and the rest of his fishing company "were up by candle light" in order to assemble at Luce's Landing.[37] On the beach they maintained a large reel on which to store the seine and a small boat to take it out. A thick fog engulfed the shore, but before it lifted they heard the boom of a cannon and knew the British were near. The farmer-fishermen immediately abandoned their fishing and set out in their boat northward into the fog. There they soon encountered an American revenue cutter, the *Eagle* out of New Haven, becalmed and much surprised to find itself within cannon range of a British warship as the fog lifted.

Before leaving shore, the fishermen sent out three messengers on horseback, Paul Revere–style, to arouse the local militia. One of these, according to a family story, was 10-year-old Herman.[38] According to a newspaper account 68 years later, at the time of Herman's death, the boy galloped his horse from house to house, shouting, "The British are here.

They [the fishermen] want every man to the Sound with his gun." One farmer did not believe the breathless boy, telling him, "Go home, mind your business, the British won't hurt you" but changed his mind when he heard the cannon boom from the British ship.[39]

Meanwhile, the fishermen, combined with the *Eagle*'s small boat, attempted to tow the *Eagle* to safety in Mattituck Inlet about two miles away, but the wind came up, causing the commander Capt. Frederick Lee to run his ship ashore about a mile northwest of the Hallock Homestead.

After beaching the *Eagle*, its crew, along with some volunteers from New Haven and the fisherman they met on shore, quickly dragged two four-pounders and two two-pounders up onto the top of the bluff, "where they were planted, and the colors near them, with a determination not to 'give up the ship.'" A three-day battle ensued. On the first day, the combined forces of the local militia, the crew, and volunteers from New Haven—armed only with muskets and the small cannon salvaged from the *Eagle*—managed to hold off several attempts by the 18-gun British warship *Dispatch* to send barges filled with marines to capture the American cutter.

On the second day, the *Dispatch* left the scene and headed to Connecticut. Thinking the battle was over, Capt. Lee sent the New Haven volunteers home, refloated what was left of the *Eagle*, and anchored it outside the sandbar, unfortunately beyond the effective range of their muskets. However, the *Dispatch* returned on the third day, this time with a larger British warship, the *Narcissus*, and a third, smaller armed vessel. By this time the Americans were out of ammunition, and facing a much larger British force they could only watch helplessly as the crew of the *Dispatch* towed the *Eagle* away. Although the incident was insignificant in the war, it left the Hallock family and their neighbors with many tales of the battle—and cannon balls they picked up in nearby fields, one of which is now displayed in the Hallockville Museum. Their neighbor, Samuel Terry Hudson, who grew up in the house that is now the museum's administration building, wrote a colorful account of the battle in 1899, much exaggerating the exploits of the local militia.[40]

Herman and Arminda

Following the obligation of Puritan fathers to provide farms for their male offspring, Zachariah II bought a 130-acre farm about a mile to the west on Sound Avenue, straddling the road now called Pier Avenue, for his oldest son Herman (1804–1881) and settled him on this "West Farm" after his marriage in 1828, at age 24, to 16-year-old Arminda Youngs.[41] Arminda was the daughter of Deacon Daniel Youngs (1766–1845) and granddaughter of Rev. Daniel Youngs, the longtime slaveholding minister of the Aquebogue church that the Hallocks all attended. Zachariah, following typical practice, did not give the young couple the deed, instead keeping the property in his own name until his death in 1854 (see fig. 1.4).

The Aquebogue Church Is Racked by Dissension

Shortly after Herman and Arminda's marriage, a bitter feud broke out in the Aquebogue church (now Old Steeple Church), which had been the Hallock family church since the First Great Awakening in the 1750s. The feud, which resulted in the founding of the first church in the Sound Avenue community and again tore the Hallock family apart, began when the Aquebogue congregation hired Rev. Evan Evans over protests from a vociferous minority. The new minister brought a controversial new covenant

Figure 1.4. Herman (A) and Arminda (B) Hallock. Photographs likely taken in the 1860s. *Source:* Hallockville Museum Farm. Used with permission.

then being adopted by many Presbyterian and Congregational churches. Sixty-one rebellious parishioners broke away to form their own congregation that kept the old covenant and old ways. After a failed attempt at reconciliation in 1831—and after being formally expelled from the Aquebogue church—the conservative dissidents built their own 32-by-42-foot meeting house about a mile to the west on Main Road. The breakaway group called themselves the Strict Congregational Church at Aquebogue, using exactly the same name as the old church.

Members of the new church lived mostly in downtown Riverhead or up on Sound Avenue, resulting in a dumbbell-shaped parish and long carriage rides for many. Consequently, three years later, the breakaway group split again—this time amicably. The Sound Avenue (Northville) part of the congregation, more than two-thirds of the total, paid $350 to the members who lived in Riverhead for their interest in the building. They disassembled the structure, moved it four miles by oxcart to North Road (Sound Avenue), and reassembled it "as their place of worship," where it has rested ever since, later serving as the Grange Hall and now a Buddhist temple (see fig. 1.5).

Thus, the church that became the center of the Sound Avenue community was born in controversy. The "great eruption"—as Halsey Hallock later called it—split both the Hallock family and the Hallockville neighborhood. Zachariah II, along with Herman and Arminda and his brother Zachariah III, stayed in the old church. We don't know if it was for theological reasons or because Herman was married to the daughter of a deacon in the church. However, Herman's uncle and aunt, John and Joanna Hallock, joined the separatists, as did their sons Isaiah, John Franklin, Daniel, and Caleb, all of whom lived near the Homestead in the Hallockville neighborhood. Daniel Hallock, a brother of Capt. Zachariah, also joined the breakaway group.

The Sound Avenue community was actually the result of not one but four rebellions to purify the church, starting with the Church of England breaking away from the Catholic church in the 16th century, then the Puritan rebellion against the Church of England, then the First Great Awakening, and finally the great eruption of 1828, when a sizable portion of the Aquebogue church walked out and founded their own true church. No wonder the people of Sound Avenue seemed to have rebellion in their genes. Although their attitudes softened in subsequent decades, the conservatism and traditionalism of the rebellious parishioners at the core of the new church also became a fundamental cultural characteristic of the Sound Avenue community well into the 20th century.

Figure 1.5. This photo shows the original 1831 Northville Church on Sound Avenue, (later called the Grange Hall and now a Buddhist temple), about 1900. The tower was added in 1859 when the building became the Northville Academy. The architecture of the building was old-fashioned, like its congregation's theology. The small-paned windows, narrow eaves, and colonial-style entablature over the doorway were reminiscent of 1730s Long Island meeting houses, not the Greek Revival or Gothic-style churches in vogue by the 1830s. *Source:* Hallockville Museum Farm. Used with permission.

The Next Generation

While their church was reeling from the schism, Herman and Arminda "set up housekeeping"—as they said in those days—in the old house on the West Farm. Less than a year after their marriage, Arminda gave birth to their first child, a daughter who died before naming. They lost the next child, a son named Charles, at three months old in 1831.[42] For their third child born, in 1832, they combined the names of Herman's mother and stepmother into Mary Christiana, but she also died three years later.[43] When another son arrived in 1833, they named him Charles, following the common custom to reuse the name of a deceased child for the next-born of the same sex. Three more children arrived over the next decade, Daniel in

1836, Halsey in 1838, and Adelia in 1841. Then another daughter, Hannah, arrived in 1850, nearly a decade later. The third-born, Halsey, went on to live in the Hallock Homestead for most of his 101 years and will be the main protagonist of our story.

Chapter 2

The Young Halsey Hallock

> It was my misfortune in boyhood to go to a district school . . . a little square pine building blaring in the sun stood upon the highway without a tree for shade or shadow near it, without bush, yard, fence or anything to take off its bare, cold, hateful look.
>
> —Composition by 16-year-old Halsey Hallock

Halsey's Birth

Herman and Arminda's third son, Halsey (1804–1881), married Emilie Wells in 1866 and the couple became the last to raise a family in the Hallock Homestead. Halsey was a successful farmer, an active member of the community, and in many ways a Puritan to the end, and his long life encompassed the evolution of Sound Avenue into a prosperous farming community that nevertheless, like the Hallock family itself, remained socially conservative and somewhat insular despite numerous connections to the modern world. Most of the older buildings that are now part of the Hallockville Museum Farm were either built, modernized, or substantially enlarged during his lifetime, including the Hallock Homestead and Homestead Barn. What visitors to the museum see today is essentially the place that Halsey and Emilie left.

Halsey was born July 4, 1838. It was the 62nd anniversary of the Declaration of Independence. Martin Van Buren occupied the White House. Victoria was crowned queen of the United Kingdom a week earlier. Halsey's parents, Herman Hallock and Arminda Youngs, still lived on the West Farm in the old Corwin house on the corner of Sound Avenue and Pier Avenue.[1]

Zachariah II, Halsey's grandfather, and his second wife Christiana were living in the original west wing of what is today the Hallock Homestead. Halsey's uncle, his father's younger brother, Zachariah III, occupied the main part of the Homestead. Following typical Puritan practice, Zachariah II still held title to both farms, something he would not relinquish until his death.

Following the relatively new practice in the community of giving children middle names, Herman and Arminda reached back to the maiden name of Arminda's mother, Jerusha Halsey (1767–1846), who came from the Sagaponack/Bridgehampton Halsey family. Arminda's step-grandmother was also a Halsey of Bridgehampton—Mary Halsey (1755–1846), daughter of Stephen Halsey.[2] With Arminda's mother and step-grandmother both still alive in 1838, it is not a surprise that this son received the Halsey middle name.

The Hallocks stayed in touch with their South Fork relatives, visiting occasionally.[3] This family connection to Thomas Halsey, one of the founders of Southampton town on the South Fork, allowed Halsey to claim forebearers among the first settlers on both of Long Island's Twin Forks—something he proudly mentioned in an interview 98 years later.[4]

The family always referred to their third son as Halsey, although on formal papers he is usually listed as D. Halsey Hallock and occasionally as David H. Hallock. His mother wanted to use the single name Davidhalsey and his parents sometimes called him that—but never David.

Halsey's Childhood

We do not know a lot about Halsey's childhood. Here is one of his recollections many decades later: "Independence Day, when I was a lad, was ushered in by the cannon's terrible roar. Another Fourth of July when I was a young lad, fireworks were shot off at Mattituck creek. I can remember hiding behind my mother's skirts as the rockets terrified me."[5] Notice he does not mention any celebration of his Fourth-of-July birthday. Birthdays were not celebrated in the community at that time. Family diaries never mention birthdays, until near the end of Halsey's long life when they suddenly started dual celebrations of his birthday and Independence Day.

Another recollection from when he was 99 years old: "As a boy of ten I went with my parents and elder brother to attend the general training day program at Greenport. From all sections of the county people came to see the militia perform their drills and maneuvers and I and the other youngsters were much impressed by the roar of cannon and the music of the fifes and drummers."[6]

The most significant local event during Halsey's childhood, the construction of the Main Line of the Long Island Rail Road through Jamesport (less than three miles away) to Greenport, occurred in 1844 when he was six years old. Melinda Corwin, the Hallocks's next-door neighbor, reported in her diary on July 27 that the "rail road passed through the island with great rejoicing." A few weeks later she went down to Jamesport to watch the train pass by, clearly a novel experience.[7] The railroad provided a fast and convenient link to New York City and its burgeoning markets and connected the Hallocks to the outside world in ways unavailable to earlier generations.

Surely young Halsey made the three-mile trip to the Jamesport station numerous times, either just to watch the trains or perhaps on his way to visit the whaling port his uncle, James Tuthill, founded a decade earlier. Halsey's aunt Polly died before his birth and his uncle James left town with his second wife about 1840 after suffering financial reverses. However, one of Tuthill's partners, Albert Youngs—Polly and Arminda's brother and thus also Halsey's uncle—still lived there and operated a general store and ships chandlery that served the entire Peconic Bay area. Although some of James Tuthill's business ventures, such as a whaling company and a steam packet line, were defunct by the time of Halsey's youth, schooners still arrived and departed frequently from the wharf in the new port, and small ships were built and repaired in the nearby shipyard. There was plenty of activity for the young Halsey to watch.

The House Exchange of 1845

The other big event during Halsey's youth, at least for him and his family, was the house and farm exchange that occurred in 1845 when he was seven. Herman and Arminda moved back to the main part of the Homestead while his brother Zachariah III and his wife Arletta took their place on the West Farm. As Halsey's daughter Bessie describes the exchange in her history of their house, which she wrote in the first-person and cleverly titled "Autobiography of an Old House": "When little George Wilson was 11 and Matilda Keziah eight [Zachariah and Alretta's children] Zachariah 3rd and his brother Herman changed farms. In 1845, Herman and Arminda came to live with me, the house where Herman was born. They brought their four lively children, Charles 12 years, Daniel 9, David Halsey 7 and

Adelia 4 years to make life merry in the old house." Why did brothers Herman and Zachariah III exchange houses and farms in 1845? Bessie remains conspicuously silent on this. Halsey claimed that "no one knows exactly why."[8] No explanation exists in the family papers, leaving one to suspect that it was something the Hallocks did not want to talk about. The two farms matched in size, with similar soils and topography; the houses were also similar, both about 80 years old with old-fashioned story-and-a-half center-chimney designs containing about five rooms downstairs and a couple of chambers upstairs under the eaves.

So why exchange houses and farms? Perhaps interfamily dynamics: a conflict between Zachariah III and his stepmother Cristiana, who was living in the Homestead's old west wing; or between Arletta and her mother-in-law; or between either of them and the *pater familias*? We do not know, but the Hallocks's silence on the issue leads us to suspect this explanation. Herman and Arminda named their first daughter Mary Cristina, combining his mother and stepmother's names, so perhaps this is an indication that they were on better terms with her.

Raising the Roof

When brothers Herman and Zachariah III exchanged houses, the Homestead still consisted of just the story-and-a-half Cape Cod likely built by Reuben Brown and his wife when they married in 1765 (now the footprint of the front part of the structure) and an even older small west wing (now the sitting room in the rear), probably dating to the mid-18th century or earlier. The only change the Hallock family made after buying the Homestead in 1801 was the addition of a small back kitchen.

In Bessie's words:

> When they [Herman and Arminda] arrived, I [the house] felt something was going to happen to my anatomy. They tore my roof off and raised me up a full story. Not satisfied with that, they made the attic high with two windows in each end so that Arminda had a big room for her loom to do her weaving. This also made an airy place winters or summers for boys sleeping quarter. I well remember the snow falling between my "ribs" on the bed cloths of the boys.

"Raising the roof" happened often on Sound Avenue in the middle decades of the 1800s. Most of the older homes were still basic story-and-a-half designs, what realtors today call Cape Cods.[9] However, as the community became more prosperous, families enlarged them by adding another floor. Sometimes they simply jacked the first floor up eight or nine feet and built a new first floor under it. Other times, they jacked the roof up and built a new second story below it. Or they simply tore off the old roof, built up the second story, and then framed a new roof above.

The Hallocks used a combination of the last two methods. They disassembled the original hand-hewn second-story framing and reassembled it on the third floor after building an entirely new second floor. Looking at the Hallock Homestead today, the first and third floors date from 1765 but the second floor dates to 1845. The floorboards of the second floor come from the 1765 house, with the walls, doors, and mantelpieces from 1845. The Hallocks installed new windows on the second floor that matched ones on the first and third levels. However, they later modernized the first floor with larger windows, resulting in the mismatched windows sizes visible today.

Numerous other houses along Sound Avenue underwent this same radical makeover in the 19th or early 20th century, including the house that Zachariah III and Arletta moved into during the farm exchange of 1845 and the Hallockville Museum's Hudson-Sydlowski House. In both of those cases, the makeover became even more extreme. They removed not only the roof but also the first-floor ceilings, leaving just the shell. Then they installed new ceilings at a higher and more elegant height, extended the side walls upward for a full second story, and constructed a new roof.

Writing many years later, Halsey wondered how Arminda, "already the mother of eight children, three of them in yonder graveyard," could consent to move "her little brood" into the old Hallock Homestead knowing that it was about to be torn apart and "renovated from foundation to attic."

Early Education

Halsey attended the one-room District 11 school that originally stood just to the west of his childhood home on the West Farm. The school was built in 1836, when Riverhead and Southold realigned district lines to create a new district entirely in Riverhead that served the eastern part of the Sound Avenue (Northville) community. The Southold residents of the original district paid the Riverhead residents $15.11 for their share of the value of the old school. Halsey's grandfather, Zachariah Hallock II, conveyed the land—adjacent to his West Farm to which he still held title, although Herman and Arminda then lived there—just enough to accommodate the school "and the privilege of going round the same to build and repair same." In consideration, Zachariah received $10 and the "ashes which shall be made in the District school house."[10] (The ashes were valuable as fertilizer.)

Halsey attended the District 11 school until age 16 in 1854, when his parents withdrew him for reasons we will see. A "composition" he wrote that year gives a remarkable description of the school:

> It was my misfortune in boyhood to go to a district school. Not but that it was the best place for me. But such a one. A little square pine building blaring in the sun stood upon the highway without a tree for shade or shadow near it, without bush, yard, fence or anything to take off its bare, cold, hateful look. Before the door in winter was the great pile of wood for the winters use. And there in summer were all the chips and scatering [sic] sticks of wood to be kicked about all summer by mischievous urchins.[11]

The other Sound Avenue school, District 10 a couple of miles to the west, was equally bleak. Halsey's cousin Henry Wilson Young (1847–1927), who attended that school and went on to be a newspaper editor in Kansas, vividly recalled many years later its "slab benches" at which he sat in the old "unpainted structure, with no grounds except the public highway in front."[12]

Here is Halsey's description of conditions inside [spellings original]:

> In winter we were squeesed into the recess of the farthest corner among little boys who seemed to be sent to school merely to fill up the chincks between the bigger boys, for certainly they were not sent for any such absurd purpose as an education. These were the great schollars. The school in winter was for them not for us youngsters. We were read and spelled twice a day unless something turned up to prevent, which did about every other day. For the rest of the time we were busy in keeping still and a time we always had of it.

He goes on to describe the rather chaotic scene that constituted education and discipline in those days:

Our shoes always would be scraping on the floor or knocking the shins of the urchins also being educated. All of our great bootes together would fill up the corner with such a noise that every ten or fifteen minutes the master would bring down his two foot ferule on the desk with such a clap that sent shivers through our hearts to think how that would have felt had it come down on our heads. And then with a look that swept us all into utter extremity of stillness he would cry! Silence in that corner.

Stillness would prevail for a few minutes but little boys memories are not capacious. Some of the boys had great gifts of mirthfullness, and some of mischief but the most had both together. The consequence was that just when we were the most afraid to laugh we saw the most comical things to laugh at. Temptations which we could have vanquished with a smile out in the open air were irresistible in our little corner where a laugh and a stinging slap were quite apt to go together. So we would hold on and fill up and hold on and fill up till by and by one of the weakest would let go a mere whifit of a laugh and then down went all the precautions and one went off and another and another touching off all the others like a pack of firecrackers. It was in vain to deny it. But as the process of snapping our heads and pulling our ears went on with primitive sobriety we each in turn with tearfull eyes and blubering lips declared we did not mean to, and that we would not do so again. And that was a fib however unintentional. For we never failed to do just so again and that about once an hour all day long.[13]

On top of all this, students needed to "shake and shiver at the beginning of school for it was very cold and to sweat and stew for the rest of the time before a great stove red hot!" Halsey suggests that "it is worth going miles to see how a school house ought to look. But generally, the barenest [sic] spot is chosen, the most utterly homely building is erected without tree or shrub for shade." He concludes, "And their [sic], those that can do no better pass the pilgrimage of their childhood education."

Halsey's younger sister Adelia retained similar memories 60 years later: "What punishments were dealt delinquents: placing of the fools cap, split quills on the ear. We have witnessed shutting up in the big desk, and when asked how he liked it the culprit would call out, 'first rate'; also the old fashioned slipper vigorously applied while the offender was bent across the master's knee; the reliable ruler always in evidence."[14] As much as Halsey and Adelia criticized their elementary educations under the rudimentary conditions of a one-room schoolhouse and poorly trained teachers, the quality of Halsey's writing indicates something quite different. Despite a few lapses from modern spelling conventions, his essay is remarkably well written, with vigorous prose and excellent penmanship.

School Books and Budgets

The annual reports of the school trustees confirm the casual and chaotic nature of schooling that Halsey describes in his essay. In 1844, with Halsey probably in first grade, the trustees reported that the school functioned for nine months with a "qualified" teacher—better than other local districts, which often struggled to find or keep teachers. However, out of the 56 children who attended the school that year, only 24 received 6 or more months of education, 14 attended between 4 and 6 months, 16 between 2 and 4 months, and 5 attended less than 2 months.

This was better than the report for the District 10 school the same year, which stated that out of the 51 students taught, only 5 attended for more than 8 of the 11 months the school held sessions, while 11 attended less than 2 months, and another 14, less than 4 months. In other words, half the students attended less than 4 months and the average student received only 4.5 months of education. Why such poor attendance? Other responsibilities, namely working on their family's or employer's farms, took up their time.

Then, as now, a combination of state support and local taxation funded the school. In 1852 the District 11 school received $54 for teacher salaries from the state. The school raised an additional $25 in local taxes, giving it a total budget of $79, excluding the special library fund. The district paid $61.03 for the teacher's salary (about $2,400 in contemporary dollars) for the 10.5-month school session.[15] The remaining $18 covered all expenses for building repair and fuel. Halsey's father served as a trustee for two years, 1846 and 1847, and "Uncle Riah" (Zachariah III), who lived next door to the school by then, served as the librarian.

The young Halsey had access to a library that grew to 153 books in 1847 and 186 in 1848. An annual state program provided an additional $8.20 in 1852 for the school library, enough to buy a dozen more. Presumably he took advantage of this resource. Books covered a wide range of subjects, ranging from classics like Plutarch's *Lives*, Bunyan's *Pilgrim's Progress*, and Benjamin Franklin's *Life* to somewhat more esoteric titles like *Natural History of Birds* or *Polar Seas and Regions*. Some were practical such as *Familiar Illustrations of Mechanics*, *Buel's Farmers Instructor*, or *Lee's Geology and Mineralogy*, and some veered more toward religion such as *Paley's Natural Theology* and *Luther's Sermons*, reflecting the rather thin line that existed between the community's church and school.

Students of Color

The school provided Halsey's first close contact with people of color. In 1844, with Halsey in first grade, the trustees of the district reported one "colored" student. By 1851 three "colored" attended Halsey's school.[16] Who are these "colored" students? The 1850 census recorded five single Black men living in the community, ranging in age from 17 to 20 and working on farms of Halsey's neighbors. The names of two younger Black people also appear: a 13-year-old boy named "That" listed as a laborer on the farm of Caleb Hallock (Herman's cousin three farms west of the Homestead) and an eight-year-old named Fanny who lived with John T. Luce, about a mile to the west. Perhaps these are two of the "colored" students in the District 11 school with Halsey in 1851. He never mentions any of them in his writings.

A Descendant of Abraham

Halsey told the story of young Jewish peddler who came to their door around 1855 when Halsey was 17 years old:

> A rather small slender boy of about 13–15 years old, with his basket, sent out from the great city into the countryside all strange and indeed frightful to him—for he is just over from the other side of the ocean. His basket filled on the start with trinkets or small household articles to eke out a living as best he can. He appears at our house just before night and timidly knocks on the door with evident fear mingled with hope upon his weary tear-stained face—asks for a place to sleep for the night—poor fellow knows full well what it is to be turned away with a cold "no." But he has found a kind heart at last in the one [Halsey's

mother, Arminda] who always had a kind heart for the poor unfortunate of God's creatures. Well do I remember how meek and disconsolate the poor boy seemed to be at the table with us that first meal. It was plainly evident that he was a descendant of Abraham the father of Isaac.

The boy was Solomon Salburg (born c. 1831). The Hallocks not only made the boy as "comfortable as possible" but, despite cultural and religious differences, they became his lifelong friends. Salburg married, settled in Riverhead, raised three children, and became one of the town's leading dry goods merchants, part of a budding community of Jewish immigrant merchants. Halsey remembered Salburg coming to the house repeatedly in later years with a "beautiful fat and sleek team of Canadian horses." Salburg felt comfortable enough to drive his "thoroughly groomed" team right into the Hallocks's barn and often stayed the day on Sunday.

Salburg left Riverhead by 1880 and moved to New York City, where his business continued to flourish. But he stopped by years later for a visit and stayed for dinner. At that dinner, Salburg told Halsey that his father Herman once offered to buy a suit from him if he would vote for Lincoln. While that transaction may not have worked out, Halsey bought his own wedding suit from Salburg's store.[17]

Herman and Arminda also befriended Jonas Fishel (1833–1909), a Jewish immigrant from Austria, who arrived in Riverhead as a 16-year-old peddler in 1849. Halsey remembered Fishel coming regularly with "box and basket" to their house. Fishel and his brother Andrew went on to run Riverhead's leading department store.[18] Many years later, after Herman's death, Arminda felt comfortable enough with the Fishel brothers to travel with them when they went to inspect their business interests in Colorado. Arminda wanted to visit her daughter Hannah, then living in Kansas "one last time." Unfortunately, Arminda did not survive the visit—and returned home in a coffin.

Tommy Pope

In another example of his mother's soft heart, Halsey tells the story about how in February of 1854 she welcomed a 13-year-old English orphan boy named Thomas Pope (1841–1932) into the household.[19] In Halsey's words, about 20 years earlier "a family of four strangers drifted into this little village, two young men, a mother and a grandmother." The mother soon died, and then the grandmother, leaving the boy's two uncles "in a strait" to find a home for Tommy. "My mother came to the rescue—although a family of five children of her own—one more would not make much difference." Tommy stayed with the Hallocks for four years, becoming an "integral member" of the family and Halsey's "running mate," despite being a few years younger.[20] Of course, like Halsey, Tommy also worked on the farm. When he moved on, Herman wrote a testimonial that Tommy was "truthful trusty and interested for his employer and when he left my family we all felt deeply interested in his welfare."[21]

That fall, as Halsey's sister Adelia later remembered, after the teacher punished Tommy "unjustly and unmercifully," their parents took her (then 12), Halsey (then 16), and Tommy out of the district school. They converted the upstairs parlor in the Homestead into a schoolroom and her oldest brother Charles, then 21, taught them there in the winter of 1854–55, along with their cousin Serepta Aldrich.[22]

In 1898, 40 years after leaving the Hallock farm, Tommy initiated a long-distance correspondence from Idaho that continued for several decades until his death in 1931. Many of the letters begin with "Dear Brother," a sign of the closeness of the two.[23] In one of his letters, Tommy described the punishment he received [spelling original]:

> You remember our brother Charles was our teacher that winter that we all quit school and converted the upstair parlor into a school room. And do you remember why your father took us out of school? You know the teacher (I forgot his name) gave me an awful licking, he had a big hickory, and he used it unmercifully first on the front of my hands and then on the back of my hands, and when we went home that night my hands were puffed up as big as two or three hands ought to be, I think if your Father could have got hold of that teacher that night, he would have fixed him so that he would not have taught school for a few days at least, anyway he took us out of school and we did not go back any more to the District school.[24]

Tommy and Halsey then attended the Franklinville Academy (in today's Laurel) for a year. Tommy worked briefly on a farm near the academy. Then, in 1859, the year he turned 18, he and his friend Charles Reeve joined 100,000 others determined to find their fortunes in the Pikes Peak gold rush. A year younger than Tommy, Reeve grew up in the Aquebogue area, the son of a boatman. Tommy and Reeve traveled west by train as far as the tracks could take them, probably somewhere in Missouri. From there they pushed handcarts with their few belongings the remaining 700 miles across the plains to Denver, then a town of just 100 people, and from there on to the gold fields around Black Hawk, about 40 miles further west.[25] Tommy and Reeve encountered many hardships in their search for riches. Reeve soon gave up and returned to Long Island, but Tommy endured the tribulations, including several insidious partners who ran off with most of his assets. He made some money buying and selling gold-bearing deposits—enough to finance his last trip east. Then he lost it all—a pattern he repeated several more times in his life.[26]

He next moved to Idaho for a new gold rush and met the same fate, but he remained there, married twice, and raised a family. He did a little of everything—farming, minor local offices, even saloon keeping—but nothing seemed to work. At one point he accumulated 1,280 acres of farmland and invested in an expensive irrigation canal, but successive years of devastating grasshopper attacks wiped him out again. As he stated in one of his letters, he started farming with about $20,000 in capital, and after five years hardly anything remained. This story about the travails of farming must have struck a chord with Halsey, who faced the vicissitudes of agriculture all his life.

Halsey's Diary

Halsey kept a diary as a teenager during 1855 and the first four months of 1856. He started again in January 1857 and made it to July that year. For 1858 only a few sporadic entries exist, and after that the diary mostly just contains notes on fertilizer usage, farm crops, and yields. Nevertheless, the diary gives us an extraordinary window into life on the Hallock farm during those early years.[27] He was only 16 when he began the diary, and his life already consisted mostly of farm work with brief interruptions for school. Most days he describes the weather and the tasks of each member of the farm's work force—himself, his father, his two brothers, and two farmhands, Tommy Pope and Tommy's uncle Henry Pope.

Most mornings that winter, Monday through Saturday, after his father Herman took them out of the district school, Halsey went to school upstairs in the east front room where his older brother Charles taught him, Daniel, Adelia, cousin Serepta Aldrich, and Tommy Pope. "We must learn all we can," he noted one day. But it was not all work and school either. The very first entry, on New Year's Day, in the evening he joined "some of the boys [who] have gone to the pond with their skates." Predictably, the next day he felt "very lame and stiff."

Lots of Church Meetings

More than anything else, the family went to church meetings, as documented in Halsey's diary. On a typical Sunday, they went to a morning service and then another in the afternoon. Often Herman and Arminda went to "Steeple Church" in Aquebogue while the younger family members go to the newer Northville (Sound Avenue) Church established in the "great eruption" of the 1830s. Both churches were Congregational. On Sunday evenings they generally attended another meeting in one of the community's two schoolhouses. Most weeks some or all family members attended one or more additional meetings either at a church or in a schoolhouse, sometimes on a Monday, sometimes a Wednesday, sometimes a Saturday.

After attending two services on a Sunday in September, Halsey commented in his diary, "We have the blessed privilege of hearing the gospel preached which is one of the best privileges." The following Sunday, "This is the Sabbath of the Lord thy God. In it thou shalt do no work & we attend church as usual and hear good enough preaching. All we want to be profited is an attentive heart & a willing mind to receive it."

On top of all these regular meetings, they attended occasional temperance meetings and special religious observances, such as the spring day of fasting and prayer that continued a tradition from colonial New England, balanced by a day of thanksgiving in the fall, also celebrated with a church service.

One of the highlights that February was a week of revival meetings in the Northville Church:

> Tuesday: The church of Northville has begun now to hold special meetings for the purpose of pleading with the Almighty to come into our midst and convert souls. This morning the meetings commenced and lasted through the day and evening.
>
> Wed forenoon: Mr. Rice gave us a short sermon. In the afternoon Mr. Reed preached, in the evening it stormed so that there was not many out but we had a very good prayer meeting.

> Thursday: There was a great deal of snow on the ground and it storms the day through, in the forenoon Mr. Rice gave us a sermon and in the afternoon too. In the evening Mr. Hale gave us a sermon.
>
> Friday: Prayer meetings all day, great signs for good, in the evening Mr. Hale gave us a short sermon. After sermon Mr. Wells requested that all that wanted to commence to serve the Lord this evening should occupy the front seats, there was a great many went forward. Great signs for good.
>
> Saturday: we attended school all day, in the evening we attended meeting and had a very interesting meeting.
>
> Sunday: we all attended meeting except Sarepta and Hannah who staid [sic] home to keep fire. In the evening we attended prayer meeting at the church of Northville

Life in Herman and Arminda's Household

The family also did a lot of visiting. For instance on a Wednesday in the middle of January, most of the family went to visit their uncle Nicholas Young (Arminda's brother) in Aquebogue. Another time they went to Jamesport to visit their uncle Rogers Aldrich, the widower of Herman's younger sister Hannah. One day Halsey wrote that "the women go visiting all afternoon." Just as often, they received visitors, generally family.

The Hallocks also frequently entertained cousins from the big city. Halsey later wrote that he was always amazed that his mother, with only "miserable conveniences for doing her work," managed not only to feed the growing family but also to provide a noon meal for all the workmen on the farm—and, in addition to that, to feed city cousins (children of two of Capt. Zachariah's daughters who moved to Brooklyn and New York) who thought nothing of taking advantage of her hospitality to enjoy country living for weeks at a time.[28] Bessie also wrote about "how the city friends and relatives with their friends did love to spend a carefree summer's vacation enjoying Arminda's hospitality." For them, the Homestead "made a very pleasing stopping place."[29]

Halsey makes some surprising little references in his diary. He comes home from Riverhead one day and casually mentions that he just had two "double teeth" pulled and another time that his mother was getting a new set of teeth.

In the entire diary, not a single holiday celebration occurs: Christmas is mentioned, but not celebrated; Easter, never mentioned; Fourth of July, never, even though it was Halsey's birthday and supposedly the biggest celebration in the community. No one else's birthday is mentioned either, and on Thanksgiving they go to meetings, no family get-together. The diary contains remarkably few references to recreation of any kind. A little ice skating. A few singing schools. One trip across Peconic Bay with other young people. Not much else.

Brother Charles Marries and Moves to Smithtown

As Bessie wrote in her "Autobiography of an Old House," in December 1854 "the first break came in the family when the oldest son, Charles [Halsey's brother] took as his wife Laura M. Wells, daughter of Deacon Joshua Wells." She added that "all the relatives gathered at an infare to celebrate the marriage." The word "infare" shows up in old dictionaries. In those days weddings generally took place in the bride's family home, as did Charles and Laura's—in her father's home about two miles west on Sound Avenue. Then the next day the groom's family welcomed the couple to their house with an infare. For the occasion, the Hallocks bought a new sofa that remains in the Homestead today (see https://hallockville.org/hallocksbook/).

Shortly after their marriage, the new couple moved to Smithtown. Seventeen-year-old Halsey helped his brother and sister-in-law move. They went to Riverhead with a cart load of belongings and traveled by train from the Riverhead station, perhaps Halsey's first train ride based on his rather breathless description: "Many eyes are turned to the east to discover the approach of the great horse & soon it is seen to approach with the speed of the wind. All onboard is heard from the head quarters which is responded from the whistle then away she moves." Halsey did not ride in the passenger compartment with Charles and Laura, but rather on the "frate" car with their furniture, barrels of supplies, "hencoops" with the hens inside, and even a cat in a bag. Once in Smithtown, a wagon took them and everything to the new farm in the Kings Park area near Long Island Sound.

Why did Charles, the firstborn, take his Sound Avenue bride to Smithtown? Perhaps, with its closer connections to Brooklyn and New York City, marketing farm produce proved easier in Smithtown. Without question, like all good Puritan fathers, Herman provided the capital to buy the farm. We know from Halsey's diary that Herman went with Charles earlier that year to Connecticut to look into buying a farm there. Then, in August, they went to look at the 155-acre farm Smithtown. A possible family connection exists, as at least seven other Hallock families lived in Smithtown at the time, including two very near the farm Charles acquired. Locals referred to the area informally as Hallocksville.[30]

School Term in Smithtown

Halsey and his sister Adelia spent the winter of 1855–56 in Smithtown, where they studied again under their brother Charles. A letter survives (the only letter) from their mother Arminda. It includes this admonition: "I trust you will try to learn all you can. You will never regret trying to store your minds with useful knowledge."

She went on to remind them not to forget "the obligations you are under to your Heavenly father" and ends by saying "[I] trust you will remember your mother." She signed simply "AH."[31]

The Franklinville Academy

Halsey's father, Herman, sent him, Tommy Pope, and Adelia to the Franklinville Academy during the 1857–58 winter term. Situated in the hamlet then called Franklinville (now Laurel) that straddles the Southold-Riverhead border along Main Road, in the days before public high schools, the academy provided a secondary education to students from throughout the North Fork and beyond. Students from too far away to walk boarded with local families. Built in 1833, it was one of several academies then operating on the East End of Long Island. The most famous and oldest was the Clinton Academy in East Hampton, but others operated in Sag Harbor and Southampton, sometimes on a rather irregular schedule as teachers came and went. Sometime after 1890, with private academies no longer needed because of the establishment of public secondary schools, the old academy building was moved back on its lot and converted into a dwelling that still stands at 2170 Main Road in Laurel.

The academy's most famous principal, Joseph Newton Hallock (1832–1913), Herman's second cousin who grew up in Franklinville, served in 1857 when Halsey, Adelia, and Tommy Pope attended. Joseph Newton had just graduated from Yale, where he was exposed to radical abolitionist thinking. He likely influenced the young Halsey's thinking about slavery and the plight of the enslaved. Joseph Newton left a couple of years later to become principal of the new Northville Academy. He later moved to Brooklyn to become editor and publisher of the *Christian at Work*, an important religious journal of its time.

Most days Halsey, Adelia, and Tommy walked three miles to school through the woods that still stood along today's Herrick's Lane. Occasionally Halsey's older brother Daniel took them by wagon, and they walked home.[32] An advertisement over the name J. N. Hallock for the spring 1857 term of the Franklinville Academy anticipated "a pleasant and profitable term" and invited "all who desire to improve and are WILLING TO STUDY."[33]

According to Bessie's "Autobiography of an Old House," Halsey's parents sent his siblings Charles, Daniel, and Adelia into "the city" for the final years of their education—either Brooklyn or New York City—the Hallocks had cousins in both places.[34] Daniel received some musical training there and learned to play the melodeon. A diary entry mentions Adelia coming home from "seminary."

Halsey's diary for 1857, though far from complete, does cover the first three months of the year he attended the Franklinville Academy, which he barely mentions except for the last day of school on March 19 when he reported that the graduation exercises held in the Franklinville Church "pass off finely." Unlike his siblings, Halsey never received any further education.

His diary fails to mention the most significant thing that happened to him there—meeting a young girl named Marietta Terry, who became his first wife three years later (see fig. 2.1). From Hog Neck (Bayview) in Southold, she boarded with a Franklinville family. The only possible allusion—an entry on July 4 that year saying he and George Tuthill went out riding. Tuthill was Halsey's best friend at the academy and also fell in love with a girl from Hog Neck. Halsey prefaces this report with the statement that "nothing much of importance had happened in the previous two weeks." But, based on an account Halsey wrote 70 years later, it appears the destination of the two young men on their July 4 ride was most likely the girls' homes on Hog Neck![35] The young men apparently either proposed or restarted their courtships that day and the two couples married in a double wedding ceremony in 1860.

Figure 2.1. Halsey Hallock (A) and Marietta Terry (B), probably taken about the time they met at the Franklinville Academy in the 1856–57 term. *Source:* Hallockville Museum Farm. Used with permission.

Scarlet Fever

A scarlet fever epidemic hit the North Fork in mid-spring of 1857. Halsey's entry on May 24 mentions attending the funeral of 21-year-old Allen Reeves and quoted the minister's text: "All men are appointed once to die." The next day, a Sunday, he reports his friend, 16-year-old Nathaniel Downs, at "the point of death" in the morning, making for a very solemn church service. Downs died that evening. The following day Halsey attended his second burial in three days. "No funeral sermon is preached on account of sickness yet in the family"—the only comment in his diary. Soon, Nathaniel Downs's older brother, George, at 19, almost the same age as Halsey, also succumbed to the epidemic. Both of the Downs boys attended the District 11 school with Halsey and were likely frequent playmates.

Scarlet fever become more virulent in the early years of the 19th century. It crashed across the country in waves, with the worst cumulating in 1858, before subsiding in the early 20th century, for reasons not clearly understood. It was a disease of young people, most common between the ages of 5 and 15, although the scourge reached both younger and older.[36] The same year Halsey lost his three friends, 10 burials of young people under 26 occurred in the Sound Avenue Cemetery—compared with one or two in most other years—most likely victims of the epidemic raging across the country.[37] Ten burials of children occurred in the Aquebogue cemetery the same year.[38] In Franklinville (now Laurel), Edward and Alma Fanning, who lived just west of the Franklinville Academy, lost two children at the same time and buried them in a single coffin with a shared headstone for "little Willie & Mary."[39]

Brother Daniel and Sister Adelia Marry

During the year-and-a-quarter that Halsey kept his diary reasonably faithfully, his brother Daniel courted Amanda Wells, a sister of Charles's wife Laura. Halsey refers casually to "Daniel and his girl" going to a temperance meeting together. Another time they arrive together at a family gathering in Jamesport. On yet another date he mentions that "in the evening Dan has gone courting."

In 1858 they married. Daniel's father Herman followed the usual Puritan custom and set the new couple up on a farm about six miles to the west in Roanoke (the area of Sound Avenue around present day Roanoke Avenue) that Zachariah II purchased for unknown reasons in one of his many real estate forays some years earlier.[40] As typical in such situations, the father Herman likely kept the deed in his own name.

Later that same year, Halsey's sister Adelia also married. As Bessie describes the occasion in her "Autobiography of an Old House," "On October 12, 1858, seventeen-year-old Adelia walked out of this house and was married to Simeon O. Benjamin in the Northville Church on the north side of the road. Simeon's niece, Adelia Youngs Dimon was her attendant and I have been told that her cousin Serepta Aldrich came on horseback, (the same horse) with her beau Richard Albertson, both from Jamesport, to attend the wedding."[41] Simeon and Adelia settled on a farm about two miles to the west on Sound Avenue. Interestingly, the three siblings—Charles, Daniel, and Adelia—all found spouses among the members of the new church on Sound Avenue, not in the older Steeple Church in Aquebogue that their parents attended.

Music

A long history of music exists in the Hallock family. One descendant of Capt. Zachariah supposedly played in the band that welcomed Lafayette back for his triumphal revisit to the United States. Zachariah II and his two sons were long remembered for their singing voices. Arminda's family was also musical, with her a good singer and passing on her musical talent to her children.[42]

Halsey's brother Daniel may have been the most musical of Herman and Arminda's children. Around 1852, when Daniel was about 16 and Halsey about 14, Daniel took his younger brother to a singing school in Greenport led by William B. Bradbury (1816–1868), who became well known as a musician, music teacher, and composer of hymns and anthems as well as a manufacturer of pianos. Halsey recalled that "all the talent on the east end were there." Halsey still remembered 75 years later that "the great piano and voices could make some noise." It was maybe the first time he heard a piano play.[43]

The incident made an even greater impression on the musically inclined Daniel. He spent the next winter in New York City "giving attention to music." He came back able to play the melodeon, a small reed organ, with the idea of introducing instrumental music to Northville Church—an idea that, as we will see, caused a furor in the conservative church.

In January 1855 Halsey and Daniel attended another all-day singing school in Greenport. They stayed overnight at a hotel, returning the next day after meeting up with friends. He went to another singing convention in Riverhead later in the year, as well as a few other singing schools. Eventually, his brother Daniel organized his own singing school for the church choir, which Tommy Pope recalled in one of his letters. Tommy also recalled their own impromptu "singing schools" while cutting trees in their woodland.

Temperance

Despite popular misconceptions, in the 17th, 18th, and even early 19th century New England Puritans did not eschew alcohol. Instead, rum and other alcoholic beverages were an important part of their meals and celebrations. Halsey's great-grandfather Capt. Zachariah Hallock's account book, kept from 1771 to 1818, shows occasional references to hard cider, and the record book of a local store shows rum as one of the few items he purchased regularly.[44] An inventory taken at his death in 1820 included casks for hard cider.[45] His son, Halsey's grandfather, Zachariah II, continued to produce hard cider on the Hallock farm for his entire life. Halsey remembered his grandfather's cider mill "built by himself by a new improved plan" and that his grandfather always kept "a couple of barrels in his cellar, a treat for his company and for himself, and sold many dollars worth of that cider made from his own orchards."[46]

This attitude began to change as the temperance movement nationally grew out of the evangelical Protestant religious revivals of the 1820s and 1830s, known as the Second Great Awakening, that fostered numerous social reform initiatives, including abolitionism. The Sound Avenue community held its first temperance meeting in 1828 in one of its schoolhouses. James Y. Downs (1813–1894), one of the local attendees, reported, "There was a pledge drawn up and it was for one year and I signed it. I think there was between 20 and 30 that signed. This put a stop to setting the bottle before men as soon as they came in. We did not think of trying to do work without rum."[47]

The movement grew rapidly over the next two decades. Halsey's brother Daniel became a strong advocate for prohibition, perhaps as a result of a revival experience at age 16.[48] While Daniel was the most heavily involved, the whole family—with the notable exception of Halsey's grandfather, Zachariah II—attended numerous temperance meetings and often heard temperance sermons in their churches. One of the ministers in Northville Church became a local leader of the crusade—perhaps one of the reasons that Daniel, Halsey, and Charles all gravitated to that church in the 1850s.

The whole church—essentially the whole community—became caught up in the temperance movement. Halsey and his brother Daniel likely attended the September 1860 meeting of the Suffolk County Temperance Society at the "elegant" new Northville Church built the year before. The correspondent for the *Sag-Harbor Express* described the meeting as the "most interesting" he attended in the 10 years since the organization's founding. The two-day session ended with a choral rendition of an ode to the tune of "For Auld Lang Syne," conducted by Joseph Newton Hallock with words he wrote specially for the occasion. Here are two verses:

> Let "auld acquaintance" be forgot—
> Rum, Brandy, Gin and Wine—
> We'll drink in the gushing water pure
> For auld lang syne.

> Ye Merry Northville girls and boys
> From morn till day's decline
> Drink sparkling water pure and bright,
> For auld lang syne.[49]

When Zachariah II died in 1854, the family quickly dismantled his cider press.[50] For the next century or more, no Hallock touched alcoholic beverages, nor did any members of the community openly do so. Indeed, well past the middle of the 20th century, all social events in the community—whether church meetings, Grange suppers, or family celebrations—were entirely dry. Even the church switched from wine to grape juice in their communion services.

No Mention of Anti-Slavery

A startling omission from Halsey's diary is the abolition movement. Even though 1855 became the year of "Bleeding Kansas" and much national ferment over the status of slavery in the Union, Halsey never once mentions it in his diary. Despite his later proud recollection that his first vote was for Abraham Lincoln, he never records attending an anti-slavery meeting. Although he occasionally notes the subjects discussed in a sermon or at the many prayer meetings and other religious gatherings, his diary never once mentions the evils of slavery. Instead, the family's main moral concerns focused on the temperance movement. Once in February 1855 they attended an anti-tobacco meeting, but never an anti-slavery meeting.

A World Unchanged

In many ways the Sound Avenue world that Halsey grew up in was unchanged from the world of his great-great-great-great-great-grandfather William Hallock in the 1640s. The Southold-born novelist George Frederick Humel, in his 1935 novel *Heritage*, wrote this description of the fictional community Norwold, a thinly disguised version of his hometown that could have described the Sound Avenue community equally well:

> Save for a slight change in high-water mark and its drift nearer the pole-star the Norwold of 1846 was the Norwold of 1646.

Its village rules and customs, as well as the daily life and deep-rooted prejudices of its inhabitants, were in all essentials what they had been two hundred years before. . . . The families which made up Norwold's hundred-odd households were, with few exceptions, the families which had founded the village in the sixteen-forties. Everyone, except by accident or intrusion, was everybody else's uncle, cousin, a'nt, gramper, gramma, heir apparent. Everybody knew everybody else's family-history for at least four generations back.[51]

Chapter 3

Love, War, and Death

Daniel, Halsey, and the Civil War

> It was as if the pitcher at the fountain was broken and its crystal contents all lost.
>
> —Halsey Hallock, about the death of his first wife

A Vote for Lincoln

Halsey Hallock turned 21 on July 4, 1859. His first opportunity to vote in a presidential election involved the momentous contest of 1860 between Abraham Lincoln, John C. Breckinridge, John Bell, and Stephen A. Douglas. Seventy years later, Halsey loved to tell his daughter Bessie's young piano students, while they waited for their lessons, about that first presidential vote—for Lincoln.[1] With his family all strong Republicans and supporters of the abolitionist cause, Halsey was in the majority in the town of Riverhead, which Lincoln carried with 69 percent of the vote.[2] As much as Halsey liked to talk about his support for Lincoln, he never mentioned to Bessie's young students that numerous ancestors on both sides of his family once owned slaves or that the town hired a substitute so that he did not need to go to war.

Love and Marriage

Just a few weeks after voting for Lincoln, Halsey married Marietta Terry. "In November 1860," as Bessie wrote, "a Franklinville Academy romance culminated in the marriage of the youngest son David Halsey to Marietta Terry, the daughter of King Hiram Jesse Terry of Southold."[3] The equivalent of high school sweethearts, Halsey, age 17, met Marietta, age 14, while both attended the Franklinville Academy. Her family lived about 10 miles away in Bayview, part of Hog Neck in Southold. Consequently, she boarded with a local family while at school. At the time, Halsey did not mention Marietta in his diary, but here are his recollections many years later:

> At the [Franklinville Academy] that winter I became attached to a girl, Marietta Terry, that came from the before mentioned homely name of Hog Neck or later called Port Tranquil. Now that was a risky thing to do. I had hardly ever been so far from home but having once broken the ice of timidity by offering my arm in the entry of the hall and meeting with no repulse and walking by her side with her gloved hand in mine, for it was cold, to Mr. Skidmore's, her boarding place. We parted little thinking of what dangerous grounds we had entered. A correspondence was kept up for two years and the affinity became more and more. Eventually my friend, George H. Tuthill thought it would be a nice way to spend our July Fourth to call and see our acquaintances. I think he had kept up a correspondence with his future wife [Nancy "Nannie" Beebe] also. Well, in November of 1860 Marietta Terry and I were married. It was a double ceremony in the Southold Presbyterian church performed by the Rev. Dr. Whitaker.[4]

Marietta Terry

Although Halsey's diary covers the 1856–57 winter term at the Franklinville Academy when he met Marietta Terry, it never mentions Marietta. Almost no other information exists about Marietta from this time. Tommy Pope does not mention her in his letters to Halsey many years later. The only surviving document is a letter written April 20, 1857, from Adelaide Hallock, a classmate of Halsey's younger sister Adelia at the Franklinville Academy, to Marietta, back at her parent's home at "Port Tranquil" (now Bayview) on Hog Neck in Southold. The winter term ended a month earlier. Adelaide, the daughter of Caleb and Almina Hallock, lived just three farms to the west of the Hallock Homestead.

The letter chats about the weather, a new scholar at the academy, a social day, and the scarlet fever epidemic coursing through the area—no news, or even mention of Halsey, except for a cryptic comment that "I have not had a chance to tell Adelia what you told me to but I will tell her the first opportunity." Could the little secret be the budding romance between Halsey and Marietta?[5] Why else did the Hallock family keep this letter?

Major Changes to the Homestead

Following the tradition of Puritan fathers, Herman needed to provide a home for the young couple. Having settled his other two sons on farms of their own, he wanted to keep Halsey on the Homestead. Herman's stepmother, Christiana, had died, leaving the Homestead's west wing empty. However, he and Arminda probably did not think it was big enough. Maybe they hoped for lots of grandchildren? Instead, they moved the small west wing, probably dating from the mid-1700s, and attached it to the rear of the Homestead, where it remains today. To make room for that wing, they detached and moved off two small wings. One became a chicken coop and the other became the washhouse and later the farm shop. To avoid blocking upstairs windows on the back of the main house, they constructed a small flat-roofed connector that caused Homestead occupants leakage problems every time it snowed.

The family then built a much larger and "more modern" wing on the west side of the Homestead to accommodate the newlyweds.[6] Halsey and his bride Marietta had the use of not only four rooms downstairs and three upstairs in the new wing but, through interconnecting doors, several more rooms both upstairs and downstairs in the old part of the Homestead.

Family and Community Divided by the War

As proud as Halsey was of his support for Lincoln, these sentiments were not popular with many others in their Sound Avenue community who strongly opposed the war and what they thought it stood for. Some neighbors even crossed the street to avoid the Hallocks. Melinda Corwin was a next-door neighbor before the Hallock brothers switched farms and a frequent visitor in the Hallock home, but as the two families drifted apart in their political views during the 1850s, records of such visits grow conspicuously absent from her diary. She demonstrated her strong anti-Lincoln views in 1861 when she lamented a "begging sermon" given by an abolitionist preacher in the Sound Avenue Church.[7]

Early in the Civil War, pro-war communities across Long Island erected "liberty poles"—basically extra-tall flagpoles—to show their patriotic support for the Union. A 105-foot-high liberty pole rose in East Hampton on May 21, 1861.[8] Another went up in Hempstead Village that year, with Southampton raising one the following year. According to Harrison Hunt and Bill Bleyer, historians of Long Island and the Civil War, it became almost a competition to see who put up the tallest pole.[9]

Pro-Union members of the Sound Avenue community decided to erect a liberty pole in front of the church. They obtained a suitable pole in Greenport and carted it as far as the Hallockville neighborhood, where they left it while waiting for the top mast to be fitted. During the night, opponents of the war stole the pole and destroyed it. The parishioners went back to Greenport, obtained another pole, and set it up.[10] It can be seen in a pencil-and-charcoal drawing (fig. 3.1) done shortly after by Sarah E. Luce, the daughter of a prosperous Sound Avenue farmer Hallock Luce.

Figure 3.1. This circa-1861 drawing by Sarah E. Luce (1838–1908) shows the second Northville Church, completed the year before, on the left, and the first church, built in 1831, on the right, with the steeple added in 1860 when it became the Northville Academy. The unusually tall flagpole in the foreground at the intersection of Church Lane and Sound Avenue was the liberty pole that caused a major controversy in the community. *Source:* Hallockville Museum Farm. Used with permission.

The flag appears to have 33 stars, the number of states from February 14, 1859, when Oregon joined the Union, to July 3, 1861.

Although authorities never definitely identified the individuals who destroyed the liberty pole, a series of articles about subsequent scandals in the Northville Church linked the perpetrators to those scandals and pointed specifically to Isaiah and Caleb Hallock, first cousins of Halsey's father. Isaiah lived one house west of the Hallock Homestead—where the Hallockville Museum's Cichanowicz farmhouse now stands—and Caleb lived two houses further west. Both were strong Copperheads, as opponents of the war became known. This incident suspiciously took place virtually in their front yard and illustrates the bitter divisions that racked the community and the nation—and the Hallock family—during those difficult times.

Many decades later, Halsey Hallock referred obliquely to "the deepest trials in Civil War Times" in the Northville Church.[11] A majority of its members supported Lincoln. Halsey told a story about two men (probably Joseph Newton Hallock and a brother) doggedly crossing fields from Franklinville to attend the Northville Church because of its abolitionist stance. However, a strong minority clearly stood on the other side.

Rev. Thomas Harris, the minister in the church during the war years, apparently supported the abolitionist cause. Samuel "Sammy" Tuthill, a Northville farmer who strongly opposed the war—and nephew of Caleb and Isaiah Hallock, making him Halsey's second cousin—reported disparagingly in his diary one Sunday in 1863 that "Priest Harris preached politics & nigger."[12] Another Sunday that year, Sammy complained in his diary about a "black abolishioner" in the pulpit. On still another Sunday he complained about a "radical abolitionist, full of higher law" preaching in the church. That July, after Sammy returned from a town meeting about Lincoln's first wartime draft, he reported (incorrectly) the burning of the draft office in Jamaica by protesters and added the comment "we hope so."[13] Although they didn't burn the Jamaica draft office—which served both Queens and Suffolk counties—rioters there, encouraged by leading Democrats, did attack the building, remove soldier uniforms, and burn those in a huge bonfire.[14] Sammy likely also heard news of the anti-draft and anti-Black riots in Manhattan—the most destructive in American history—at the same meeting. His strong sentiments about the draft and the war are clear!

Sammy Tuthill frequently attended Democratic caucuses and anti-war rallies that year and the next, including a "peace meeting" in Riverhead that featured speakers from as far away as Illinois and lasted all afternoon and well into the evening. Just before the election of 1864, he attended an anti-war assembly held in the Northville Church's lecture room—"quite a full meeting," according to Sammy. He attended anti-war events with his uncles Caleb and Isaiah Hallock, Isaiah's son George C. Hallock, and a first cousin, Eugene Hallock—all immediate Hallockville neighbors of Halsey and his family.

Halsey likely participated in a special town meeting February 17, 1864, called to decide what action the town should take to fill its quota in the president's recent draft. At that meeting Benjamin F. Wells, one of the local Copperhead leaders, dramatically offered a resolution: "Whereas war in all its aspects is dreadful and terrible and all its acts and tendencies are to death and destruction, therefore, resolved by the people of this Town . . . [we] are utterly opposed to a further prosecution of this most wicked and unrighteous war."[15] James Harvey Tuthill (1826–1894), a Riverhead lawyer, then amended the resolution to strike out everything starting with "utterly opposed" and replaced it with the words "heartily and forever in favor of the prosecution of this war until this most wicked rebellion can be entirely subdued." Thus amended, the resolution passed, although the numbers for and against were not recorded.

At a subsequent special meeting that April, as the *Suffolk Weekly Times* reported, "The Copperhead raised his snakish head and began to hiss" when Wells introduced a similar resolution: "Whereas a further prosecution of the War leads only to a larger expenditure of blood treasure and destruction, therefore Resolved that the people of this town no longer desire its further continuance and earnestly invokes a Suspension of hostilities and return to peace." After this resolution failed 90 to 25, the meeting adopted a resolution urging the "most vigorous prosecution of the war" and an amendment to the Constitution abolishing slavery, "the cause of the war."[16]

In the 1864 election, Halsey undoubtedly voted for Lincoln again, but the president's popularity ebbed a bit locally. He carried Riverhead with only 55 percent of the vote, and in the election district that included Northville, Jamesport, and Aquebogue, Lincoln retained an even slimmer 52 percent majority. The "Peace Party" (i.e., Democrats) got 48 percent of the vote—truly a community and a family divided.

Support for the War Did Not Lead to Volunteering

Even though a decisive majority of Riverhead's voters initially supported the war and the Republican party, this did not translate into large numbers of the town's young men volunteering for service. Only somewhere between 75 and 83 men went to war from Riverhead during the entire war—an extraordinarily low number—only about 2.5 percent of the town's population of 3,044.[17] The North as a whole sent an over 11.1 percent of its population to fight, more than four times as much as Riverhead. Even fewer served from Riverhead's "old families"—less than one out of every ten eligible young men. None of the young men in the Sound Avenue community, including Halsey and his two brothers, volunteered in the war's early years, despite their strong abolitionist leanings. Of the 27 young Hallock men living in the town in 1860, only one ever served at any point in the war—and only after he was drafted—Halsey's older brother Daniel Y. Hallock.

Marietta's Brother Charles Terry

Although most of Halsey's immediate family and community avoided serving in the army, he and Marietta still had a personal connection to the war—Marietta's brother Charles E. Terry, who enlisted at age 18, in September 1862, as a private in the New York 127th Infantry Regiment (known as the Monitors), along with a number of other young men from Southold. Terry "was just a boy [who] had been induced to join as Southold got up a company to all go together," Halsey recalled many years later. "Oh how she [Marietta] would pray for his safe return."[18]

Terry served for the duration of the war until mustered out as a private in June 1865. His unit, initially assigned to the defense of Washington, saw action in northern Virginia and after August 1863 in a series of engagements in and around Charleston, South Carolina. Although not one of the more bloodied units in a bloody war, the regiment nevertheless lost about 130 of its members, out of the thousand in a typical regiment, to either battle casualties or disease.[19]

Halsey's Brother Daniel Goes Off to the War

On July 1, 1863, Halsey and his two brothers traveled to Jamaica, in Queens County, to register for the nation's first wartime draft at the office that served all of Long Island except Brooklyn. Daniel became one of 1,120 unlucky men, out of 4,024 enrolled from Suffolk County, chosen in the first lottery that September.[20] (See fig. 3.2.)

Figure 3.2. Daniel Y. Hallock, circa 1864, with his wife and two sons (A), and then in uniform (B). These photos were probably taken on the same day as keepsakes for his family before he went off to war . . . just in case. *Source:* Hallockville Museum Farm. Used with permission.

Unlike most other draftees, despite his responsibilities taking care of a farm and a young family, Daniel enlisted in the Eighth New York Heavy Artillery as a private on February 1, 1864. We don't know why he volunteered rather than waiting to be called or finding a way to avoid service. He was always something of a dreamer and idealist.[21] However, the motivation may have been partly financial. In addition to his salary of $13 per month and a $100 bounty for volunteers, the town of Riverhead offered a $400 bonus to anyone who volunteered, a not insignificant sum in those days, and another $5 per month to a wife of a soldier plus $1.50 per month for each child.[22] The first-year package totaled $752—well more than the $300 to $600 in value of farm crops that many young farmers in the area could produce at the time.

A number of his letters to his parents and brother Halsey survive.[23] The Eighth New York Artillery, initially stationed guarding a hospital near Fort McHenry in Maryland, moved to the northern Virginia theater in May 1864, where it saw heavy fighting. Daniel fought in the Battle of the Wilderness, Gen. Ulysses S. Grant's first foray into northern Virginia.[24] The unit went on to fight in battles of Cold Harbor, Ream's Station, Thatcher's Run (Hatch's Run), and others. However, Daniel did not participate in most of this fighting. Starting in early June 1864, he spent nine months in military hospitals. Although initially disabled with severe diarrhea, in later letters he describes his diagnosis as "nervous prostration" or "a case of genuine nervousness." He spent most of that time at Lincoln General Hospital, the largest of the Civil War hospitals, located just 15 blocks east of the Capitol in Washington, DC.

He rejoined his unit in March 1865, the final month of the war, just after his comrades fought in the battle of Thatcher's Run.[25] However, the Eighth New York was heavily involved in the war's last campaign. Indeed, Daniel was just 28 miles from Appomattox, on a forced march from Petersburg, when news of Lee's surrender arrived on April 9, 1865. A dramatic letter to his parents dated April 17, 1865, from Burksville, Virginia, describes his elation at the "crowning victory of the war" and the "good prospect of the complete overthrow of the rebellion." He added that "in the mercy of God I have been enabled to participate in this last movement and have been spared to see victory crown our arms."[26]

Altogether, the regiment, which numbered about 1,000, lost 372 of its members to battle-caused deaths and another 298 to disease. The unit mustered out on June 5, 1865, although Daniel and some of his comrades served a few more months in another New York unit.

Elisha Wells

Herman and Arminda also received personal communications describing the horrors of the war from two other soldiers. The first was Elisha Wells (1830–1895), a friend of the Hallock family. His wife, Maria Skillman Hudson, grew up near Herman. Notorious as the "town drunk," during the Civil War Elisha hit a real low.[27] A court removed property from his name and appointed Herman and another friend to look out for Maria and their seven children. On December 31, 1863, at age 33, realizing he needed to do something to pull his life together, Elisha walked to New

York City. There he met a man from Connecticut who took him to New Haven and enlisted him in the Second Connecticut Heavy Artillery. Elisha likely received a sign-up bonus in Connecticut, but his granddaughter Lois Young claimed that "certainly his wife never saw any of it."[28]

In his 18 months in the army, Elisha wrote occasional letters to his "Dear Friend, Mr. Herman Hallock," who served as guardian of his affairs. Elisha saw plenty of action, including the battle of Cold Harbor where 10,000 Union men lost their lives in half an hour. His regiment alone lost 400 men in the fortnight before the first letter in June 1864. Elisha's letters home did not varnish the truth. "No man can realize what a battle is except one that has been in one," he wrote. "Those who have never been south can form no idea of the horrors of war." He added, "If I ever live through this war it will be a wonder. The chances are ten to one against me."[29]

The second letter, dated December 26, 1864, was more confident. Now stationed at Fort McMahon in front of Petersburg, Virginia, he thought the "Rebs" could not last much longer there and that as a whole "the rebellion is about to cave in."

If Elisha's purpose in enlisting was to get his life back in order, it appears to have worked. One of the letters mentions sending $25 to his wife and asks Herman to check on whether she received the funds. He returned from the war as a reformed man and farmed successfully until his death in 1895. He remained close to the Hallocks, and his son Charles married Halsey's daughter Eula in 1891.

James Henry Tuthill

Arminda also corresponded with her nephew, James Henry Tuthill (1834–1925), the son of her brother-in-law James Tuthill, founder of the whaling port of "James Port"—today South Jamesport. Tuthill served in the Union Army from 1862 through 1865. Like Elisha Wells, Tuthill did not attempt to minimize the horrors of war in letters to his aunt. He served in most of Gen. Philip Sheridan's bloody Shenandoah Valley campaign that began in September 1864. That November he wrote of persevering "through fields of carnage and blood." He seemed particularly distressed by the behavior of some of his fellow soldiers: "As a Soldier I have had much to resist in order to live as I would die. In battle while leaden hail fell thick and fast, men would plunder, men would fight with fearful oaths, some seem lost as men, and transposed to demons." Wounded and assigned to slightly safer duty as a general's clerk during his recovery, with just eight months left of this three-year enrollment, he told his aunt that he looked forward to coming home.[30]

A Substitute Dies for Halsey

Halsey escaped the draft in the first two rounds, but that changed either in the May or July 1864 lotteries in response to the president's call for an additional 500,000 men. However, instead of enlisting like his brother Daniel, he allowed the town to hire a substitute in his place—something neither he nor the family ever mentioned after the war.

The wartime draft acts specifically allowed for the hiring of substitutes to serve in place of men drafted. On eastern Long Island, this became a way for the local Republican majorities to retain support without putting their sons at risk. Riverhead, like many other area towns, decided to hire substitutes for any who chose not to serve. The town raised the money by borrowing from its residents. Herman loaned the town $200 in the first round of fundraising. Halsey's uncle, Zachariah Hallock III, loaned $200 in 1864, and several relatives and many others in the town made similar loans.[31] Altogether Riverhead raised $103,886 in bonds to pay for the hiring of substitutes for anyone who wanted one and bounties to those who enlisted—an amazing amount of money for the town, nearly 30 times its annual budget before the war.[32]

J. Henry Perkins, Riverhead's wealthiest citizen and the town's treasurer, went to New York City to hire a substitute. A receipt in the collection of the Riverhead town historian shows that on September 22, 1864, he paid Oliver E. Vail $2,000 to hire substitutes for Halsey Hallock and another Riverhead draftee, Elisha E. King.

Providing substitutes became a lucrative business during the Civil War. Agents scoured the poorer parts of New York City and Brooklyn for young men, often recent immigrants, willing to enlist for a fee. Early in the war, a substitute cost $300, but as the conflict ground on, agents offered up to $500. However, the agent charged Riverhead $1,000 for Halsey's substitute—a tidy profit indeed!

The substitute for Halsey, a 24-year-old blue-eyed, brown-haired German immigrant named Erich Bartels, traveled to Jamaica, Queens, to enlist on September 21, 1864, as a "volunteer" in Halsey's stead.[33] Just a month later, Bartels received a mortal wound in the battle of Boydton Plank Road, also known as Burgess Mill or First Hatcher's Run and part of the bloody siege of Petersburg, Virginia. Bartels lingered in the regimental hospital in Petersburg for over five months before dying on March 31, 1865.[34] The official cause of death—"Vulnus Sclopet"—the abbreviation commonly used in Civil War records for the Latin term *Vulnus Sclopeticum* for "gunshot wound." Ironically, Halsey's brother Daniel was stationed in the same place. One wonders if either of the Hallock brothers ever met Bartels or knew of his death—certainly something the Hallock family never acknowledged.

Neither Halsey nor anyone else in the family ever talked about why he, unlike his older brother Daniel, chose not to serve in the army when drafted: maybe the family thought one brother in the war enough; maybe his father needed him home on the farm; maybe he and Marietta already knew too much about the horrors of the war from her brother Charles and his brother Daniel—and the letters from Elisha Wells and James Tuthill. Or perhaps Halsey and Marietta already knew she was expecting, with their long-awaited first child due in less than seven months.

Death of Halsey's First Wife

The nation plunged into grief with the death of President Lincoln on April 15, 1865. Just four days later Halsey suffered a second, much more personal loss when his wife, Marietta, died in childbirth.

After their marriage, as Halsey later wrote, he and Marietta "lived as happily together in [their] humble home as ever a young couple can."[35] But as he noted, "Perhaps in the wife's heart especially there was one thing lacking as was most natural": the lack of a child during the first four years of their marriage, a delay quite uncommon in those days before any practicable birth control. When Marietta finally became pregnant after such a long wait, their expectations soared. As he remembered nearly 60 years later:

> As we were looking and anxiously awaiting the happy result, it was as if the pitcher at the fountain was broken and its crystal contents all lost. The dear little expected one, she lay on her mother's arm and such was destiny or divinity. Friends do you know what [this] means to a young man? Some do. I cannot forget. [Some] may say I am indulging in sentimental feelings, wondering back to days long since passed, [but these memories] bring deep feelings of joy and sadness. My heart swells and my

eyes suffuse with tears. . . . How sad the memories of that spring. The whole nation was in mourning for the president, Abraham Lincoln, who was laid to rest in those same days.[36]

Halsey always called her "my dear heart Marietta." They buried her in the Terry family plot in the Southold cemetery—in a single coffin with the stillborn daughter in her mother's arms. For the rest of his long life, Halsey visited the grave and Marietta's family every time he went to Southold, often taking his second wife along.

> It would seem I and all were stricken at this time as never before. It has not been an easy task for me to write the above. I have a tender heart and tears are very near the surface and I have very little privacy. I know that I am pursuing a course that you seldom see in print. When I came to my senses, I felt like one dead. All fond hopes crushed with a feeling of helplessness and despondency. But I was young and possessed of a good share of energy—had a good home—father and mother in the same house and, of course, I was comfortable—but oh so lonely and desolate.

While waiting for a brighter day to dawn, he moved back to the east side of the Homestead to live with his parents. The new west wing, where he and Marietta lived so happily, stood empty for the next year and a half.

Halsey liked poetry and probably knew Walt Whitman's famous poem about Lincoln's death:

> When lilacs last in the door-yard bloom'd,
> And the great star early droop'd in the western sky in the night,
> I mourn'd—and yet shall mourn with ever-returning spring.

One wonders how Halsey faced each successive spring, with its fresh reminders of the double loss whenever he saw Whitman's "lilac bush, tall-growing, with heart-shaped leaves of rich green" that still grows just east of the Homestead, right outside his bedroom window.

Chapter 4

Last Family in the Homestead

1866–1885

And here begins the dawning of my second life.

—Halsey Hallock

Halsey's Second Marriage

Despite Halsey's desolation at the death of Marietta, soon "hope again began to kindle, there might be a brighter day dawning." Just over a year and a half later, on November 15, 1866, he married again, this time to the 19-year-old Emilie Jane Wells (1847–1932). Sixty-six years later, about the time that Emilie died, he wrote this:

> And here begins the dawning of my second life. I had lived out my first life, in the most favorable circumstances from the beginning to the end and it is but as a tale that is told. The tree that is cut down is not dead soon puts forth its strength in a new growth.
>
> It took but little encouragement on the part of those that were older to start the slumbering but beautiful coal of hope and love again into a glow of life. All the inevitable past was unchangeable. A new step of adventure was before me and once the step was begun the flame began to burn all new and delightfully beautiful. What a beautiful flower, love and hope

combined make—what a dreary world it would be without it. Yes, there was a beautiful blossom of a girl of the same stock as my brothers' choices—the daughter of their only brother. I had never met her and she looked so young and beautiful—had I the courage, audacity to make any advancement in that direction. Faint heart never wins, the venture was taken and bless the Lord proved a success.[1]

Halsey claimed not to have noticed Emilie before, but she was the daughter of Joshua Minor and Betsey Wells, prominent members of the community and the niece of both of his sisters-in-law (his two brothers married Joshua Minor's sisters, making Emilie's sisters-in-law also her aunts). Moreover, she was a member of the Northville Church, she lived just two miles west on Sound Avenue, and she was his second cousin.[2] Incidentally Emilie's mother's middle name was Hallock.

Emilie

Halsey was 28 at the time, nine years older than Emilie. He recalled later that "wags" commented about the nine-year difference in their ages: "All the little birds of gossip were set busy. That old fellow, why it can't be true, too much difference in their ages and such like." But in many ways they shared a lot in common beyond their background and family connections.

Emilie received a similar elementary education in the District 10 school and then attended the new Northville Academy in 1862 and 1863. Coincidentally, the principal of the academy during Emilie's student years was Joseph Newton Hallock, the same liberal-leaning Yale graduate who served as principal of the Franklinville Academy five years earlier when Halsey attended.

While a student at the Northville Academy, Emilie started a "Forget Me Not Album" with poems and notes written mostly by school friends—a precursor to the modern yearbook custom. The first entry records an ode "To Emilie" by J. Newton Hallock, the principal of the Northville Academy, followed by autographs, notes, and sentimental poems from 50 of her friends and classmates, as well as from ministers in the Northville Church, all written in 1862 and 1863. Most of the verses seem highly sentimental and carefully rhymed and metered—but with not a single reference to the bloody Civil War then in progress.[3]

However, Emilie clearly shared Halsey's views on the war. In 1862, while "editress" of *The Seminary Bell*, Northville Academy's student newspaper, she wrote: "Let us be thankful that as the eighty-sixth anniversary of American liberty draws nearer and nearer, we feel more and more assured of the safety of our glorious Union, for which our ancestors bled, and suffered and which our noble volunteers are striving to perpetuate. May we all be grateful for the success which attends them and for the many blessings we enjoy as a nation."[4] Another indication of her political proclivities comes from a remarkable letter Emilie received from a French-born Civil War soldier. Emilie sent a care package that randomly found its way to 27-year-old G. A. Gaston Jacquemin-de-Zouval at General Hospital at David's Island, New York Harbor. In his thank-you letter dated July 27, 1865, he told of being inspired by his own "great-father," who left France to fight with Lafayette "in 1770" [*sic*] for the freedom of America. "I think it was never so nobler a cause than the one you have been fighting, for it is self freedom, Your Union, Your Country, Your so noblest institutions in all your Liberty, Celestial gifts that God in his mercy has given to all, to you particularly, in this blessed Country." The letter became a treasured keepsake in the Hallock family. No record can be found of this young soldier, but there is ample documentation of French soldiers participating in the war.[5]

Wedding

Emilie and Halsey married the morning of November 15, 1866, in the home of the bride, as was customary on Sound Avenue. Their 66-year marriage proved a long, happy, and loving one, with relatives remembering them holding hands to the end. As strong as his attachments to his second wife, he never gave up his feelings about his first wife. Whenever they went to Southold, he took Emilie to Marietta's grave and to visit her parents. Halsey spoke of having two fathers-in-law. In 1872 he mentioned in his diary visiting both "Father Wells" and "Father Terry."[6] Marietta's parents in turn always referred to Emilie as their "dear daughter."[7]

This description survives of Halsey and Emilie's wedding:

> Emilie Jane Wells married David Halsey Hallock on Thursday morning at 8 o'clock, November 15, 1866. The day was cloudy and showery. [The] marriage took place in the parlor of her girlhood home between the front windows (the west front room). The

wedding breakfast was served before the ceremony. Rev. John A. Woodhull performed the ceremony and the couple were attended by Simeon O. Benjamin and Adelia J. Benjamin [Halsey's sister and her husband]. Those present were all of the Wells family then born, Herman W. Hallock and Arminda Hallock, parents of the groom and the Misses Maria "Libby" and Lorenia Benjamin, cousins of the bride. The bride was attired in her traveling dress, a red merino with red hat trimmed with black velvet bands, flat white velvet flowers and wide white satin ribbons to tie under the chin. She wore as a cloak a three-quarter length black garment trimmed with black velvet and beads galore. The groom wore black trousers, a dark purplish coat and a flowered velvet vest.

The bride's trousseau included a slate blue silk dress and a golden-brown silk which cost $50.00 it being at the time of the inflated prices during the Civil War.[8]

The description seems a little confusing. Most likely she wore the golden-brown silk dress—costing about $800 in current dollars—for the wedding. The traveling dress served for their honeymoon trip.[9] No wedding photographs were taken, but Halsey and Emilie went to a Riverhead photography studio soon afterward for the pictures (fig. 4.1).

Halsey and Emilie's Wedding Trip

After their wedding, Halsey and Emilie Hallock embarked by train from Riverhead on a trip through upstate New York and as far west as northern Ohio—a voyage that would have been unlikely or impossible a generation earlier.[10] They traveled with his sister Adelia and her husband, Simeon Benjamin, and stayed mostly with relatives and acquaintances—apparently all Halsey's and Simeon's relatives and acquaintances, not Emilie's.[11]

The newlyweds spent their first night with his cousin, Mrs. Matilda Platt, in Brooklyn.[12] The next morning, the party took the train to Elmira, New York, where they spent two days with Simeon's 72-year-old uncle, also named Simeon Benjamin. This Simeon Benjamin (1792–1868), the son of a Northville farmer, became a wealthy man, first as a shop owner in Riverhead during the war of 1812, then as a merchant in New York City, and finally as a developer, banker, and entrepreneur in the booming new town of Elmira. He helped found Elmira Female College (now Elmira

Figure 4.1. David Halsey Hallock (A) and Emilie J. Wells (B) around the time of their marriage, 1866. Halsey was proud of his resemblance to his hero, Abraham Lincoln. He is wearing the flowered velvet vest mentioned in the description of the wedding. *Source:* Hallockville Museum Farm. Used with permission.

College) in 1855, the first rigorous postsecondary institution for women in the country, and became its principal benefactor, giving it the equivalent of several million dollars during his lifetime. He also generously supported other religious and charitable institutions in that city.

Sixty-six years later, Halsey still remembered a dinner he and Emilie ate with the "millionaire" as "quite an experience for farmers from Northville." The meal was at the home of the millionaire's son-in-law, also a wealthy man, who happened to be a state senator. The young country couple, not accustomed to such sophisticated company, suffered a few embarrassing moments when they did not know how to handle the fancy foods served at the dinner!

From Elmira, the party took the train 90 miles further west to Friendship, New York—also on the main line of the Erie Railroad—where Halsey's youngest sister Hannah and two other North Forkers attended the

Baxter Academy of Music. The school, founded by James Baxter in 1853, claimed to be the first and the largest music school in the United States. It seems remarkable that Arminda and Herman Hallock sent, or could afford to send, their youngest daughter to this distant school.

From Friendship, the party proceeded 250 miles further westward by train through Cleveland, Ohio, and on to Elyria, on the shore of Lake Erie. The newlyweds stayed nearby with Nathan Tuthill, another elderly uncle of Halsey's brother-in-law Simeon Benjamin. Later the party stayed with David Conklin, who moved west a few years earlier after selling his house in Jamesport to Jedidiah Hawkins so the latter could tear it down and build the mansion that now serves as the Hawkins Inn. The honeymoon party also stayed with members of the Young and Hook families, all farmers who migrated to Ohio from the North Fork in the previous decade or two. Halsey and Emilie brought back some pebbles from the shore of Lake Erie as a memento.

Finally, the party took a sleeping car back to Buffalo, where they stopped to see Niagara Falls, "the best of all the sights we have seen." Niagara Falls became the honeymoon capital of the nation by the mid-19th century. The Erie Canal made access relatively easy in the 1830s, and good railroad connections made it even easier after 1843.[13] There the couple bought a pincushion as a memento.[14]

Quite likely neither Emilie nor Halsey had traveled off Long Island before. Halsey had only been as far west as Jamacia, Queens, where he registered for the draft, and Emilie perhaps never beyond the East End of Long Island! Halsey ended his account of the trip saying that they arrived home "in pretty good condition to go to work."

Romantic Words in Emilie's "Forget Me Not Album"

In 1867, a few months after their wedding, Halsey added his own verse to the album—as always, demonstrating his romantic bent:

Dear Emilie

That our lives may be
one continual flowing
stream of purist love,

> sympathy, affection and
> Union of heart—and
> that we may ever be
> shielded from all the
> evils of life by our Heavenly
> Father is the fervent desire.
> And Prayer of your Loving
> Husband
> —D. Halsey Hallock

While the verses in these albums often lack originality—just copied from then-well-known poets—these appear to be Halsey's own words. Similar words apparently did not come as easily to Emilie, as it took her another year to compose four stanzas of "Lines to My Husband," beginning with:

> Let the world hoard ill-gotten gains,
> And miser-like recount her store,
> Thirsting amid a sea of wealth
> To grasp <u>one</u> ocean more;
> But I've a treasure dearer far
> Than land or wave impart,
> And not for worlds would I exchange
> The wealth of his loving heart.

Again, these words appear to be her own, not copied from a favorite poet.

A New Family

After their honeymoon trip, Emilie and Halsey settled into the new west wing of the Homestead built six years earlier for Halsey's first marriage and "set up housekeeping." Two and a half years later, Emilie gave birth to a son named Halsey Winfield Hallock (fig. 4.2), the first of five children (figs. 4.3 and 4.4). Using surnames as first names was common in the area. One neighbor was Wells Hallock, another Hallock Luce. But Halsey as a first name seems especially common.

Figure 4.2. Halsey Winfield "Hal" Hallock (1869–1957). Firstborn child of Halsey and Emilie. It was common for very young boys to be put in a dress. Hal never married and lived in the Homestead with his two unmarried sisters until his death at age 88. *Source:* Hallockville Museum Farm. Used with permission.

Figure 4.3. Eula Hallock (1871–1968) (A) and Georgia Irene Hallock (1875–1916) (B), the second and third children of Halsey and Emilie. Eula married farmer Charles S. Wells in 1891. Georgia married master builder Henry F. "Harry" Corwin in 1897—the last two wedding ceremonies to take place in the Homestead's east front parlor. *Source:* Hallockville Museum Farm. Used with permission.

Figure 4.4. Bessie Leona Hallock (1880–1966) (A) and Ella Arminda Hallock (1885–1985) (B), Halsey and Emilie's fourth and fifth children. Both never married and lived their whole lives in the Homestead. Bessie was a talented and trained musician who served for 50 years as the organist and choir director of the Sound Avenue Congregational Church and gave private piano lessons to all the young girls from the neighborhood. Ella was the last of her family to occupy the old Homestead, until she moved out in 1979. *Source:* Hallockville Museum Farm. Used with permission.

Changes in the Homestead

Halsey and Emilie lived for seven years in the new west wing of the Homestead, with their two young children, Halsey (Hal) born in 1869 and Eula, in 1871. Then in 1873, Halsey and Emilie moved to the larger, old part of the Homestead and Herman and Arminda moved to the newer-but-smaller west wing. We do not know why they changed places. With only two children at the time, Halsey and Emilie had plenty of space for their young family. Maybe everyone anticipated future additions. Another possible explanation suggests that Emilie found it embarrassing to walk past her in-laws' sitting room windows every time she needed to go to the shared outhouse. Exchanging living quarters solved that problem![15]

This exchange of living quarters soon set off a major wave of interior renovations. In Bessie's words, "In a short time alterations were made in the east side." Before the renovation, the main block of the first floor still retained its colonial-era configuration, with a large chimneystack, about six feet square, in the center that contained fireplaces opening into parlors on each side and a large walk-in fireplace opening into the original kitchen behind.[16]

Emilie and Halsey removed the obsolete large central chimney and the adjacent steep winding stairs to make room for a more elegant entry hall and straight stairway that still stands today. However, the limited space necessitated a rather narrow balcony on the second-floor level. Although they removed the old chimney and fireplaces, they left the original fireplace mantlepieces in the two front rooms on both the first and second floors.

The colonial-era kitchen became a sitting room and eventually Bessie's music room, which the Hallockville Museum now interprets as a dining room. Instead of using the large central chimney, they tucked a small chimney into the corner of the front room to service the stove in the new sitting room—the latest in heating technologies in 1873. The mantelpiece they built behind the stove remains visible today, but with a radiator installed in front.

This modernization included replacing all of the old nine-over-six windows on the first floor with larger six-over-six units; replacing all the interior doors, trim, and even floorboards; and installing pocket double doors between the front and back rooms on the east side to create a large space for family gatherings and parties, but still allowing the rooms to be separated in winter to make heating easier. Essentially, they totally modernized the front part of the house, leaving none of its colonial-era fabric visible.

These changes gave Emilie a chance to redecorate the entire downstairs—faux graining all the new interior doors to look like more expensive wood; painting the rest of the woodwork; papering the walls using the latest patterns; and covering the new wood floors with wall-to-wall Brussels carpeting still there today. At the same time, they consolidated two upstairs bedrooms into one larger one to make room for two closets and added several more closets downstairs, another touch of modernity lacking in the 1765 house.

When they finished, the front of the house contained three formal rooms—the west front room, which served as a "best parlor" with the fanciest decor and nicest furniture, and two parlors (also called sitting rooms) on the east side connected by the new double sliding doors—the Homestead that visitors to Hallockville see today.

About the same time, the Hallocks modified the back wing, which was the oldest part of the Homestead, moved in 1860 from the west side to make way for the new wing. They increased the ceiling height—originally about seven feet, typical of the colonial period—to a more fashionable eight and a half feet (Halsey stood six feet) to make this a more elegant dining room (latter used as their main sitting room). They also raised the roof above to accommodate a room for hired help. A stylish Gothic dormer provided light for that room and served as an architectural focal point for visitors coming up the walkway from the horse block. In 1884, a recently arrived Bohemian couple, Josephine and Joe, worked on the farm and lived in that room, leading it to be referred to today as the Homestead's "Bohemian room."[17]

To replace the colonial-era kitchen, the Hallocks attached a lean-to shed onto the back of the rear wing.[18] Emilie wanted something more up to date than the old kitchen with its walk-in fireplace and open hearth that her mother-in-law had used. She wanted a stove. But a stove needed a much narrower chimney to draw properly. Thus, like many of their neighbors faced with the same problem, they simply built a new kitchen on the back with a new appropriately sized chimney. They designed the new kitchen to accommodate the most modern of modern conveniences—a cooking range at stand-up height. They also installed a dry sink (i.e., with no running water, but with a drain running outside) with a waist-high counter, something else not in the original colonial-era kitchen. Halsey was very proud of this "modern" kitchen, which visitors to the Homestead can still see today.

Because the kitchen was not one of the formal rooms that guests saw, and because it was only a place for the women to work, the Hallocks did not make any effort to make this room stylish. Instead, they reused pieces salvaged from the modernization of the front. For instance, the west window, a nine-over-six unit with wavy crown glass, is likely an 18th-century window salvaged from the renovation of the front part of the house.[19] Similarly, the floorboards are wide planks, of the type used in the 1760s, not the 1870s, again likely recycled from the front part of the house. The door to the back staircase also is a colonial-era piece reused in the kitchen. The rest of the room remains very simple, with the exterior sheathing serving as interior walls and simple plank doors, all in sharp contrast to the detailing in the front of the house.

A diary entry in 1873 recorded spending $4.75 for "ceiling stuff"—the narrow wood pieces, then called "ceiling board" but today known as wainscotting, used on the new walls and ceiling—from the Hallett planing and molding mill in downtown Riverhead.[20] This mill, constructed in 1868 by

Charles Hallett on the Peconic River waterfront (now parking lots), was Riverhead's largest manufacturing operation, with 50 employees operating 30 woodworking machines driven by a 60-horsepower steam engine. In addition to the wainscoting, the mill also produced moldings, window sash, shutters (then called "blinds"), and other fancy woodwork, some of which likely appeared in the front part of the house.[21]

The Hallocks worked to keep not only their house up to date but the furnishings too. An 1875 advertisement for S. B. Halsey of Watermill listed Herman Hallock as one of 25 buyers of a "silver tongue organ" that year, though it remains uncertain who played that organ, perhaps Halsey's sister Hannah when at home from teaching in the South. The recently formed local chapter of the Patrons of Husbandry (Grange), meeting in the old Northville Church, also bought an organ that year.[22]

Standard of Living

Fragmentary accounts for 1876 and 1877 reveal a markedly different economy than that experienced by their ancestors at the beginning of the century. The farm still produced most of what they ate but was also much more integrated into the market economy. The Hallocks could buy nutmeg, pepper, chocolate, rice, and cinnamon—and even candies and peanuts from the little Taft Candy Store that is today a Riverhead town landmark. Their diary shows them occasionally purchasing oysters and clams, rather than digging them on their own.

The Hallocks no longer dressed in homespun. Instead, they bought silk, cashmere, calico, lace, "cambrie," flannel, "cord," muslin, and "col jean" cloth as well as buttons, thread, "narrow alpaca braid," and other trimmings. They still sewed all of their own clothes, both for men and women. However, sewing no longer took place entirely by hand. According to an entry in the family account books, the Hallocks bought a new Wilcox and Gibbs sewing machine for $65 in 1872.

Occasional manufactured items show up in the records. Emilie got a new summer hat from Mrs. Ketcham in Riverhead for $2.50. They now bought manufactured shoes for their kids instead of homemade, as in the days of Capt. Zachariah. And there was an occasional splurge, such a damask tablecloth for $11.26.

Most of their shopping occurred in downtown Riverhead, generally at merchants such as Fishel, Perkins, Vail or Brown & Jackson, with occasional purchases at Van Tuyl in Jamesport. The accounts also show occasional transactions with peddlers. For instance, in July 1877 they purchased lace from a peddler named Salter for 16¢. The same month they bought five pairs of stockings from another peddler and a broom from another. They also gave 5¢ to a beggar.

The accounts often record selling butter to Fishel, Brown & Jackson's general store—today the Star Confectionary. They sold about 15 pounds of butter every 10 days or so. At 20¢ per pound, the income was significant. The $13.49 they spent to attend the Philadelphia Centennial Exposition was the equivalent of 66 pounds of butter, or about a month-and-a-half's production. Occasionally they sold a few crates of strawberries, cherries, and apples. Unlike in Capt. Zachariah's day, all the transactions appear to be in cash—no more keeping a ledger and settling up occasionally.

Sister Hannah Volunteers after the War

Halsey's youngest sister, Hannah Jemima "Jennie" Hallock (1850–1908; fig. 4.5), remarkably went off to music school in Friendship, New York, where

Figure 4.5. Hannah Jemima Hallock, known as Jennie, Halsey's youngest sister who volunteered to teach former slaves in the deep South after the Civil War. *Source:* Hallockville Museum Farm. Used with permission.

Halsey and Emilie visited on their 1866 honeymoon. Even more remarkably, Hannah went from there to teach at Talladega College in Alabama and Straight College in New Orleans—both founded by the American Missionary Association, a radical abolitionist offshoot of the Congregational Church that focused on educating freedmen in the aftermath of the Civil War.

One of the few organizations at the time run by Blacks and whites together, the Missionary Association, founded over 500 schools and 11 colleges throughout the South during and after the Civil War. It also created the Freedmen's Aid Society to recruit Northern teachers like Hannah.[23] Teaching in Alabama and Louisiana was a remarkable venture for Hannah, one with considerable risk given conditions in the postwar South, with frequent threats and sometimes real violence against former enslaved and the white Northerners who tried to help them. However, her work in the South fits in with the Hallock family's abolitionist reputation. Halsey's diary records that he made small donations to the "Freedman's Relief Society" (National Freedman's Relief Association) in 1864 and to "Aid to Freedman" (probably the Freedmen's Aid Society) in 1867, $1.50 and $1, respectively.

A Troubled Romance

Hannah was entangled in a problematic romance while teaching at Talladega and Straight. Hannah met Marshall P. Dedrick while studying at the Baxter Academy of Music in Friendship in 1866. He was from Friendship and about eight years older. According to Bessie's account in "Autobiography of an Old House," the west wing of the Hallock Homestead, where her parents lived after 1873, "was from time to time regaled with [Hannah's] experiences and . . . the problems of romance [that] culminated in a marriage in the fall of 1880" to Marshall, who Bessie describes as an acquaintance made in Friendship.[24]

When Hannah married Marshall in 1880, he was 37 and had a four-year-old son, John, from a previous marriage. The chronology presents an interesting problem. Marshall married his first wife, Mary Rockwell, sometime before 1870. In 1876, they moved to Kansas and had John. About 14 months later, another child, an infant daughter, was born but did not survive. The mother died in December 1878, 15 months after her daughter.[25]

Almost immediately after his first wife's death, Marshall sent his son to live with Hannah's parents in the Homestead, where Bessie recalled that "little 4-year-old John Dedrick stayed with the Hallocks for a year and made things lively before his new mother, Hannah and Marshall his father married." A brief item in Halsey's diary for 1880 indicates that the Hallocks charged Marshall $20 to board John that year.

It remains unclear where Hannah lived at that time, or if she was with Marshall. Somehow the college relationship survived his marriage to Mary and rekindled within a year of Mary's death, leading to John's board with the Hallocks in 1879, Marshall and Hannah's marriage in 1880, and Hannah's move to her husband's farm in Kansas.[26]

Wider Horizons: Centennial Exposition in Philadelphia

The Hallocks's horizons expanded in the second half of the 19th century. Not only did they travel across New York and Ohio on their honeymoon trip in 1866, but a decade later, in October 1876, they joined the 10 million visitors at the Centennial Exposition in Philadelphia, where they were exposed to the latest in fashion, technology, and agricultural science.

The Hallocks went to Philadelphia by train. The whole trip lasted four days. According to their diary, roundtrip tickets cost $7.60 and other incidentals cost $5.89. They came back with a toy for Eula, a book for "Hallie," and another for Eddie (Terry), the 10-year-old son of a local farmer living with Herman and Arminda and working on the farm. They also recorded 30¢ spent on the trip for candy and chestnuts as well as $3.25 for a new bag for "Emmie."

Deaths of Herman and Arminda

Halsey's father Herman "left his earthly abode for the better land" on November 11, 1881, leaving just Arminda in the west wing. Herman's will left the Homestead farm to his youngest son, Halsey.[27] It specifically noted that the father had given his two older sons, Charles and Daniel, "all that I expected to give them" and that they could expect no further bequests. In essence, Herman had accomplished the main duty of a good Puritan father—establishing all of his sons on farms of their own, first helping Charles acquire the farm in Smithtown, then giving Daniel the farm in Roanoke, and finally giving Halsey the Homestead farm. Arminda received $50 annually and all his railroad bonds, an indication that the Hallock farm was sufficiently prosperous for Herman to do a bit of investing. Arminda also received two cows "of her choice," a mare, buggy, and harness. Halsey was to provide her "annually from products of the farm," all the wood, wheat, corn, beef, pork, eggs, fruit, and vegetables "that she may need and require." She also had use of the west wing of the Homestead, where she and Herman lived.

In the spring of 1882, again in Bessie's words, "Arminda felt she must see her younger daughter, Hannah, now living in Belle Plaine, Kansas. Arminda had an additional reason for her trip, a new grandson named Herman Hallock Dedrick, born in December 1881, and named after his grandfather, her late husband. She bravely undertook the long journey in company with the "Fishel boys" who were on their way to Denver, Colorado."[28]

The Fishel boys were sons of Jonas Fishel, a Jewish immigrant peddler that the Hallocks had befriended years earlier. He went on to operate what became Riverhead's largest department store.[29] Two of Jonas's sons, Arthur and Gilbert, moved to Denver, where their father maintained interests, leaving the Riverhead store to their brother Edwin. This explains why the Fishel boys could accompany Arminda on her visit to see her daughter in Kansas. That Arminda felt comfortable making such a long and difficult journey in such company indicates the close relationship between the Hallock and Fishel families—one of old Puritan stock, the other of recent Jewish immigrants.

Unfortunately, again in Bessie's words, Arminda "was fatally stricken with a stroke out there [in Kansas] and never returned alive. She was brought back and laid beside her dear husband in the Aquebogue Cemetery." Sadly, the grandson Herman survived less than two months beyond his grandmother.[30]

Writing in the 1930s, Halsey recalled his mother's parting words as she left on her fatal trip to Kansas: "Halsey don't let the place run down—keep it up." He remained proud to think that if her spirit could visit the house again, she could see how "that lone boy of hers and his children have kept up the old home place."[31]

Chapter 5

Scandals in the Church

A church notorious for the pugnacious character of the flock.

—*Brooklyn Daily Eagle*[1]

Even though they had one of the finest churches on Long Island [and lived in] an unusually wealthy farming district . . . the people seem to be belligerent.

—*Long Island Traveler*[2]

A Dispute over a Melodeon

A correspondent for the *Sag-Harbor Express* in 1860 described Northville (later Sound Avenue) as "one of the pleasantest villages on our Island, and far removed from all those haunts of vice, and scenes of dissipation . . . which abound in some villages."[3] But this prosperity and lack of temptation did not lead to social amity. The Northville Church was born in acrimony when its members walked out of the Aquebogue Church in what Halsey Hallock called the "great eruption" of 1829, essentially a controversy between modernizers (Aquebogue) and conservatives (Sound Avenue). With this background, it did not take long for the members of the new church to start bickering amongst themselves.

The divisive nature of the congregation first manifested itself in a dispute about whether to allow a melodeon into the church, an innovation championed by Halsey's brother Daniel Hallock. In the 17th century, Puritans banned the use of all musical instruments except the tuning fork.

This prohibition continued in many North Fork churches well into the 19th century.

Melodeons became widely available and affordable in the 1850s. The player used two foot pedals to operate a bellows in the back of the box to make its sound by blowing or sucking air through vibrating reeds. The first advertisement for Carhart's patent melodeon appeared in the Sag Harbor *Corrector* in 1850, stating that these instruments could play four or five octaves with a "very pleasing sound."

James Y. Downs, a neighboring farmer, recorded in 1854 and 1855 that Daniel's proposal became a "a trial to the church." While some members wanted to introduce instrumental music into the church, others felt "very much grieved" by the idea. Some called it a "desecration." Bessie Hallock wrote years later that it resulted in a "furore [*sic*]" in the congregation. "What a commotion it caused, that such a worldly device should be tolerated in the sanctuary." After all, only a generation earlier this church had split from the Aquebogue Church to keep their "Strict Congregational" heritage, and now a majority of the members wanted to modernize!

As Halsey recalled many years later, "The little box was tremblingly allowed" inside the church walls. A special church meeting in 1855 passed a resolution in favor of "the melodeon which has caused so many unpleasant feelings." At the end of the meeting, 30 members of the congregation signed a resolution protesting the melodeon and appealed to the minister, Rev. John O. Wells, but he advised Daniel to "hold fast" and the melodeon stayed. Daniel became the first melodeon player.

The 30 opponents of the melodeon included at least 11 of the 31 founding members of the church, with an average age of 45 years. Among them were Isaiah Hallock and his wife Elizabeth, cousins and next-door neighbors of the Homestead Hallocks. Although the reformers won the day, the split between modernizers and traditionalists persisted and continued to fester over the next three decades.

Erection of a New Church Divides the Congregation

A proposal in 1859 to erect a new church and rent part of the old building as an academy also proved controversial, with many members of the congregation thinking the old one good enough. The architecture of the new church, with its Italianate features, stained glass windows, and tall steeple, was much more modern than the vernacular meeting house design of the old building (actually only 28 years old) and likely part of the reason for the vigorous objections from more conservative parts of the community (see fig. 3.1, chap. 3). The previous edifice, the simple vernacular structure that still survives as the Sound Avenue Grange Hall (now a Buddhist temple), exhibited virtually no architectural ornamentation and no steeple, keeping with the church's adherence to its old-fashioned Puritan theology. In the end, 72 families signed up to support the new building and 69 actually paid, in amounts ranging from $5 to $200. Herman remained a member of the Aquebogue Church, but his brother Zachariah III signed as one of four at the $200 level. Not surprisingly, 8 out of the 17 families that opposed the melodeon are also missing from the list of supporters for the new building. As usual in the community, Hallocks predominated, with 12 of 69 contributors.

Slavery Further Divides the Church

Just as it divided the nation, the question of slavery divided the Northville congregation in the decades before the Civil War. Although the majority, including the Homestead Hallocks, sided with the abolitionist cause, a strong minority thought otherwise. The liberty pole smashing incident early in the war was but one manifestation of these divisions. The Hallocks's neighbor Melinda Corwin, who commented derisively in her diary as early as 1837 about an anti-slavery lecture in the Northville Church, in 1863 noted being "weary of the wicket war." Later that year she decried a "political harangue" in the church. In 1864 she deplored the reelection of Lincoln. In 1865 she reported "a stranger in the pulpit betting [sic] for freedmen."[4]

The majority of voters in the election district on the east end of town, which included Northville, supported Lincoln in both 1860 and 1864, but a vocal minority voted against him and strongly opposed the war. The church membership apparently split in the same way. Although in the minority with her anti-war opinions, Melinda Corwin had plenty of company in the bitterly divided Northville Church. Nearly 70 years later, Halsey Hallock still referred obliquely to the church's "deepest trials in Civil War times."[5]

The Organ Smashing Incident

The congregation elected Halsey Hallock as a deacon in April 1865. Years later he recalled feeling "as unlikely and as unhappy in that position as you can imagine. It was troublous times." He had also just lost his first wife. The next major controversy erupted a month later.

The church's sewing society raised money to buy a pipe organ, which the church installed in the balcony of the new building. Sammy Tuthill, a cousin of the Homestead Hallocks, reported in his diary that the organ "finished [and] goes well" and mentioned the instrument's music again the next Sunday. Another member recalled many years later being "on the spot" as a 12-year-old boy when the organ arrived and that it was "used with excellent effect."[6]

The following Saturday evening, a month and a half after the end of the war at Appomattox, some dissident members of the congregation entered the church and tossed the new organ out of the balcony, "damaging it extensively." Melinda Corwin, in her diary, referred to it—perhaps approvingly—as "a great smashup at the church." Another member, Lucius Hallock (1853–1933, a more distant cousin), observed in a letter to Halsey nearly 70 years later, "Before the next sabbath [the organ] had overleaped the breastwork and spread itself all over the pews below which effort proved to be its undoing." He added:

> There was however some Deviltry going on especially in connection with the Civil War, and the significance of the term "Copperhead" was well known in those days. The good name of "Hallock" was not free from this stigma and your Father, 'Herman' told my Father 'George W.' that his life was not free from danger, as he passed out through the wood in the night to attend a prayer meeting for the success of the Union forces during the Civil War.[7]

This was only a decade after the controversy about the melodeon. Somehow, opposition to instrumental music in the church became intwined with opposition to the war. Many years later a minister in the church attributed the incident to someone having played "Johnny Get Your Gun" on the church organ. No such song existed until long after the war, but the phrase "Johnny get your gun" was widely used as a Civil War recruiting slogan. The inference assumed a widely shared belief that the opponents of the Civil War were also enemies of the organ.[8]

The First Attempt to Burn the Church

Feelings continued to run strong. January 22, 1866, someone bored a hole into the back wall of the new church and attempted to use flammable material either to set it on fire or blow up the building.[9] Sammy Tuthill, a church trustee and Hallock cousin, recorded in his diary, "The church has been set on fire but went out."[10] That same day Melinda Corwin recorded in her diary that "fighting in this church terrible."[11]

Fingers pointed at Isaiah Hallock, Halsey's cousin and a next-door neighbor, who earlier opposed the melodeon and was implicated in the liberty pole incident. Two days later, on January 24, 1866, Sammy Tuthill, who was Isaiah's nephew, recorded in his diary, "Uncle Isaiah arrested by church off[icers] & cong[regation]." Exactly what they arrested Isaiah for remains unclear, but presumably something connected with the organ smashing and incendiary incidents. It is also not clear who arrested Isaiah. Officers of the church? Under what authority?

No matter what the issue, the church seemed to be divided. In 1871, they considered hiring out the seats in the church—a common practice in the area—as a better way to raise money for paying the minister than by seeking donations. However, according to trustee Sammy Tuthill, the discussion devolved into a "high old time" and the final vote split almost evenly—14 for renting and 15 against.[12]

A Brief Revival

In January of 1872, a traveling evangelist, Rev. Potter, spent the week at Northville. Halsey noted in his diary that "I trust that a large number of Souls have been born into the kingdom." The *Sag-Harbor Express* reported that Potter converted over 200 "during his labors at Northville," a number that seems rather exaggerated.[13] The paper also claimed that Potter's effort helped settle "old troubles"—something the community desperately needed—and removed "hard feelings." The same source mentioned the case of "two sisters, who had not spoken to each other for six years, brought together and a reconciliation effected."[14] Unfortunately, however many souls may have been saved, the week of revivals did not result in reconciliation among the community.

More Mysterious Incidents

Another mysterious incident occurred around 1873. When the parishioners came to church one Sunday morning, they were horrified to find bold black letters painted on the white front of the academy building (the old church) across the street to the general effect that one of their neighbors "mourned the loss of a lady porker"—presumably a euphemism for something a bit saltier.[15] In yet another incident, miscreants attempted to break up a temperance meeting by tossing in live skunks. The church tried to reconcile everyone by clearing the names of those accused of upsetting the organ, attempting to burn the church and tossing skunks, but this also proved controversial.[16]

Throughout this period, Halsey served in various leadership roles in the congregation, sometimes as deacon, sometimes as presiding officer of church meetings, and sometimes as trustee. In 1875 the congregation elected him deacon again—just in time to be caught up in the continuing controversy over the proposal to rent or sell pews. This time the congregation voted in favor, and Halsey purchased pew no. 15 for $450.[17]

The Reverend Wright

These internal divisions came to the fore again in 1877, shortly after the congregation hired a new minister, Rev. Henry Newman Wright, who had a somewhat vague background. Wright arrived in Northville on January 14, 1877, and preached for two Sundays before the congregation voted to give him a call on January 23. As usual, Halsey stood in the middle of things. He signed the minutes of the meeting that passed the motion "to raise sufficient amount of money to obtain Mr. Wright." The trustees met to "bargin [sic]" with Mr. Wright on a salary—agreeing on $700, with an effort to raise $800—and circulated a "signment" to secure the necessary funds.[18]

All went well until the trustees attended a meeting of the Congregational Association (a coordinating group of leading Congregational clergy and lay people for the county) on February 28 at "South Road" (the Aquebogue Church). At the meeting, Sammy Tuthill, along with head trustee George Mitchell Terry and several of the deacons (probably including Halsey Hallock), learned about a letter with damaging information about Wright. The Association immediately voted to expel Wright and to withdraw his certificate as a minister.

Tuthill does not say what was in the letter, but the trustees and deacons met that evening to discuss the situation and agreed to let Wright continue to "minister the sacrament," despite his being defrocked by the Association. A church meeting on March 3 only discussed electing deacons and new members, with no mention of the problems with Wright. The trustees apparently still retained enough faith in Wright that on March 9 they authorized an advance on his salary for him to purchase furniture at Fishel & Brothers in Riverhead and on March 14 they held a "donation" to raise money for his salary.

The deacons and trustees then organized a special meeting on April 17 "to obtain the advice of the church regarding the ordination of Reverend H.N. Wright." Wright attended and offered a prayer at the beginning. The congregation did not decide about Wright but rather adjourned after some discussion with a motion to wait until after the next meeting of the Congregational Association.[19]

Wright continued to preach at Sunday services until May 1, when church leaders called another special meeting. Wright apparently did not attend this time. After hearing the contents of "certain letters in their possession touching on the character" of Wright, the congregation passed this resolution:

> We the members of the Northville Congregational Church in Church Meeting assembled to look and inquire into the scandalous reports about our Minister Bro. H.N. Wright, which has come to us from so many reliable sources, that in our belief is of such a disgraceful character, and also his course of conduct since he has been with us—and his uncommon way of explaining the Bible, which is so different from that of our Fathers and also our own belief of Bible truth and for the welfare of a Christian church.[20]

After determining that Wright "has shown himself unworthy of the confidence and respect of the people," attendees rejected by a large majority a resolution to allow Wright to continue to preach on an interim basis "until measures can be taken which shall result in his dismissal." Instead, they voted by secret ballot to ask the trustees "to use their discretion in disposing of Mr. Wright"—with 13 in favor and one blank. It appears that the members supporting Wright stayed away from the meeting.[21]

Tuthill's diary describes the May 1 session as "a high old time." After that meeting, Tuthill and the other trustees met at George M. Terry's house and decided to dismiss Wright. They walked across the street and served him notice to vacate in 30 days. He served them notice that he would continue preaching.[22]

With a nose for scandal, the *Brooklyn Daily Eagle* quickly picked up the story. With Wright in the pulpit for only two months, according to the

Eagle, letters from previous parishes led the trustees "to the conclusion that he was quite unfit for the Christian ministry, and the sooner they got rid of him the better. But Mr. Wright refused to quit and told them that the accusatory letters were 'only sap, and that only sapheads would pay attention to them.'"[23] The Wright question divided the community—just like earlier controversies over music, a new building, and the Civil War—with some ardent partisans supporting him and many others opposed. The trustees tried locking him out of the church on Sunday. On May 6, Halsey Hallock wrote in his diary, "The Northville Church kept locked to keep out the notorious H. N. Wright."[24] Unable to gain entry to the church, Wright resorted to preaching to his supporters outside.

The Church Is Burned

Trustee Sammy Tuthill lived within sight of the church, about a quarter mile to the east. On the night of May 14, a Monday, he awoke to a cry of "fire," and seeing a big glow out his bedroom window, "ran out the west door and found it was the church in flames. At 1 o'clock (in the morning) everything was down." Two days later this brief story ran in the *Brooklyn Daily Eagle*: "The Congregational Church in Northville, Suffolk County, one of the largest and finest on the Island, outside of this city, was burned to the ground on Monday night. There had been serious differences of opinion between the members and the pastor, and the burning is believed by many to be the work of design."[25] The following day, the *Eagle* ran a lengthy story about how the church hired Rev. Wright without adequately checking his background and then tried to fire him after receiving letters informing them he was "quite unfit for the ministry." "For many weeks the conflict raged. Whenever the trustees attempted to enter they were pulled down the steps by the partisans of the minister, and when [Rev. Wright] essayed an entrance, these guardians of the fold seized his coat tails and forced him back, 'hind foremost,' as the saying is." According to the *Eagle*, Wright then uttered "mysterious warnings" that if he could not occupy the pulpit, no one else would. Allegedly he warned that "if they persisted in their shameful treatment of him, he would show them the biggest fire and smoke ever seen in Northville." The *Eagle* does not explicitly state that Wright burned the church down but says that the prophesy "seems to have been the causes of its own fulfilment" the following Monday night, as "the prophetic parson gazed calmly from the window on his church in flames."[26]

Take the *Eagle*'s account with considerable skepticism. This was, after all, the age of yellow journalism, and the *Eagle* was not known for sticking meticulously to the facts of a story.[27] For instance, only eight days elapsed between the trustees shutting Wright out of the pulpit and the church burning down, not the "many weeks" claimed by the *Eagle*.

No one could prove definitely that Wright burned the church. Halsey Hallock reported in his diary on May 14, "Northville Church it is believed was set on fire & burned to the ground."[28] Later Sammy Tuthill testified in a trial in one of several lawsuits that resulted from the incident that Wright threatened "fire and smoke" at the parish meetings after being dismissed.[29]

The *Eagle* went on to say this was not the first church the "delightful firebrand" burned down: "Strangely enough, this was the second time that Mr. Wright has invoked fire from heaven upon his enemies." His previous church in Edwards, New York, "was mysteriously destroyed by fire, not without a pretty general suspicion that the parson himself was guilty of this ecclesiastical arson."[30]

The Next Day

Trustee Tuthill stayed at the destroyed church for the rest of the night. The next day a crowd gathered in front of Wright's house and, according to Tuthill, "they gave it to him pretty hard." Later, he and his cousin, fellow trustee Eugene Hallock, went in and told Wright that "he had to go" and watched him "pretty close." Then Tuthill and Hallock went to the church's lawyer and arranged for the sheriff to come and arrest Wright and his wife. The sheriff took Wright to Riverhead but, according to Tuthill, on "examination" the justice acquitted Wright in full. Tuthill noted that reporters from the *Eagle* attended to get the story.

The Trustees Evict Wright

Over the next month, Tuthill attended numerous meetings and visits to their lawyer about what to do. On May 23, the Congregational Society voted to raise by subscription $5,000 to be used as a reward for the "infamous villain or villains" who "burned the church to the ground."[31] After a few Sundays without services, the church began meeting in the west schoolhouse and finally in the lecture room of the original church building (then used as the Northville Academy). Tuthill notes occasionally that Wright did not come.

Even after firing Wright and despite allegations he burned the church down, the trustees still could not get rid of him. He demanded that they pay his full year's salary even though he had only preached two months. He and his wife barricaded themselves in the parsonage and refused to leave. This culminated on July 4 when head trustee Terry decided the time had come to put Wright out of the parsonage. According to Tuthill, he and Terry gathered a group of men: "At 10 o'clock we met & went in & told him that we had come to help him move & went to work & took his things out into the street nice and careful with no damage whatever & watched them rest of day." The weather was nice and dry, so Tuthill went home to make hay in the afternoon. He barely got in one load when he received word that "Riverheaders were coming down to put things in again" and said "We got our company together & stood guard." They arranged for a constable to come from Mattituck, who stayed there until one o'clock in the morning. Some of the party stayed all night.

Wright and his family spent the night with James H. Wells, their next-door neighbor. The next day Tuthill and a few others carted Wright's things off, presumably to the station in Riverhead. Halsey Hallock merely recorded in his diary that on July 4 "the Notorious Wright moved out of the parsonage"—without stating that the move was totally involuntary!

During the next few days Tuthill checked on the parsonage a couple of times. Meanwhile, Wright filed charges of illegal entrance, assault, and battery against them. And then, for good measure, Wright sued the trustees for a year's salary and $3,000 in damages and demanded that they give him a good character recommendation when he applied for another pulpit!

The Press Could Not Get Enough of the Story

Southold *Watchman* called this incident "the glorious fourth at Northville," reporting that when Wright and his wife refused to leave and barricaded themselves inside, the trustees sent a "groceries boy" with a basket of goodies to the back door of the parsonage. The *Brooklyn Daily Eagle* provided even more details—likely mostly imagined—that the basket "included coffee, mixed pickles and half a dozen tins of sardines." The *Eagle* claimed that the trustees rushed in behind the decoy to evict the parson and his wife.[32] The *New York Herald* ran an article about the incident under the headline

"Turning Out a Parson: Rev. Henry Newman Wright Dislodged by the Church Trustees."[33]

A few days later, the *Eagle* revised a few details of its story, under the headline "Pius War," saying that instead of a boy with groceries, it was the "colored" sexton of the church (a nonexistent position) with some spring vegetables.[34] Embellishing the story still further, the *Eagle* added other details, all of dubious veracity. Supposedly Mrs. Wright punched one of the trustees and gave him a black eye. The story also claimed she was still in her nightgown when the good trustees evicted her, even though it occurred in the middle of the day.

Wright had a pugnacious reputation himself, according to the *Eagle*. About a year earlier when he was a candidate for the ministry in Rockville Center, allegedly he decided to eliminate his main rival for the job by punching him in the face. The *Eagle* called this "a display of muscular Christianity" on "this Island of saints."[35] Great language!

Lawsuits Continued for Four More Years

The incident resulted in a blizzard of lawsuits that continued four more years. Northville was a litigious place and so was Rev. Wright. The church accused Wright of burning its building down. Wright accused the church of wrongful termination, wrongful withholding of pay, and wrongful eviction.

Wright's case against George Terry, the head trustee, played out before a packed courtroom in Riverhead for two days in October 1878. As the judge summarized the case, without question the trustees proceeded within their legal rights when they dismissed Wright and did not owe him for any services beyond the date of his dismissal, even if there was a written contract, which apparently there was not.

Moreover, the judge instructed the jury that the trustees acted equally within their legal rights when they evicted Wright and his family from the parsonage. The judge used an analogy that if you had a servant in your house and dismissed her from service, you would be perfectly within your rights to evict her from the house. Basically, the only question the judge left to the jury remained whether the defendants used unnecessary force in removing Wright and his family and whether they did any harm to his furniture "more than was necessary in removing it in a decent and orderly and proper manner."[36] The jury, "after a brisk trial," ruled in in favor of the trustees.[37]

94 | A Farm Family on Long Island's North Fork

Libel Lawsuit against the Church

At the annual parish meeting on January 29, 1878, while Wright's lawsuit wound its way through the courts, along with hiring a new minister and organizing a subscription for a new organ, the members of the congregation voted to censure Halsey's cousin Eugene Hallock who "has by his actions since the burning of the church <u>assisted</u> and <u>defended</u> [underlining original] H.N. Wright and is still in our opinion assisting him in the prosecution of a large amount of the Parish." The congregation also likely implicated Isaiah and Caleb Hallock, Eugene's uncles and Halsey Hallock's cousins once removed.[38] The same meeting voted "to bring the church burner to justice," without explicitly naming the culprits.

This action triggered Eugene, Isaiah, and Caleb Hallock to file a lawsuit claiming the trustees and deacons, including Halsey Hallock, libeled them. The lawsuit asked for $10,000 in damages for expelling them from membership and intimating "they were connected with the church burning and organ destruction some time ago."[39]

Sammy Tuthill reported hearing about this lawsuit in his diary on March 27, 1878, when he met with George M. Terry, the head trustee. He noted that he was included in the slander lawsuit, which he thought must be a mistake as Caleb and Israel were his uncles and Eugene was his cousin.

For Halsey, this was not only an intra-family squabble but also a neighborhood fight. Isaiah Hallock lived next door to the west (where the museum's Cichanowicz House now stands). Caleb lived two farms further west. Eugene, Halsey's second cousin, lived three farms to the east.

More Lawsuits

Some of the same plaintiffs also sued a well-known New York–based church journal, the *Christian at Work*, which just happened to be edited by Joseph Newton Hallock, a slightly more distant cousin who grew up in Franklinville, served as principal of the Franklinville Academy while Halsey attended, and later became principal of the new Northville Academy. Because of his connections to Northville, he took a more than casual interest in the disputes in the church there.

An article in the *Christian at Work* insinuated that the same people bore responsibility for destruction of the liberty pole and likely served as "accessory" to the organ tossing, church burning, and other incidents. The *Christian at Work*'s editor then asked, "Who are they?"[40]

Although not explicitly named, Caleb Hallock felt threatened enough to sue the *Christian at Work* on June 6, 1878, for defamation, asking $10,000 in damages.[41] He and his brother Isaiah and their nephew Eugene may very well have been involved in the liberty pole incident. It took place virtually in front of their homes. They were certainly Democrats and opposed to the war. The church had "withdrawn fellowship" from all three men. Other indications show Caleb as a relatively litigious man who often got into disputes with neighbors over livestock and such matters.

Isaiah, Caleb, and their wives were among the group of conservatives who broke away from the Aquebogue Church in 1829 because they thought it too progressive. Apparently, once again they could not accept changes taking place in the church. Isaiah and Caleb both formally withdrew from the congregation in 1879, according to church records, but withdrawal is almost certainly a euphemism for the de facto expulsion.

As if this were not enough, Wright filed a new lawsuit against trustees of the Northville Church in April 1879. This time he claimed that the public reading of the derogatory letter about him "so injured" his standing as a minister "that he has been unable since to obtain a situation." He claimed $25,000 in damages. Lawsuits continued until the final one was dismissed in 1882.[42]

Trying to make sense of all this, the Southold *Traveler* connected the disputes over Wright directly back to those over the Civil War and the organ smashing incident. The *Traveler* further claimed that the same faction threw rotten eggs at the church's minister and tried twice to blow the place up. The *Traveler* noted that "even though they had one of the finest churches on Long Island" and lived in "an unusually wealthy farming district . . . the people [of Northville] seem to be belligerent." The *Traveler* went on to say that two factions still existed in the church, with each still accusing the other of burning the place down.[43]

The *Brooklyn Daily Eagle* went even further, noting the contentious disagreements were not entirely Wright's fault. According to the *Eagle*, the church at Northville was "notorious for the pugnacious character of the flock" and Wright misfortunately fell into this caldron of partisan bickering. "The shepherd was soon threatened with personal violence by Democratic saints for not being a Democrat partisan, and by Republican believers for not aiding their party." According to the *Eagle*, one side threw the organ out of the balcony while the other threw rotten eggs at Rev. Wright and even threw a skunk into the church.[44]

Wright went on to be ordained as a Congregational minister at a church in New Lots, Brooklyn, in 1881. Although the Long Island Association of Congregational Ministers had censured Wright, the New York and Brooklyn Association repudiated that determination.

News of the incident spread far and wide. Even the *San Francisco Chronicle* ran an article, reprinted from the *New York Times*, under the heading "Why a Church Was Burned: A Novel Way of Getting Rid of a Pastor." The account started with a description of Northville as a "prosperous Suffolk County village" in "one of the finest agricultural regions of Long Island" where the farmers seemed "exceptionally well off." The article speculated that prosperity "seems to have made the people belligerent" and that troubles in the church were a frequent occurrence.

Sensationalism from the *New York Times*

New York Times reports about the Northville affair were even more fanciful and exaggerated than those in the *Brooklyn Daily Eagle*. For starters, the *Times* got the denomination of the church wrong, calling it the "Independent Methodist Church at Northville."[45] It went on to embellish all the details. It claimed that a large crowd gathered on the day the trustees locked Wright out of the pulpit and seemed "well pleased with the subsequent performance." It claimed that the trustees called Sheriff Smith and "a posse of deputies" to maintain order and claimed that holes had been drilled in the floor of the church to make it burn faster. Here is one example of the *Times*'s embellishments:

> Early in the morning a detachment of Trustees occupied the front steps of the meeting-house, with the determination of dying, if necessary, at their post. The minister, with a small column of personal friends, stormed the steps with a heroism which was worthy of the highest admiration. . . . The combat raged long and furiously. At one time the storming party would drive the enemy from their intrenchments, only to be driven out in turn by the ferocious charge of the rallied and indomitable Trustees. So much valor, stubbornness, and Christian zeal has seldom been displayed. . . . Skirmishing went on all over the village during the

rest of the day, and the quiet of what is frequently called "our American Sabbath" was diversified by the shouts of victorious Trustees, and the bugle-call of the fierce minister's partisans.

In yet another fanciful detail the *Times* added that Rev. Wright discovered the fire himself and sent his son out to sound the alarm because he feared that if he went himself, his enemies would burn his parsonage down![46] All of this goes well beyond the colorful language that characterized the yellow journalism of the time. Indeed, it appears that the *Times* reporter took a few secondhand facts and made up the rest. It made for a good story but strays far from the firsthand reports of Sammy Tuthill and others on the ground at the time in Northville—very different from the careful fact-checking that characterizes the *Times* today.

A Revival Gets Out Of Hand

The scandals did not end with Wright's departure. The church quickly hired a new minister, Allison O. Downs, and raised money for a new organ. Naturally, Halsey Hallock remained in the middle of things and chaired the special meeting that agreed to hire Downs.[47] They ordained the new minister in February 1878, nine months after the notorious fire. Downs, perhaps best known as an ardent temperance advocate, decided he needed a "season of revival" to exorcise the place from its tumultuous past. The revival took place in the Northville Academy building, the old church, which the congregation used for services until funds could be raised to build a new edifice.

Apparently, the teacher in the one-room school in the western part of Northville, "Professor Brewster Hampton Saxton," got a little too enthusiastic at the revival and began to behave rather eccentrically. This included breaking into song and prayer in the middle of lessons but went far beyond that. According to the *Brooklyn Daily Eagle*, Saxton "began to evince extraordinary fondness for the little girls, and supplied them liberally with oranges and candy . . . [so all the] mothers kept their precious daughters at home."[48] The boys got "cuffs" and oaths, leading fathers to keep them at home too. The school's trustees decided to get rid of him but that set off another legal struggle—between this school and the teacher.

The school may not have been easy for any teacher to manage, especially in a litigious place like Northville. The previous year, the school trustees brought in a new teacher "who could govern the school." But one of the parents, Manly W. Downs, soon charged the supposedly mild-mannered young woman, Lizzie Griffing from Shelter Island, with assault and battery and had her arrested at the school and brought before a magistrate in Riverhead. Her alleged crime: she whipped the hands of Downs's nine-year-old daughter and kept her after school. The newspaper editor, who had known Griffing since she was a little girl, found the whole situation amusing and ludicrous.[49] In the end, this case became just another example of the litigiousness of the Northville community.

A New Scandal

It only took a few more years for the new minister, Allison O. Downs, to become enmeshed in a scandal of his own. In 1884, while he attended a temperance convention in Orient, his 26-year-old wife, Clara Downs, eloped with a 54-year-old deacon who lived across the street, George Mitchell Terry—the trustee who led the struggle against Rev. Wright a decade earlier. The Downses had been married for seven years and had two young children including a new baby girl.

Naturally there was a Hallock connection. When she eloped, Mrs. Downs left her baby with Edna Hallock, the wife of George C. Hallock who lived four houses west of the Homestead Hallocks. Mrs. Downs said she intended to visit a friend. Instead, she got on a train with Terry and left for New York City.[50] Again, the *Brooklyn Daily Eagle* could not resist the story, running it under the headline "Parson Downs / He Wants a Divorce Because His Wife Eloped With Deacon Terry."[51]

According to the *Eagle*, Deacon Terry had $7,000 in cash from the sale of his mother's farm to fund their travels. Apparently, no one had any idea where the couple went, although the article speculated Florida, where Mrs. Downs had a sister who allegedly "eloped with her sister's husband."[52] The *Eagle* claimed that others thought they left for Europe because "Mrs. Downs was never done expressing a desire to see Paris." The *Eagle* also claimed that "Deacon Terry was a conspicuous man, tall, stout and with black-gray chin whiskers nearly two feet long, of which he was ridiculously proud." The paper wondered what she saw in him. Supposedly the "popular clergyman," Rev. Downs, seemed "heart-broken" over the infidelity of his wife. The *New York Times* added the detail that Mrs. Downs was "a very prepossessing blond" and noted that she was also active in church affairs.[53]

Scandals in the Church | 99

So how did this one turn out? As recalled by a neighbor many years later, "Mrs. Downs got wild when she realized what she had done."[54] In its usual colorful language, the *Eagle* reported that she "discovered her error" and now had a "desire to resume business at the old stand." The *Eagle* also reported that "Mrs. Terry has forgiven the deacon" and was willing to live with him again.[55] However, it appears that the eloping couple's return may not have been entirely voluntary, as one of the other deacons of the church, Hallock Luce, pursued them to Virginia and may have compelled them to return.[56]

The people of Northville were not as accommodating as Mrs. Terry. Sammy Tuthill recorded in his diary that his neighbors greeted the Terrys with "full wagons of serenaders" the night he returned from the elopement.[57] Serenading couples on their wedding night with loud singing and noise makers was a raucous local custom that Tuthill mentions a few times. Presumably this serenade for Terry was more of a taunt than a celebration. Two nights later, the neighbors serenaded the Terrys again. One Long Island newspaper reported that "certain parties at Northville have taken the trouble on themselves to nightly meet adjacent to the house of Mr. Terry and make night hideous with their threats, etc."[58] The *New York Times* referred to it as a "tin can serenade."[59]

The community remained clearly upset. Sammy Tuthill, who worked closely with Terry to settle the earlier scandal, reported in his diary that on December 29 he attended an "indignation meeting" at the church over Terry's return to Northville.[60] Naturally, this being Northville, there ensued a lot of disagreement. Some supported Mrs. Downs, others supported Mrs. Terry.[61] They voted for a resolution condemning Deacon Terry, then on a revote they tabled the motion but also voted to publish the resolution in the *Riverhead News* and the *Traveler*.[62] The following week, the *Eagle* reported that the community remained "all tore up" about the affair.

This being litigious Northville, everyone went to the courts in "a perfect tornado of litigation." Rev. Downs quickly filed for divorce from his wife and custody of their children. He also filed a $20,000 lawsuit "as an injured husband" against Deacon Terry. Mrs. Downs somehow also filed a suit against Deacon Terry (her erstwhile lover). In addition, Mrs. Downs's mother filed a lawsuit against both Rev. Downs (her son-in-law) and Deacon Terry (her daughter's erstwhile lover).

The *Eagle* quoted Mrs. Downs claiming that Rev. Downs "was not a Christian husband," and snidely pointed out that she eloped with a "Christian deacon!" The *Eagle* snuck in the comment that Northville was "not unacquainted with arson, burglary and slander"—obviously an allusion to the previous scandals in the church with which its readers were familiar. The *Eagle* even stated that the "Northvillians" would "probably burn up [their] church again" in defense of their good name.⁶³

The *Eagle* could not leave the story alone. Just a week later the paper reported that Deacon Terry decided to leave town again, this time alone, to escape all of the legal problems his elopement caused, including another lawsuit from his own mother, claiming that the money he used to run away was actually her money—the proceeds from the sale of her farm to Halsey's brother-in-law, Herbert Wells.⁶⁴

The only reference to this whole affair in the church records was a resolution in early 1885 that expressed "our deepest sympathy to our pastor in his great difficulties and our fullest confidence in him as a minister of the gospel." The same meeting adopted a similar resolution extending "our deepest sympathy to our sister Mrs. [George] Mitchell Terry in her great affliction," with any notice of the earlier meeting apparently expunged from the church records.⁶⁵

Deacon Terry's whereabouts remained unknown, but he sent a letter to his wife in early February asking for her forgiveness "saying he has been living two lives and could not withstand the fear of exposure." Mrs. Terry was supposedly willing received him back and forgave him fully.⁶⁶

Was the Christian minister as eager to forgive his wife? Of course not. He filed his divorce case within a few days of his wife's elopement with the deacon.⁶⁷ The courts moved quickly and Rev. Downs obtained his divorce barely two months later, granting him not only a divorce but also custody of the two children. Mrs. Clara Downs went to live with her parents in Bridgehampton.⁶⁸

Is that the last we hear of all this? No. Just a week later the *Eagle* reported Deacon Terry returned to town and proposed to live there with his wife despite public protests and a resolution of the community denouncing him.⁶⁹ When that proved untenable, the couple stayed together as husband and wife but moved to Brookhaven Town, where they were still living 30 years later.

Less than a year afterward, Rev. Downs remarried, this time to Liela Downs, daughter of Nathaniel and Rachel Downs, who lived about two miles to the west near what is now Northville Turnpike.⁷⁰ The reverend was from a Southampton branch of the Downs family and not closely related to the Northville family of the same name. Downs stayed in the pulpit for another 11 months, until November 1886, when he and the new Mrs.

Downs left suddenly for a church in Michigan. In the process he somehow left the Northville Church with a $700 debt.[71]

Three years later, a rather different story emerged. It turns out the real philanderer was Rev. Downs! According to an article appearing in the *Eagle*, while Downs was the pastor at Northville "he earned a reputation as a bicycle rider and spent much of his time traveling about the country." His bicycle was a big wheel—introduced just a few years earlier—the latest craze among young men. By the mid-1880s the local papers had frequent references to bicycle trips, bicycles for sale, bicycle races, and even bicycle tours from New York City.[72] Apparently, Rev. Downs's bicycle trips were not entirely innocent. The *Eagle* strongly implies that he visited Lelia, whom he married so soon after his divorce. As the *Eagle* put it, "Parson Downs got a divorce and promptly married the very woman who had bred such intense jealousy in Mrs. Downs."

To summarize, Rev. Downs goes bicycling and has the first affair. This causes his wife, Clara, to run off with the Deacon Terry. The deacon and his wife then get back together, but they leave town. And Rev. Downs gets to keep his children and marry his mistress as if he were totally blameless!

Another Falling Out

Less than 10 years later, in 1895, members of the Northville congregation suffered another major falling out when the new minister in their church, Rev. T. H. Griffith, introduced a new order of worship with responses from the congregation. The *Brooklyn Daily Eagle* in its usual vivid style reported that "the descendants of the Puritans claim [the new service] is too decidedly ritualistic leaning towards Episcopalianism."

Church attendance started to dwindle until finally the deacons held a "largely attended" meeting of disaffected members at one of their homes. When a committee appointed at the meeting met with their pastor, he "treated them very coolly" and termed their criticism of the new order of service an insult.[73] The deacons then passed a resolution rejecting the new order of service and the pastor responded by offering his resignation effective a month later.

Then, on a Sunday night, Griffith launched a jeremiad against the congregation, assailing them "in most bitter terms," according to the *Eagle*. He even threatened to provide evidence that would send one member of the congregation to prison if he did not stop his attacks, adding that the unnamed sinner "was bound for perdition anyway." One never knows how much of the *Eagle*'s accounts to believe, but a *Suffolk County News* article about "trouble in the Congregational church of Northville" confirmed that the flock rejected his new order of worship as being too Episcopalian: "The domanie got mad and talked very plainly, intimating that certain ones in his congregation should be placed behind stone walls."[74]

Halsey Hallock again found himself in the middle of the controversy. The *Eagle* provided a list of supporters and opponents of Griffith, with Halsey listed as one of two supporters. The dozen opponents included his brother Charles, his brother-in-law Simeon O. Benjamin (married to sister Amelia), and another brother-in-law, Leslie Terry (Emilie's brother's brother-in-law).[75]

Why All the Scandals and Controversy?

That there could have been so much conflict and animosity in a place like Northville is astounding. Visitors always described it as prosperous and pleasant. The population was remarkably homogenous. In the 1860 census, of the 337 individuals who lived in Northville, 308 or 91.4 percent, were native-born whites, with only 14 nonnatives, mostly Irish laborers and their families, and also 15 Blacks, mostly young farm workers or servants.[76]

If we exclude the Black and Irish laborers on the fringes of the community, the homogeneity becomes even more remarkable. Except for the minister's family, all of the native-born whites come from New York State, and almost all of these descend from the original Puritan settlers of Southold town, with many complex interrelationships through marriage. And all engaged in the same occupation—farming.

Economically, the community appears rather egalitarian: no unusually large or wealthy farms; no farmers in a tenant situation. According to census data, the average farm was worth just over $4,000, with most in a narrow range from $2,000 to $8,000. Of the ones worth less, most belonged to children of farmers who eventually stood to inherit substantial property. Only a few were worth more than twice the average.

A strong conservative streak—first manifested in 1829 when a group of 61 dissidents broke away from the Congregational church in Aquebogue—runs through most of the later crises. The conservatives, while not a majority, were definitely a strong minority: Melinda Corwin calling an abolitionist sermon "beggarly"; Caleb and Isaiah Hallock supporting the anti-war party during the Civil War and probably responsible for the liberty pole incident; and people opposing instrumental music in the church and later tossing the organ out of the balcony. These same people became supporters of Rev. Wright—perhaps because the others opposed him—and they probably made up the core group who attacked pastor Griffith over something as seemingly innocuous as introducing a congregational response into the order of worship.

In all of this, Halsey and his branch of the Hallock family sat on the liberal end of the spectrum, at least for their community. They supported abolition, voted for Lincoln, favored musical instruments, and willingly allowed a new form of worship.

Rewriting Their History

Despite all these scandals, the Northville Church managed to write the less savory parts of its past completely out of its history. For instance, in a lengthy address on the history of the church delivered by Deacon Chauncey Howell, a Hallockville neighbor and blood relative of the Homestead Hallocks, at the dedication of a new church building in 1904, Rev. Wright's name is simply omitted from the list of ministers who served the congregation.[77] Similarly, there were no references to the organ smashing incident, the first attempt to burn down the church, the Terry/Downs scandal, or any of the other controversies that afflicted the congregation over the previous three-quarters of a century. Instead, the address ended by claiming that "when the full history of our church shall have been written . . . it will be plain to all that we have been Divinely led."

Twenty-five years later, in a paper read at the centennial service for the church in 1929, Halsey Hallock, then age 91, was a little more forthright, recalling, "Our church has come through rough seas, but thanks be to God, we are and have been for many years sailing under a banner of peace."[78] The church records remain nearly silent, simply stating that "for a short time in 1877 [Wright] was acting minister."[79] A rumor persists that a 20th-century historian of the church intentionally destroyed what records did exist of those events.

Chapter 6

Life in the Homestead

1885–1920

My dearest Bessie
Your eyes are as true blue
As my love is for you.

—Bessie's cousin, Nina Benjamin

Bessie's Album

In 1886, six-year-old Bessie received a little autograph book as a Christmas present from her eight-year-old cousin Nina Benjamin (1879–1944). After a bit of verse by Nina follows this little rhyme from Bessie's father Halsey:

My Dear Bessie
The Good Book says
Remember now thy creator
In the days of thy youth.[1]

And one from her mother, Emilie:

Dear Little Bessie
Be a good girl and you
Will be a true woman.

School

The Hallock children all attended the one-room District 11 school a mile walk to the west. For Hal, Eula, and Georgia, it remained the same "little square pine building [with] its bare, cold, hatefull look" their father attended. However, in 1888, with Bessie in second grade, the trustees lengthened the building to provide room for a coatroom, raised the roof, added a bell tower, finished the interior with ceiling board, and installed new seats and desks—"modernizing" the old structure in every way (see fig. 6.1).[2] Bessie graduated from the school in 1895 at age 14 and Ella followed four years later.[3] She possibly skipped a grade because her neighbor "Aunt" Frances Hallock taught her how to read before she started school.

Figure 6.1. The District 11 school in Northville (Sound Avenue), built in 1836 and much renovated in 1888. Photo circa 1900. Halsey attended the school in the 1840s, and later all of his children received eighth-grade educations here. It stood originally on the northwest corner of Pier Avenue and Sound Avenue (next to the house where Halsey was born). *Source:* Hallockville Museum Farm. Used with permission.

Many years later, Ella recalled the one-room building "with the old pail and dipper." She remembered it being so cold that the ink froze in their ink bottles, forcing the students to warm them in the sand under the stove. "The ground turned into a lake every time it rained. The boys had to row us up to the school steps, which of course was great fun." She remembered playing "prisoner's base" in the road in front of the school.[4] The building still stands today, behind the first farmhouse south of Sound Avenue on Manor Lane.

After completing eighth grade in the one-room school, Hal and Eula attended the Northville Academy, which reopened in 1882 after being closed for almost a decade. According to entries in the Hallock diaries, "Hallie's" bill in 1885 was $14.85 and Eula's, $19.32. In 1891 the diary shows an entry of $7 for Georgia's tuition at the Franklinville Academy, and the following year, $9 to "Mr. [W. S.] French" for her tuition there.

Riverhead opened the public Union School in 1871, downtown, just east of the Methodist church on Main Street. It offered a two-year secondary program that gradually put the old private academies out of business. Bessie was among seven members of the graduating class of 1897, the only one from Sound Avenue.[5] She served as the class secretary and helped devise the class motto: "No Footsteps Backward." Three years after graduating, she returned to the one-room District 11 school as the teacher for the 1900 school year.

In 1899, Ella attended the same Union School in Riverhead for a week before the new Riverhead High School opened on Roanoke Avenue. With the new building, the school extended its curriculum to a four-year program, but Ella stayed only for two years, never graduating.

The school belonged to the district that served downtown Riverhead, but the outlying districts, all independently organized, could pay tuition for their students to attend. The distance being too far for daily commuting, Ella boarded with the Ernest and Grace Duryea family on Court Street four days a week. Many years later she still remembered getting up at six o'clock on Monday mornings to bicycle from the Homestead to the school in downtown Riverhead when unlucky enough to not get a ride with her uncle Addison Wells.[6] That was a seven-mile trip, on unpaved roads, on a one-speed bicycle, in all weather!

Bessie and Ella went to New York for music lessons once a week. That was "when the train took only two hours to get there," Ella commented many years later. Bessie took piano, Ella took violin. "We were in all the plays and recitals for the church," as Ella recalled. "There was the Literary Society and the Christian Endeavor. I was in the choir. They were pleasant days and busy ones."[7]

Two Sisters Marry

Eula Hallock (1871–1968) married Charles S. Wells on December 10, 1891, in the Homestead's east front room, following the local custom for weddings to take place in the home of the bride. Diary entries that October show expenditures for Eula's "wedding outfit," including $17.50 for a cloak. One local paper reported, "We understand that the happy couple will go directly to housekeeping."[8] They originally settled on a farm further west on Sound Avenue, but later bought the south half of the Homestead farm.

Eula and Charles's two daughters became a frequent presence on their grandparents' farm (see fig. 6.2). Eula inherited her parents' longevity gene and lived to age 97. Her daughters Irene Hawkins and Lois Young lived to be 95 and 94, respectively. Lois became one of the founders of the Hallockville Museum and for many years served as its collections curator.

Georgia (1875–1916), the third child of Halsey and Emilie, married Henry F. "Harry" Corwin in 1897, one of several carpenters in the Corwin family business that specialized in large structures such as churches. Their work took them all over the area and required long absences from home. When Georgia's health deteriorated, Harry decided he needed to

Figure 6.2. Picnic at Hallock Pond with Eula (Hallock) Wells and Ella Hallock; their mother, Emilie Hallock; and Eula's daughters, Irene and Lois, on July 4, 1924. Bessie Hallock photo. *Source:* Hallockville Museum Farm. Used with permission.

stay nearby. So he switched careers and in 1908 started the Crescent Duck Farm in Aquebogue on the family's sandy land. Now the last duck farm on Long Island, it is operated today by third-, fourth-, and fifth-generation descendants of Georgia and Harry.

Georgia died from cancer in 1916 at age 42, leaving three sons—Fennimore age 18, Lloyd age 12, and Halsey age 7. While their mother was ill and after her death, the two younger boys lived for a while with their grandparents in the Homestead, making the place lively with children's voices for the last time (see fig. 6.3).

A Family Reunion and Other Excursions

After the Civil War, Halsey's brother Daniel returned to his farm but soon turned his mind to inventing and manufacturing better farm equipment. He was always mechanically minded, and perhaps his wartime service in an artillery unit whetted his appetite for more. In the 1880s he gave up

Figure 6.3. Halsey Hallock in 1918 with his grandson Halsey Corwin, who lived with the Hallocks for a few years before and after his mother's death. Bessie Hallock photo. *Source:* Hallockville Museum Farm. Used with permission.

farming and moved to Southold, where he became a full-time manufacturer best known for his patented potato diggers. In the 1890s Daniel moved to York, Pennsylvania (leaving his wife behind on Long Island), and established D. Y. Hallock & Sons, which successfully manufactured agricultural equipment on a larger scale and distributed nationwide over the next few decades.

In 1898, Halsey and his brother Charles and sister Adelia Benjamin traveled from Long Island to York, Pennsylvania, where their brother Daniel lived, for a family reunion that brought together all the siblings, including their sister Hannah, then living in Illinois (see fig. 6.4).

Excursions to New York City, Brooklyn, or elsewhere, as well as leisure trips closer to home, became more frequent. Each year the Hallock family attended the annual Suffolk County Fair in Riverhead. In 1910 they heard Theodore Roosevelt speak there.

The Methodist camp meeting in Jamesport in August became another annual highlight. Although the main feature was supposedly the preaching and singing in the central tent, these meetings served as a major social

Figure 6.4. Hallock siblings at their last reunion in 1898 in York, Pennsylvania: (rear, left to right) Halsey, Adelia (Benjamin), Charles (sitting), Hannah (Dedrick), and Daniel. *Source:* Hallockville Museum Farm. Used with permission.

gathering, complete with ice cream and fancy women's hats. The Hallocks occasionally joined Sound Avenue neighbors at the Old Landing Club, a social club on the shore of Long Island Sound organized by local farm families.

They also enjoyed sailing outings on Peconic Bay with their uncle Dan Downs (Emilie's brother-in-law). Ella recalled one such trip in 1910: they left their horse in the Miamogue Hotel stable in South Jamesport, where it became violently ill from eating baling wire and died. In 1901, the Hallock girls joined many of their neighbors on an excursion to Hartford, Connecticut, from the recently constructed Iron Pier on the shore of Long Island Sound only a mile from the Homestead. In 1909, they took a three-day excursion in a launch from Mattituck Creek to Norwich, Connecticut, and probably took similar excursions organized by the Sound Avenue community (see fig. 6.5).

Figure 6.5. Hallock family portrait, 1910. Emilie and Hallock Halsey; their only son, Hal; and their four daughters, Georgia, Ella, Bessie, and Eula. *Source:* Hallockville Museum Farm. Used with permission.

Quakes and Blizzards

On August 10, 1884, the Hallocks experienced an earthquake their neighbor Sammy Tuthill recorded in his diary.[9] With an estimated magnitude of 5.5, the earthquake was centered off Coney Island.[10] Although felt on the entire East Coast, it was strongest on Long Island and nearby Connecticut. On February 28, 1925, the Hallock diaries include another earthquake—one strong enough to shake the house and that "made everyone feel sick."

From March 11 to 14, 1888, a severe nor'easter, brought 40 to 50 inches of snow driven by high winds. The Great Blizzard of '88—one of the worst ever to strike the Northeast—was especially severe on Long Island. The Southold *Traveler* reported drifts over 15 feet, and the village got cut off from all communication for four days following the storm. According to Ella Hallock, "Our folks didn't try to dig to the outhouse, they tunneled out to it."[11]

The Hallocks Continue to Enlarge and Update the Old Homestead

During the final decades of the 19th century and the first of the 20th, as both the farm and the community became more prosperous and more closely connected with the rest of the world, the Hallocks continuously enlarged and updated the old Homestead, installing "modern" conveniences and trying to conform to the latest styles.

They installed fancy maple wainscoting on the walls and ceiling of their sitting room in the late 1880s. Called "ceiling board" at the time, these narrow pieces of machine-made molding gave the appearance of linen-fold paneling.[12] Similar woodwork, probably from Hallett mill in Riverhead, appeared in many other dining rooms of the period along Sound Avenue in the final decades of the 19th century. Later, when the wood darkened with age, the Hallocks painted it white to brighten the space. They conceived of this as their new dining room, but over the years used it mostly as their favorite sitting room with the dining table folded into the center of the room except for big family dinners.

This room, originally located on the west side of the house but moved to its current location in 1860, was the oldest part of the house, dating to the mid-18th century. After all the changes, including raising the ceiling, replacing the floors, installing ceiling board, and adding the gothic window upstairs, Halsey said of this room, "As far as the timbers of that little home is concerned the timbers are the same, just like the Irishman's jack knife. The same old knife but it has had a new blade and a new handle."[13] He referred to a saying popular in the late 19th century about an Irishman with an old knife from his father. It received five new blades and three new cases but remained the same old knife. Indeed, this room is like that, everything visible on the outside and the inside has been completely changed—the doors, windows, layout, location, and finish materials.

As the century neared its end, the Hallocks added a downstairs east bedroom. Located just off their sitting room with a nice south facing window, a downstairs bedroom must have been a great convenience to Emilie and Halsey in their final decades.

When the Hallock women got tired of having to traipse out to their washhouse to do the weekly laundry, they also added a shed on the back of the "modern" kitchen to accommodate a laundry room and a pantry in 1894, allowing the women to do their wash in a more convenient location just steps from the kitchen range where they heated the water. This also gave the menfolk exclusive use of the former washhouse for their farm shop, where they could repair and service equipment.

Under the new washroom they dug a cistern and lined it with cement. Gutters directed rainwater from the roofs into this cistern. The Hallocks used cistern water for most domestic purposes, such as cooking, washing hands, and washing clothes. They preferred mineral-free rainwater to hard water, from the well west of the sitting room, that would not make soap suds with their homemade soap.

With a limited supply of cistern water, the Hallocks carefully conserved its use. Estelle Evans, one of Bessie Hallock's piano students in the late 1920s, recalled not being allowed to touch the piano until she washed her hands. Ella would lead her into the washroom, pump just an inch or so of water into a pan, and have Estelle put her hands flat in the bottom of the pan to wash them. The author's grandmother, who grew up in a similar Sound Avenue farmhouse, remembered that they let their cistern go dry once each summer so they could sweep it out.

The West Wing Moves across the Street

With Herman and Arminda in their graves and Eula and Georgia married, Halsey and Emilie and the three children who never married did not need so much space (see fig. 6.6). In 1903, like true Yankees, not liking to leave a resource unused, the Hallocks detached the large west wing of the

Figure 6.6. This is the only surviving photo of the Homestead before 1903, when the Hallocks detached the 1860 west wing (in foreground of photo) and moved it across the street. Photo taken by Emilie's nephew, Horace J. Wells. *Source:* Hallockville Museum Farm. Used with permission.

Homestead and moved it across the street. They rented it for a few years and then in 1906 sold it and the farmland on the south side of Sound Avenue to their son-in-law, Eula's husband, Charles Wells (see fig. 6.7).[14]

Charles gradually accumulated 120 acres of former Hallock land, but living across from the in-laws may not have worked out well. In 1914 he sold out to two Polish immigrant farmers, Frank Cichanowicz and John B. Doroski, and moved to Southold.[15] The house burned down on a cold winter night, December 28, 1938, and was replaced by a smaller one-story house that still stands on the site.

After removing the large west wing, the Hallocks enlarged a small room on the west side of the original Homestead to create a second downstairs bedroom with generous south and west facing windows. To protect the view of the street from their sitting room window behind, they ingeniously sliced off the corner of this extension, hiding the diagonal wall in a new closet. They needed to be able to see their neighbors going by on the road!

After all these changes, the Homestead that museum visitors see today contains 12 rooms—three bedrooms upstairs, two more downstairs,

Figure 6.7. The former west wing after it was moved across the street in 1903 and converted to a separate house for son-in-law Charles and daughter Eula Wells. Bessie Hallock photo. *Source:* Hallockville Museum Farm. Used with permission.

two parlors in the front, a third parlor that doubled for music lessons, a sitting room–dining room, kitchen, washroom, and small room under the eaves to accommodate hired help. In addition, the Homestead contained two pantries downstairs and a large storeroom upstairs, as well as a huge attic on the third floor and, surprisingly for a house of its age, 12 closets.

The family continued to modernize and make changes into the first decade of the 20th century. Telephone service came to the Homestead in 1903, provided by local Baiting Hollow and Roanoke Telephone Company founded in 1900 by Sound Avenue farmers Henry R. Talmage and Charles H. Warner. Initially the company had 20 subscribers, all on one line. To "dial," one turned the crank to ring a bell in the operator's home down the street. She plugged you into the line of whomever you wanted to talk with.

Not quite done with improvements, in 1906 they acquired a new kitchen range. Ella told a story about how her parents assembled the stove outside and then could not get it through the door. That caused a good laugh. They added a pump to the well at the side of the house the same year. Likely this was a hand pump with a long rod connected to the pumping mechanism 60 feet down in the well.

In 1907, like many other Sound Avenue farm families in that period, they added a porch to the front of the house—fashionably called a piazza. With traffic on Sound Avenue limited to pedestrians and horse-drawn carriages, this would be quite pleasant and sociable, although that soon changed with the arrival of the automobile.

After Bessie nearly asphyxiated her sister and herself twice with the woodstove in their sitting room, the family installed central heating. They enlarged an old root cellar to make way for a coal-fired furnace in 1907—a gravity hot water system with all the return pipes sloping back to the furnace. The following year they climbed up to the third floor to dump buckets of water into a large funnel to fill the system and fired it up. But it was never too effective in the uninsulated house, as Bessie wrote, "My poor old frame was and is hard to heat but furnishes plenty of fresh air to help stave off colds." The author remembers visiting the Hallocks many years later and finding both the radiator and the stove in front of it going full blast in an attempt to keep the sitting room warm.

After decades of additions, modernizations, and improvements, with the occupants all growing older the Hallocks suddenly stopped making changes after 1907, leaving the Homestead essentially as visitors to the Hallockville Museum see it today, except for some basic electric wiring after electricity became available in 1926.[16] The wiring—generally one light and one outlet in every room—cost $271.87.[17] Their first electric bill: $1.80. They installed an electric pump in the well and rudimentary plumbing in the house—a single faucet in the kitchen and a toilet and tiny sink with just one faucet in a closet off the east bedroom—cold water only! The house never had a bathtub or hot running water, even though the Hallocks lived there another 50-plus years.

Cars

Ella recorded her first automobile ride November 4, 1905, with neighbor Clifford Hudson, but the family did not rush to acquire a horseless carriage. Indeed, two years later they bought another new surrey. In 1915, in a freak snowstorm on Easter Sunday, April 4, the Hallocks took the sleigh to church, according to the diaries. In a poem she wrote in 1916, Ella still drove a carriage. But their first car, a Ford Model T, likely came shortly thereafter (see fig. 6.8). Surprisingly, only Ella ever learned to drive, making her siblings and parents reliant on her for chauffeur service.

Figure 6.8. The Hallock's Model T Ford is shown here in a 1924 picnic at Hallock Pond. Bessie Hallock photo. *Source:* Hallockville Museum Farm. Used with permission.

The family diaries do include the purchase of their second Ford car in 1921 for $585. Later they switched to Chevrolets.

Women's Organizations Blossom

Gradually, as the century ended, the church reduced the number of Sunday services to just one in the morning, but at the same time a whole new nexus of church-related activities developed, especially for the women—part of an explosion of women's organizations happening across the nation as they exerted more agency in their lives. The Ladies Mutual Benefit Society came first, organized in 1876 with an official mission "to collect money for church purposes." According to its constitution, "Any Lady may become a member of this Society by the payment of twenty-five cents and a fee of five to be paid at the first meeting of each month." The record book indicates they diligently collected the 5¢ at each meeting! By 1880, 37 members, including Emilie Hallock and her mother, Betsy J. Wells, took turns meeting in each other's homes. The society was as much social as it was religious. Their constitution required that 10 minutes of each meeting be devoted to business. We can imagine what the ladies spent the rest of their time doing!

The church also formed a Women's Home Missionary Union in 1888 that met monthly to raise funds for "home missionary purposes." The members read articles about the importance of work with "mountain whites" and "American negroes," as well as international missionary efforts in India, Africa, and elsewhere. Again, the Hallocks took leading roles. For instance, in 1921 Ella participated on the Service Committee for Near East Relief.

Young Ladies' Busy Workers Society

Women of the community also began organizing secular groups. They started a group called Young Ladies' Busy Workers Society of Northville before 1886. The members, mostly young women, including Eula Hallock, who joined in 1889 at age 18; her sister Georgia, who joined in 1890 age 15; and Henrietta (Terry) Wells, Emilie Hallock's sister-in-law. The group's name may say it all. Members met twice weekly in each other's homes. The minutes for May 17, 1890, record that the society "met with Miss. Eula Hallock, quite a number present." They organized "novelty box socials," picnics, an annual strawberry festival, and even an art gallery (with nominal admission) for George Washington's birthday. They held regular business meetings, although the subjects of the business seldom registered in the minutes, which often reported with frank honesty "no report read, no business conducted."[18] It seems fairly obvious that the main purpose of the meetings was social. Generally they brought their sewing, although the minutes of one meeting recorded that they played Ouija instead.

Among its endeavors, the group prepared and sold *The Practical Cook Book*, published in Jamesport by Epher Tuthill, who ran a printing press as one of the many businesses in his Main Road store. The *Long Island Traveler* noted, "It is very certain that no better investment of 50 cts. can be made."[19]

Woman's Christian Temperance Union

We have seen that temperance activities became an important part of the local church's program beginning in the 1840s, with a focus on men. A group called the Sons of Temperance still met in the Sound Avenue Hall in 1868.[20] However, in the following decades, temperance became more of a women's movement. "Aunt" Frances Hallock founded the local chapter of the Woman's Christian Temperance Union (WCTU) in 1896 with

18 members and held the initial meeting in her house. The WCTU met monthly. After prayers and singing, the women read articles to each other about the success of the temperance movement and sent delegates to various county and state conventions. As was the case in many other organizations for women, the most important function of WCTU meetings appeared to be providing ways for women to get together. The meetings often ended with a "social" or an "entertainment," and the minutes contain frequent votes of thanks for the refreshments.

On a national level, the WCTU, founded in 1873, spearheaded the crusade for Prohibition. Members advanced their cause by entering saloons, singing, praying, and urging saloonkeepers to stop selling alcohol. The WCTU also played an important role in the struggle for women's rights and suffrage after Frances Willard became its president in 1879. However, the Sound Avenue chapter appears not to have engaged directly in any of these activities.

Bessie Hallock served as president of the local chapter for 30 years, starting about 1919, the year the country adopted Prohibition. In 1925 Bessie co-led a WCTU meeting on work for soldiers and sailors, something with which she had remarkably little experience. Other programs that year focused on citizenship, social morality, and Americanization—belying the anti-immigrant strain in the temperance movement. In 1930 she served as part of a delegation to the organization's state convention in Johnstown and reported back that "there is a flood tide of revolt against the wet candidates that have been picked to lead the old parties in this state."[21]

Children and Young People's Programs in the Church

For the first time, the church organized separate activities for children and young people—part of the invention of childhood that occurred in Victorian times. The Sunday school movement reached Sound Avenue in the 1880s. Frances Hallock (whose washhouse is now located behind the museum's Hudson-Sydlowski House) taught for so many years that virtually everyone in the community called her "Aunt," the customary way to address the primary Sunday school teacher. Ella and Bessie Hallock also both served as Sunday school teachers in the first decades of the 20th century. Both also served as delegates to County Sunday School Conventions and helped organize the annual Children's Day, a new celebration in the church.

As teenagers and young women, the Hallock girls participated in the Young People's Society of Christian Endeavor (YPSCE), which operated in the Sound Avenue Church from 1888 to 1945. Founded in Maine in 1881, within 25 years it quickly grew into a global phenomenon with 70,000 societies and a membership over three million young people worldwide. It was a nondenominational organization, a way for churches to reach out to and organize young people—a precursor of the youth fellowships later popular in many Protestant denominations.[22] Both Bessie and Ella often led YPSCE meetings and served as delegates to county and state conventions.[23]

But YPSCE was by no means entirely religious. As in women's organizations, the social committee played an important role. In 1912 the society presented the play *Fifteen Miles to Happytown*, with Ella the general manager and Bessie the musical "directress."[24] In February 1914 the society met "at the home of Miss Ella A. Hallock" for a musical and literary program followed by social games and refreshments.

A Very Active Social Life for the Young Misses Bessie and Ella

If the community news columns in the local papers are to be believed, Ella and Bessie led very active social lives in their late teens and early 20s. Music remained at the center of both girls' activities. They both studied in the city and both gave lessons, although it became a profession only for Bessie. A formidable musician, Bessie also served as the organist and choir director of the Sound Avenue Church for 51 years, starting at age 20. In a 1916 account of an elaborate double wedding in the Sound Avenue Church, the local paper noted that Bessie not just played the organ but she "presided at the organ."[25]

Ella played the violin (see fig. 6.9), often in small ensembles with her sister. She was also a key enabler of her sister's church music work. As she wrote many years later, "Music played quite a part in our household. Bessie with fifty-one years at the church organ. My part for many years before electricity took over, to pump the organ for her midweek practicing—then on Sunday to sing in the choir and sometimes to assist with the violin. Brother Hal said he never lacked for music in the home."[26]

Ella and Bessie also joined something called the RLHA club. It is unclear what the initials stood for, but it appears to be an all-women organization. For instance, the Sound Avenue correspondent of the *County Review* reported on July 28, 1907, "The Misses Bessie and Ella Hallock entertained the R.L.H.A. Club Friday afternoon" at the Sound Avenue

Figure 6.9. Ella with her violin on the Homestead's front porch. Bessie Hallock photo. *Source:* Hallockville Museum Farm. Used with permission.

Hall, where they participated in a series of duets, trios, and quartets with other musicians. The program ended with Bessie playing a voluntary on the organ. The news report of next meeting simply stated, "The R.L.H.A. club met with Miss Elizabeth A. Howell last Friday afternoon. An interesting program was presented after which dainty refreshments were served." At a meeting of the club at Mrs. Lulu Luce's, Bessie played a piano solo and in a piano duet. Ella played in a violin trio. "The Misses Bessie and Ella" hosted the next meeting. The club continued to meet for several years, at least through 1910.[27]

In 1914 Bessie led a nine-person orchestra at the entertainment following a strawberry supper sponsored by the Ladies Mutual Benefit Society. At a "musical evening" at the home of Mr. and Mrs. W. H. Howell, Bessie and Ella played a piano and violin duet and a piano duet.[28]

Literary Society and a Lyceum Club

Ella and Bessie also helped found the Sound Avenue Literary Society. Ella was the initial secretary in 1905, with her sister Bessie also an active member from the beginning. The two often performed musical numbers as part of the programs. Ella sometimes played violin and other times played piano two-hands with her sister. A 1906 article refers to the Literary Society and a play to be performed at the next meeting by the Lyceum Club of Sound Avenue, *A Man in the Case*. Both Ella and Bessie appeared in the cast—Ella as a "wealthy lady to the manor born" and Bessie as her orphan niece.[29]

A June 1907 meeting again featured the Hallock sisters as key parts of the program, with Bessie performing a piano solo and Ella as part of a violin trio. The next meeting would occur at the home of "the Misses Bessie and Ella Hallock." According to its record book, the society lasted seven years.[30]

A Sound Avenue Tennis Club

In a sign of how much Sound Avenue changed, in approx. 1910 residents organized the Ariston Tennis Club, possibly named for the ancient king of Sparta, with Mr. and Mrs. Charles Young in the lead. The club built a private tennis court near the Young house a few miles to the west of Hallockville. At its 1914 annual meeting, the club elected Bessie as its president.[31] Bessie recorded in her diary that she played weekly matches at the club's court from 1910 to 1917. Although the club was small, the couple-dozen members engaged in the normal social activities in addition to playing tennis. It existed until at least 1919.

A Typical Day for Ella

In 1914, when Ella's father suggested she write down everything she did in a typical day—"she would be surprised at how much she accomplished"—she responded with a poem entitled "The Account of Saturday, November 28, 1914, Is the Tale That I Now Relate":

> My mother dear had gone away
> So I wondered how I'd best spend the day.
> At 5:30 o'clock, I arose from my bed
> And, O, my eyes felt as heavy as lead.

I combed my hair and put on my clothes
Before Bessie Leona [Ella's sister] stretched, grunted and rose.
I hoped the two boys would just lie still,
But for early rising they need take no pill.
When I'd washed and lowered myself downstairs,
I was followed down by two white bears.
While I got breakfast in the din of a zoo,
I put the pumpkin on to stew.
Bessie did the chores in bedrooms four
Then told the kids to get dressed some more.
After the animals and keepers were fed,
I proceeded then to mix the bread.
I punched it here and I punched it there
Till I thought it was kneaded pretty fair.
I then set it by the stove to rise,
And proceeded to mix up crust for the pies.
I rolled out the flour and placed it on plate
And thought it'll not hurt if they have to wait.
Dried limas were washed and put on to cook
While I, for a while, the kitchen forsook.
I then started out for a cold ten mile drive
Taking Bess to give lessons and a boy that is five.
We made several calls on the way up the street
And when we met Helen, I purchased some meat.
Was out on the road an hour and a quarter,
Which you see made the morning that much shorter.
I then fixed the pumpkin and filled up the pies,
And on them, I'll tell you, there weren't any flies.
Of potatoes, I peeled a heaping big pan
While with a caller my tongue swiftly ran.
The brussel sprouts I fixed with care,
So that on lice we need not fare.
Then molded the bread into white loaves four
And set it back to rise some more.
Took out the pies with a smile on my face
And put in two more right on the same place.
Creamed chicken I next turned to prepare
The meat from the bones I firmly did tear.
Gave the vases of flowers some good fresh water
And did numerous other things that I'd oughter—

Took out the pies and put in the bread
So that seven hungry mouths might be fed.
I then let out a loud yell for dinner,
Which brought them in—each saint and sinner.
The youngsters were told to wash hands and faces
Before, at the table, they took their places.
On every face was a satisfied look
When to play and work their way they took.
I then from the oven took the staff of life
Which looked so good, I looked at it twice.
I now scraped and washed up the dishes
And also formed a few little wishes.
With a look at the clock I began to sweep
I'll tell you right now, I did not creep.
The kitchen then I dusted with care
When I got through, it looked pretty fair.
Right then I saw coming my music scholar,
So I poked up my hair and pinned up my collar.
I started right in with the musical lad
And when we got through, it didn't sound bad.
I then went up to change my dress,
And looked rather better then, I guess.
I hastily put on hat and coat
And wondered if women will ever vote.
A pie I tied up to carry away,
And two were gone of those made that day.
A beeline I made for Aquebogue,
Was glad it was this side of Quogue.
Well, we lastly got to the home of Harry,
As mother was ready, we did not tarry.
I then came home and unharnessed my steed,
And put up the wagon that we didn't need.
We lit up the lamp and I combed mother's hair
Because she had letters to read, she didn't care.
The men now came in and got neatly dressed,
For we all were invited out as guests
Up to Aunt Delia's for a very good supper
We smacked our lips both lower and upper.
We surely did have one great big treat
For Aunt Delia as hostess, you can not beat.

When we got home and dropped into bed
I slept just as soundly as though I were dead.[32]

The two little boys are Ella's nephews Lloyd and Halsey Corwin, the younger sons of her sister Georgia who was ill and died two years later. The boys, then ages nine and five, spent a lot of time with the Hallocks while their mother struggled with her cancer and then after her death. Ella made the 10-mile morning drive with horse and buggy—an hour and a quarter roundtrip—as their first car was still several years in the future. The second drive in the afternoon to pick up her mother, who was visiting her ill daughter Georgia, in Aquebogue was four miles each way—almost as long.[33] For supper, they visited Aunt Delia, Halsey's sister Adelia Benjamin about two miles to the west. Total distance traveled that day—about 22 miles.

Women's Suffrage

The diaries of Sound Avenue men contain frequent references to voting, but no references to women's right to vote. The Hallock women all joined the WCTU, which supported suffrage for women, but it does not appear a theme of any local meetings that the Hallocks attended.

The only exception is one line tucked into Ella's 1914 poem. After baking bread, cooking pumpkins, dusting the kitchen, creaming chicken, and checking the water in the flower vases, she finally gets a chance to change her dress to go to Aunt Delia's house for supper: "I hastily put on hat and coat / And wondered if women will ever vote."

New York became the first eastern state to grant full suffrage to women in 1917, and the following November the sisters recorded in their diary "first time women could vote in U.S. elections." We assume that Ella, Bessie, and their mother all voted for the Republican candidates that carried the town and county. Most certainly they did not vote for Alfred E. Smith, the Catholic anti-Prohibition Democrat who narrowly won the governorship of New York that year.

Why Did They Never Marry?

It seems surprising that three out of Halsey and Emilie's five children never married. However, Sound Avenue remained a small community with limited opportunities to meet eligible partners outside the community. We

Figure 6.10. Bessie and Ella Hallock as young women. *Source:* Hallockville Museum Farm. Used with permission.

do not know about Hal, but Bessie and Ella both were attractive, talented, and seemed interested in finding a mate. In 1920, Bessie, already 40, even served on a committee with Mabel Hallock, Elizabeth Howell, Olive Hallock, and Meta Conklin to organize an "unmarried women's social" at the Grange Hall.[34] Amazingly, despite this gallant effort none of these five ever found a husband.

Bessie was perhaps more focused on her career in music, but it seems more surprising that Ella never found a husband. Described as a "tall and slim red-headed young woman," she was "musically talented, playing the violin and singing with a pleasing contralto voice."[35] She was vivacious and outgoing, always a good conversationalist. We know she was a good cook and good with a needle—requisite skills for matrimony in those days, and yet she never found a partner. What happened?

Even though one might expect a shortage of young women, given their frequent death in childbirth, the opposite seemed to be the case in the early 20th century Sound Avenue community. The 1920 federal census returns reveal a severe shortage of men in Bessie and Ella's 30 to 39 age bracket: only two unmarried men versus eight unmarried women—six never married and two already widowed. It is possible than World War I deaths accounted for some of the missing men, but farm boys were not that likely to serve. More probably some of the young men left the farm for better opportunities in more urban areas.

The only reference to a suitor in the Hallock diaries is a cryptic mention on June 18, 1905, that "Charles Brady called in to see me."[36] Brady worked as a farm laborer on the Eugene Hallock farm, just to the east of the Homestead. Already about 50, he had worked on that farm for at least 25 years, probably one of the young boys who came out from the city in the 1860s and 1870s to work on local farms but never left. Ella must have been perplexed or amused. He certainly was not her equal in ambition, status, education, or probably anything else. Indeed, this may be why she recorded the event. He remained a lifelong bachelor, and she would die a spinster.

Many years later, when her cousin Virginia Wines asked about marriage, Ella, then in her 90s, responded in typically upbeat fashion: "Where there is life, there is hope."

Chapter 7

The Hallock Farm

To stay alive through the Revolution
You had to have a bit of scrawny land to rake something into,
A cow that gave a little milk every two weeks,
One miserable hen that might lay an egg once in two weeks
. . . and rum.

—Halsey Hallock, speaking about his
great-grandfather, Capt. Zachariah Hallock[1]

By the time Capt. Zachariah Hallock died in 1820, the Hallock farm was already beginning to modernize and improve. He may have ducked the American Revolution, but he participated fully in the early stages of the agricultural revolution that swept the East Coast in the late 18th and early 19th centuries.[2] The presence of horses in the 1820 inventory taken after his death indicates that he was well along in the transition from oxen to horses, which, while more expensive to obtain and keep, are much more efficient. Another important indicator is that the inventory includes the manure in the barnyard, appraised for $24 (about $500 in today's dollars), almost as much as his two-year-old mare, signifying that Zachariah and others farming in the area had moved beyond the wasteful practices of earlier centuries that left Long Island's sandy soils seriously depleted and were now carefully husbanding this valuable resource to maintain soil fertility.

By the early 19th century, farmers on the East End of Long Island began using menhaden (also called mossbunkers)—an abundant bony fish not fit for human consumption—as fertilizer. The fish, combined with intensive use of farmyard manure, allowed local farmers to restore the fertility of easily depleted Long Island soils and laid the basis for the agricultural prosperity that followed later in the century. Capt. Zachariah's 1820 inventory includes shares in two fishing companies—one on Long Island Sound and the other on Peconic Bay.

Many days were devoted to preparing equipment as well as to the actual fishing—a complex community activity. Normally, 12 to 16 men owned "rights" in a fishing company equipped with a seine up to half a mile in length, two or three boats, a reel to wind the net on, and a fish house. This practice continued well into Halsey's youth.[3] He described it as an all-week undertaking, with the men leaving home Sunday evening with their pail of "grub." When successful, he recalled, they could land 500,000 fish in a month. The fish all needed carting back to the farm. Each farmer's wagon was carefully measured by volume so he could get his fair share. Wagons carried one to two tons, or about 2,000 to 4,000 fish.

The Farm in Halsey's Youth

The first definitive glances at the Hallock farm are two sketch maps drawn by Halsey in his diary in 1859 and 1860 and data reported to the 1860 federal census (copies available at https://hallockville.org/hallocksbook/). The census shows 175 acres—125 improved and 50 unimproved—with a value of $8,000 ($250,000 in current dollars). Halsey's map for 1859 shows slightly less—a total of 154 acres. The missing 21 acres are possibly the Roanoke farm on which brother Daniel had been settled. Halsey's 1860 map shows about 106 acres used for crops, mowing, pasture, and other improved land and another 48 acres of woodland.

Notes on the edge of Halsey's 1860 map list the animals and crops produced that year. The Hallocks managed with just three horses in 1859 and four in 1860. Their 14 cattle included 7 "milch cows" (i.e., milk producing), mainly to produce butter, valued at $140 that year (over $4,000 in current dollars). Many years later Halsey's daughter Ella recalled that "Mother was forever making butter."[4] The remaining cattle were presumably either calves or yearlings. The family butchered just one animal. Livestock included 26 sheep and 15 swine, but the sheep produced only four pounds of wool apiece, less than half of modern standards.

The farm had between 80 and 100 chickens that produced $170 worth of eggs that year (over $5,000 today). Their four-acre orchard yielded $40 worth of apples. Altogether, Halsey calculated that they either sold or consumed $2,000 worth of produce (about $63,000 in current dollars).

Corn and oats were the principal grain crops, producing 350 and 400 bushels, respectively, in 1859 and 400 and 225 bushels, respectively, the following year.[5] Wheat came in a little less at 280 bushels in 1859 and 130 in 1860. The farm produced only 10 bushels of rye in 1859 and 40 the next year. The biggest crop was hay, with 35 tons recorded—the equivalent of 1,500 standard bales today, about 35 wagon loads—enough to stack one bay of the Hallock barn (about 12 by 30 feet) 24 feet tall.

Potatoes were just beginning to become an important crop at that time. The farm reported just 100 bushels in 1859—about three tons—probably a bad year. If we assume that the family could eat 20 bushels with 20 bushels necessary for seed, that left only 60 bushels to sell. Only two wagonloads. Not a lot. The following year Halsey recorded harvesting 600 bushels (18 tons) from three acres—a more respectable yield.

Potatoes were labor intensive. Halsey described as a boy using the traditional planting method where they dropped seed potatoes into every third furrow made by the plow.[6] In the fall, the Hallock men dug all the potatoes by hand with pitch forks, "picked" them into baskets, carted them to the barn, and dumped them into the cellar. When the market was right, they shoveled the many tons of potatoes into baskets, lifted the baskets back up the cellar stairs, graded them to remove spoiled tubers, put them in barrels, and loaded the heavy barrels onto waiting wagons—all backbreaking hand labor—before finally sending them off to market.

In Halsey's childhood, they still did most of the work by hand or with primitive horse-drawn tools. The year started by carting manure out from the barn and dumping it in small heaps throughout the fields. Next, they spread the manure by hand. In 1855, Halsey recorded that he, his brothers, his father, and two farmhands hauled an incredible 240 cartloads of barnyard manure. They also spent an amazing amount of time fishing, sometimes with huge catches that they used for fertilizer.

In April, they started plowing—with a boy, perhaps the young Halsey, to guide the horses and a man to guide the heavy plow. Next they broke the lumps with a harrow dragged behind the horse. In early April they began planting potatoes. In late April and early May they planted corn—23 acres of it in 1859. The process involved first digging a large hole for some fish manure, then dropping a handful of seed, covering it, and stomping on the hill with their shoe to firm up the soil and retain moisture.

That was the easy part. As Halsey described it, "After the corn is through the ground, the fight is on. Start in with the horse with the boy [probably himself] on his back, of course, to keep him somewhere between the rows and the larger boy (if there is one) to hold the handles of the old harrow. . . . Then the whole force was put on with their hoes to cut and slash around the hill to kill the grass, weeds and worst of all sorrel."[7] Halsey and his brothers repeated the harrowing and hoeing several times through June, July, and August. Halsey remembered years of "fiercely hot days in the corn, pulling or chopping the weeds." Harvesting was no easier. They cut and stacked the corn stalks, then after a month or so they removed cobs, carted them to the barn, and eventually husked them, all by hand. They also tied the stalks into sheaves and carted them to the barn to use as fodder. Halsey remembered being a "champion corn husker" who could manage up to "100 bushels between sleeps." Of course, the workdays were long, generally 12 hours. The cobs could be fed directly to chickens, hogs, and horses. But for domestic consumption it had to be shelled with a hand-cranked mill, or perhaps just using the blade of a shovel turned upside down.

Accelerating Agricultural Change

Like many other parts of the country, the rate of agriculture change began to accelerate in the Sound Avenue community during Halsey's youth. In perhaps the biggest change in the 1850s, the Hallocks, like their neighbors, started purchasing fertilizer materials. They bought ashes and bonemeal from New York City and guano imported from islands off the coast of Peru.[8] Halsey's 1855 diary contains 22 references to guano. They carted at least six tons of it by wagon from the train depot and the port in Jamesport and sometimes from Riverhead. They used it mostly on potatoes and corn. In 1860, Halsey recorded that guano and other purchased fertilizers cost $380 (about $12,000 in current dollars)—a very significant investment at the time. In the 1860s they also started using "fish guano," a waste product of factories that produced oil from menhaden. By 1864, eight or ten such factories existed on the eastern end of Long Island.[9]

Halsey's youth also witnessed the introduction of manufactured farm machinery. Typically, the Hallocks became early adopters. Although Cyrus McCormick invented his mechanical reaper in 1831, it took him nine more years to sell his first machine, and not until the mid-1850s were the design and manufacturing problems sufficiently solved to make practical machines widely available.[10]

In 1854, the first reapers were trialed in the community, deemed unsatisfactory, and sent back.[11] Just two years later, Halsey's diary records that on July 14, 1856, "Dan [his brother] goes to the depot after a reaper. He gets home about sundown. Then we set it up ready to start in the morning." It was a John H. Manny combined mowing and reaping machine that cost $135—probably more than the value of all their other equipment combined.[12] The machine's ability to both harvest grain and cut hay made it doubly useful. Herman and his brother Zachariah II purchased it jointly, making them one of the first on Sound Avenue to own such a machine.[13] The following day, Halsey recorded, "This morning start the machine in the grain on the hollow lot. Afternoon, bind and cart 32 shock today." Always mechanically inclined, Daniel proved the appropriate son to send for the machine. He eventually left farming and turned to the commercial manufacture of farm equipment in York, Pennsylvania.

Besides the reaper/mower, a number of other new or improved machines soon appeared in Sound Avenue fields. Starting in the 1850s, portable horse-treadmill-powered threshers replaced the older, stationary, sweep-powered ones. Self-scouring steel teeth replaced cast-iron teeth on cultivators.[14] By the 1860s, seed drills, mechanical corn shellers, and self-rake reapers all came into common use in the area. Plows with double moldboards made their appearance in the 1870s.

The pattern of adoption remained similar for all of these machines. Inevitably, the Hallocks and other Sound Avenue farmers waited until after the experimental stage passed. Then, if it made economic sense for the area, they adopted it rapidly.

Visitors to the Hallockville Museum Farm today think of it as quaint and old-fashioned and never changing, but during the years between Halsey's birth and his early adulthood, the farm and the surrounding community changed rapidly. The arrival of the railroad in 1844 facilitated shipping of local produce, connecting the Hallocks to urban markets. They began to use fertilizers from Peru and other faraway places. They started buying manufactured machinery from Illinois.

Far more important than the local rail connection was the tremendous growth of the New York City market. Hay, the principal energy source of the city's transportation system, became the most valuable cash crop in the area. Potatoes, a relatively inexpensive way to feed that growing urban population, also rapidly gained in importance.

The railroad also expanded their horizons. Farmers began to travel to New York City and beyond with some frequency, as Halsey did on the wedding trip after his second marriage in 1866. The railroad also allowed

Halsey's brother Daniel to take music lessons in New York City and his sisters to study there.

The railroads became just one aspect of a growing communications network that tied local farmers closely to the rest of the country. Agricultural magazines began to circulate in the area. In February 1856, Halsey sent away for a subscription to *The Cultivator*, one of the earliest agricultural magazines. Halsey, only 17 years old at the time, clearly wanted to be on the forefront of developments in scientific agriculture, with an annual subscription for the cost just 50¢ per month.

These same forces led a group of progressive Sound Avenue farmers to start the Riverhead Town Agricultural Society in 1863. Often called the Farmers Club, for the next 75 years it met in the Northville Academy building (originally the 1831 church and later the Grange Hall), providing a venue for discussing ways to improve agricultural practices, with Halsey likely an early member. Starting in 1865, the Suffolk County Agricultural Society organized annual fairs at Riverhead, providing yet another opportunity for farmers to see all the latest techniques and equipment. The Hallocks seldom missed attending and became frequent exhibitors.

Peak Years on the Farm

The 1880 federal agricultural census shows the Hallocks with 126 acres—75 acres tilled, 16 acres of permanent grassland, 30 acres of woodland, and another 5 acres listed as "other," probably Hallock Pond and surrounding wetlands. About 40 acres along Herricks Lane had previously been sold as small woodlots (see fig. 7.1).

In 1880, the largest crop on the farm, in terms of acreage, was hay, with 15 acres. In the middle decades of the 19th century, hay became the single most important crop on most Sound Avenue farms, not only providing fuel for the farm's horses and food for its cattle and sheep but also providing the main cash crop—shipped by rail to a ready market in New York City where the transportation system relied on "hay burners."[15]

That same year the Hallocks also grew ten acres of field corn, seven acres of wheat, and four of oats. The Hallocks still raised only three acres of potatoes, the same as 20 years earlier, which produced about 600 bushels. The four-acre orchard with 150 trees still provided apples, although with their grandfather's hard-cider press closed after the family joined the temperance movement, one wonders what they did with the fruit. Following the typical

Figure 7.1. In the late-19th century, the Halsey Hallock farm contained over 160 acres and stretched from the shore of Long Island Sound to about six-tenths of a mile south of Sound Avenue, a total length of about 1.5 miles. It was a typical "bowling alley" farm, to use the local term—long but narrow. Halsey sold the parcels south of Sound Avenue to his son-in-law Charles Wells in 1906, leaving just the 60-acre parcel north of Sound Avenue. Notice all the other Hallock names—grandchildren or great-grandchildren of Capt. Zachariah Hallock and their Howell cousins—that led to the neighborhood being called Hallockville. Hallock State Park is today the northern portion of all these farms. *Source:* Matt Kania, Map Hero, Inc.

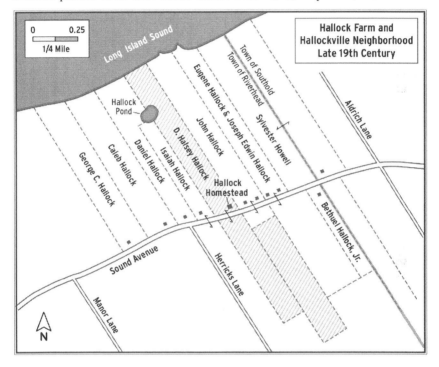

rotation of the time—corn the first year, followed by potatoes, then wheat or other grain, and finally three or more years of hay and grazing—they likely used the remaining 32 acres to graze livestock, building up the soil for future cultivation.

Over the next two decades, potatoes became the most important crop on the Hallock farm and in the area. An 1890 article from the Southold *Traveler* noted that no Northville farmer planted less than 8 to 15 acres of potatoes, and some planted 30 or 40 acres.[16] Potato growing did have its challenges. Perhaps the most serious was the arrival of the Colorado potato beetle on Long Island in 1875. These voracious insects could demolish entire fields of potatoes in a matter of days, necessitating the use of pesticides such as Paris Green, an arsenic compound. In June of 1892, the *Traveler* reported that "potato bugs are very severe, and the expense and work of poisoning is a great 'cut' to the profits." And the following month, the same paper reported that in Northville "the fleas [probably potato leafhoppers] on the potato vines are very numerous in this locality and the vines are fast succumbing to their ravages."[17] Cauliflower, cabbage, and strawberries were all introduced into the area in the second half of the century and became significant sources of profit for many local farmers, but the Hallocks mostly stuck with potatoes, corn, wheat, and hay.[18]

Changes in Agriculture

Farming changed dramatically in Halsey's lifetime. For the Riverhead Agricultural Society's 50th anniversary in 1917, his nephew Horace J. Wells spoke about the short list of farm implements he remembered belonging to his own grandfather, Joshua Wells (1785–1866), in the 1850s—just hand tools such as the sickle, cradle, and scythe and a few simple horse-drawn tools such as primitive hay rakes, plows, harrows, and wood frame cultivators.

Horace went on to describe all the amazing improvements during his lifetime, each bringing a major saving in labor and increase in efficiency. For instance, his grandfather's hay rake—dragged by long ropes behind a horse—required a boy to control the horse and a man walking behind to operate the rake. When the rake filled, the boy backed the horse a few steps and the man lifted the rake, leaving a pile of hay to be forked by hand into a wagon. Around 1850, the sulky rake—so called because of its two wheels and a seat like a sulky—came into use, which required only one man to operate and allowed him to ride instead of walk behind.

Other riding machines appeared on the farm for cultivating, mowing, planting potatoes, and cutting grain. In particular, the reaper for harvesting grain saw continuous improvements that enabled it not only to cut the stalks of wheat, rye, and oats quickly but also to bind stalks into bundles that could easily be loaded on a wagon and carried to a threshing machine. The only function of the operator was to drive the horses (see fig. 7.2).

Perhaps the most significant new labor-saving device for a potato farmer like Halsey was the Hudson Bicycle Cultivator invented in the 1880s by

Figure 7.2. Halsey Hallock driving his reaper-binder on his 80th birthday, July 4, 1918. Bessie Hallock photo. *Source:* Hallockville Museum Farm. Used with permission.

S. Terry Hudson, who lived in the Hallockville Museum's Hudson-Sydlowski House (advertisement for the Cultivator at https://hallockville.org/hallocks-book). Like the sulky rake, Hudson's machine allowed a man to ride rather than walk behind and allowed him to steer the machine using bicycle-like pedals, hence the name Bicycle Cultivator.

By the end of the century, Hudson manufactured hundreds of these machines each year and licensed to other manufacturers for nationwide production. His cultivator even won a medal at the Paris Exposition in 1889. "It took some years to get used to the idea of paying a man real money for anything as easy as riding," according to Halsey's nephew Horace J. Wells. "These machines were used by the owners of the farm, as it was considered immoral to let a hired man use one."[19]

Threshing saw similar improvements. After the Civil War, portable horse-powered threshing machines appeared in the Sound Avenue community, and then steam-powered machines, and by the time Horace is writing in 1917, gasoline powered machines. He claimed one of those machines could thresh more grain in a day than was grown in the town a century earlier. Over the same period, most other farm tools also saw substantial improvements, enabling farmers like Halsey to do more work faster and with less labor.

Even the animals on a farm improved considerably. At the beginning of the 19th century, the Hallocks, like everyone else, raised traditional general-purpose mixed-breed cattle used for milk, meat, and as draft animals. By the end of the century, local farmers gradually replaced these old-fashioned cattle with breeds carefully developed for milk or beef production. As Sammy Tuthill, who also prepared a paper for the Agricultural Society's 50th, wrote, "No bull or cow is now considered worthy of mention which has not a long pedigree."[20] Halsey's cattle routinely won prizes at the annual Suffolk County Fair in Riverhead. For instance, in 1893 he won a first prize for his "fine lot of Guernseys."[21]

The 1876 Centennial Exposition in Philadelphia symbolized the change in perspective that took place among Sound Avenue's farmers during the previous decades. Halsey and Emilie Hallock and several of their neighbors went to Philadelphia and saw all the latest industrial and agricultural equipment on exhibit. They connected with agricultural information from all over the country and became essentially modern in their approach—adopting new machinery as rapidly as it was introduced, using their land as intensively as possible, and utilizing much larger amounts of capital in their operations. Most important, they actively searched for the latest scientific and technological developments that could make their production more efficient and profitable.

Appearance of the Farm

Sammy Tuthill also wrote about how the physical appearance of farm fields changed over that 50 years. Long Island farmers never had enough stones to build stone walls like in New England. Instead, Tuthill described boundaries commonly marked by a trench on one side and a mound on the other, with trees on the mound loped down to form a hedge. By the middle decades of the 19th century, split-rail fences, generally with rails made of chestnut, became the norm, with many surviving into the 20th century (see fig. 7.3). Tuthill recalled "many a day have I sat on the sharp edge of a split rail while my ancestors diligently plied the broad-axe to sharpen the ends."

In the early 20th century, barbed wire partially replaced split-rail fences, but it was never totally satisfactory on Long Island where the salt in the air quickly caused the wire, with inadequate galvanizing, to rust. Within a

Figure 7.3. Hal Hallock watching a newborn calf west of the Homestead Barn, 1932. Notice the long runs of split-rail fence in the distance. Bessie Hallock photo. *Source:* Hallockville Museum Farm. Used with permission.

decade or two, even these fences gradually disappeared as agriculture shifted to row crops like potatoes and cauliflower—grown with mechanized equipment that did not require fencing. Photos of the Hallock farm in the early 1920s reveal some rail fencing still standing on the front portion of the farm, nearest the barn, but unfenced open fields on the rest of the land.

Changes in the Landscape

In Halsey's youth, the Hallockville landscape contained far fewer trees compared with the present day. Most area farms had been clear-cut more than once, with the wood used to construct buildings, build fences, cook, and provide fuel for hungry fireplaces in winter. Any excess brought good money as cordwood in New York City, making it perhaps the most important cash crop in the early 19th century. Even the hedgerows and fence lines contained far fewer trees than today, since the constant grazing by sheep and cattle prevented regeneration of saplings.

The north end of the Hallock farm, today part of heavily wooded Hallock State Park, had been cleared entirely in Capt. Zachariah's day for cordwood and pasture. In the 1850s the Hallocks even tried planting corn in the hilly and thin soils between the pond and the bluffs—an experiment not repeated. The Hallocks continued to graze cattle and sheep on that part of the farm, but toward the end of the century they gradually allowed the pastures and fields nearest the Sound shore to grow back into woodland. Early 20th-century photographs show the area around their pond (now part of Hallock State Park) still partially cleared, but with scattered glades of trees, mostly Eastern Red Cedars typical of early succession woodlands. Writing in the 1930s, Halsey expressed his amazement at how rapidly cedar trees overtook the area in the previous 40 or 50 years. He assumed that large colonies of what he called "cliff swallows"—probably the bank swallows that still colonize the clay pinnacles in the area—were responsible for spreading the seeds, but all swallows eat bugs, not seeds.

Mechanization, a Road Not Taken

As Horace J. Wells and Sammy Tuthill wrote in 1917 about all the amazing improvements that occurred in agriculture on Sound Avenue in the 50 years of the Agricultural Society, they seemed totally unaware of the seismic change about to occur: the introduction of tractors and mechanized agriculture.

In 1911, a notice appeared in a local paper for an exhibit of Avery tractors at the Suffolk County Fair.[22] This appears to be the first reference to tractors in Riverhead. In a microcosm of this rapid transition, the local agent for Avery tractors, George Morell, was the son of a carriage maker, William Morell. The Avery company originally produced large steam-powered tractors, some weighing as much as 25 tons. It introduced a lighter gasoline machine in 1910, but these still weighed several tons and were more suited to expansive Western prairies than smaller Long Island fields. Halsey and his family undoubtedly saw the exhibit, but they remained uninterested in buying one of the ungainly new machines.

By 1915, machines appeared that were more suitable for local conditions. An article that year in a local paper reported:

> Considerable interest was shown yesterday at the Aquebogue station when W. L. McDermott unloaded from the freight cars the new tractor and thresher purchased by George Naugles and Mike Backowsky. Many of the local farmers who were on hand were most enthusiastic in their comments concerning the tractor.

This feature foretells a new era in farming in this section. For heavy work the possibilities of the tractor replacing the horse with less expense and greater efficiency can be appreciated. . . . Messrs Naugles and Backowsky have the good wishes of all for the success in their new enterprise.[23]

The tractor, likely the first tractor purchased in the town of Riverhead—a Mogul 8-16 introduced just that year by International Harvester—was a single-cylinder, kerosene-fueled machine that claimed 8 horsepower at the drawbar and 16 horsepower for belt-driven work. Rated for two-bottom plows, it sold for only $675, not much more than two good horses. At 5,000 pounds it was considered a relatively light machine compared with the earlier monsters.

Interestingly all the players in this story were Hallockville neighbors. Until 1913, William L. McDermott, the tractor dealer, son of Irish immigrants, lived two farms to the west on the former Daniel Hallock farm. George Naugles, a recent Lithuanian-Polish immigrant, lived across the street from McDermott and had a mechanically inclined 20-old son. Mike Backowsky, another Polish immigrant, farmed around the corner on Herrick's Lane and also had a son of similar age and interest.

However, the Hallocks—on the leading wave of every agricultural innovation over the previous half century—let this one pass them by completely. They never acquired a tractor or any other motorized farm equipment. While they continued farming until about 1926, they stuck to their horses, even while everyone around them started buying tractors. Halsey, who was 77 by 1915, was possibly past the age for experimenting with new technologies. His son Hal, already 46 and still a bachelor, probably did not think too much about the future either, as he never learned to operate a tractor or drive a car.

Hallock Homestead Barn

As the farm changed and grew over the course of the 19th century, the Hallock family continually enlarged, modified, and even moved their barn. The story is complicated but worth telling because the barn—properly decoded—remains a physical manifestation of the rich history of the property.

In Halsey's youth, the original colonial-era English-style barn stood near the road, due west of Homestead sitting room windows according to

Bessie. At just 1,000 square feet, this barn was large enough to accommodate the simple farming tools of the day and enough hay and feed for a few farm animals. Like all old English-style barns, a style brought by the area's early Puritan settlers from East Anglia, the broad side faced south to take advantage of the warming winter sunlight. Before Halsey's birth, the family moved their threshing barn from the south side of the street and attached it to the main barn. At some point they also added a shed to the south side of the original barn, visible in Halsey's 1860 sketch (https://hallockville.org/hallocksbook/), expanding its area by about a third.

In 1866, the family moved the whole barn about 200 feet to the northwest, positioning it further away from the Homestead. This kept the barnyard smells from wafting into open windows on prevailing southwesterlies. Positioning it further back from the road also allowed more room for livestock on the warmer southern side of the structure.

Creating a potato cellar may have been an even more important reason for moving the barn.[24] Potatoes needed to be stored below ground to prevent them from freezing in the winter when the price was likely the highest. As that crop became more important, the Hallocks needed more storage space than the small root cellar under the Homestead. It was likely easier to dig a cellar and move the barn on top of it than to try to dig a cellar under the barn on its existing location. They dug a 300-square foot cellar that could accommodate 40 tons of potatoes, about what the Hallocks reasonably expected to grow on the four or so acres they typically planted during that time period. They also dug two cisterns that collected all the runoff from the barn roofs and offered an easy way to provide water for Hallock livestock—a relatively new technology at the time and still visible in the Homestead Barn. Halsey's diary recorded spending $440 for digging a cellar and two cisterns, including all the masonry work.

Moving barns was not unusual. In 1878 the *Long Island Traveler* reported that James Y. Downs, a Sound Avenue neighbor, "moved his barn some rods from its former site on the highway and built a large addition"[25] Emilie's brother, Edward "E. P." Wells, also moved his barn to place it on a hillside where a new cellar could be easily accessed from the lower level.

After moving the barn in 1866, the Hallocks added a lean-to shed, covering the back portion of the new cellar. Over the next few decades, as the farm became more prosperous and its agriculture more intense, the family continuously enlarged and modified the structure. Around 1880 they moved the east wall of the barn out and built two new bays onto the original three-bay structure. This allowed them to more than double the size of the potato cellar. The addition also included new horse stables and a workspace for sorting potatoes at the entrance to the cellar. However, the main purpose of this addition, and many of the subsequent ones, was increased storage space for hay, now the most important cash crop and essential for feeding the farm's horses and livestock. Around the same time, they extended the low cow shed further east across the front of the new bays and added a small shed to the front of the threshing barn.

In the next two decades, Halsey replaced the older one-story front lean-to shed with a much larger two-story shed visible today, allowing expanded hay storage on the second level and room for cows and sheep below. The first decade of the 20th century witnessed even more changes to the barn. In 1901, according to an item in the local paper, Halsey added two new sheds to his barn—one on the west end to provide more space to store machinery and produce and another across the front to expand the sheltered area for livestock. The newspaper article reported "Boss Harry Corwin," Halsey's son-in-law, "being in charge of the work."[26]

In 1904, when ice destroyed the ill-fated Iron Pier (actually mostly made of wood) the Hallocks, who were stockholders in the pier company, salvaged material from the wreck and built a new, much larger and more modern east shed, replacing a smaller shed that previously stood in the place. The wing provided space to accommodate the wagons and farm equipment, now much larger and more numerous. This wing also made sorting and loading potatoes brought out of the cellar more efficient. The large loft area overhead accommodated the empty barrels needed for shipping. Doors on both the front and back allowed wagons to be driven through.

This is the barn that visitors see at the Hallockville Museum today, except for the loss of one shed across the front (see fig. 1.1, chap. 1). Despite all the changes over the years, every new section incorporated older timbers. For instance, the shed addition behind the main threshing floor, probably added after they moved the barn back in 1866, contains one roof rafter, reused upside down, that shows the notched lath style typical of the 1600s and early 1700s. Similarly, the main tie beam in the east wall of the circa-1880 addition is actually the original tie beam from the east wall of the 1765 barn—but installed backward. The current front shed of the barn also contains many timbers recycled from earlier incarnations of the building, including hand-hewn posts on the west wall and floor joists supporting the loft overhead. They did not throw away anything that could be reused!

The Farmyard

The farmyard witnessed an equal number of changes in Halsey's lifetime. Capt. Zachariah's old shoemaker shop arrived outside the kitchen door, now repurposed as a milk house with a basement below, while Halsey was still a child. The outhouse that visitors see today—with three seats, two for adults and one smaller one with a built step for a child—shows evidence of construction in the 1860s or 1870s, although it undoubtedly replaced an older structure. Conveniently it featured two doors, one in the front and one on the side, to allow escape if it should blow over. It had a cement-lined pit with an access hatch behind for shoveling out the residue, probably the latest in outhouse design at the time. Not far from the outhouse, the Hallocks built a smokehouse (see fig. 11.1, chap. 11)—carefully separated from any of the other outbuildings because of the danger of fire but convenient to the kitchen.

The combination woodhouse and washhouse that now stands just to the left of the outhouse went through several incarnations during Halsey's lifetime. The western half possibly started life as a wing on the Homestead, and after being moved to its current location became Arminda and Emilie's washhouse. Diary references indicate that Herman often helped Arminda with her laundry chores and that Halsey did the same for Emilie. The chimney accommodated a woodstove for them to boil water provided by the cistern underneath.[27] After 1894 when the family built a more convenient washroom shed attached to the Homestead kitchen, the building became the farm shop—probably a shared use in the past.

The original roofline of the washhouse was lower and symmetrical, but later in the 19th century, after the Hallocks moved another structure with a salt-box roofline up against the old washhouse, they raised the roofline of the original building to match the newer addition. The new part—possibly Grandfather Zachariah's old cider mill—became their woodshed to store the firewood that fueled not only the kitchen stove but also stoves in the sitting room and parlors (see fig. 7.4).[28]

When the Hallocks moved the small west wing of the Homestead to the rear, they removed the 1801 back kitchen and converted it to a chicken house, a little to the east of the smokehouse. Later they built a second chicken house further back behind the smokehouse. Finally, when the Hallocks acquired their first Model T Ford around 1920, they built a simple garage just to the west of the washhouse/shop. Later, as the family's cars grew longer, they added a few more feet on the back end.

Figure 7.4. Bessie titled this photo "Humble Equipment." It shows her brother Hal in 1926 bringing in a load of wood to the Homestead with a mule cart. The workshop/woodhouse is behind the cart, the shoemaker shop to the right, and the back end of the garage to the left. *Source:* Hallockville Museum Farm. Used with permission.

Gradually other new buildings appeared near the barn. A corn crib stood next to the east end of the barn for safely storing ears of corn. The current structure is a replacement moved from another farm. Next east of that stood the pig house, now reconstructed on the original foundation. Early photos show at least one more building to the east.

The Hallocks continued to add other buildings behind the barn to accommodate the ever-growing need for places to store machinery and keep livestock. Bessie's photographs show three connected buildings behind the east end of the barn that she called Peter Tumbledown's Outfit and another shed-like building further back that possibly sheltered cattle or sheep (see fig. 7.5).[29] At its peak in 1910, the Hallock farm contained at least 19 buildings (see map in fig. 7.6).

Ella also recalled an icehouse behind the barn. Likely a low structure, mostly underground, it does not appear in any of Bessie's photos and no longer exists. They carried the ice down from the pond on a low "truck" (actually a sleigh) and covered it with straw.[30]

Figure 7.5. Bessie labeled her 1923 photo of these three structures behind the Homestead Barn "Peter Tumbledown's Outfit." Bessie Hallock photo. *Source:* Hallockville Museum Farm. Used with permission.

Figure 7.6. Buildings and fence lines on the Hallock farm at its peak, circa 1910. The Homestead, barn, outhouse, shop/woodhouse, and garage still stand at the Hallockville Museum Farm. The corn crib, smokehouse, and chicken coop have been replicated. *Source:* Matt Kania, Map Hero, Inc.

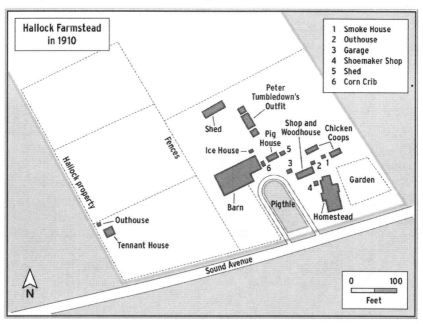

Help on the Farm

The Hallock records contain frequent references to hired help. As previously related, the orphan boy, Tommy Pope, and his British-born uncle, Henry Pope, lived and worked on the Hallock farm in the 1850s.[31] In 1867, Emilie's younger brother John Horace Wells (1852–1921) came to live with them and work on the farm. From a big family that ultimately included seven sons and two daughters, clearly his father's 100-acre farm was not big enough to divide between them. At age 15, with his father's consent, he decided to leave home and work for another farmer, saying it would be better for him and "would give the younger brothers at home a better chance." The first year on the Hallock farm he received $91 for seven months' work. He worked for the Hallocks for five years and for other farmers eight more years, then taught school for a few terms before saving enough money to get married and buy a farm of his own in 1884 when he was 32 years old.[32] One of his younger brothers, Clarence, born in 1863, followed the same trajectory: working on the Hallock farm for a few years and delaying marriage until age 30, at which time he moved to Smithtown and rented a farm there.[33]

Starting about 1874 and lasting beyond 1880, 10-year-old Edward "Eddie" Terry came to work on the Hallock farm. The son of a Mattituck farm family, he lived with Herman and Arminda in their part of the house. In 1883, a family diary mentions that "colored Jack Thompson here part of this year," but no additional information can be found about him.

In 1884 the Hallock diaries record that a Bohemian couple slept in the little room over the back wing. Unfortunately, all we know about them are their first names, Joe and Josephine. They likely immigrated that year, part of a small wave to the New York area during the 1880s and 1890s from Bohemia, then part of Austria and now the Czech Republic. Many settled in scrubby land in the southern part of the town of Islip that they renamed Bohemia in 1885. Joe and Josephine probably only spoke German and Bohemian (Czech), which the Hallocks did not speak, although by that time a few German-speaking farmers had moved into the area. It must have been an interesting cross-cultural experience for the Hallocks—and also their first contact with Eastern European immigrants.[34] It would not be the last, as a wave of Polish immigrants flooded into the community in the following decade.

Tenant House

The family diaries show that they began work on a tenant house in 1906, most likely to accommodate a family of Polish immigrants. It stood somewhere "near the west line," but no photos survive. Ella Hallock told a story about the mother of the Polish family complaining that "the house was too tight."[35] According to the Hallock diary, they painted their tenant house gray in 1926, the same year their own house was painted that color. A 1926 diary entry includes a Williams family in the tenant house, likely a Black couple, John and Viola Williams, who show up in Riverhead in the 1920 census. Then in 1929, the Hallocks sold the tenant house to Jim Young, who moved it to Westphalia Avenue in Mattituck.[36]

A Model of Sustainability

Like most 19th-century farms, the Hallock operation was a model of sustainable living, in line with the motto "Waste not, want not." No garbage truck ever visited because there was no garbage to cart away! No electric lines. No gasoline engines. "Reduce, reuse, recycle" was part of the culture, not a slogan. The farm could have been "zero waste" certified. They didn't know the terms sustainability, recycling, or ecological. These words hadn't been invented, but they definitely described the way the Hallocks lived.

Farming with horses was totally sustainable. The only fuel Old Nell needed—hay and oats—grew right on the farm. No need to buy any gasoline and other fossil fuels. She was born right there, too. About the only things they ever paid cash for were harnesses and an occasional new set of horseshoes.

Nothing was thrown away: if ripped—mended; socks with holes—darned; old clothes—cut into little pieces and sewed into quilts or woven into rag rugs; and old wool—cut into really thin strips to make hooked rugs.

They were frugal with everything: old tin cans were flattened and used to patch the kitchen floor; soured milk was used in a recipe for sour milk cookies; leftover meat was used to make hash; grease from cooking became the basis for breakfast gravy the next morning; and leftover potatoes—they had endless recipes for those.

Old newspapers never went in the trash but found use as wrappings, as spills (tapered paper rolls) for lighting oil lamps, under rugs to keep the drafts from blowing through the cracks between the floorboards, and to light the kitchen stove every morning. Any left over after all that, into the outhouse for you-know-what.

Their four cisterns provided what might be called a rainwater collection system. The kitchen sink and washroom tubs both drained through the walls into buckets to be reused on their gardens—today's graywater recycling system (both of these drains as well as the roof gutters feeding the cistern are visible to the right of the cover photo of the Homestead's "kitchen end"). Nothing wasted on the Hallock farm, not even their wastewater!

The pigs constituted a recycling system in themselves. The Hallocks gave the pigs food garbage from the house. Instead of throwing away potatoes unfit for sale, Halsey's father Herman cooked them in a big pot and gave them to the pigs. In return the pigs gave the Hallocks the most delicious bacon, which Halsey's mother Arminda cured herself in the smokehouse.

Chickens were another essential form of recycling on the farm. The Hallocks fed them food scraps from the house and weeds from the garden. Besides producing eggs and meat, the chickens also gave them manure—the very best fertilizer. The chicken coop was conveniently located next to the vegetable and flower gardens for when they needed a little extra nutrient for a prized flower or plant.

The outhouse also fit into what we might call a "sustainability system" in two ways. First, in the days before toilet paper, they saved old corn cobs or old newspapers to be used for the same purpose. The bin for corn cobs still survives just inside the front door. Around to the back one can see the second form of what we would call recycling. Beneath the seats was a cement-lined pit, shoveled out from time to time and used like farmyard manure to fertilize their fields.

Every year they carted hundreds of cartloads of barnyard manure out to their fields and used ashes from their stoves to provide potash. More ashes came from New York City to use as fertilizer, as well as fish scraps left over from the local menhaden processing industry. A careful pattern of crop rotation helped maintain soil fertility. In essence, the Hallock farm used what a century later we consider "green" and "organic" practices, with both on-the-farm and wider recycling systems that disappeared in the 20th century but are today coming back into favor.

Chapter 8

Sound Avenue Prosperity

> By Industry we thrive. Economy is wealth tis said & some have found it out.
>
> —Diary of Sammy Tuthill

One of the earliest descriptions of Northville appears in Nathaniel Prime's 1845 *History of Long Island*. Writing two decades before the Civil War, he described Northville simply "as a small settlement on the north side of the island about two miles from Upper Aquebogue."[1] He called the church's congregation, which he conflated with the community, "small," with just 40 families, and "strictly independent." This last characterization was to prove accurate for the Sound Avenue farming community over the next century. Whatever the circumstances, Sound Avenue was always a community slightly apart, somehow seeing itself as a little superior to its neighbors, and definitely independent! It was also a community optimistic about its economic prospects. When the Northville community wanted its own post office in 1838, it was forced to use the name "Success" because of the other Northville upstate. However, while Success described the economic aspirations of the Hallocks and their Northville farmer neighbors, residents never thought of it as the real place name, and it fell out of use after the discontinuance of the post office in 1880 (see fig. 8.1).

Change Accelerates after the Civil War

In 1860, a travelogue in the *Sag-Harbor Express*, one of the few newspapers at the time on the East End of Long Island, provided this description of Northville:

Figure 8.1. Doodle featuring the Success name used by Northville's post office between 1838 and 1889, by Addison J. Wells, a schoolteacher brother-in-law of Halsey Hallock, dated 1878. *Source:* Hallockville Museum Farm. Used with permission.

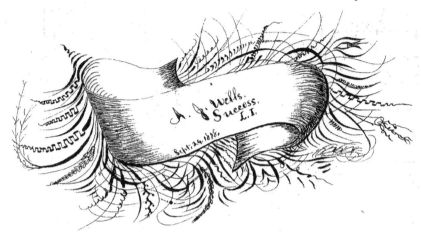

We now start afresh and soon find ourselves in the flourishing village of Northville—where judging from appearances every man has an independent fortune. We saw in passing no less than *four* new houses in the process of erection. . . . I am told that since the Long Island rail road has been built these farms have doubled in value, and they produce nearly twice the quantity of crops more particularly the potatoe [*sic*], which brings the ready cash as soon as dug.

We see in this locality no walls broken down, or gardens overgrown with weeds but everything looks thrifty, and betokens wealth. The spacious mansions occupied by these farmers and their families, are almost without an exception, *well painted* and the grounds about the houses tastefully ornamented with flowers, and shaded with fruit or ornamental trees, showing they have refinement and cultivated tastes and are able to *enjoy* as well as to *accumulate* property.[2] (Italics original)

A house being built by Daniel Y. Downs (see fig. 8.2), and later owned by Halsey's brother Charles, was likely one of the four new structures mentioned by the *Sag-Harbor Express* correspondent. The first detailed map of the community, part of a map of Suffolk County produced in

Figure 8.2. This house built by Daniel Y. Downs, later acquired by Halsey Hallock's brother Charles, was probably one of the large new houses along Sound Avenue that so impressed the *Sag-Harbor Express* correspondent in 1860. *Source:* Hallockville Museum Farm. Used with permission.

1858 by J. Chace of Philadelphia, shows almost 70 homes, most in a tight linear arrangement along Sound Avenue.[3] Eight Hallock families are lined up just west of the Southold–Riverhead town line—all grandchildren of Capt. Zachariah Hallock and source of the Hallockville name. Well over two-thirds of the houses sat on the north side of the road, in the typical colonial orientation facing south. Very few homes existed in the western third of the area where the water table was deeper. Before technological improvements to cement made cisterns feasible, a farm needed either a pond or a well as a source of water. In most of Northville, the water table is about 50 to 60 feet down, but in the western reaches, nearer 100 feet, making dug wells more difficult.

An 1873 map shows about 75 houses in the two Northville school districts.[4] In his 1874 *Sketches of Suffolk County*, Richard M. Bayles (1846–1930) wrote the following:

> About three miles east of Wading River a settlement of farmhouses begins, and extends without any remarkable interruption,

in a continuous line to the eastern limit of the town, and beyond. This settlement lines the North Country Road a distance of about twelve miles . . . passing through a section occupied almost entirely by rich, highly cultivated and productive farms. . . . The inhabitants are almost exclusively farmers, and the appearance of fruitful fields, and large, well filled barns, granaries and stock-yards, which are common all through this section, speaks in evidence of the success with which agriculture is carried on.

[Northville] is one of the most pleasant and attractive rural settlements on the island. The location is elevated and remarkably healthful.[5]

In 1876, George Miller confirmed this description in the brief paper "History of the Town of Riverhead": "No part of the town of Riverhead has increased so much and so rapidly in agricultural wealth as Northville. That village and the whole extent of the north road to Wading River, prove that the early historians of the town misconceived the character of a large part of the lands in the town not then brought under cultivation. They are in fact valuable for that purpose and have been much improved within a few years."[6] In 1885, Bayles described Northville again: "The soil is rich and well cultivated, the large homelike appearing farm houses with their surroundings of overflowing plenty testifying to the general prosperity of the people and the success of their efforts at improved cultivation of the soil."[7] He listed the population as 469. It is not surprising that Bayles said all these nice things about Northville. Before going on to a career of teaching and writing, he was educated at the Northville Academy under the direction of Joseph N. Hallock.[8] At the time, he likely met Sammy Tuthill, whom he later credited with assisting him with information about Northville.[9]

They Are All Hallocks!

In the middle of journalistic fulminations about the scandals in the Northville Church, the *Brooklyn Daily Eagle*'s wide-eyed reporter noted that "all the people are related" and "most of them are of the Hallock family."[10] All of this turns out to be accurate, or only slightly exaggerated. The 1860 census reveals that just six family names—Hallock, Benjamin, Wells, Luce, Downs, and Terry—constituted 75 percent of the farming households in Northville, with the Hallock family as 20 percent of the list and controlling the same proportion of the community's wealth.

These six families, all descended from the area's 17th-century Puritan settlers, were all interconnected with the Hallocks and each other. For instance, Halsey and Emilie, Hallock's closest relations by marriage—brothers- and sisters-in-law and spouses of aunts and uncles—included six connections to the Wells family, five connections to the Benjamin family, and five to the Terry family, and two connections by marriage back to other branches of the Hallock family.

Demographics

A young community in 1860, Northville's demographics mirrored those of many developing countries today. Even excluding the 44 unrelated young people working as farm laborers or servants, nearly half the population was below age 20 and three-quarters below 40. Only a few made it beyond age 70, with the oldest being an 82-year-old woman.

The community experienced the high levels of infant and child mortality typical of the era. For instance, that same 1860 census reports 11 infants of less than a year, but only 52 children between one and nine; whereas, based on the number of infants, there should have been about a hundred. Most of the "missing" children undoubtedly succumbed to the many childhood diseases and frequent epidemics that remained the scourge of the times, such as the scarlet fever outbreak that took two of Halsey Hallock's teenage friends in 1856. Records in the Sound Avenue Cemetery indicate that from its opening in 1832 until the end of the century, infants under a year old constituted almost a quarter of the burials, with nearly half children or teenagers.[11]

Sound Avenue Mobility

With the multigenerational history of the Hallock family, we tend to think of this as a very stable community. But a great deal of outmigration occurred over the years. Four of Capt. Zachariah's daughters ended up in Brooklyn. Halsey's brother Charles moved to Smithtown in 1856, although he moved back to Sound Avenue in 1891. Halsey's other brother, Daniel, moved first to Southold and then to York, Pennsylvania, where he manufactured farm equipment—although his wife never made the move. Halsey's sister Hannah, after a stay in the deep South, married Marshall Dedrick and moved with him first to Kansas and ultimately to Chicago. In 1869 Halsey's cousin George Wilson Hallock (son of Zachariah III) sold his farm to his brother, Zachariah IV, for $6,000 and bought a much bigger farm of some 200 acres in Smithtown.[12] John Morse Hallock, Halsey's next-door neighbor to the east, sold his farm in 1912 and moved to a bigger farm in New Jersey. This constant out movement is one of the main reasons so many farms were available to the new Polish immigrants who arrived on Sound Avenue around the turn of the century.

Factors Driving Prosperity

Several factors drove the growing prosperity of the Sound Avenue community. The increasing use of all kinds of fertilizers—first fish; then Peruvian guano, fish guano, bone meal, and ashes; and finally manufactured products—sustained agricultural production on the area's easily exhausted loamy soils. The rapid increase in the population of New York City—from just over 60,000 at the beginning of the 1800s to over 300,000 by 1840 and over 600,000 by 1860—provided markets for Sound Avenue's farmers. In particular, the wave of Irish immigration to the city expanded the demand for potatoes, a crop uniquely suited for local soils.

Transportation improvements also played an important role in the emerging prosperity. First came the development of a new port, called James Port, on Peconic Bay in the 1830s. Its wharf facilitated shipping produce by water to New York and New England markets and allowed ashes and other fertilizing ingredients to be brought in cheaply. Completion of the Main Line of the Long Island Rail Road through to Greenport in 1844, with stations located in Riverhead, Aquebogue, and Jamesport, barely two miles from Sound Avenue, provided faster and relatively inexpensive access to the booming New York City market.

The Hallocks were not unusual in their prosperity. A surviving tax list from 1902 for the District 11 school district indicates Halsey Hallock's property was assessed at $6,300. Out of 57 properties, his was fifth highest. However, many others were not that far below. The two highest: Charles Hudson a little to the east at $8,400 and John Hallock next door at $8,000.

A New Church and an Academy

The new Northville Church in 1859 was a sign of the community's increasing prosperity and modernity. Unlike its predecessor, it featured a "spire pointing heavenward." Architecturally up to date in the then-popular Italianate style, it featured round-top windows, a fancy rose window, and brackets under the steeple eaves (left building in fig. 3.1, chap. 3). Both the idea of a new church and its modern design proved controversial, but the forces of progress won, as we have seen.

Another sign of the transformation taking place occurred in 1859 when a group of progressive farmers in the community organized an academy in the upper part of the old church building. Before public high schools, private academies such as this provided the only secondary education available. It was a very forward-thinking enterprise for the Sound Avenue community. But like most other modernizing initiatives in the community, strong opposition emerged among some of the more conservative church members to giving over the second floor of the former church to the academy.

The Northville Academy organized as a joint stock company, with shares selling for $10 each. Samuel Hudson (father of S. Terry Hudson), whose house is now the Hallockville Museum's administration building, led the effort. As with everything else in the community, numerous Hallocks participated. Ten family members subscribed, including 21-year-old Halsey, his brother Daniel, his cousin George Wilson, and his Uncle Zachariah. His future second wife, Emilie Wells, studied there and her father subscribed.[13] The academy's founders not only paid $215 to local builder Nathan Corwin for building a second floor in the old church, but paid another $140 to Corwin to erect a totally unnecessary steeple and an additional $35.85 for a bell (right building in fig. 3.1, chap. 3).[14]

Joseph Newton Hallock, a second cousin of the Homestead Hallocks, became the first principal. He grew up in Franklinville (now Laurel) and graduated from Yale College in 1857 and Yale Seminary in 1860, where he likely picked up some modern liberal ideas. He served as principal of the Franklinville Academy when Halsey attended. Something of a radical for his day, certainly an abolitionist and strong supporter of the temperance movement, his appointment is another indication of the forward-looking ethos of the majority of Sound Avenue's farm families.

An 1861 advertisement for the Northville Academy in a Greenport newspaper claimed that, although just a year old, the academy was twice as large as any other academy in the county. It guaranteed "practical discipline and thorough scholarship." Its 1861 catalog stated, "Students are prepared for college" and "Rates $3.50 per term. Board $1.75 to 2.00. Washing 25c extra." A flyer for the fall 1862 term advertised, "Board is cheap and tuition low."[15]

The academy's handbook bragged, "No place in the Country is healthier, or more free from immoral and vicious influences. There are no grog shops or taverns in the village, and the only places of public resort are our Schools and Churches. The people are thus naturally cheerful, sober and industrious, and no better place could be found for parents to send their children."[16] The previous term 50 students attended, according to the 1861 catalog, 18 male and 32 female. For the next term, the school expected 50 males and 38 females and added a teacher of "practical and ornamental penmanship." According to the catalog, "The course of instruction embraces all that is essential or of a practical and thorough English Education and includes a preparation in the classics and Higher Mathematics for admission to any class in any of our New England colleges."[17] An August 1863 article reported 174 students, 92 males and 82 females.[18]

The curriculum may have been exacting, but attendees were also able to demonstrate a lighter side in their literary efforts. While a student there in 1861, Emilie Wells (later Halsey's second wife) edited the student paper called *The Star Spangled Banner*. One of the offerings included this playful ditty that started:

> We caught an eel the other day.
> And where d'ye think we met such luck?
> Why, no where else, of course, you say,
> But on the creek at Mattituck.

In 1862 Emilie became "editress" of the school literary magazine, *The Seminary Bell*. She promised to fill its pages with "choice poetry and prose" by the students. One example was a brief essay "Blackberry Path" about a berry picking outing to "Northsides" where one of the young men lagged behind—supposedly to help one of the young ladies with her basket—to find out where she lived.

The following year, Ellen B. Hallock (daughter of John and Frances Hallock, who lived next door to the east of the Homestead) served as the "editress." She included such choice riddles as:

Why is Mr. Reeve like a pair of eye-brows? Because he is placed over pupils.

What is the difference between the labors of a farmer and that of a seamstress? One gathers what he sows and the other sews what she gathers.

Why is a 4-quart dish like a side saddle? Because it holds a gall-on.

The Northville Academy flourished for a few years and then ran into administrative difficulties and closed in 1873. It reopened briefly in 1882 before closing for good in 1890 as public high schools began to take the place of private academies.[19]

The Third Church

After the Northville Church burned in the mysterious 1876 fire many blamed on Rev. Wright, it took the congregation four years to rebuild, partly due to their lack of insurance, a mistake not repeated. The depression following the financial panic of 1873 also made it harder to raise money, as did dissension in the congregation.[20] They finally managed to raise the $10,000 needed and finished a new church on January 13, 1881. The list of families who agreed to contribute—naturally maintained by Halsey Hallock—shows 69 donors. Of these, 14 are Hallocks, more than any other family name.[21]

Ever frugal, they purchased the plans from Philadelphia architect Benjamin D. Price, who specialized in mail-order designs "of moderate cost" in a variety of popular styles. By 1891 he boasted that 600 sets of plans had been sold to churches around the country. That year his catalog featured about 100 designs and variations, with many selling for between $10 and $20.[22]

The congregation hired Riverhead's leading architect, George H. Skidmore, to supervise the construction. The new building (fig. 8.3), even more modern and up to date than its predecessor, featured stacked Gothic windows, an even taller spire, an organ located front-and-center, and lots of elaborate interior woodwork.

Figure 8.3. The elaborate interior of the new church erected in 1881 shows how far the congregation had come from the simple Puritan features of its first building just 50 years earlier. It also demonstrates the community's determination to be up to date with a design reflecting their prosperity. Despite the divisive scandals in the 1860s and 1870s, by 1885 it had 158 members during the pastorate of Allison O. Downs, making it the largest church in the town of Riverhead. Source: Hallockville Museum Farm. Used with permission.

A Fourth New Church in 1904

In 1881, on a Sunday evening just a year after the third church's dedication, the sexton hoisted the 72-inch kerosene reflector lantern to the ceiling, with all 32 burners lighted, and the rope broke, causing it to come crashing to the floor. Fortunately, no serious damage occurred.[23] But the luck did not hold. Lightning struck the steeple in 1901 and the church burned to the ground. This time the congregation carried adequate insurance. Again, they did not choose a local architect but rather an architect from Queens to design an even more modern building, completed in time for its dedication on August 25, 1904: "A handsome and roomy new church which has been built by the progressive people of Sound Avenue to take the place of the house of worship destroyed by lightning in 1901. . . . The new church is complete in every detail. . . . It is one of the finest structures of its kind to be found in any rural community of the State."[24] The *Brooklyn Daily Eagle* called it "the handsomest and most thoroughly modern church of any in a thoroughly rural community on Long Island, if not in New York State." The building sported two spires, the tallest 85 feet. "From its organ to its coal bin, everything is of modern design and handsome execution."

Although Gothic in its inspiration, the building design was very "modern" for its day.[25] The auditorium had pews laid out in an asymmetric partial semi-circle on a sloping floor—known as the Cleveland Plan—with the choir, organ, and pulpit located in one corner on a curved dais. Large sliding doors allowed the adjacent lecture room to open into the main auditorium, providing seating for 500. The new building boasted a gas lighting system, with an acetylene plant located in a small brick building off the southwest corner of the church.

Small diamond-shaped varnished wood shingles, with occasional diamond patterns in a lighter color wood, covered the interior walls. The column-free interior featured a domed ceiling covered in blue-painted tin with wood ribs. Incorporated into the attic was a sophisticated ventilation system. A room above the main vestibule housed a magic lantern–type projector. The varnished pews featured Gothic arches on their ends. Despite all the Gothic touches, no crosses or other religious symbols were incorporated into the architectural design—a nod to the congregation's Puritan heritage.

The building cost $15,000—about $500,000 in today's dollars, thanks to what the *Brooklyn Daily Eagle* characterized as "liberal" contributions from those Sound Avenue farming families. The ever-frugal farmers saved money by doing much of the work themselves, including digging the cellar and raising the frame. Local carpenters Elbert Fanning and Fred Moseley did most of the remaining work. Of course a Hallock served on the building committee—Halsey's nephew Herman. Membership reached 190 with average attendance of 200, but these represented only 14 families. The *Eagle*'s article about the new church gleefully noted that the Hallock, Wells, and Youngs families—all descended from the first settlers of Long Island—formed the core of the church.[26]

New Schoolhouses

The community's efforts to modernize their schools provide additional evidence of their progressive bent. When the first school appeared in the community, soon after the state passed legislation in 1812 establishing a statewide system of common school districts, it was a no-frills structure. By the 1860s, that building, which became the District 10 school, the western of two schools in the community, seemed small and outdated. The district called a special meeting of legal voters late in 1864 "to consult in relation to building a new school house." It took another nine years to actually get the new school built. They choose a new site a bit further west (a little east of Northville Turnpike where the Highlands at Aquebogue is now located), purchased the land in 1871, and finally raised the new building on March 4, 1872.[27] Henry Wilson Young, who described the original school he attended as a boy as an "unpainted structure with no grounds" with slab desks inside, called the new building, where he taught for a year in 1873, "a more modern structure" with ample grounds, larger windows, and a higher ceiling.[28]

Not to be outdone, trustees of the other district in the east part of the community (District 11) decided to update their school at a special meeting in 1888. They replaced all the windows with larger units, raised the roofline "up sharper," jacked the building higher off the ground, built a new foundation, and enlarged the classroom. They covered the interior walls with fashionable varnished wooden "ceiling board" (what we call wainscotting), added a bell cupola, and replaced the old plank desks with new desks made in Grand Rapids, Michigan (see fig. 6.1, chap. 6).

The following year, in a sort of contest, the western district decided it too needed more space and wanted something more modern. The district hired Elbert A. Fanning, a local carpenter, to take out the coatrooms in the front of the building to create a larger classroom and built a new shed with boys' and girls' entrances and coatrooms on the back. As the other district did the year before, Fanning also lined the walls and ceiling with "ceiling board" with a natural wood finish and added a bell cupola to the roof. District 10 also replaced its plank desks with more comfortable factory-made units.

New Union School

In 1909, as educators began to question the wisdom of eight grades in one room, and as both Northville schools became overcrowded, the two districts considered merging but voted it down. However, the New York State commissioner of education forced the merger anyway. For the next two years, the old one-room schools accommodated just four grades each, with the upper four grades in the Sound Avenue Hall. Finally, in 1911, the consolidated district completed a four-room school halfway between the two old schools, a more modern structure in the then-fashionable Colonial Revival style. (See fig. 8.4.)

Unfortunately, the new school burned to the ground on February 18, 1916. According to the *Riverhead News*:

> Nothing but a heap of ashes is left of our beautiful new schoolhouse. While school was in session on Wednesday morning at about 11:40, a noise was heard in the cellar. Miss [Helen] Gillespie [the principal] and one of the larger boys went down to investigate, and, according to reports, found the top of the furnace blown off and the beams overhead on fire. The school was immediately emptied and assistance summoned, but the flames spread too rapidly to be checked. By 1 o'clock, the building was entirely consumed.

Figure 8.4. The first Union School built by the combined Northville school districts in 1911. It burned in 1916. *Source:* Hallockville Museum Farm. Used with permission.

The newspaper article is perhaps a sanitized version. According to local legend, the students went sleigh riding on a hill across the fields north of the school and stoked the furnace too much before leaving.[29] At any rate, all hundred children escaped the blaze. Some of the older boys managed to save most of the library books by tossing them out of the library window while the fire blazed.

The community built an even more modern new school the same year. Like the previous building, it contained three classrooms downstairs and a fourth classroom, plus a 35-by-80-foot auditorium with stage upstairs. The *County Review* described the new Colonial-style building with typical exuberance, saying that "few rural communities in the State can boast of a handsomer or more up-to-date school building" that complied in every detail with the latest requirements of the state's education department. The architect, William Sidney Jones, carried on the practice of Riverhead's leading architect George H. Skidmore. The paper noted drinking fountains in the corridors, lavatories in the basement, and running water supplied from "compressed air tanks"—all major upgrades from the old one-room buildings. Because Sound Avenue still lacked electric service, the school had its own power plant and water supply. The heating system used steam, with fresh air admitted through grills directly into classrooms as needed.[30] In 1927 the district added another classroom to the rear of the building.[31]

Riverhead Town Agricultural Society

At the close of a temperance meeting on Christmas Day in 1863, George Wilson Hallock (Halsey's cousin) asked farmers to meet and organize a Farmers Club. Although called the Riverhead Town Agricultural Society, it met in the Northville Academy and most of the members came from Northville. Naturally, Halsey became one of 23 founding members, along with four Hallock cousins.[32]

The society served as a forum for the area's progressive farmers to discuss the latest developments in agricultural practice. It also functioned as a cooperative for the purchase of fertilizer and other supplies delivered to the dock in Jamesport.

At a typical meeting in 1886, naturally a Hallock presided as president, Halsey's cousin Henry L. Hallock. The farmers present briefly discussed a letter received from congressman Perry Belmont about tariffs and debated whether to join the Farmer's Alliance, a somewhat radical national organization that worked to oppose railroad monopolies. (They did not join.) The rest of the meeting focused on the question of the day: "What is the best fertilizer for potatoes?" Fifteen of the farmers present described their experiments with different types of fertilizer, their favorite brands, and their theories on how best to utilize fertilizer.[33]

Formally incorporated in 1867, the society served as a major social nexus for farmers. In addition to regular debates about the best farming methods and trials of new plows and reapers, the society also found time for social events like its annual oyster supper, which actually featured oyster stew. In 1908, Halsey reported going to New Suffolk for 25 gallons of oysters for the supper.[34]

Sometimes the entertainment consisted of playing "42," a trick-taking game locally popular because it was played with dominos rather than cards, which were still considered sinful in this community with its strong Puritan legacy.[35] The society, often referred to simply as the Farmers Club, celebrated its 50th anniversary in 1917 and its 75th in 1937 when it claimed to be the oldest farmer cooperative in the United States (see fig. 8.5). By that point, they met in the kitchen of the Sound Avenue Hall (former academy and first church, then used by the Grange). Estelle Evans recalled her

Figure 8.5. Meeting of the Farmers Club, also known as the Riverhead Town Agricultural Society, in the kitchen of the Sound Avenue Hall (a.k.a. Grange Hall), 1933. *Source:* Collection of the author.

father, Leslie T. Wells, always going to Aquebogue to buy ice cream for the Farmers Club meetings.

First RFD Route and the Sound Avenue Name

The community took another step into the modern world in 1899 when it became the first rural free delivery (RFD) route on Long Island. The post office set up its first experimental RFD route in 1896—part of a nationwide effort by farmers organizations to get the same free mail delivery that cities and towns enjoyed since 1863. The RFD system was still considered experimental when the Riverhead Town Agricultural Society led the effort to create the new route, noting that the new system could save local farmers the need to drive three, four, or five miles to the nearest post office to pick up mail. The innovation aroused considerable interest across Long Island, with numerous front-page articles in the local press.[36] The national introduction of parcel delivery in 1913 made the service even more valuable by facilitating the delivery of national newspapers and magazines and even mail-order baby chicks.

Creation of the RFD route necessitated renaming North Road to avoid confusion with other roads of the same name. Again the Agricultural Society took the lead and decided to change the name of the village to "Sound View" and the road to "Sound View Avenue."[37] However, the new name was quickly shortened to "Sound Avenue." The church quickly dropped the problematic Northville name and became Congregational Society of Sound Avenue in 1904.[38] Soon Sound Avenue also became the name that most people used for the community, although the school retained the Northville moniker.

The RFD route started in Riverhead, went up Roanoke Avenue, east along the newly renamed Sound Avenue to Herrick's Lane, down Herrick's Lane to Main Road (then called South Road), and back to Riverhead, a total of about 20 miles. The route served 172 boxes on Sound Avenue, one for each home. However, instead of placing boxes in front of the houses, the route used the "cross roads" system with all boxes clustered at the intersections. The box for the Hallocks was located at the corner of Herrick's Lane, a short walk away. Long Island's most famous photographer of the era, Hal B. Fullerton, photographed one of the clusters of mail boxes on Sound Avenue soon after they were erected in 1899.[39] Despite post office regulations requiring standard boxes, the original homemade wooden ones stayed in service for many years.[40] A month after the inauguration of the new route, the post office reported that it had already delivered 5,000 pieces of mail to Northville farmers.[41]

Iron Pier

Perhaps the most audacious effort by the progressive Sound Avenue farmers was the construction of the Iron Pier. They organized a joint stock company, the Northville Pier and Land Improvement Company in 1899. The company planned a pier extending 396 feet into Long Island Sound and supported by iron pilings. The stockholders thought it would "boom the community" by allowing cheaper transportation of farm produce and easier passenger connections to Connecticut.

The company sold shares for $100 each and applied to the state for an underwater land grant extending 500 feet into the sound. It selected as its contractor Henry Case, who had recently built a similar pier on Coney Island.

The company was truly a Hallock enterprise, as Halsey's second cousin, Henry L. Hallock, then the town supervisor, served as its president. Signatures of Herman H. Hallock, Halsey's nephew, and William McDermott, a Hallockville neighbor a few houses to the west, also appear on the stock certificates.[42] Naturally Halsey Hallock was a shareholder. The company built the pier at Luce's Landing—the north end of Henry L. Hallock's farm—one of the few spots in Riverhead where a break in the cliffs made it possible to drive a wagon down to the Long Island Sound shore. He also donated the land for a new town road leading to the pier, today named Pier Avenue.

From the beginning, the project faced skepticism and bad luck. Many Sound Avenue neighbors scoffed at the very idea, saying that no pier could ever withstand the ravages of storms and ice on the exposed shoreline. Initially the work progressed smoothly, but then a sudden northeast gale storm swept the deck planking off a raft being towed from New York City, forcing the directors to hire someone to collect the lumber along the beach and bring it to the site.[43]

Then Case encountered financial troubles and abandoned the job, causing the directors to finish the project themselves using a local contractor. Amazingly, the cost, projected to be $14,500, came in closer to $10,000, mostly because Hallock kept expenses under control.[44] It was completed in July 1900, except for wooden pilings along both sides of the pier intended to protect it from ice. For some reason—perhaps to save money—they were never installed, leaving the structure vulnerable to winter storms. The pier was never much of a financial success. At low tide the water depth at the end of the pier was only nine feet, making it difficult for large boats to approach.

The Iron Pier met its end the night of February 13, 1904. An unusually cold winter froze the sound three to five feet thick. Then, after a warm spell allowed the ice mass to float freely offshore, high winds and strong tides drove that ice sheet back against the pier, which sheared the pier from its footings, casting it up on the beach.[45] The directors gathered the materials into piles and auctioned them off in 1905 for a total $125.[46] Halsey Hallock used some of the salvaged wood to construct the new shed at the east end of his barn.[47]

Telephone

In yet another connection to the modern world, telephone service came to Sound Avenue in 1901, just 25 years after Alexander Graham Bell invented the instrument. In 1900 Baiting Hollow farmer Henry R. Talmage installed a private line from his house to his father's next door. The following year he and neighboring farmer Charles H. Warner organized the Baiting Hollow and Roanoke Telephone Company as a joint stock corporation. They began service with 20 subscribers on a single line running along Sound Avenue—creating tempting opportunities to listen in on each other's calls. Warner and Talmage not only managed the company but cut the trees on their own farms for the poles, strung the wires, and troubleshot the equipment. The company tried to keep rates affordable—just $1 a month, about $24 today—but with service by party line and no free long-distance calling!

Telephone lines reached the Hallock Homestead in 1902. The Hallocks experienced a run-in with the system in 1907 when a low-hanging line caught the top of their buggy and ripped if off.[48] Eventually the company expanded service to most of Riverhead and beyond, with connecting lines to surrounding companies. When sold in 1917 to the New York Telephone Company for $26,707 (about $650,000 in current dollars), there were 200 customers and 121 stockholders.

Electricity

The ultimate connection to the modern world, electricity, did not come to most of Sound Avenue until 1927, 45 years after Thomas Edison's Pearl

Street power station in New York City. Electric service arrived in downtown Riverhead in 1893, with rival companies supplying AC and DC current. But it took another 34 years of agitation, naturally led by the Riverhead Town Agricultural Society, to get power to all of Sound Avenue, just three miles away. When power lines still had not reached the community in 1926, the *County Review* wrote, "Electricity is no longer a luxury. It has become one of the prime necessities and is nowhere more urgently needed than on the farms . . . which make Sound Avenue so important and valuable a part of our township."[49] Finally, the following April the *Review* reported the encouraging news about poles for the power line being placed along Sound Avenue and that it anticipated "the work will be carried through without serious delay."[50]

Electric service enabled Sound Avenue farmers to install electric pumps in their wells, which in turn allowed many, like the Hallocks, to install indoor plumbing for the first time. It also allowed the Sound Avenue Church to install an electric organ blower, making obsolete the role of organ pumper and relieving Ella Hallock of the chore of pumping for her sister Bessie's weekly rehearsals on the church organ. One observer wrote nostalgically at the time, "One is reminded of the amusement furnished to the younger portion of the congregation in the good old days, when the organ pumper [usually a man or boy during church services], on occasion, shut off in the side room, went to sleep during the sermon and failed to respond to his signal. Those days are no more. Thus one by one a machine age takes the joys out of life by making everything exact, efficient and scientific."[51]

The Great Race

In 1909 the Hallocks's then-new front porch became their private spectator gallery for the only legal motor race ever to take place on Sound Avenue—probably 10 years before the Hallocks owned a car. Organized by Riverhead hotel owner Frank J. Corwin and other local promoters, the race ran a nearly 23-mile course that started on upper Roanoke Avenue, then east along Main Street and Main Road to Mattituck, where it took a hairpin turn onto Sound Avenue. From there it ran past the Hallock Homestead back to Roanoke Avenue. The cars, all stock cars that could be purchased from a dealer, ran either five or ten laps, depending on their size and horsepower (see fig. 8.6).

With 16 entries and staggered starts, race cars would have passed the Homestead about 120 times. The fastest car, a Buick driven by Louis

Figure 8.6. Number 7 passing the Sound Avenue house of Emilie's brother, John Horace Wells, on the straightaway in the 1909 race. This postcard image was not of the actual race but a promotional item staged before the race and apparently given away in large numbers. Notice the recently erected telephone poles on the right side. *Source:* Hallockville Museum Farm. Used with permission.

Chevrolet, with average speeds of 70 miles per hour overall and 76 miles per hour on one lap—setting a world record for a road race even though none of the roads were paved. Imagine how fast these cars must have driven on the Sound Avenue straightaways! Remarkably, only one accident occurred, when a car lost a wheel and overturned, killing its mechanic, on Sound Avenue at Jacob's Hill about two miles east of the Homestead. While the race was a technical success and much enjoyed, it was a financial failure for the promoters since most spectators watched from roadsides along the route—like the Hallocks did—rather than paying to sit in the grandstands on Roanoke Avenue.[52]

New Polish Neighbors

As late as 1880, the community remained remarkably homogeneous. The federal census of that year listed 347 individuals living in or near Northville.[53] White, native-born residents constituted 91 percent of the total—almost all descendants of the Puritans who settled Southold two centuries earlier.

There were only 18 foreign-born laborers, servants, or their offspring—mostly Irish, but a few from other Western European countries. That census also revealed 11 Black farm laborers and one Native American.

The Hallocks's neighborhood began to change significantly in the 1880s with an influx of immigrants from Poland and other parts of Eastern Europe. In 1892 the *Long Island Traveler* noted that "there are quite a large number of Polanders" already living in and around Northville.[54] The 1900 census, the next available, shows a much more diverse community, with Polish immigrants constituting almost a quarter of the population. Mainly they were single young men, although there were about a half-dozen families. Most left their home country, then part of the Russian empire, either for economic reasons or to escape the military draft. After arriving on Long Island, initially most either worked as farm laborers or as household help. Halsey Hallock briefly employed Alex Romanowsky as a farmhand and later had another Polish family in the new tenant house.

Although these newcomers all started as laborers, part of the 2.5 million Polish immigrants who came to America by 1930, they quickly began buying up local farms. They came well equipped for farming on the North Fork. Poland stood at the heart of Europe's potato growing area, so they brought with them potato growing skills and experience. Three recent Polish immigrants had already acquired their own farms on Sound Avenue by 1900, and by 1930 Polish families with names such as Naugles, Trubisz, Cichanowicz, and Sydlowski owned over 70 percent of the farms in the Hallockville neighborhood.[55]

George Naugles (1864–1920), part of the earliest wave of Polish immigrants, became the first to buy a farm in the Hallockville area. According to census records, he arrived in 1888 at age 24 and became a citizen in 1895 at age 30. Although he immigrated from Poland, technically then part of Russia, the family was ethnic Lithuanian and his name was originally Jersey Nauwialis ("No-VAL-is"). According to family legend, the Northville school simplified the name to Naugles, and Jersey became George.

By 1902, he already owned a small farm on the south side of Sound Avenue a little west of the Hallock Homestead. Within a dozen years, he bought two more farms on the north side of the road that once belonged to the brothers Caleb and Daniel Wells Hallock, cousins of the Homestead Hallocks. A barn built by the Naugles family, after the fire consumed their old barn in 1936, was moved to the Hallockville Museum in 1999 and now stands on the west end of the museum's campus.

Immediately to the west of the Homestead, Konstanty and Adela Cichanowicz in 1923 bought the 35-acre Isaiah Hallock farm. Konstanty had immigrated from Bialystok, near the northeastern border of present-day Poland, in 1902 at age 22. Adela came from Pietrylowicze, a small town of about 140 people 40 miles south of Vilna in an area then part of the Russian Empire and now in Belarus. The old Hallock house had burned down in 1915. The Cichanowiczes initially lived in a small outbuilding that they called "the little Hallock house." But by 1930, the hardworking family saved enough money to build the four-square Cichanowicz farmhouse that is still in its original location as part of the Hallockville Museum complex. Konstanty and Adela's daughters took piano lessons with Bessie in the Homestead. The Cichanowicz children and grandchildren continued to farm that property and several others nearby, including the Hallock Homestead farm, until nearly the end of the 20th century.

Another typical Polish immigrant success story is that of Kazimierz Trubisch. Born in Pietrylowicze, the same small town in what is today Belarus, as Adele Cichanowicz, at age 25 he arrived at Ellis Island on the *SS Cleveland* from Hamburg in 1910 with only a few dollars in his pocket. Immigration records indicate that his father funded the trip. He soon changed his first name to Charles and Americanized the spelling of his last name to Trubisz.[56]

After working on local farms for eight years, he was able to purchase the former Bethuel Hallock farm just east of the Hallock Homestead in 1918. This farm had stayed in successive generations of the Hallock family since Capt. Zachariah Hallock acquired it in the late 18th century. But John Morse Hallock, the last of the Hallock line to live there, sold the farm in 1908 and moved to New Jersey. The initial buyer, probably a speculator from New York City, held it for only a few years before selling it in 1912 to Halsey Hallock's only son, Hal.

Very impressed with the industrious young Charles Trubisz, the Hallocks sold him the farm in 1918. The Hallocks, however, did not provide financing. Instead, a professional mortgage lender in Huntington provided the $7,000 mortgage, which Trubisz managed to pay off in just a few years. Trubisz soon married the daughter of another Polish immigrant family that lived down the street. Naturally, like other nearby Polish families, they sent their daughters next door to the Hallock Homestead for piano lessons with Bessie.

The little white house that stood across from the Hallockville Museum until about 2015 (visible on far right in Bessie's photo of 1930 Sound Avenue in fig I.1) tells a different side of the Polish immigrant farmer story—a family that left a farm laborer situation in the hamlet of Orient at the eastern tip of the North Fork and tried to establish themselves in farming but failed in the difficult economic climate of the early 1930s. John and Annie Trykoski bought this land, originally part of the Hallock farm, and built this house in 1928, leaving the Homestead Hallocks surrounded on all three sides by new Polish immigrants. One of the daughters remembered the Hallocks across the street as a "wonderful" family. She said that when the Hallocks baked bread, one of the sisters would bring them over some. In turn, when they made pies, they would make an extra one for the Hallocks.

Like so many of the other Polish immigrant families, the Trykoskis took out a mortgage to buy the farm. They also borrowed from a neighbor to build the barn. However, the Depression years proved very difficult for farming. Even though, according to the 1930 census, his wife Annie and their oldest daughter worked as "pickers" on a duck farm—plucking the feathers from slaughtered birds—to bring extra income into the household, the family was unable to make the payments and consequently lost the house and farm in 1932. They moved back to Orient, where John Trykowski again became a laborer.

The Homestead Hallocks also interacted extensively with another Polish immigrant, John Sydlowski. When they gave up farming around 1925, they initially rented the farm to Sydlowski. The following year, when the former Samuel Terry Hudson farm just west of the Carey Camp Road became available, Halsey Hallock's son Hal accompanied Sydlowski to the lawyer's office to assist with the purchase—yet another sign of how impressed the Hallocks were with their new Polish neighbors and, in this case, the tenant on their farm.[57] The Hallockville Museum moved the Hudson-Sydlowski House to its campus in 1988, where it now serves as the museum's administration building.

As immigrants from Poland inundated the community, they were met with mixed reactions by the old families of Sound Avenue. On one hand, local farmers clearly welcomed them as cheap farm help in an area with little other labor available beyond the family. They were also more than happy to sell their farms for what seemed like amazing prices. On the other hand, the newcomers were foreigners, did not speak English, practiced the Catholic religion, and drank alcohol. All of this must have been an immense shock for the insulated and inbred Sound Avenue community of Puritan descendants.

There were certainly many incidents with immigrants slighted or discriminated against. A close reading of the local press shows some interesting trends. Even though about a quarter of the local population was already Polish in the first decade of the 20th century, the weekly Sound Avenue columns in the local papers almost never mentioned them. Those columns reported regularly on social and church events in the community—who was visiting whom, who was traveling where, what happened at church meetings, and so on. But not a word about any of this for the Polish community living among them, not even wedding announcements.

The few times they received mention they were often referred to as "Poles," generally in the context of one of the old families selling their farm to "a Pole."[58] Interestingly, the Polish immigrants did not refer to their Protestant neighbors as "Americans," but rather as "Yankees" or more often as "English," perhaps a sly dig that the ancestors of these Puritan farmers had once been immigrants too. The "English" displayed a certain begrudging admiration for the work and success of the Polish newcomers, but it was often mixed with an element of condescension. In fact, the Polish immigrants provided a safety valve for Sound Avenue's younger generation to escape from the land and move on to more lucrative non-farming pursuits.

The Agricultural Society, the Grange, the Literary Society, and of course the Sound Avenue Congregational Church and all its affiliated organizations had no Polish members. When Sound Avenue incorporated as a village in 1920, none of the village officers were of Polish descent. But the schools became the great mixers. Students formed lasting friendships across ethnic lines. Within a generation, there would even be several marriages between second- and third-generation Polish and their Protestant neighbors.

A Neighborhood Rum-Running Operation

In a minor diversion from their farming, some of the Polish immigrant families living in the Hallockville neighborhood engaged in a little rum-running operation during Prohibition. The Naugles family led the operation, but the Cichanowicz and Trubisz families also participated. Fast boats delivered the bootleg alcohol, brought by sea from Canada to the Long Island Sound beach on the north end of the Naugles farm. There the enterprising farmers rigged a primitive inclined railway to haul it up the steep cliff, where they loaded it into fast cars for delivery to a thirsty New York City market.

According to Naugles family lore, when their old barn burned down in 1936 at the height of the Great Depression, the profits from the rum-running operation allowed them to build the handsome new barn now owned by the Hallockville Museum. The Hallockville Museum's Cichanowicz farmhouse was also likely built with proceeds from the rum-running operation.

The Hallock family in the Homestead lived right in the middle of this operation throughout the Prohibition era, with the Trubisz family on one side and the Cichanowicz family on the other and the Naugles families just down the street. The Hallocks had been enthusiastic supporters of the temperance movement since the 1840s. They lived in a town that voted dry in every election since early in the 20th century, and their Sound Avenue community—at least all of the Protestants in it—remained totally dry. During most of this period, Bessie served as president of the local chapter of the Woman's Christian Temperance Union. However, there is not a single mention of the local rum-running operation in anything Halsey or his daughters wrote or said. They certainly never reported the operation to authorities or took any steps to impede its operation. This is one of the many interesting unspoken contradictions that characterized the community.

Village of Sound Avenue

Sound Avenue farmers always demonstrated an independent streak. In 1921 it became literal when they declared their independence from the town of Riverhead and incorporated as the Village of Sound Avenue. As usual, the Riverhead Town Agricultural Society—mostly a Sound Avenue organization—led the effort. Local farmers long agitated for better roads, which came to mean well-oiled roads that allowed them to carry three times as much in their horse-drawn wagons. With the advent of automobiles and trucks, the condition of the roads became even more important. Heavy cars often inflicted severe damage during late winter thaws.

Sound Avenue farmers claimed that they contributed $4,000 for the support of highways in the town but received little benefit. As the *County Review*'s Sound Avenue columnist put it in February 1921, "The dissatisfaction with the condition of our local roads which for a number of years has been more or less vocal, but wholly unorganized, was brought to a focus by the fact that during the past year all the road oil that came to Sound Avenue was what was brought in on the tires of automobiles from the puddles in the village streets."[59] The advocates of incorporation, led by John R. Reeve, a farmer who also operated the first garage on Sound Avenue, hoped for better roads at lower taxes, as well the purchase of firefighting apparatus for their new "city."⁶⁰

Put to a vote on October 22, 1921, in a rare display of near unanimity, village incorporation carried 28 in favor to 2 against—the only village ever incorporated within the town of Riverhead. "It is one of the wealthiest farming communities in the State and it is expected that progressive policies will be adopted," the *County Review* wrote.⁶¹ The only non-farm residence on the village's assessment roll was the church's parsonage.

In the first village meeting that year, John T. Downs, a retired successful farmer, was chosen as president. The voters thought so highly of him that they also elected him treasurer, leaving him to choose which position he wished to occupy. The most critical position in the village, that of highway commissioner, went to John R. Reeve, the principal organizer of the effort to incorporate. Not surprisingly, Reeve and Downs lived next door to each other.

The *Brooklyn Daily Eagle* could not resist poking fun at the Village of Sound Avenue, with only 544 residents. An article accompanied by a cartoon prodded, "Nothing to do and all day to do it in, seems to quite truthfully describe the life of John T. Downs, 'mayor' of Sound Avenue village."⁶² (Downs actually served as the first "president" of Sound Avenue.) The *Eagle* slyly noted, "As village president he stands unique in many respects. . . . No controller to 'yawp' at him . . . no boro hall . . . no police department . . . no board of estimate to get in hot water with . . . no subways to stew over." The *Eagle* compared Downs's job with that of the mayor of New York, noting that in Sound Avenue there were "no fire regulations because there is no fire department, no sidewalk complaints because there are no sidewalks, no one calls him up to say that the sewer is plugged up or the electric light wires are down or that the stores are charging too much, for there are no sewers, no electric lights, [and no stores]."

Although the village claimed a population over 500, only 20, including Hal Hallock, showed up at the first budget vote in April 1922—all males, even though New York State gave women the right to vote in 1917. The voters were also all of "English" descent, even though Polish immigrants made up roughly 57 percent of the new village's population and already owned 36 of the 88 farms and rented another dozen or so more.⁶³

Ever undecided about the village name, voters changed it from Sound Avenue to Northville by a vote of 49 to 41 at the annual meeting in 1929. The following year, when their dream of better roads and lower taxes did not work out, Sound Avenue farmers voted 61 to 2 to surrender the charter and unincorporate—another rare display of near unanimity.⁶⁴

People of Color

People of color constituted a significant minority of the Sound Avenue community from its beginnings. In the 18th century, numerous neighbors and relatives of the Homestead Hallocks owned slaves. After the gradual end of slavery in the early 19th century, most of the former enslaved quickly moved away, likely to communities with larger populations of Black people. However, when the new church in Northville was formed in 1831, the membership roll included two "colored" persons, Brister and Phillis Young. Brister was the son of Brister and Zipporah, who had been slaves of Rev. Daniel Youngs, the longtime minister of Aquebogue Church and great-grandfather to both Halsey and Emilie Hallock. Only one other person of color ever became a member of the church, shortly after the Youngs. Their tenure did not last very long. Brister soon died, Phillis moved to Greenport with her son John Youngs, and the other person of color left for an unknow destination.

However, there continued to be a presence of "colored" people in the community, mostly young single men and women employed as farm laborers or household help. In 1840, Hallock neighbors and relatives Samuel Tuthill, Abraham Luce, and William Benjamin all lived with "colored" girls between 10 and 24 in their households. John F. Hallock (living next door), John T. Luce, and Jabez Corwin lived with young men of similar age. The same pattern applied in the rest of Riverhead Town, occasionally with non-white workers younger than 10 years old. As we have seen, Halsey's first experience with someone of color probably occurred in his elementary school.

Child Laborers from the House of Refuge

As Sound Avenue farms became more prosperous in the mid-19th century, farm labor increasingly became a problem. Farmers sometimes hired sons of their neighbors and relatives, as did the Hallocks. Irish immigrants also sometimes provided a source of farm labor. Poor children from New York City and Brooklyn, often Black, provided another major source of labor.

The 1860 census lists eight young Black boys and three girls, all under 16, living in the community. One of the young men worked on the farm of John F. Hallock, immediately east of the Homestead. Another girl and boy worked on the farm of Daniel W. Hallock, two doors to the west. The Hallocks's cousin, Samuel Tuthill, had an 8-year-old Black boy working on the farm to whom the census taker assigned the Tuthill family name, in an eerie reprise of the practice of assigning last names of masters to their slaves. Another area farmer, John H. Wells, lived with a 14-year-old boy named Richard, to whom the census taker assigned the Wells family name. The census also lists 9 unrelated white boys ages 1 to 17 and one 9-year-old white girl.

Many of these young workers came from the New York House of Refuge, a juvenile reformatory and a product of an early 19th-century reform movement to separate young boys and girls from adult prisoners. Established in 1824 in Manhattan, the House of Refuge moved to Randall's Island in 1854 and operated until 1935. It was considered a model institution and acclaimed by visitors such as Alexis De Tocqueville, Frances Trollope, and Charles Dickens. The inmates were mostly children picked up for minor crimes but also included children placed by pauper families. The reformatory had the authority to bind out inmates through indenture agreements as "apprentices" on farms, and sometimes whaling ships, to get them as far away from the evils of the city as possible and supposedly to learn a trade and prepare for adulthood.[65]

In 1864 Samuel Tuthill recorded in his diary that his neighbor Isaac Reeve brought four boys from the House of Refuge, including a 13-year-old named Charles, to work on the Tuthill farm. Over the next several years, Tuthill also recorded various farm tasks that Charles helped with and that Charles went to school, although it is not clear how much. But trouble was brewing. In April 1868, Charles stole some tobacco and then lied about it. The following month, Charles ran away. Tuthill spent the next several days searching for Charles, going as far as Wading River and Bellport, all to no avail. He then went to Riverhead and placed an advertisement in James B. Slade's recently founded *Riverhead News* for the runaway boy—just as enslavers a half-century earlier placed advertisements for runaway slaves. Tuthill also sent a letter to the House of Refuge about the runaway boy, but Charles never returned.

For some reason, the 1865 New York State Census does not list Charles in the Tuthill household. But it does list as "hired help" a 13-year-old from Kings County, Zachariah Miles, possibly the same boy. Young boys, and sometimes girls, show up in many other Sound Avenue farmhouses in that census. The state census does not list race. It is not clear how many of these young boys and girls came from the House of Refuge. Runaways may have been fairly common. For instance, an advertisement appeared in the *Long-Islander* in 1869 for a "Mulatto girl aged about 16 years" who had run away from a Huntington subscriber who said she was "apprenticed to the house keeping business from the House of Refuge, Randall's Island."[66]

The same year Charles ran away, Tuthill recorded in his journal that he "brought two niggers" as farm workers to his cousin Elisha Wells—who wrote the Civil War letters to Herman Hallock—likely from the House of Refuge. The two boys probably did not stay, as they do not show up on the federal census in 1870, although a young white farm laborer named Innocence Nois is listed.

Early in 1869, Tuthill tried again. He recorded in his journal that "my boy come this PM got by D W Reeve from House of Refuge. Says he is twelve years old a mulatto color wool head . . . my boys name is Henry Lang."[67] There are diary references to him going to church and school, but he is generally just called "the boy." The 1870 census lists him as Henry Lung, age 16, and says he is white. The same census also lists a young girl, Mary Withall, age 13, as a domestic servant. Quite a few other Sound Avenue farms hired similar help either on the farm or in the house—generally teenagers, sometimes as young as 11, usually white but sometimes Black. They were generally born in New York State, but one Black teen came from Virginia.

Racism

Despite the relatively small number of Black residents, the white residents blamed them for three out of the four robberies reported in the final decades of the 19th century. The first involved a "young colored boy" named Herbert Spencer, who worked on the farm of Halsey's cousin, Henry L. Hallock. Allegedly Spencer broke into the Hallock home in 1881 and stole a "small sum" of money while the family attended church. Even though an article in the *Sag-Harbor Express* indicated that "there was no proof of burglary," the court sentenced Spencer to two years in Sing Sing prison.[68]

Samuel Tuthill's diary is replete with other racist references. In one 1863 entry he complained that the minister Rev. Thomas Harris had "preached politics & nigger." He also complained about a guest speaker at a prayer meeting being a "radical abolitionist, full of higher law." In 1864 he noted sarcastically that "niggerism [was] preached" at a church meeting by someone as "black as thunder." He objected in 1865 to a preacher from the Freedman's Aid Commission—at the same time the Homestead Hallocks were supporting the organization.

Frequent entries also appear in Tuthill's diary using the N-word. In 1868, he reported that his father-in-law's "nigger ran away to day with his boots on."[69] In 1870, he mentioned that "a nigger come here & ate breakfast wanted to hire out at $10 per month." Tuthill did not hire the man. In 1874 he recorded attending a concert in Riverhead of "niggers from South." In 1885, he reported that his boys went to "a nigger concert in the Lecture Room."

In 1881 Tuthill, attended at least two cakewalks at the Northville Academy, and additional ones in subsequent years. He often served as one of the judges.[70] The history of the cakewalk is complicated. It may have begun in the antebellum South as a way for slaves to satirize the fancy dancing at the parties of their white masters. After the war—and especially after one was featured at the 1876 Centennial Exposition in Philadelphia—cakewalks became immensely popular with white audiences, a way for whites to cast ridicule and condensation on the dancing of Black Americans. Typically, the dancers (or walkers) were Black, although whites sometimes participated in blackface. The judges, usually white, awarded a cake to the winner, hence the name.

The earliest reference in Suffolk County newspapers happened to be in Riverhead in 1873. The article revealed its racist roots in the very first sentence: "A genuine darkey 'Cake Walk' took place 'over the river' on Friday evening at the house of Mr. Hicks, colored."[71] The prize, a large cake. The paper conspicuously mentioned that the female half of the winning couple weighed nearly 300 pounds. "Over the river" referred to the area now called Riverside, at the time the home of a small community of African Americans who moved out from Brooklyn or New York City to work in Riverhead's hotels and as domestics in homes. "Mr. Hicks" was William Hicks, who became well known in the area for organizing cakewalks, including some that Tuthill attended in the Northville Academy.

Perhaps the most egregious account of a cakewalk described an 1886 event at Terry's Hall in Riverhead that Tuthill could have attended. The Riverhead correspondent to the *Sag-Harbor Express* wrote that "it was a nigger affair run on nigger principles." He added that "the doors were thrown wide open to every dusky skin that presented itself." That fall, the same correspondent described another "darkie cake-walk" in Riverhead.[72]

Tuthill, one of many local Copperheads during the Civil War, stood on the opposite side of the fence from Halsey Hallock and his immediate family—a divide that became more obvious as scandals rocked the community in the 1860s and 1870s. We have no record of the Homestead Hallocks ever attending one of these cakewalks. Halsey never used the N-word in his diary or any of his writings, instead sticking with "colored," a term then considered neutral and respectable. At a 1906 meeting of the

Literary Society, one of the songs featured was "Nigger Loves Possum" sung by "five young ladies." Perhaps it is just coincidence, but neither Bessie nor Ella participated in that performance.[73]

In 1923, the Hallocks recorded being invited to a meeting of the Klu Klux Klan but noted in their diary that they "did not go." This was the peak year of Klan organizing in Suffolk County, and its core anti-immigrant, anti-Jew, and anti-Negro message appealed to many in the area. In an effort of appeal to another favorite villain, the Klan also promoted its stance against alcohol. That year, the *County Review*, one of two newspapers published in Riverhead, carried 67 articles mentioning the Klan. Although the paper took a strong editorial stance against the Klan, stating that the country was "no place for religious intolerance or racial bigotry," most of the news items were about meetings all over the county. Local ministers, including from the Hallocks's Congregational denomination, often addressed or hosted these meetings. There was a small meeting in Riverhead in April and two huge September and October meetings in Flanders (about a mile from downtown Riverhead), both with thousands of attendees. Even closer, the *County Review* reported two meetings in Jamesport in October, one in a large field and another in Mechanics Hall. Another Jamesport meeting followed that December. Likely these were the meetings to which the Hallocks were invited, just a few miles from home. Jamesport had an active Klan chapter and the Hallocks undoubtedly knew some of them, but there is no evidence of Klan activity on Sound Avenue.[74]

The Strange Tale of Chloe Luce

Bessie Hallock, one of the final three unmarried siblings to live in the Homestead, compiled records of all the burials in the Sound Avenue Cemetery. Her list includes only one non-white person: "Chloe Luce (colored)" who died in 1889 at age 70. Whereas for everyone else in the list Bessie documented their spouses and parents, all she says about Chloe is that she "lived with Caleb Hallock."

Who is Chloe Luce? And why is she buried in the Caleb Hallock plot in the cemetery? She was born about 1819 to a slave woman belonging to Rev. Abraham Luce, who donated the property for the first Northville Church. Under the gradual emancipation laws then in effect, Chloe and her mother automatically became free by 1827.[75] The 1830 census lists a free "colored" female between 10 and 24 and another between 36 and 55, presumably

Chloe and her mother, still in the Luce household. The 1840 census shows a "free colored" woman between 16 and 24, again corresponding to Chloe's age, still living in Luce's household. Luce's daughter Almina, just four years younger, grew up with Chloe. When Almina married Caleb Hallock in the early 1840s, she presumably brought Chloe with her. The next three federal census returns all show Chloe living there, generally listed as a servant.

When Chloe died, Caleb's nephew, Sammy Tuthill, recorded that they gave Chloe a "full service" with "many present" and buried her in "a fine casket." They engaged the Tuthill brothers of Jamesport, the leading undertakers in the area. They brought in Rev. Robert Weeks, the minister in the Episcopal church in Greenport, to which Caleb shifted his allegiance after the expulsion of him and his brother Isaiah from the Northville Church due to their seditious actions in the 1860s and 1870s. Caleb also hired "Professor [Arthur M.] Tyte," Riverhead's leading musician, to provide music for the service.[76] They gave Chloe a nice gravestone, similar to many others in the cemetery, and buried her in their own cemetery plot, not in the Potters Field.

All of these actions are even more remarkable as Caleb Hallock, unlike his cousins in the Homestead, opposed abolition, did not vote for Lincoln, thought fighting a war to free slaves a terrible idea, and remained against the efforts of the Freedman's Bureau to help the former slaves after the war. He was a virulent racist. When one of his barns burned down in 1885, without evidence he blamed it on "young niggers fooling with matches."[77] And yet this same family obviously showed great affection for Chloe, a former slave girl.

The Great Migration

By 1900, immigrants from Poland and elsewhere in Eastern Europe filled many of the farm labor positions, but there were a handful of Blacks in the community, now all from Virginia, including a 23-year-old young man and a 28-year-old woman on the farm of John Morse Hallock, next door to the east of the Homestead.

Then, starting in the relatively prosperous 1920s, an influx of African American farm workers arrived on Sound Avenue—a tiny tributary of the Great Migration. Almost all came from Virginia, mostly from a small area centered on Cumberland, Fluvanna, and Powhatan counties. The number of African Americans in the town of Riverhead grew from only eight in 1920 to 93 in 1930, or about 15 percent of the total population. Most of these were listed as living in "rear" or "tenant" houses on area farms.

Prosperity and Modernity

At the beginning of 1864, Sammy Tuthill wrote inside the cover of his new journal: "By Industry we thrive / Economy is wealth tis said & some have found it out." He attributed this quote to Sarah Luce, the young daughter of a neighboring farmer. This may sum up the worldview of Sound Avenue farmers of the time, with their focus on prosperity and economic success. They were not alone; the whole East End experienced a remarkable period of success, as the *Brooklyn Daily Eagle* observed in 1908: "There is hardly a farmer down that way that has not his farm paid for and a good big bank account and money on bond and mortgage. They have made money out of potatoes, cauliflower, asparagus, cabbage and cabbage seed and a few other crops of lesser importance. As an evidence of the thrift of the inhabitants, the Riverhead Savings Bank has considerably over $5,000,000 on deposit [about $160 million today], and the Southold Savings Bank is only a very little below it."[78]

One surprising way that Sound Avenue farmers demonstrated their prosperity—besides building large, handsome homes—was the color they painted barns. In many parts of the country red was the choice color for barns because iron oxide (otherwise known as rust) was the least expensive pigment. However, most Sound Avenue barns were painted white, gray, green, or some other color. The author's great-grandfather, Herbert Wells, a brother of Emilie Hallock, always painted his barns and outbuildings a rich cream because he "didn't want to look cheap."

With this new prosperity came connections to the modern world. Some of the connections were technological—the railroad, the telephone, the automobile, and finally electricity. These connections helped break the old ways of thinking and brought a sense of modernity, as demonstrated in the designs for the various new churches and schools, in the movement to start an academy, and in the much-expanded travel horizons for the Hallocks and their neighbors. No longer an isolated, backward-looking community of the early 19th century, the people of Sound Avenue now looked forward to a prosperous future, although still retaining much of their conservative ethos.

Chapter 9

Love, Courtship, and Marriage on Sound Avenue

Today is Christmas. We got up quite early this morning. Pa and Leslie moved the cook stove out in the washhouse. I suppose it has been the most eventful day of my life. At seven o'clock in the evening I was married.

—Henrietta Terry

Love in the Sound Avenue Community

Contrary to popular assumption, the Puritans always believed in romance as the basis for marriage, even in the 17th century when they were hanging witches. Parents did not arrange marriages for their offspring. What is striking about love and courtship in the Sound Avenue community is how free it appears to have been. Parents expected teenagers and young adults to develop romantic relationships on their own. Young people met in school, in church, or at social functions.

Even in the 17th century, Puritans were not puritanical in the modern, everyday sense of the term. They considered sex an important part of marriage and talked about it quite openly. They were also generally quite successful in confining sex to the marriage bed. Rates of illegitimacy and of children born substantially less than nine months after marriage remained remarkably lower in Puritan New England than in most other parts of colonial America.[1]

These unwritten social mores—the rules and boundaries of courtship—continued to be so strong that there seems to have been surprisingly little need for supervision of the actual dating. In the Sound Avenue environment, children, even young adults, were seldom out of sight. Moreover, expectations to find a proper partner were well established. The author's search through genealogical records, comparisons of birth and marriage dates, cemetery records, local diaries, and even the scandal-laden yellow press failed to uncover a single incidence in the Sound Avenue community of a child born out of wedlock or unseemly soon after a wedding. While it is likely these things would stay hidden, it seems impossible they could be that well-hidden!

Oldest Account of a Wedding on Sound Avenue

The first account we have of a wedding in the Hallocks's community comes from the diary of Ruth Jessup (1786–1868), who became the second wife of Herman's cousin Noah Youngs (1788–1853) in 1825: "This day I have voluntarily renounced the name of Jessup, and in its stead taken that of Youngs. [I] have quit the bleak and barren shores of maiden land, launched on the sea of uncertainty for the continent of matrimony."[2] Ruth turned 39 later that month, and this was her first marriage. Noah was 37. His first wife, Keziah Reeve, died just two years earlier, leaving him with two young children that needed a mother. Unfortunately, Ruth's marriage led to heartbreak. On October 13 the next year she wrote, "This day the Lord has given a son to my bosom a lovely little babe . . . I fear that its life is not to be long." Two days later she wrote again, "This day I am called upon to resign my son."

Courtship on Sound Avenue

Surprisingly few firsthand accounts of courtship exist. Halsey Hallock's diary for 1856 provides a few brief glimpses of his brother Daniel's courtship of Amanda Wells, the younger sister of Laura Wells, who married his older brother Charles two years earlier. Halsey never mentions Amanda by name but speaks casually of "Daniel and his girl." They apparently spent a lot of time out alone. They went to many meetings together, especially temperance meetings; they stopped at the home of an uncle in Jamesport during a family visit. The descriptions are all very matter of fact, just an everyday normal event. Daniel and Amanda married two years later.

Seventy years later, Halsey said this about his older brother's marriage: "Prior to the Civil War Daniel began to notice that Deacon Wells [father of his brother Charles's wife] had another daughter, Amanda, of the proper age and I can imagine that Bro. Daniel saw that she was fair to look upon and of sound physique and of royal good stock and as most natural led to a tie-up and union of forces."[3] The references to "sound physique" and "royal good stock" are striking. It makes one wonder about the criteria for a life partner, and how much of that involved romance. At least Halsey mentioned that she was "fair to look upon."

Halsey's teenage friend Tommy Pope was also something of a lady's man. In his second letter to Halsey, he mentioned always being attracted to red-haired girls and asked about "his old sweetheart" Addie Hallock. He asked again in subsequent letters about what happened to her. Then in a latter letter, he added, "I used to think there was no other girl on earth that was quite as good as her" and cryptically wondered if it was his fault that they did not get married—despite the fact that Addie was only 14 at the time. This is another example of the casual relationship scene in the community at the time.[4]

Startlingly, as we have seen, Halsey's diary does not contain a single mention of his own future wife, Marietta Terry, even though it covers the period when he met her at the Franklinville Academy and began their four-year courtship. However, from his account many years later, we know that the courtship started with him asking if he could escort her back to her boarding house after school and continued by mail for a couple of years until finally he and a friend took a Fourth of July carriage ride to Southold to visit their sweethearts.[5]

Halsey's cousin Sammy Tuthill was equally elusive in his diary about his courtship. The entry for November 13, 1866, starts as usual with his farm work—in this case carting and husking corn—and then suddenly announces that "at 7 o'clock pm I was married to Salem Wells youngest daughter Eliza." Salem Wells was Tuthill's next-door neighbor, so he certainly knew Eliza since his boyhood. Nevertheless, even though his diary is quite complete from its beginning in 1863 three years earlier, there is not a single reference to Eliza until he suddenly announces their wedding![6]

Melinda Corwin's diary contains another brief account of a Sound Avenue courtship: Daniel Tuthill's courtship of her 26-year-old daughter, Fanny. She noted for January 20, 1867, that "Daniel Tuthill is in the parlor." Melinda does not record why Tuthill visited, just that he managed to get there all the way from Orient in a blizzard even though the road was not dug out. In February, there is another entry: "Dan Tuthill this evening." By April frequent references appear to "D.T." In June we get this entry: "Stormed all day. D.T. in the parlor. We have an application for our dear Fanny." Finally in December: "Fanny was married this morning at ½ past 8 to D.T. Tuthill. May the good Lord Bless and prosper her and make her useful and happy and also the companion she has chosen."

While this was very much a "parlor courtship," by the 1880s a regular dating scene existed on Sound Avenue. Emilie Hallock's future sister-in-law, 19-year-old Henrietta Terry, one July night in 1883, when her younger brother Leslie did not get home after a church meeting until midnight, commented casually in her diary that "I think he must have went home with some of the girls."

That October an entry from 19-year-old Henrietta mentions that her neighbor Ekford Hallock attended the fair "with a girl I did not know," adding that he and his previous girlfriend Edith "must have dissolved partnership." A month later she notes that Ek and Edith were back together again at the county's bicentennial celebration in Riverhead, adding "so I guess he will carry the day." She was right. They married several years later and spent the rest of their lives on a farm on the corner of Doctor's Path and Sound Avenue, not far from the Terry home.

Another time, Henrietta spotted another friend Herman with a girl named Edith all afternoon, commenting, "I guess that is a made up match." In the fall of 1883, Henrietta's sewing circle helped organize a series of "sociables"—get-togethers with supper included—at member's homes. These undoubtedly provided opportunities for young people to meet, socialize, and pair up.

Henrietta Terry's Courtship and Wedding

By far the best documented Sound Avenue courtship and marriage is Henrietta's own. She started keeping a diary in 1883 as a girl of 18 and concluded in 1884 as a married woman of 20.[7] The small diary in her fine hand traces her courtship, engagement, and marriage to Herbert Wells, one of Emilie Hallock's seven younger brothers.

Herbert, who Henrietta always refers to in the diary as "Hurb," first called on her in July the year before she started her diary. The courtship lasted about a year and a half. Much of it took place in the parlor of her parent's house. Generally, he came by about once a week. Here are the first four entries:

January 14: Hurb came up this evening.

January 21: Hurb came up about five O'clock and staid [*sic*] until past twelve.

January 28: Hurb came up in the evening.

January 30: Hurb came up in the evening and we went to Riverhead. The wagon spring broke as we were turning the corner by George Aldrich's. We went in and got his carriage and went on. The lecturer did not come. Misunderstood the night. We got home about nine o'clock.

By February, she recorded, "We are having splendid evenings now." Sometimes Herbert stayed for the entire evening. Once, when he stayed past one o'clock in the morning, she used mirror writing, her favorite tool when she wanted to keep something secret, to confide the time to her diary.

The other major part of their courtship, including their very first date, consisted of carriage rides to church meetings. (See fig. 9.1 for another example of courtship by carriage ride.) Sometimes these meetings occurred on Sound Avenue in the Northville church or the local schoolhouse. Often they did not go to the closest meeting but rather to ones in Riverhead, Aquebogue, and sometimes far beyond. Occasionally they went from one meeting to another—or no meeting at all. For instance, on March 25 she wrote, "In the evening Hurb and I went down to South road [the Aquebogue church] expecting to go to meetin there but when we got there we changed our minds and went to River Head to the Congregational church." On the way to these meetings and between meetings Herb and Henrietta enjoyed a lot of alone time in the carriage—often an hour or more each way—in winter, snuggled under a warm blanket. Indeed, this seems to have

Figure 9.1. Sherwood Tuthill, son of Sammy Tuthill whose house is in the background, in 1891 courting future wife Nelly Brown. Likely Herbert courted Henrietta in a similar carriage. *Source:* Hallockville Museum Farm. Used with permission.

been the whole point. Henrietta never once comments on the content of any of these meetings, but later that year when she prepared a large hair wreath to enter in the Riverhead County Fair, along with samples of hair from all her relatives and friends, she crafted the central flowers out of hair from the tail of the horse that pulled their carriage to all those meetings. Of course, Henrietta never says exactly what they did on those trips! But clearly they enjoyed a lot of unsupervised alone time—in some ways the equivalent of "parking" after the advent of the automobile. Amazingly, parents felt comfortable letting their sons and daughters spend all that time alone and go unsupervised on social outings, to plays and concerts, and even on excursions across Long Island Sound or to the city.

In May Herbert took her to a convention of the Suffolk County Temperance Society in Southold. Sounds dreary, even if the *Brooklyn Daily Eagle* promised the convention would "be of unusual interest," but it was their first overnight trip together, and at the time such gatherings were considered social events.[8] They stayed with Halsey Hallock's brother

Daniel, then living in Southold, where he manufactured farm equipment. Daniel's wife, Amanda Wells, was Herbert's aunt. Herbert and Henrietta went to the convention the first evening and reported it was poorly attended. The real attraction of the trip came the next day: a leisurely carriage ride out to Orient Point, stopping along the way to visit several old friends. Henrietta called it a "splendid drive." On the way back they "had a chance to see Greenport." They attended the convention again that evening before driving home arriving about eleven o'clock in the evening.

The next day they traveled again—first going down to Peconic Bay, then climbing up a hill (perhaps Sharper's Hill in Jamesport). From there they went to New Suffolk, where Henrietta had never been. On the way home they stopped for supper at the Hallock Homestead with Halsey and Emilie (Herbert's older sister). The roundtrip was over 39 miles—likely seven or eight hours together in the carriage.

Occasionally, Herbert took Henrietta to social events. On April 5 that year, they went to an "Old Folks Concert" performed by a Mattituck group. She did not get home until midnight, so was "dreadful sleepy" the next morning. The concert was part of a movement that began in Boston in the early 1850s under the leadership of Robert "Father" Kemp and remained popular for the rest of the century. As exercises in nostalgia, performers dressed in period costumes, the programs used old-fashioned language, and the songs came from those supposedly sung a century or two earlier. A correspondent in the *Long Island Traveler* claimed to be "very well pleased with everything" at the concert except that there were not enough doughnuts to go around.[9] A flyer for a similar "Old Folks Concert" performed at the Jamesport and Aquebogue Congregational Churches in April 1880 featured "Ye singers . . . arrayed in ye costume of ye Olden Time" and, like the Mattituck concert Henrietta and Herbert attended, doughnuts and apples were served at intermission.

On May 5, Herbert and Henrietta planned to go to a performance of *Uncle Tom's Cabin* in Riverhead—probably presented by a New York–based company, likely in blackface, that also performed in Sag Harbor and Babylon that month—but it rained so hard they stayed home.[10] This performance could have occurred in the recently constructed Vail Music Hall on Peconic Avenue, now a town landmark, or one of the other three halls in downtown Riverhead that hosted such entertainment.[11]

Here are three entries from July:

July 1: It is one year ago tonight since Hurb first asked me for my company. I was expecting other company so could not except [*sic*] of his.

July 8: Hurb come up while it was raining in the afternoon [regular writing]. Stayed until almost two O'clock [mirror writing]. Well do I remember the reason why [regular writing].

July 22: It is one year ago to night that Hurb first come here. We went down to South road church. I little thought then he would be coming a year from that time.

What kept Herbert there so late on July 8? Possibly it was the night they became engaged, which she does not specifically mention in the diary. Soon thereafter, he brought Henrietta a "beautiful bouquet from his mother." A few weeks later he brought her a "'splendid' half bushel of pairs [*sic*]." In September, he brought a "splendid" watermelon and stayed again until two o'clock in the morning.

Three August Excursions

That August, as the courtship heated up, Herbert invited Henrietta on three separate excursions. The first, by boat to New Haven, was delayed for a couple of days by rough weather, but they finally made it. The very next day, even though she woke up feeling sick, she went with Herbert and two other couples for a ride over to the ocean shore at Westhampton Beach. They took their "dinner" (always the noon meal in a farm community) and enjoyed it on the sand. Although Henrietta recorded that there were many others on the beach and in "bathing" when they arrived, she did not say that she and Herbert went in the water. She noted specifically that she sat on the wagon's bench with Herb while he drove over. The trip required three and a half hours each way, with only about two hours on the beach, so the carriage ride seems to be the main event. They made it a real outing by stopping in Riverhead for ice cream on the way home. A week later came the biggest excursion of all, a one-day whirlwind tour of Brooklyn and New York City.

As part of the courtship, Herbert took Henrietta to the Jamesport Camp meeting. This was an annual August week of revival meetings with sermons and singing, but she does not comment on any of those activities. Like many teenagers, she only comments about which of her friends attended, what they wore, and the lack of ice cream! Instead, Herb took her down to the "port" to get ice cream. Somehow, they did not get home until one o'clock in the morning although the camp meeting itself undoubtedly ended hours earlier.

Then we get this intriguing entry: "October 14: Hurb come up about four O'clock we were going up West and then back to meeting but the weather did not permit. In the evening the moon come out and it was beautiful. It served us as a light. We could hardly agree on some points tonight." Sounds like a lover's quarrel. What makes it especially intriguing is that she tore the next two pages out of the diary, something she did several other times when things did not go well.

Making Her Wedding Dress

Exactly when did Herbert pop the question? Henrietta never mentions an engagement or setting the wedding date. But on November 7 this entry suddenly appears: "Went to Mrs. Mosleys to see about hats and went by Brown & Jackson to get me a plum colored silk dress [material]." Brown & Jackson was one of Riverhead's leading general stores. Its new Second Empire building with a mansard roof, erected just the year before, still stands on the corner of East Main Street and Roanoke Avenue, occupied since 1917 by Star Confectionary. The material needed ordering. They went a week later to pick it up but discovered that an exact match to the sample was not available. She sent again for something similar.

The following week, she reported that her friend Carrie had "come up early this morning" and "cut out my silk dress," adding that Carrie and Johnnie (possibly Herbert's brother John Horace Wells) will be standing up with her at the wedding. Henrietta and her mother worked on the dress for the next week, but on November 30, Henrietta reported, "Ma worked on my silk dress all the forenoon. In the afternoon I pulled the bastings. The wide box pleeting looked like a fool. It stood out almost straight. Ma went to work and ripped it all off. We didn't know whether we could get the creeses writ or not." She and her mother went back to work and two days later reported, "It looks real nice now." The final touch—they added some white lace picked up in Riverhead that week (see fig. 9.2).

Figure 9.2. There were no wedding photos, but on April 30 the next year Henrietta had this photo taken of her wearing the plum colored dress in a Riverhead studio. *Source:* Collection of the author.

Preparing for the Wedding

Preparations began to heat up in mid-December:

> December 12, 1883: Ma made one plane cake this fore noon. It was quite good. In the after noon she made another and tried to make it a little better and it all went down heavy. I set down this forenoon and wrote twenty four invitations and come to find out I had written them all on the back of the sheet. I set down and cried I felt so bad.
>
> December 13: Ma made another cake. It is better than the first. I finished writing the invitations.

December 14: Ma made six plain cakes today. I guess they are quite good. Today I have been addressing the envelopes, and sent to Riverhead by Pa and got one doz sheets of paper and six envelopes more because I made a mistake in writing some of the first.

December 20: For a wonder it is pleasant this morning. The snow is five or six inches deep. Ma and I have been making the ribbon cake. I think we had pretty good [luck] and she made five cakes for the perimid cake. In the evening Pa killed eleven roosters and we plucked and Ma dressed them. About five o'clock I went over to Mrs. [Halsey] Benjamin's. They had a bundle they wanted me to bring home. It was a present of two woolen blankets or sheets from Uncle Halsey. They are very nice ones.

December 21: Ma made three more plain cakes two of them I think is real good. Then we made the gray icing for the ribbon cake. In the afternoon I picked all the chicken meat off the bones and fixed it to press.

December 22: I don't think it has snowed at all today. The only day this week it hasn't. Ma washed this forenoon. I cleaned up all around down stairs. Pa has been glewing the parlor chairs. It has been pretty cold, but beautiful sleigh riding. Ma has been icing cake again tonight. She fixed the two cakes for the ends of the table. I am dreadful tired and sleepy tonight.

December 24: It has been unpleasant all day in the forenoon it rained but Pa, Ma and Leslie [her brother] went to River Head. [Leslie] got me two vaces for a present. Ma got a glass pitcher. I made a cake while they were gone then I done the ironing. Leslie has been over to Mrs. Benjamin's after some things. He got some box wood and we were going to fix it into wreaths in the evening.

The Wedding

Sound Avenue weddings in this era seldom took place in the church. Most occurred in the bride's family home. Henrietta's wedding occurred in her parent's front parlor. The ceremony itself was brief—just the requisite vows recited with the minister. Describing a similar parlor wedding a generation later, one of Henrietta's granddaughters, Estelle Evans, said, "It was so short we didn't even have time to cry."

> December 25, 1883: Today is Christmas. We got up quite early this morning. Pa and Leslie moved the cook stove out in the washhouse. I suppose it has been the most eventful day of my life. At seven o'clock in the evening I was married. We set the table before Carrie got here. When she come she fixed the lace for my neck. She brought me a pickle caster. It is very pretty. About five o'clock it commenced to snow & snowed quite hard for about two hours. But all that live within five miles of here come except five. Eighty-five in all got here. Mr. Downs [minister] got here awful late, but when he did come it did not take him long to tie the knot. I didn't mind it as much as I expected I should. I got lots of presents and they are just lovely. I didn't mind the rest half as much as I thought I was going to. I believe they had all gone home by half past one. Grandpa and Grandma staid all night.

Significantly, Henrietta does not mention any Christmas celebrations—they remained Puritans, after all—although they did make some boxwood wreaths. It sounds like a good party, with some guests staying past one o'clock in the morning! What did Henrietta imply when she wrote "I didn't mind the rest half as much as I thought I was going to"? Was she simply referring to the party? Why would she mind that? Or was she referring to her wedding night?

Her entry the following morning starts, "we Did [capitalization original] not get up very early this morning." The word "we" is in small script, uncapitalized, as if inserted at the beginning of the sentence as an afterthought. They did not go on a honeymoon. Instead, she spent the morning washing dishes and helping clean up the house. They had "lots of bisquit cake and every thing else" left over.

The Infare

That evening, Henrietta and Herbert attended the customary infare at his parent's house—the party traditionally held to welcome to new couple back to the groom's family house. We have seen that the Hallocks held a similar party in 1854 when Halsey's brother Charles married Laura Wells. Herbert's brother, "Johnnie" [John Horace Wells], picked them up about five o'clock. Along the way, they stopped and picked up Carrie, his girlfriend. "They made quite a large party. I believe fifty-four set to tables. We had a splendid time." It is unclear how they managed to seat so many in the Wells house, which was not that large. Even more impressive, 16 managed to sleep there that night.

The Serenade

Curiously, Henrietta's diary does not mention the wedding serenade that occurred that evening. We know about this from an entry in Sammy Tuthill's journal: "Jim went eve to Serenade to [Joshua] Minor Wells. Herbert Wells was married last night. Danl Still Terrys daughter. Home at 10 OCl. No cake."[12] James Evans, in his "Nawth Fawk Tawk," calls the serenade "a raucous departure from Puritan decorum." He describes it as a "holdover from truly ancient days, when well-wishers sought to make sure the consummation of a new marriage was free of evil spirits." Elsewhere in the country, this custom was called a shivaree, belling, or horning. The evil spirits part seems unlikely, as the Sound Avenue community showed no evidence of a belief in superstition. Rather, the tradition seems to have been an example of their capability for pure fun. Here is Evans's description: "Serenaders with pots, pans, horns, bells and other noisemakers approached the newlyweds' window in silence. When they judged the young couple would least like to be distracted, they made as much noise as they could. After a good laugh, they might leave, but if they felt especially festive, they might prolong the cacophony until their victims arose and invited them in for some refreshment."[13] Technically, the serenade should have occurred the night before, but weather perhaps delayed the revelers until the infare night. Given the hour, this sounds more like party crashers rather than sleep interruption. The last note in Tuthill's diary entry—"no cake"—is especially interesting. Apparently the serenaders expected refreshments, but the Wells family provided none.

At Tuthill's own wedding 20 years earlier, the serenade was much more raucous, although not unexpected. On his wedding day, after carting and husking corn and picking up a friend at the station, the only bit of wedding preparation he mentions is that in the afternoon they "picked up things ready for Serenading." He and Eliza married that evening at seven o'clock.

He noted the house "well filled" and that after the ceremony: "Every thing went on finely. There was big doings out of doors. Tar barrel burnt, fence torn down, buildings moved &c cider drank, cake eaten & old pork from Mattituc."[14] Quite a party indeed! Sounds like the serenade got a bit out of hand, with fences torn down and buildings moved. Presumably these were small buildings. But at least they had cake, unlike at the serenade for Herbert and Henrietta. The next day Tuthill went back to "muxing around" in the barnyard as if nothing had happened the day before! ("Muxing around" was regional dialect for what we would call "messing around" today.)

Local papers on the East End are full of references to "good old callithumpian serenades" following a wedding or return from a honeymoon.[15] The revelers serenaded the author's own grandparents after they returned from their honeymoon in 1916: "Mr. and Mrs. L. Leland Downs arrived home Sunday evening after ten days of pleasant sight-seeing in Washington. They were promptly serenaded in thorough-going fashion on Monday night by a company of very noisy and very hungry boys."[16]

Henrietta and Herbert Set Up Housekeeping

Herbert and Henrietta lived with her parents for the next nine months. The diary is mostly about the routine, everyday aspects of life. However, she mentions going to Riverhead to have a picture taken of her in her wedding dress—not with Herbert. And she does exchange at least one of her wedding gifts—the pickle caster from her best friend Carrie.

In February Herbert arranged to buy a circa-1820 house and farm from Henrietta's aunt Frances Terry. Completing the transaction and getting the house ready took several more months, but on September 10 she finally reported in her diary: "Today Herbert & I move into our house to make a home of our own for us as long as our lives are spared us." On moving day, they went to Riverhead with four wagons to bring back the furniture they acquired to furnish their new home. A painted bedroom set—the least expensive in the company's catalog—that was part Henrietta and Herbert's furniture purchase is now on display at the Hallockville Museum's Homestead.

After moving in, with a house of her own to take care of, Henrietta stopped keeping a diary except for a brief period many years later. Herbert and Henrietta lived in that house for the next 37 years until she died at age 57. Herbert lived another 15 years.

Although Henrietta's 1884 diary contains cryptic references such as "one month time . . . not yet" disguised in mirror writing, indicating she thought she was already pregnant, apparently that was not the case. At least four pregnancies ended sadly before the birth of her first surviving child, Leslie Terry Wells, in 1892, eight years after her marriage. Daughters Mary Hallock Wells and Ella Estelle Wells followed in 1896 and 1901, respectively.

Chapter 10

Holidays and Entertainment

A gay old time.

—Samuel Tuthill's description of a temperance meeting

In the 18th and early 19th century, the Sound Avenue community celebrated almost none of the holidays we know today. Social life was mostly limited to church meetings and family get-togethers, barn raisings, weddings, and similar community events. Not until the second half of the 19th century do we begin to see at least sporadic references to Thanksgiving and—still later—Christmas. Neither, however, looked much like modern holiday celebrations. We also start to see parties, organized social events, and other evidence that, despite their Puritan heritage, Sound Avenuers knew how to have a good time.

Fourth of July

For much of the 19th century, the only holiday the Sound Avenue community celebrated somewhat regularly was Fourth of July. In his old age, Halsey still remembered his first visit to Greenport as a boy on Independence Day, also General Training Day, with the "awful sound" of the militia standing in a line and firing their guns all at once and the "cannon's terrible roar."[1] On the occasion of their father's hundredth birthday, July 4, 1938, his daughters Bessie and Ella wrote the following:

We were surprised to find that fireworks were used on Fourth of July in his early childhood. He tells of one such occasion when a crowd assembled from all the surrounding countryside to witness the display on John Franklin Hallock's hill near the Sound cliffs [next farm east of the Homestead]. Some of the older boys, to add to the illumination, hoisted a tar barrel up a tall pole on the next hill northwest, and set fire to the barrel causing a brilliant light that was seen for a long distance on land and sea; thus adding to the perturbation in the breast of this small boy.

One of the incidents of the occasion—some of the young ladies whose family arrived with a spanking team and a fine carriage, on their return were obliged to come into the house to rid themselves of grasshoppers and like that had hopped and crawled out of the grass into their skirts quite to the discomposure of the young maidens. The long, full skirts of that era making very efficient insect traps. The stylish equipage of Mr. Dimon [owner of what is today called the Jamesport Manor] was frequently seen on the highways and in all the east end villages, and we doubt if his fashionable daughters did ever again suffer such an irritating experience in all their travels.

On a previous Fourth of July, he remembers going with his family and meeting with others to see fireworks on the high ground southwest of Howard's branch of Mattituck Creek. He was so small he was frightened by the, to him, awe-inspiring exhibition, and took refuge behind his mother's skirts.[2]

On July 4, 1839, Melinda Corwin reported "a great display of fireworks" at the new village of Jamesport, "artillery company fired guns a good many times." She claimed the display "far exceeded anything done in Jamesport before." However, she did not report any repeat shows in subsequent years except for 1855 when July Fourth fell on a Sunday, that Monday she reported "plenty of powder burnt today" and 116 people sitting at tables for a picnic.

When other local diaries mention the Fourth of July, it is generally just a regular workday, although occasional outings and other gatherings occurred. For example, Ella Hallock recalled the holiday in 1916 when they left their horse tied to a tree and took boat rides from Laurel to Riverhead. Stranded by the tide, they did not get back to the horse until midnight.[3]

Christmas

Christmas, Thanksgiving, and other supposedly "traditional" holidays are thought of as always existing, but the Sound Avenue community celebrated none of these at the beginning of the 19th century. Christmas, as known today, is essentially a Victorian invention. New England Puritans strongly opposed the holiday, which they considered a pagan and popish introduction. Massachusetts banned Christmas in 1659: "That whosoever shall be found observing any such day as Christmas or the like, either by for-bearing of labor, feasting, or any other way, upon any such account as aforesaid, every such person so offending shall pay for every such offense five shillings, as a fine to the county"[4] Although Massachusetts repealed the law 22 years later, Christmas remained little celebrated in Puritan New England until the middle decades of the 19th century, and even longer in the conservative towns on the East End of Long Island.

But this began to change after Prince Albert, the husband of Queen Victoria, set up a Christmas tree in Windsor Castle in 1841. Engravings of the scene, widely circulated in magazines on both sides of the Atlantic, quickly led to the adoption of the custom by the more up-to-date citizens of urban areas. Meanwhile, literary figures like Charles Dickens in England and Washington Irving in New York consciously invented Christmas "traditions" to create a respectable middle-class family holiday that could compete with the rather raucous year-end celebrations favored by the lower classes.

References to Christmas remain scarce in East End newspapers through the 1850s, with only an occasional advertisement for cakes and other sweets. The first Christmas event advertised in the Sag Harbor *Corrector* is a "sale of useful and fancy articles" to raise money to help paint the Bridgehampton Presbyterian Church in 1850. The next issue contained a similar advertisement for a Christmas day fair conducted by the ladies of the Sag Harbor Methodist Church with "useful and ornamental articles" offered for sale.[5] For the rest of the decade, although the *Corrector* published an occasional Christmas poem or story and a few holiday advertisements, no reference appears to any local Christmas events or celebrations.

Christmas began to creep into the area during the next two decades. By 1870, the children of the Presbyterian Sabbath School in Sag Harbor held an annual Christmas tree festival with a large tree erected in front of the pulpit. The same issue of the *Sag-Harbor Express* reported that the Presbyterian Sunday School in Bridgehampton enjoyed a Christmas tree in the parsonage, with a table of tempting eatables. Even the Sunday school of the Riverhead Congregational Church had a Christmas tree.[6]

These new "traditions" trickled down to the conservative Sound Avenue farming community even more slowly. Melissa Corwin never mentions Christmas in the diary she faithfully kept from 1837 through 1868 (see winter photo of the Corwin house in fig. 10.1). While other diaries kept by Sound Avenue farmers often note Christmas day, until the late 1870s it remained just a regular workday—a day to chop wood or clean out the hen house—as the following diary entries for December 25 indicate:

1822: "We thrashed." (Diary of Noah Youngs, a cousin of Zachariah Hallock II)

1846: "We went to Zachariah Hallock's." (Zachariah III, brother of Herman Hallock) "Their little boy was sick." (Noah Youngs)

1847: "We covered hen roost and thrashed." (Noah Youngs)

1855: "Christmas. It storms all day. PM old Mr. Hallock comes to see us." (Diary of Halsey Hallock)

Figure 10.1. Melinda and Jabez Corwin, whose diary never mentions Christmas, lived in this typical Sound Avenue farmhouse. Built in 1859. Photo circa 1930. *Source:* Hallockville Museum Farm. Used with permission.

1863: "I went to the pine woods with uncle Caleb C. Wells to measure bounds, got home at noon, PM I and Jane went to Uncle Isaiah [Hallock, cousin of Herman Hallock] they were not home & we went on to Franklinville & to Mattituc to the smith shop then come home, eve I went to Farmers club, at Lecture room." (Diary of Samuel Tuthill)

1867: "Wednesday Christmas we cut wood in woods AM PM carted 2 loads Mr Downs way at 4 ocl I & Eliza went to D W Reeves to wedding of his daughter married to Isaiah Seymore Corwin good many there." (Samuel Tuthill)

1869: "Saturday Christmas I & boy carted 4 loads of manure from horse stable down south for potatoes & load of wood home from woods am pm we cut in woods." (Samuel Tuthill)

1873: "Christmas—Mr Hunt come & threshed rye—cut locust tree in front of old house & in hedge—Sarah was here sewing & finished Eliza's dress eve went to prayer meeting." (Samuel Tuthill)

Christmas became a federal holiday in 1870, but a Christmas tree did not appear on Sound Avenue until 1877 when Sammy Tuthill reported that community members packed the District 11 school on December 24 to see their first one—36 years after Victoria and Albert's tree. However, Tuthill did not report any other holiday celebrations. His diary entry for that year reads, "Christmas. We muxed around home. Holed 2 posts & made some fence by stack yard. pm rigged Lila off riding. I whet saws & did notions." For some reason, Christmas became a popular time to get married, perhaps because it occurred at the end of the outdoor work season. Herman and Arminda Hallock married on Christmas Eve in 1828. Sammy Tuthill's dairy mentions attending a Christmas day wedding in 1867. As we have seen, Emilie's brother Herbert Wells married Henrietta Terry on Christmas day in 1883.

During the last two decades of the century, a few Christmas "traditions" begin to creep into Sammy Tuthill's diary references. He occasionally mentions "keeping Christmas" with family dinners, buying oranges, and even exchanging a present or two. But just as often, as happened in 1888 when he recorded taking hay to a dealer, there is no mention of any Christmas festivities. Not until 1898 does he mention a Christmas tree in a private home, when his son Sherwood put one up for his three-year-old son Rollo. The following year Sammy recorded, "We kept Christmas pretty well" with a "meal of ducks & fowl."

Initially, Christmas arrived on Sound Avenue only as a secular celebration. The church did not observe the day until well into the 20th century, although it did decorate with greens as early as 1884.[7] Really conservative families such as the Hallocks never fully embraced the holiday. No Christmas tree ever graced the Homestead until after it became a museum in the 1980s. Halsey and Emilie's daughter Eula, born in 1871, always remembered that about the only Christmas present she ever received as a child was an orange.[8]

Although a Christmas tree never appeared in the Homestead, Santa visited at least once. According to an article in the *Long Island Traveler*, on Christmas day 1878 Herman and Arminda celebrated their 50th anniversary with a big party. The highlight occurred when a "living, moving, ponderous form enveloped in robes and furs appeared at the door" and "old Santa Claus" distributed gifts to all, supposedly running a bit late on his usual Christmas Eve errands the day before.[9]

All of this began to change early in the 20th century. In 1910, the Sound Avenue column in the *County Review* reported, "The Christmas season will be celebrated here with the usual club and family gatherings." But these celebrations still did not make it to the church, where "in accordance with its custom of many years" the Sound Avenue Sunday School "will not hold any special celebration of the season." Annual "Christmas exercises" or "Christmas entertainments" occurred at the new Union School, but not until 1914 did the church hold a Christmas service, with "sermons by the pastor and special music by the choir"—of course led by Bessie Hallock.

Fast Days and Thanksgivings

Thanksgiving, at least the so-called traditional holiday meal we think of today, came equally late to the Sound Avenue farming community. Of course, Thanksgiving has long roots in this country. In the early 1600s, the Puritan settlers brought with them the practice of declaring occasional days of thanksgiving in response to providential events, generally in the fall. They also followed a parallel practice of annual fast days in the spring. These fast days continued to be observed on Sound Avenue throughout the 19th century. Melinda Corwin recorded attending a fast day at the church in 1844.¹⁰ The local paper noted the annual declaration of a fast day in the church as late as 1913.

The classic Thanksgiving—a big family meal followed by games and entertainment—became well established in New England by the early 19th century, spreading rapidly to other states. Many governors declared annual days of thanksgiving, including New York's in 1817, generally for a Thursday in November or early December. However, the Sound Avenue community did not pay much attention. For instance, in 1849 Noah Youngs noted November 29 as Thanksgiving Day but does not indicate any activity beyond normal farm work.¹¹

The first reference to a Thanksgiving service on Sound Avenue appears in 1855, when 17-year-old Halsey Hallock recorded in his diary for November 29: "This is thanksgiving day & we attend meeting."

Sarah Josepha Hale began her ultimately successful campaign for an annual national Thanksgiving Day in 1837, in editorials in her magazine *Godey's Lady's Book*. Abraham Lincoln declared two in 1863, the first in August following the Union victory at Gettysburg and the second starting the annual tradition of national Thanksgiving in November. That same year, Melinda Corwin, a Sound Avenue neighbor, recorded in her diary: "Roast turkey first time on Thanksgiving at Rosie's [her daughter]. Went to church and heard a " 'political harangue.' " (She was not a fan of Lincoln!) Although she kept a diary from 1832 to 1867, this is the only reference to Thanksgiving.

Sammy Tuthill, in 1863, noted March 19 as the fast day and added that "Priest Haris preached politics & nigger." That same year, presumably on the day that Lincoln proclaimed, Tuthill wrote, "Thanksgiving Day. Went to Pond Quoge [Ponquogue] to the lighthouse & carried Mr. Halleck to Riverhead got home at 1/4 to 8." In 1864 Samuel Tuthill does not mention Thanksgiving, but the next day he "went to George M Terrys to a party. Good time. Home at 1 ocl." In 1865, "Thursday thanksgiving . . . funeral of James Harvey Williamson at our church & buried."

In 1866, Tuthill's journal first mentions turkeys. A few days before Thanksgiving, he carried 14 turkeys, weighing 140 pounds total, and sold them to a Riverhead merchant for $25.20. That year, on Thanksgiving, "We butchered 2 hogs—done at 9 ocl; hung them in the south barn & went over & helped press hay. At 12 past 1 I & Eliza went down to Uncle Daniel C Terrys to Thanksgiving dinner. His children & Elisha & his wife were there. I got home at 12 past 5 ocl meeting at church at 11 ocl but few there." Here are his Thanksgiving entries for the next few years:

[1867:] Took care of things & went to Father Wells & ground axes & went in the house a while come back & went down the woods to cutting firewood it soon begun to rain so we come home & cleaned 40 bushels of oats & put in red houses carted sorgum leaves in hog pen.

[1868:] I & Eliza went over to her folks and ate dinner roast goose pm I come home & rigged off to Riverhead & met Mr. Smith at the cars & come back home brought the mail up, went to work, took care of things went to store for kerosene & got ready & went to wedding to Joseph Wells. . . . Large company. Good table.

[1869:] I took care of things & cut wood in woods am & boy pm i went to JH & J Henry Wells to DC Terrys. Ellen here to dinner roast duck. Cold [weather].

Very few references to Thanksgiving appeared in the local press during most of the 1870s, only reprints of presidential proclamations and similar items. Local diaries stayed equally silent. Most years Sammy Tuthill's diary does not record any special dinners or other celebrations, although he often went to a prayer meeting at the church. However, in 1879 the *Long Island Traveler* (Cutchogue) published a long list of who visited whom for Thanksgiving, indicating that the tradition was seeping into the East End of Long Island but still not the Sound Avenue community.

In 1883, Henrietta Terry recorded in her diary, "Today is Thanksgiving. . . . Pa and Ma went to meeting I did not." She spent the day sewing and doing other normal housework—no mention of a special dinner. Throughout the 1880s, Tuthill's Thanksgiving entries primarily focused on work, although once he mentioned they "had a fowl for dinner" and then spent the afternoon husking corn. Not until 1888 did he record that they "had dinner of turkey" on Thanksgiving Day.

By the 1890s, after the deliberate introduction of the pilgrim story of the "First Thanksgiving" in school lessons, the tradition gradually spread in the community, with local papers frequently reporting church services and who came home for Thanksgiving. However, secular events, such as the "two-mile race between one of our village bicyclists and a running horse for a purse of $20," the *Long Island Traveler* reported in 1894, remained equally likely.

By the early 1900s both the local papers and local diaries frequently mention church services and spending Thanksgiving with families. The Sound Avenue column of the *County Review* listed young people home for the holiday. In 1904, the Riverhead Town Agricultural Society, meeting in the Sound Avenue Hall, debated the best way to celebrate Thanksgiving—gunning or clamming—perhaps the equivalent of today's football games.

Even though a local paper reported six million turkeys shipped nationwide for Thanksgiving in 1905, the bird only made an occasional appearance on local tables. For instance, Mary Downs reported having Thanksgiving dinner in 1915 at her Aunt Lizzie Terry's (Emilie Hallock's sister-in-law). The menu:

> Scalloped potatoes
> Macaroni and cheese
> Cold boiled ham
> Piccalilli and cucumber pickles
> Rusks and butter, tea, sweet potatoes
> Peaches (canned), chocolate layer cake and apples[12]

The rusks served with butter at that dinner are similar to our rolls. Estelle Evans, a grandniece of Emilie Hallock, recalled this about Thanksgiving dinners in the early 1920s:

> We always sat around Grandma Wells's table [Henrietta Terry Wells, Emilie's sister-in-law]. We always had pressed chicken, because that was easy. It could be prepared in advance. We didn't worry much about vegetables, because there was plenty of that in the pressed chicken. It was served with a soup. Grandma Wells made very nice mashed turnips, she knew how to mix them with mashed potatoes to make them real good. We almost always had yellow Jell-O for dessert, because that was light. Later in the evening, we had a little ice cream.

Pressed chicken was a favorite make-ahead dish, often served at picnics and even weddings, as we have seen Henrietta Wells help prepare it for her own wedding in 1883. The dish is basically cut up chicken pieces with some vegetables added to cooked-down stock and gelatin, packed in a mold. After it jelled, it could be sliced and served on lettuce with mayonnaise.[13]

The dessert Jell-O was patented in 1897 and promoted as "America's most famous dessert" after 1902.

A much more traditional Thanksgiving dinner showed up in a turkey supper at the Sound Avenue Hall in 1926. Emilie's niece, Mary Downs, recorded the following to serve 150:

> Fruit cocktail
> Turkey
> Potatoes
> Turnips
> Sweet potatoes
> Gravy
> Butter and rolls
> Pickles
> Fruit salad
> Crackers
> Apple pie
> Ice cream
> Coffee[14]

Although the new Polish immigrants on Sound Avenue brought their own Christmas traditions, Thanksgiving remained something of a mystery to them. Florence Zaweski Gajeski, who grew up just to the west of Hallockville, remembers Thanksgiving as "not a big deal" in the early 1940s. "It was a very busy time for the farm because we may still have had cauliflower, cabbage or sprouts in the field to be harvested. I remember my mother killing a chicken for dinner. . . . We did have turkey later, as I grew older." Similarly, the Trubisz family, who lived just east of the Hallock Homestead, barely celebrated in the early 1950s. "Really do not remember Thanksgiving being an event," recalls Anthony Trubisz. "Guess we were still in our busy season with cauliflower, Brussels sprouts and last of potatoes. Also, being mid-week, the family did not get together as a group—unlike Easter and Christmas which were big events."[15]

Easter

Surviving diaries of the men and women who lived on Sound Avenue do not contain a single reference to Easter for most of the 19th century, either as a special religious day or as a secular celebration. Unlike Christmas, which was often noted if not observed, Easter was not even acknowledged—another part of the Puritan effort to do away with the Anglican high church celebrations. Indeed, 17th-century Puritans in New England considered Easter the "devil's holiday" and studiously ignored it as part of their efforts to eliminate all "popish" rituals and holidays.[16]

A search of local papers reveals that no one celebrated Easter on the East End of Long Island before the Civil War. After the war, notices of Easter services begin to appear, first in Episcopal and Methodist churches and finally in the old-line Presbyterian and Congregational churches descended from the original Puritan tradition.

Easter was not celebrated in the Northville Church until 1881, when the innovation prompted a special mention in the *Long Island Traveler*: "Northville: Easter day was observed here for the first time in the history of the church society, and was termed a new thing by many of our people."[17] The article went on to describe Northville Church members as "dissenters of the fourth or fifth degree from the Apostolic Church of Jesus Christ." This is actually true in that the Northville Church split from the Fanning Church that split from the Aquebogue Church that split from the Jamesport Church, itself a descendant of the Puritan church that split from the Church of England that in turn split from the Catholic church in the time of Henry VIII. The article claimed that "it appears to have been a rule of the early dissenters to get as far away from the church as possible." The *Traveler*'s correspondent added that within his memory "the observation of Easter at this place would have been denounced as idolatrous and a relic of Popery" and "it is encouraging to know that many of the dissenting bodies of Christians are each year approaching nearer to the true church." Most likely the correspondent was Sammy Tuthill, who in the aftermath of the many scandals in the Northville Church flirted with Episcopalianism. That year, he approvingly recorded in his diary that his niece "went to meeting" on Easter Sunday and "there were decorations for Easter, flowers, etc., and Easter sermon."

A few years later, the *Traveler* devoted most of its front page to a lengthy article about the origin and significance of Easter.[18] Toward the end of the century, East End shops advertised Easter bonnets and special Easter neckwear for the men. Churches offered extravagant floral decorations and special music. Newspaper accounts indicate family members coming home for the holiday.

However, the Easter bunny never made an appearance on Sound Avenue and there are no records of Easter egg hunts or similar secular Easter customs in the 19th century. Moreover, the Sound Avenue Church still kept its distance from Easter symbolism. For instance, none of its buildings incorporated a cross or any other Christian symbols, and not until the 1950s, in the author's memory, did the congregation hang a wooden cross on an interior wall.

Parties and Entertainments

Despite their ethos of hard work and their religious pietism, life on Sound Avenue was not all dreary church services, fast days, and temperance meetings. Even the temperance meetings were not exactly dreary—and sometimes could be a "gay old time," as we have seen. Sound Avenue also had a party scene by the second half of the 19th century. It is not clear how many young Halsey attended, but his neighbor and second cousin, Sammy Tuthill, reported numerous parties in his diary.[19] In 1863 Sammy, at that time still single, reported several parties at the home of fellow church trustee George Mitchell Terry—who later got caught up in one of Sound Avenue's most notorious scandals when he ran off with the minister's wife. One of Terry's parties lasted until one o'clock in the morning. The following year, 1864, he attended at least nine parties at seven different homes. Some were surprise parties. One party at "Uncle Isaiah's"—Isaiah Hallock, who lived just west of the Homestead—featured music and dancing. Even if they did not attend, Halsey and his first wife Marietta must have heard the music wafting across the fields.

In subsequent years, Sammy's diary ticks off numerous other parties, many at the home of George Mitchell Terry. In 1866, while still a young bachelor, Sammy attended five parties in January alone. He did not get home until three o'clock in the morning from a party at Uncle Isaiah's that again included music and dancing.

The parties continued after his marriage in 1866. His journal recorded a party neighbor Jabez Corwin's house featuring "Silas with fiddle," and a few months later "music over to Mr. Downs." Winter—slack season for farmers—was the main party season, but occasional parties occurred in the fall too. Tuthill usually recorded having a good time. By 1873, he sponsored his own parties in the "old house," presumably the house of his father-in-law, Salem Wells, who died that year. Each featured dancing. For one party he recorded that a "Nig fiddles." At the same party he reported making $2 in rent—presumably admission payments from guests.

Tuthill's diary is incomplete during later years, but in 1887 he recorded that they "fixed the house for a party" and invited 50 guests, although more came and the party did not break up until two o'clock in the morning. Eugene Hallock, Halsey's second cousin and near Hallockville neighbor, played fiddle at the party. Many years later, former Sound Avenue resident Clarence B. Wardle recalled a fiddler in the community, probably not Eugene, who everyone said was an infidel, the only person who did not go to church.[20]

Surprisingly, none of the parties celebrated birthdays, which were never mentioned in 19th-century diaries. Halsey Hallock's diary does not even mention his own birthdays. Although his Fourth-of-July birthday provided a cause for a double celebration, no record of such an event occurred until his 99th year!

There were lots of other activities. They enjoyed occasional picnics on the shores of Peconic Bay or the Atlantic Ocean and boating trips on local waters. In the winter, sleighing provided a big treat, although not without its dangers. For instance, in 1886, the local paper reported "Miss Nannie Benjamin" (Halsey's niece Nina Benjamin, daughter of his sister Adelia) thrown out of a sleigh, suffering a "severe contusion" of her right shoulder.[21] By the 1880s, community members enjoyed annual strawberry festivals in the Sound Avenue Hall (the original church and later academy), as well as the annual oyster suppers sponsored by the Farmers Club.

Mary Downs, a niece of Emilie and Halsey, kept track of Sound Avenue social gatherings in her record books during the early 1900s. The numerous events included "Y" meetings (Youth Temperance Council), Christian Endeavor suppers with entertainment, "rag sewing" parties at various homes (probably rag rugs), Grange suppers, Home Bureau suppers, Men's Club (Farmers Club), Larkin Club, church dinners, and Sunday school picnics. Included also were numerous family gatherings and even surprise parties for birthdays, which were finally being celebrated on Sound Avenue.[22]

Barn Raisings

Another event that brought everyone together was a barn or house raising. For instance, in 1849 Noah Youngs mentioned in his diary that they went to the house raising for Albert Benjamin.[23] When they raised the new church on the south side of Sound Avenue in August 1859, 500 people attended the event and enjoyed a dinner afterward under a large tent erected in the field just to the west. When Herman Hallock, son of Halsey's brother

Charles, erected a new barn in 1915, photographs show dozens of men enjoying the traditional meal that followed (fig. 10.2).[24] The Homestead Hallocks are likely in that picture.

Excursions

With the coming of the railroad and improved steamboats, excursions became popular. In 1883, Emilie Hallock's brother, Herbert Wells, took Henrietta Terry on two excursions in August alone during their courtship. The first, as we have seen, was a boat trip across Long Island Sound to New Haven, turned into something of a misadventure.[25]

"Hurb" also took her on an excursion to the city on August 22, 1883. She got up early and she and "Hurb" caught a 6:15 a.m. train to Flatbush. From there they went across the Brooklyn Bridge, which opened earlier that year, and took a trolley up to Central Park. They then went back downtown to climb to the top of the Independence Building (118–120 Broadway) and do a little shopping. Before returning to Riverhead they somehow managed to also visit Greenwood Cemetery, a scenic spot in Brooklyn that was also the site of George Washington's 1776 loss in the Battle of Long Island.

Figure 10.2. Communal meal following a barn raising at the Sound Avenue farm of Halsey's nephew Herman W. Hallock in 1915. *Source:* Collection of the author.

Soon after the completion of the Iron Pier in 1900, many local residents, including Bessie and Ella Hallock, went on a day trip to Hartford, Connecticut, on the steamer *Nonowantic* of Port Jefferson, all for the price of $1.[26] Although it was supposed to be a day trip with return the same evening, the engine of the old steamer leaked so badly that passengers watched an oxcart pass them as they proceeded up the Connecticut River. They reached Hartford so late that the passengers only had half an hour on shore with no time to buy any food.

On the return trip, by the time they reached Saybrook at dusk, the tide was too low to clear the notorious bars at the mouth of the Connecticut River, forcing the captain to dock at a coal yard while waiting for the tide to rise. Some of the young men aboard climbed ashore through the coal yard and stole some tomatoes from a market garden to provide their only sustenance. The *Nonowantic* finally made the voyage back across Long Island Sound the following morning, arriving to wagons filled with worried relatives waiting for its passengers. Ella and Bessie were not so lucky. They remembered walking two miles in their long dresses up the dusty road from the pier to the Homestead.[27]

Sound Avenue Grange

The Grange became the main center of social life in the community in the early 20th century. It was officially the Patrons of Husbandry, a fraternal and social organization for farmers with roots in the social activism of the 1860s and 1870s.

The first Grange on Sound Avenue, the Pioneer chapter, appeared in 1873, only the 25th local Grange to be organized in the entire United States. Samuel Terry Hudson, whose house is now the Hallockville Museum's administration building, served as the chief organizer and first master. The Grange accepted men and women as equal members from the beginning, one of the first organizations to do so. Halsey and Emilie Hallock were members. He recorded paying dues of $2.50 in 1874 and 1875. From the beginning, it served as both a professional organization for farmers and a social organization. Halsey recorded in his diary, "May 12, 1874—Went on Grange excursion to N.Y. City, $6 fare."

The local Grange reorganized in 1879 after a few years' lapse but again failed to endure. Indeed, all 12 Granges organized in the 1870s on Long Island soon closed, along with about half in the rest of the state.

After being dormant for three decades, the local chapter revived as Sound Avenue Grange No. 1277 in 1912—the second of 15 new Granges organized on Long Island between 1911 and 1916 in the second wave of Grange creation. New Granges also appeared in Mattituck, Southold, Wading River, and numerous other farming communities as far west as Hicksville, Massapequa, and Medford. The original roll book shows 79 charter members—42 men and 37 women. By 1920, another 105 joined, mostly farmers or housewives but an occasional teacher, "school marm," or "scholar."[28] However, none of the Polish immigrants who had acquired so many Sound Avenue farms became members, nor did any of the Black laborers who came up from the South in the Great Migration.

The Grange claimed three main objectives: education, inspiration, and recreation, but the Sound Avenue chapter seems to have focused on the recreation aspect, although it did occasionally get involved in advocating for or against particular policies.

Like the Masons and other fraternal organizations, the Grange used a blackball box to vote on new members. They put it on the central lectern in the middle of the Grange assembly, then everyone walked by and put either a black or a white marble in the chute. If a proposed member received a single black ball, he or she was not admitted, giving rise to the phrase "to blackball someone."

Also like the Masons, Gangers gradually advanced through the seven degrees of membership. Some officers had colorful, agriculturally linked names (e.g., Pomona, Ceres, and Flora—positions all held by women) after the Roman goddesses of fruits, grains, and flowers. The minutes of a typical meeting on September 25, 1917, report the lecturer's hour "opened by Bro. H.R. Talmage not telling what he didn't know about the raising of cauliflower." The minutes always referred to members as "brother" and "sister." Dues were inexpensive, initially 30¢ per quarter ($7.06 in current buying value).

The original 1916 *Minute Book of the Sound Avenue Grange* provides a good example of the variety of programs: August 1, the "Humorous Program," featuring songs, readings, and a "Burlesque Grange" that "was very funny"; August 15, the annual picnic at the Old Landing Recreation Club on the Long Island Sound beach; September 15, "Ceres Night" (named after the goddess of grain), featuring a judging of baked goods that were later served as refreshments (see fig. 10.3).

Grange meetings were secret, with a password required for admittance by the ceremonial doorkeeper. After the formal meeting, as these programs

Figure 10.3. This 1920s photo of a Sound Avenue Grange meeting in the upstairs room of the Sound Avenue Hall (original 1831 church) shows the officers on the left holding their staffs. Note the men in suits and ties, the central podium, and the wood stove that heated the building until the installation of coal-fired steam system in 1928. *Source:* Hallockville Museum Farm. Used with permission.

illustrate, some form of edification or entertainment always followed. It was the latter, of course, that made the Grange so popular, with programs like "How to Keep a Good Wife Sweet" and "Hot Weather Food and Drinks." In a 1931 article, Olin P. Tuthill explained why his Grange membership was the best investment he made the previous year. Among the "lively programs" he includes a popularity contest, dances, plays, picnics, an old-fashioned spelling bee, and a night playing "42"—often followed by refreshments, always homemade.[29]

In 1945, the entertainment for one meeting consisted of a fashion show where Grange members supposedly wore clothes of a half century earlier. Most years, members put on a play, one of the highlights of the Grange's social season. In 1940 they did *Little Miss Hitch-hiker*, an obscure 1936 comedy by Robert St. Clair. Other highlights included annual Grange picnics in the summer and Grange suppers in the winter.

Despite its emphasis on fun and entertainment, the Sound Avenue Grange still reflected the community's Puritan roots. Game nights featured "42" played with dominoes, never games with cards, which were still considered vaguely sinful. Of course, although some Grange members drank coffee, alcohol of any kind never appeared.

The Great Christian Endeavor Horse Race

Horse racing seems like a far reach from the Puritan beginnings of the Sound Avenue community. But by the end of the 19th century, some of the young men there seemed inordinately fond of fast horses. In 1899, they organized a real horse race at the oval track of Suffolk County Fair Grounds in Riverhead, with seven entries, all from Sound Avenue. There was even a prize purse of $50.

Most of the young men involved were part of the Christian Endeavor Society connected to the Sound Avenue Church, and thus they were friends and acquaintances of the Hallocks. John M. Hallock, the ringleader, lived next-door to the east, the son of Sunday school teacher "Aunt" Frances and John Hallock; William McDermott lived just three doors to the west; and Charles S. Wells was their son-in-law.

The *Brooklyn Daily Eagle* had a field day with the story, running a series of three articles about the race "planned by sport loving young . . . Christian Endeavorers." The *Eagle* claimed that the six young men recently bought fast horses and regularly raced them up and down Sound Avenue in informal heats, despite the strong opposition of their minister, Rev. M. H. Fishburn, who preached several sermons against the practice.[30] The *Eagle* noted that the race was "Much to the astonishment of the church-going people [of Northville]."

Another New York paper claimed that some of the so-called trotters were actually "plough horses" and thus forgiven if they violated the trotting rules. The article describes Northville as a farming community and "as about as lively a place as one could find," saying the race grew out of a friendly challenge between the boys of the Christian Endeavor after the "Luce boys" appeared on Sound Avenue with their plough horses hitched to sulkies. Soon others followed suit, with "Charley Wells" (the Hallock's son-in-law) turning his farm horse into a black gelding named Major and Johnny Hallock (their cousin and next-door neighbor) turning out Alice B. and Edson Young, who lived about two miles down the road, turning his "old market nag" into a trotter named "Daisy B." Amazingly, she came in fourth in the actual race![31]

According to the *Eagle*, "all of Northville" and "a good part of Riverhead" attended the race. The Christian Endeavor girls sported their badges and "gave Johnny Hallock's black mare Alice B the handkerchief salute for winning first money in three straight heats." McDermott's black mare Olba D. came in second, and son-in-law Charles Wells's black gelding, Major, came in second to last.[32]

Whether these were real racehorses or just old plow mares is hard to tell. At any rate, the Sound Avenue men apparently knew how to have some fun! Both John M. Hallock and his neighbor to the east, Eugene Hallock, developed a taste for fine horses. He laid out a half-mile track on his farm in 1910 and joined the new Riverhead Driving Club in 1912. Even Halsey Hallock himself displayed a fondness for fast horses. According to his granddaughter Lois Young, he "loved to race his horses home from church—until [the family] finally told him it was unseemly behavior for a deacon."[33]

Chapter 11

What Did the Hallocks Eat?

> O yes, those nice fat slices of sausages, I mean mother's sausages, not the kind the meat shop hands out.
>
> —Halsey Hallock

What did the Hallocks eat? The answer to this question depends on the period. However, the family's diet was always part of the self-sufficient and sustainable way of living practiced on most pre-20th-century farms, with the preponderance of their food coming from their fields and gardens or the cows, pigs, and chickens in the barnyard. Although by the late 19th century store-bought luxuries and specialty items began to show up in recipes and on the table, the farm still provided vast majority of the grains, meat, dairy products, eggs, and vegetables that constituted the bulk of the diet.

Many insights about the foodways of the Hallock family are tucked into diaries, account books, and surviving childhood recollections. Estelle Evans, a grandniece of Halsey and Emilie, compiled much of this material into a remarkable cookbook, *Receipts and Reminiscenses of the Hallock Family and Friends*.[1] "Receipts" is an old-fashioned term for "recipe." Evans collected old recipes from the extended Hallock family and their community, editing where necessary to make them comprehensible. She also included information about the sources of each recipe, often naming a person, and as the title implies, providing their "reminiscenses," a term used by the Hallocks but less common today.

Capt. Zachariah and Hannah's Table

In Capt. Zachariah's lifetime (1748–1820), virtually everything the family ate grew on the farm. The only purchased consumables: a small number of semi-luxury items like tea, sugar, molasses, spices, and rum, as shown in his account at James Fanning's store in Aquebogue from 1795 to 1805.[2] The only additional purchased edible that shows up in the inventory after his death in 1820—salt.

Scattered throughout the inventory are clues to what appeared on the family's table. He grew corn, rye, wheat, and oats, as well as a few potatoes. Since the tidal mill in Mattituck was not built until the year he died, he carted the wheat and rye to one of the mills in Riverhead to be ground into flour. He or Hannah made cheese, as indicated by the cheese press listed in the weaving shop. The inventory lists 14 sheep, 9 lambs, 5 pigs, and 7 piglets, as well as a few geese, some "fowls," and, surprisingly, three turkeys. The inventory also included a barrel of beans, a cask of buckwheat, two hams, and a bushel of corn in the west chamber.

Throughout the inventory are indications that they frequently enjoyed seafood on the table—an eel spear and a clam rake in the shoemaker's shop, along with some corks for a seine and a quarter interest in a 12-rod (200 feet) seine. No evidence exists of Zachariah hunting. No gun, ammunition, or other equipment appears in the inventory and no references to hunting or guns appear in any family diaries or memoirs.

Corn

Well into the 19th century, with corn as the primary grain grown on the farm, it is not surprising that corn became the most common food on the Hallock family table, usually made into samp. They pounded corn in a mortar and then winnowed it to remove the hulls—a technique the early settlers learned from the Native Americans—then soaked it overnight before cooking several hours with field beans and salt pork to make samp, often also called corn mush or corn porridge and sometimes locally referred to as "Sam porridge."[3]

Halsey recalled that in his childhood a neighbor owned a mortar made out of a log set on end and hollowed, with a pestle attached to a limber pole to allow it to be pounded up and down. When the corn was "sufficiently cracked, not too much," his mother cooked up a huge pot of samp in the open fireplace—enough so that "she could dip out of that pot for several days"—an appetizing meal that "grew better with age," Halsey remembered, even to nine days old "as the little ditty has it."

Samp was a full meal by itself, and if cooked for Saturday's noontime dinner, it could be rewarmed for Sunday dinner, served following the afternoon church service. Cuyler Tuthill, a son of Halsey's Franklinville Academy friend, also fondly recalled the samp of his childhood: "Well seasoned with field beans and a chunk of salt pork, [samp] was a full dinner, satisfying any hungry man."[4]

Samp has nearly dropped out of the culinary lexicon today, but *Receipts and Reminiscenses* offers four different samp porridge recipes, including one from a "Grandma Hallock." All similar, they start with the pounded corn meal that Halsey remembers. Most of the recipes include beans and some combination of pork hocks, corned beef, corned pork "from a barrel in the cellar," or chicken. Potatoes or turnips could be added at the end. The only other flavoring was salt and pepper. According to Grandma Hallock, "When it was properly cooked it was fit food, even for the minister, who sometimes got it warmed over for Monday dinner when he called."[5]

Interestingly, samp porridge is one area where Long Island cuisine diverged from New England. An important staple of the diet early Puritans brought from England was "pease porridge," basically made by boiling dried field peas most of the day. In Massachusetts, this dish gradually evolved into Boston baked beans, as beans replaced peas, and molasses, which was readily available from the production of rum, was added.[6] However, on Long Island, where molasses was not as readily available, the recipe went a different direction. Samp made from corn replaced beans as the basis of the dish, although beans might still be included. However, treatment remained the same—baked on Saturday to provide a cold dinner on Sunday when there was less time to cook and likely eaten on subsequent days, just like in the "Pease Porridge Hot" nursery rhyme.

Corn also made it to the table as Indian pudding—another recipe with deep roots—made with cornmeal, milk, and molasses.[7] Its origins also go far back in New England culinary history, when they substituted corn meal (Indian flour) for wheat flour in that favorite British dish, hasty pudding. The two versions printed in *Receipts and Reminiscenses* include sugar, probably something not in the original recipes as sugar was more of a luxury then. *Receipts and Reminiscenses* quotes a woman who grew up in Peconic in the 1870s fondly remembering coming home from the long service at the church in Southold to a Sunday noon dinner of warmed over "Sam porridge" followed by Indian pudding. "What more could mortals ask for?"[8]

Occasionally they harvested a few ears of field corn still in the milk stage for corn-on-the-cob. John T. Downs, a Sound Avenue neighbor of Halsey Hallock, recalled an old man saying "it hurt his feelings to see the women going into his corn field and breaking off corn for the table" that he raised for his cattle and hogs. Our modern sweet corn did not arrive until the 20th century.

Potatoes

Potatoes came into the local diet late in the 18th century. They appear just once in Capt. Zachariah's account book. By the middle of the 19th century, potatoes were a mainstay of the diet, often eaten three meals a day. The very first line of the first letter Halsey's brother Daniel wrote after joining the army in 1864 mentions the variety of potato he ate for dinner—Peach Blows. He added that a typical dinner of potatoes, "a good piece of roast pork," and bread was "a meal not to be despised."[9] His letters contain several other references to potatoes, including for breakfast, as well as inquiries about how they were growing on Long Island.

By the end of the 19th century, potatoes were the main crop on most eastern Long Island farms, including the Hallocks's. Not surprisingly, *Receipts and Reminiscenses* includes a dozen recipes featuring potatoes—everything from potato pancakes to potato bread and even a dish called red flannel hash, which added chopped beets and cabbage to the usual meat-and-potato hash ingredients, about three-parts potato to one-part meat and smaller quantities of cabbage and beet. In other words, it was mostly potatoes with a little meat for flavoring. Another variant on hash, something one Sound Avenue farmer called "Bobby Squeak," was actually "bubble and squeak"—a Scotch recipe combining leftover meat, cabbage, and potatoes from Sunday's dinner to be served on Monday and Tuesday.[10]

A dinner (always served at noon as the main meal of the Hallocks's day) or supper seldom passed without some form of potatoes on the table. Potatoes often appeared on the breakfast table too. Estelle Evans remembered her grandfather, one of Emilie Hallock's younger brothers, preparing breakfast for himself as a widowed old man. First, he warmed up some potatoes left over from the previous day's dinner and supper. Then he cooked "some grease" in the frying pan, adding flour and then water to make a gravy, which he poured over the leftover potatoes.[11]

Molasses

In Capt. Zachariah's day, sugar was expensive—molasses, cheaper. The small amount of sugar he purchased at the Fanning store was likely used just for sweetening his tea. Molasses was the main sweetener available for his wife Hannah to use in her cooking. Throughout the 19th century, general stores in the area often advertised having "new crop" New Orleans molasses. By the end of the century, the three main stores in Riverhead—Terry and Wells, Nathan Corwin, and David F. Vail—offered as much as 50 barrels of molasses for sale at the curb in front of their buildings every fall. Farm families purchased molasses by the gallon and sometimes by the barrel, not in the small 12-ounce bottles common today.[12]

Not surprisingly, *Receipts and Reminiscenses* contains a number of molasses recipes including four cakes, several cookies, and of course Indian pudding. One of the cookie recipes, given in two versions, comes from Mary Hallock Luce Terry (1837–1925), the mother of Emilie's sister-in-law Henrietta Terry Wells. Although it is hard to know the exact age of some of these recipes, they date to at least the late 19th century. Piano students of Bessie Hallock in the 1920s and 1930s remembered her sister Ella bringing out molasses cookies as a treat after their lessons.[13] Their brother Hal complained about the students eating all of "Ella's 'lasses cookies." School children visiting the Hallockville Museum Farm today still bake cookies from this recipe on the old woodstove in the Homestead kitchen.

Meat

Throughout the 19th century, the Hallocks not only raised all their meat on the farm but also butchered it themselves. Butchering hogs and cattle generally occurred late fall or early winter, with ham and bacon smoked and hung in the attic and pork salted down in a barrel or, toward the end of the century, canned. An account of the Hudson farm about a half mile to the east in the early 19th century indicates that "for the winter supply of meat" they typically killed three or four large hogs, one "beef," and three or four sheep.[14] Probably the Hallocks followed the same pattern. Most farmers also made their own sausage. Ella Hallock's friend Hattie Aldrich recalled "an old man [who] said that it tasted so good that he wished he had a throat a mile long and he could taste it all the way down."[15] Fresh meat was a rare treat, only available at butchering time.

Halsey recalled that "pork, corn and rye were [his ancestor's] main dependence for a cold winter diet." Halsey described the pig as "the most productive of all animals" and its meat as "delicious" and "pure gold." When explaining how his great-grandfather, Capt. Zachariah, managed to survive the difficult times during and after the Revolutionary War, Halsey claimed that "credit must be given to that much abused animal called the hog—hog and hominy were the main-stay existence foods."[16] Later, writing as a nonagenarian, he remembered most fondly from his childhood: "Those fine slices of home cured ham hot from the stove. Yes, home cured and smoked in the old smokehouse. O yes, those nice fat slices of sausages, I mean mother's sausages, not the kind the meat shop hands out that are of [illegible], well you may call it what you please, but it doesn't come up to mother's not by half a long way."[17]

In those days, a smokehouse was an essential piece of equipment on any farm. Without refrigeration, they couldn't keep fresh meat for long, except in the winter. The smoke treated the meat and kept it from spoiling. Arminda smoked lots of ham, bacon, and sausage in their smokehouse. Smokehouses, which often caught fire, were generally located a safe distance from the main house and barn but close enough that women could carefully tend the fire. The Hallocks's smokehouse is immediately behind the kitchen, next to the chicken coop (see fig. 11.1).

Estelle Evans remembered that in the attic of her grandfather (Herbert Wells, Emilie's brother):

> There were three or four strips of tin nailed onto roof beams in the east end of the attic. Protruding from those beams were heavy iron hooks. When the beef was smoked in the smokehouse Grandpa Wells would take the thin smoked strips and punch a hole through one end of the strip. A piece of binder twine was pulled through the hole and tied together to make a loop. This loop was hung over the hook and the beef hung there all winter.[18]

The only meat regularly served freshly killed was chicken, often old laying hens that required several hours of slow simmering to make them palatable

Figure 11.1. Bessie Hallock's photo of the family smokehouse under a sweet apple tree behind the Homestead. The current smokehouse on the Museum Farm is a reproduction of the original. *Source:* Hallockville Museum Farm. Used with permission.

(see fig. 11.2). Of course, they needed to be plucked and dressed on the farm too. Five days before her Christmas wedding in 1883, Emilie's future sister-in-law Henrietta Terry recorded in her diary that "in the evening Pa killed eleven roosters and we plucked and Ma dressed them." The next day Henrietta recorded that she picked all the meat off the bones to get it ready to make pressed chicken. The recipe begins with reducing the stock left over from boiling the chicken, adding a little gelatin, and combining the coarsely chopped chicken with a little salt, pepper, celery salt, and onion juice. This was pressed into bread tins, chilled, and later sliced for serving.[19]

Although turkeys appear in Capt. Zachariah's inventory, they remained uncommon. Even after the ritual of family Thanksgiving dinners gradually developed in the second half of the 19th century, turkeys rarely appeared on the menu. In 1863, Hallock neighbor Melinda Corwin recorded in her

Figure 11.2. Halsey Hallock feeding his chickens. Bessie Hallock photo, 1913. *Source:* Hallockville Museum Farm. Used with permission.

diary that she experienced her first roast turkey at a Thanksgiving dinner at her daughter Rosie's house.[20] However, this was possibly her only Thanksgiving turkey. Other local diary entries seldom mention turkey. Instead, Thanksgiving dinners—when they occurred at all—generally featured ham, duck, or some other meat.

Seafood

Given that the North Fork is virtually surrounded by water, it is not surprising that seafood played an important part in the local diet. Clams were abundant in the waters of Peconic Bay. Halsey, in his diary in the 1850s, mentioned going clamming several times a year. Tommy Pope, the 13-year-old orphan who came to live with Herman and Arminda in 1854, recalled 40 years later "the clam stews we used to have at home, and I have never had any since that tasted so good. Whether it was the cooking or the clams I know not but am inclined to think it was in the cooking."[21]

Receipts and Reminiscenses contains nine recipes for stews, chowders, and fritters, and even a pie made with clams. One of the chowder recipes comes from Herman Hallock, son of Halsey's older brother Charles. Interestingly, it is basically what today we call Manhattan clam chowder—which is made with tomatoes and carrots instead of the milk or cream that characterizes New England clam chowder—not what we call Long Island clam chowder, which is basically a blend of the New England and Manhattan varieties.[22] The cookbook includes a similar recipe from Ada Belle Wells (1866–1917), whose family lived next-door to Emilie Hallock's childhood home.

The cookbook contains two clam stew recipes, including one from Ella Jane Hallock (1872–1936), the daughter of George C. Hallock who lived four doors west of the Homestead. Both are very simple concoctions made of stewed clam juice, minced clams, butter, and rolled crackers for thickening. One version adds milk, making it a little like the New England version of clam chowder but without the potatoes and salt pork.[23]

Other seafood also played an important part in the local diet. Writing in 1906 about his boyhood on Long Island several decades earlier, the Kansas newspaper editor Henry W. Young recalled seafood as always available, including "plenty of oysters, crabs, eels and escallops."[24] The Hallock family diaries in the 1850s, however, mention oysters only as a once-a-year treat and never mention eeling or crabbing, even though both were common in the area.

Fish also constituted an important part of the diet, with a long tradition dating back to the first settlement days. In the early 19th century, farmers organized into companies to catch fish for fertilizer. The main catch, menhaden, was inedible due to its bony nature, but undoubtedly a side catch of blue fish and other local delicacies made their way to the table. Surprisingly, the Hallock diaries do not mention any fishing solely for food.

The Hallocks might have enjoyed a recipe called "custard fish" that comes to us from Florence M. (Downs) Benjamin, a second cousin of Ella and Bessie who grew up a mile to the west. It is basically a custard made from milk and eggs into which they flaked dried codfish.[25]

Vegetables and Fruits

Vegetables mentioned in *Receipts and Reminiscenses* include parsnips, asparagus, beets, and turnips. By the end of the 19th century, asparagus became a locally important commercial crop. The Hallock girls remembered picking asparagus on the farm of their neighbor, Benjamin Laurens Hallock. In the 1880s cauliflower also became an important crop on local farms because the nearness to the ocean moderated the climate, allowing Long Island farmers to grow this crop over a longer season than available to competitors further inland. No tomato recipes appear in *Receipts*. John T. Downs attributed their local introduction to the same Brooklyn-born farmer who brought strawberries in 1854, but they did not become a central feature of the cuisine.

Most of the recipes attributed to the *Practical Cook Book*, published in 1886 by the Young Ladies' Busy Workers Society of Northville, are for fruit desserts.[26] There is a recipe for rhubarb mince pie that includes raisins, molasses, sugar, pounded crackers, and "spice to taste," with everything measured in "coffee cups." The whole recipe only required two lines of text. This recipe indicates the much larger role of store-bought ingredients by the 1880s—the only homegrown ingredient in the pie was the rhubarb.

Wild berries provided a seasonal treat. (Cultivated blueberries and blackberries did not arrive until the 20th century.) Henry W. Young in 1906 wrote about his great-grandfather Rufus Youngs (1748–1828), Capt. Zachariah's brother-in-law:

> Other recreation Rufus had, after the harvest was gathered in, taking an occasional half day off to go blackberrying. In tangled thickets along the cliffs near the Sound this fruit grows wild in great profusion, and the only drawbacks about getting them are torn clothes, scratched fingers and a few wood ticks. Then the native forests which still cover so considerable a portion of the eastern end of the island are in places full of little huckleberry bushes, where the fruit hangs so thick that with a dishpan and a small stick one can gather a bucket full in a few minutes. If more were gathered than could be consumed at one time, the residue was dried in the sun.[27]

Wild berries might end up in a steamed berry pudding, such as this recipe handed down by Emilie's sister-in-law, Henrietta T. Wells:

2 cups flour
1½ cups milk
¼ teaspoon salt
2 teaspoons baking powder
1 cup berries[28]

Everything was mixed together and then poured into a tin pudding mold with a tight cover and steamed for about three-quarters of an hour. Surprisingly, no shortening is involved. Also note the use of the word pudding, part of the area's old English linguistic legacy, basically a synonym for dessert, not at all what we call a pudding today.

The *Practical Cook Book* also contains a recipe for blackberry steamed pudding that involves boiling blackberries with a little sugar and water in a sauce pan, covering that with a crust made of flour, milk, and a little lard.[29] The leavening of "cream of tarter [*sic*]" and baking soda indicates a recipe that dated from before the invention of modern baking powder in the mid-19th century.

Cherries were also a common fruit. In the same diary entry that recorded the birth of Halsey Hallock on July 4, 1838, next-door-neighbor Melinda Corwin mentioned that "cherries were beginning to be ripe," a couple of weeks later than typical in the 21st century. The *Practical Cook Book* contains a simple recipe for cherry pie—just cherries, sugar, and flour.[30] In the 1830s the frugal people of the new settlement of Jamesport (now South Jamesport, which was founded by Arminda Hallock's brother-in-law), planted cherry trees along their streets. Similarly, soon after his second marriage, Halsey planted cherry trees along the roadside in front of the Homestead.

The Hallocks maintained an apple orchard throughout the 19th century. However, Hattie Aldrich, a neighbor, recalled most of the crop as "common apples, not very good"—good enough for cider and drying, not for fresh eating, but presumably good enough for cooking.[31] Bessie specifically labeled the apple tree that appears next to their smokehouse in a few of her photos as a "sweet apple tree" (see fig. 11.1)—presumably to differentiate it from the ordinary apples in their orchard. *Receipts and Reminiscenses* includes a recipe for "Ella May's Sugary Apple Muffins" made by Halsey's niece, Ella May (Benjamin) Hallock (1865–1953), daughter of Halsey's sister Adelia. The Hallock farm had several pear trees. Aldrich remembered the pears as often very good and better than the apples. Some farms also grew a few peaches, trees started by planting pits.[32]

Strawberries

As the 19th century progressed, new fruits and vegetables were introduced. John T. Downs recalled that the first strawberries grown in the area were planted by a farmer who moved from Brooklyn in 1854. Although small, wild strawberries were native to North America and occasionally picked, cultivation did not begin until the early 19th century with the first hybrids and only took off after the introduction of the Wilson strawberry in 1851.[33]

Within a few years, eastern Long Island became a major strawberry growing area. Commercial production started around 1865 among a few of the Hallocks's neighbors. New York and other rapidly growing urban centers on the East Coast, especially Boston, provided strong markets. In her diary for 1883, Emilie Hallock's future sister-in-law, 18-year-old Henrietta Terry, recorded picking strawberries throughout June—generally 30–40 quarts a day, but one day she picked 100 quarts and was quite impressed with herself.[34] It was the only form of farm work she mentioned in her diary! Most of the berries went to market in Riverhead, but toward the end of the season the family canned some of the harvest.

Another neighbor, Sammy Tuthill, mentions going to Jamesport to buy strawberries in 1865 and again in 1869, perhaps as a special treat. By the 1870s, Tuthill family members went to neighboring farms to pick strawberries, but not until 1881 does he grow them himself.[35] The Hallocks grew strawberries only on a small scale, perhaps in the garden, but an occasional crate or two went to a Riverhead merchant in the late 1870s, according to the family diary.

Strawberries soon became the centerpiece of an annual June festival in the Sound Avenue Hall organized by Ladies Mutual Benefit Society of the Northville Congregational Church. Sammy Tuthill recorded one in his diary on May 3, 1885. These festivals continued from the late 19th century through the 1930s. Entertainment followed the meal, including plays, musical numbers, readings, and other examples of local talent. According to Mary (Wells) Downs, a niece of Halsey Hallock, the food secured for one of the of the last festivals in the 1930s included 3 crates of strawberries, 30 quarts of ice cream, 15 pints of cream, 39 packages of rolls, 10 pounds of sugar, 8 pounds of butter, 2 pounds of coffee, 10 devil cakes, and 10 white layer cakes—all this for 155 attendees.[36]

We even have Ella Hallock's recipe in *Receipts and Reminiscenses* for "cream biscuits" to go with the strawberries to make shortcake:

1 quart flour
1 teaspoon salt
2 teaspoons baking powder
3 cups sweet cream[37]

Interestingly, no shortening, lard, or butter is involved—just lots of cream!

Pies and Cakes

Tommy Pope, the 13-year-old orphan who came to live with Herman and Arminda Hallock in 1854, still recalled a half century later the pumpkin pies Arminda made, saying he "never found any pumpkin pies that equaled [hers]" and "in fact it seems to me that she cooked better than anyone else."[38] Pies appeared on the table often—with seasonal fruit such as rhubarb, cherries, or apples—seemingly the most common, everyday desserts. *Receipts and Reminiscenses* contains 11 dessert pie recipes, as well as savory pies such as chicken or clam. One of Emilie's nieces, Mary (Wells) Downs, recalled that they made enough pies to last a week and kept them on the floor in their front parlor—a room otherwise seldom used except for special occasions and ones where children were not allowed. It is not surprising that when Ella sat down to write her poem about a typical day in her life (see chapter 6), she chose a day that featured pumpkin pies.

In a recollection of the Hudson farm, a little to the west, in the early 19th century: "After harvest when the apples were ripe [we] would pick up a basket full, peel, slice and place in a large dripping pan and cover with a crust and bake. This was the family supper"—in essence a classic slump or grunt.[39] Sometimes also called cobblers, with a simple biscuit topping and fruit below, these did not require an oven and could be baked over an open fire.

Receipts and Reminiscenses features 32 cake recipes. Many appear to be for special occasions, not common desserts like the pies. The wedding cake recipe for Halsey and Emilie's daughter Eula used 10 eggs, made 96 pieces, and required three or four hours to bake.[40] One wonders if most of these recipes appeared after the advent of stoves in the mid-19th century. Baking a cake in a woodstove was hard enough, with its uneven and uncertain temperatures, but baking a delicate cake over an open fire is even more difficult. In a sponge cake recipe from Emilie's sister, Ella (Wells) Downs, Emilie's daughter Ella added the notation that "a sponge cake must be handed lightly. In those days one was careful about walking across the floor while baking was being done."[41] Emilie's niece, Mary (Wells) Downs, recorded that in the 20 months after she returned from her brief college experience at Alfred (and before she married), she made 286 cakes including 66 plain and 67 either chocolate or devil.

Lard and Suet

Lard and suet often appear in the old recipes. Lard, fat rendered from a pig, was widely used as shortening in pie crusts, cookies, cakes, or deep frying. Of course, it was made on the farm too, by cooking fatty parts of a pig in an iron pot until rendered or "tried out," as women of Arminda's generation said. The remaining pieces of brittle meat, called cracklings, could be added to bread or fed to the chickens.[42] Emilie's sister Ella (Wells) Downs left us a pie crust recipe that starts by pouring boiling water over the lard and then beating it until creamy before adding flour, salt, and baking powder.[43]

Suet, the hard fat from cattle or sheep, was used like lard for pie crusts or deep frying. One favorite in the author's family was suet pudding, with a recipe from his great-grandmother Henrietta Terry Wells, sister-in-law of Halsey and Emilie. The age of the recipe is belied by the use of molasses as the only sweetener and baking soda rather than baking powder—as well as by the use of the term "pudding." A little cinnamon, cloves, or nutmeg provided flavoring.[44] It was steamed in a tightly covered tin pudding mold—standard equipment in late-19th-century Sound Avenue kitchens. Unlike fine cakes, these puddings could be easily cooked in a pot of water over an open fire in the days before cook stoves appeared in the middle of the 19th century.

Bread

All bread was homemade. Laura Downs (1898–1997), a second cousin of Ella, recalled that her great-grandmother, Laura Terry Downs (1815–1894), made yeast from hops. "Grandma would keep some dough to start the next [batch] and occasionally, by mistake, they would have sour bread."[45] A recent donation to the Hallockville Museum even included a tin container used by Emilie's brother Herbert Wells for steaming stale bread back to life.

Alcoholic Beverages

Before the Hallocks joined the temperance movement in the 1840s and 1850s, alcoholic beverages appeared regularly on their tables. Apple cider—the hard form—was important to Capt. Zachariah, and it would continue to be for his son, Zachariah II. The inventory taken after Capt. Zachariah's death includes several cider barrels, either empty or full, as well as a cider mill outside in the yard. His account book also contains an occasional reference to selling cider. In the 18th and early 19th centuries, hard cider, the beverage of choice for many including John Adams, was considered much safer to drink than water. Rum also shows up in the 1820 inventory, and the Fanning store records indicate that Zachariah often purchased rum there.

Only one recipe appears in *Receipts and Reminiscenses* for an alcoholic beverage. It is Ruth Jessup Youngs's instructions for making beer, dated circa 1830—before the temperance movement took hold in the community. Ruth Jessup Youngs was the second wife of Capt. Zachariah's nephew, Noah Youngs. Her recipe calls for boiling kiln-dried hops and then putting them in a "fresh rum barrel" with hot water, molasses, homemade yeast, and a little cream of tartar, cinnamon, cloves, and ginger. Her instructions: "Let it stand two days without a vent [presumably fermenting], then confine it, and drane [*sic*] it out without a vent. It will keep through the summer."[46]

The author's grandmother, Halsey's niece, recalled that they stored the fresh cider out in the barn where it fermented naturally. According to her recollection, the "menfolk" waited for the sweet nonalcoholic part of the cider to freeze around the outside of the container, leaving the alcohol still liquid in the center. Supposedly the men poured off the alcoholic part and thawed the rest for family consumption. One wonders what the men really did in the barn with that alcohol!

Sarsaparilla

The Hallocks also probably gathered the roots of sassafras—that still grow on the farm—to make into a refreshing beverage similar to noncarbonated root beer. Cuyler B. Tuthill, the son of Halsey's friend George Tuthill, who grew up on a Jamesport farm in the 1860s and 1870s, recalled:

> It was my Father's habit, on a pleasant Summer afternoon, to quit his afternoon farm chores, have an early supper, leaving a sturdy work horse tied nearby with spring seats in a light wagon, then all aboard for the Bay!
>
> Such an event was always enjoyed by all. The shore was a fine sandy place for capers, and all on our own property. The farm, one mile long, stretched to the Peconic Bay shore. Here

we were free to ramble to our hearts content. When father was ready, his call brought us all back soon, for we must reach another wooded marshy spot, for gathering armfuls of sarsaparilla roots. That occupation proved good fun, with the anticipation of our reward when we returned home; here Mother waited with a tub of water for cleansing the roots; then a kettle of boiling water in which they were fully boiled, after which the fine flavored juice, being sweetened, was stored to cool. It was healthful and a very enjoyable beverage, especially in haying times.[47]

What Tuthill referred to as "sarsaparilla" was actually the sassafras tree (*Sassafras albidum*), not sarsaparilla (*Smilax ornata*), a tropical plant that does not grow on Long Island. Sassafras is common and often found in woodland edges and disturbed areas such as the west hedgerow at the Hallockville Museum Farm. In the 19th century, the noncarbonated (and nonfermented) root beer, although made from sassafras, was often called sarsaparilla.

Canning

Although the process of canning fruit and vegetables dates to the early 19th century, only in the last two decades of the century, following the invention of the Mason jar, did home canning became an important part of food preservation on the farm, peaking in the early decades of the 20th century.[48] Home canning was always done in glass jars, not the tin cans used in commercial operations for which the process was named. Virtually everything got canned. In 1922, Elma Downs (a Hallock neighbor and cousin) recorded canning an astonishing 501 jars of produce. In addition to the usual peaches, pears, cherries, and apple sauce, she also canned numerous vegetables such as asparagus, corn, green beans, spinach, peas, and tomatoes and even sweet potatoes, cauliflower, carrots, and kohlrabi. In addition, she canned 23 quarts of fresh pork, 7 of sausage, and 21 of boneless chicken, as well as seafood such as clams, oysters, and scallops.[49]

The canning process was relatively simple but labor-intensive and could easily be a whole-day of work. The main steps were peeling and preparing the fruit, vegetables, or meat; loading it into a jar with sufficient liquid to cover; fastening the lid with a rubber seal; lowering the jars carefully into a large pot of hot water; and boiling for 15 or 20 minutes. Screw-on tops were invented first, but Downs and most of her Sound Avenue neighbors preferred the jars with glass lids clamped against a rubber seal. She liked to place them upside down briefly in a hot water bath—a method not recommended today. The heat expelled air from the jar. Subsequent cooling created a vacuum that pulled the lid against the rubber, making a tight seal. Although in 1921 the Department of Agriculture recommended the use of pressure cookers for canning all meat and non-acidic vegetables, Sound Avenue women apparently mostly ignored that advice.[50]

Seasonal Cooking

On the Hallock farm, cooking relied extensively on seasonal ingredients. Evans organized her cookbook by season, since that was the way they cooked. There was no fresh lettuce in the middle of the winter trucked in from California or fresh grapes from Ecuador.

Early spring meant asparagus and rhubarb. June brought strawberries and the first peas. Cherries came soon afterward. Summer brought wild blackberries and blueberries (or huckleberries). Fishing seemed most common in the spring; clams, easiest to gather in warmer weather. Summer meant lots of fresh vegetables from the garden, corn-on-the cob from the field, and the first new potatoes. Fall brought pumpkins, squash, cauliflower, Brussels sprouts, broccoli, cabbage, various root vegetables, and more potatoes. The new potatoes, cabbage, squash, turnips, carrots, and beets—or some combination thereof—could be all cooked up together with beef brisket to make a "boiled dinner."

Some things were stored for the winter, especially root crops like potatoes, parsnips, turnips, and carrots. The Homestead has an 18th-century root cellar under the original kitchen designed to keep these crops from freezing—originally 10 by 10 feet and accessed by a hatch above. Later, when the Hallocks moved the shoemaker shop to its current location next to the Homestead kitchen, they built a cellar below that could be used to keep milk and dairy cool in the summer and root vegetables from freezing in winter—all conveniently accessible just outside the kitchen door.

Winter was butchering season. Fresh beef and pork were available and could be kept for a while in cold places. It became time to eat all those root vegetables so carefully stored in the fall, and time to use the fruit and vegetables canned in the summer.

Persistence

Many of these foodways persisted into the author's childhood in the 1950s and 1960s. A large home freezer supplemented traditional canning, but still many a day was spent preserving the bounty of summer to carry the family through the rest of the year. Fruit and vegetables were never bought. Milk came from an uncle's cow, never pasteurized. Meat also came mostly from pigs and steers butchered in the family. Eggs came from a flock of chickens in the backyard. The diet was still mostly seasonal. For instance, the family only ate strawberries in June—never purchased from a supermarket. But, in season, the family ate strawberry shortcake as the main course at dinner—always served with traditional biscuits and milk or cream over the fruit, never ice cream.

Potatoes continued to be a mainstay at every dinner. Pasta rarely made an appearance. The only nontraditional dish was an occasional lasagna. Old family recipes, such as suet pudding, appeared frequently, eventually finding their way into Evan's *Receipts and Reminiscenses*. The author's grandmother still baked pies for the family every week, although instead of her original woodstove she now used a kerosene oven in her "backplace." He also remembers her enjoying an occasional can of samp—a taste no longer shared by anyone else in the family. The family and virtually the entire Sound Avenue farming community—at least the Protestant part of the community descended from the old families—also still stuck to their temperance roots and never served alcohol in any form.

Chapter 12

Retirement and Old Age

> Through winter's cold and summer's heat I still am here and hard to beat.
>
> —Halsey Hallock, at his 100th birthday

As the Hallock family members remaining in the Homestead gradually grew older, they stopped updating their house, stopped adopting new farming technologies, and stopped trying to be modern. In 1920 Halsey turned 82, Emilie 73, and their only son Hal was already 51. They never mechanized the farm and never bought a tractor or any other form of motorized farm equipment. They continued with horse-drawn agriculture until about 1925 and then gradually withdrew (see fig. 12.1). Hal kept some sheep and a

Figure 12.1. Halsey W. "Hal" Hallock, about 1925, driving his last load of corn to market. Bessie Hallock photo. *Source:* Hallockville Museum Farm. Used with permission.

few chickens for a while longer but gave that up entirely by the 1930s. His niece, Lois Young, remembered him as "the laziest man I ever saw."

The Hallocks initially rented the farm to the Polish immigrant John Sydlowski, who would later buy and live in the house that is now the Hallockville Museum's visitor center. Later the Hallocks rented to two other Polish immigrant families—the southern half to the Cichanowicz family who lived next-door to their west, and the northern half to the Trubisz family to the east.

Years later, one of Halsey and Emilie's grandnieces, Lillian Hallock Sirrine (1917–1992), told this story about Hal, probably in the late 1920s:

> Cousin Hal didn't have a tractor—so he borrowed [her brother] Harold Hallock's horse. I don't remember how the horse got down to the Hallock place, but I vividly recall how it was brought back to 83 Sound Avenue. Ella driving the car and Hal sitting in the back seat. Plodding slowly behind the car was the horse. Cousin Ella, seeing the owner of the horse said, "Times have changed, horse power towing a horse, 'stead of a horse pulling a wagon."[1]

Sirrine also recalled her experience in the late 1920s taking music lessons from Bessie:

> My mother thought I ought to take piano lessons—who from? None other than Cousin Bessie. As I went up to the door, I didn't need to knock, as Cousin Ella had seen me and opened the door. Her greeting made me glad that I took piano lessons, and her saying, "Saw you coming up the walk and I knew you'd—" She never finished, as Cousin Bessie would say, "Tut, tut, it's time for your lesson. Afterwards you'll have time to do what Cousin Ella was going to say."
>
> The aroma that hit my nostrils made me wish Cousin Bessie hadn't appeared on the scene. After the lesson, out to the room where Cousin Ella was with her father—whom I called Uncle Halsey—and she beckoned me to follow her to the kitchen. She handed me a glass of milk, and on the table was a plate of warm molasses cookies. While I was enjoying everything, Cousin Ella's brother, Cousin Hal, came in—he wasn't one to waste words. Talking to me, Hal said, "Now, don't you go and eat up all of Ella's 'lasses cookies. But you can drink all the sheep milk you

want." That day I didn't finish the glass of milk I'd been served. Cousin Ella insisted, "Hal was only kidding—he's a great kidder." As serious as Cousin Hal spoke, to me he wasn't kidding.

Another of Halsey and Emilie's grandnieces, Marie Wells Remer (1925–2015), a granddaughter of Emilie's brother Herbert, also remembered taking piano lessons in the Homestead in the 1930s:

> As a young girl, going to Uncle Halsey's for piano lessons with Cousin Bessie was really memorable. These first cousins of my mother (Cousin Hal I barely remember), and Uncle Halsey, opened up another world to me. They always seemed so dignified, so full of pleasant visiting and knew so much of family histories. It was intriguing, after the music lesson was over, to sit and listen to the visiting and then, to confirm a date of birth, marriage or death that was being discussed. Cousin Ella would open up the desk on the west side of the sitting room to find the book with the proper information. It seemed to me I had never seen such a wonderful desk with so many pigeon holes holding so much information. [The desk, handmade by Halsey, visible on left in Bessie's photograph in fig. 12.5, is still in that location in the Homestead.]
>
> The music lessons were all business. Cousin Bessie was an exacting and talented teacher. Her metronome was brought out so perfect time would be kept. There were scales, the graded Williams study books. Single selections she ordered were added and at times we played duets. I could bring two pieces of my sheet music. I used "In an Eighteenth Century Drawing Room" and "Little Old Lady." This seemed especially wonderful to me.[2]

Looking back many years later, Irene Wells Hawkins (1903–1998), daughter of Eula and granddaughter of Emilie and Halsey, remembered:

> There have been many happy family parties in the Hallock house. I remember the dining room table drawn out full length in the dining room covered with a white linen tablecloth. Aunt Ella presided at the end of the table dipping the mashed potatoes, turnips, dressing and chicken, goose, lamb or whatever was available at the time and passing bowls of gravy, vegetables,

etc., and entertaining us with a lively conversation at the same time. Then when it seemed impossible to eat another bite, Aunt Ella, Aunt Bessie and Grandma, after clearing the dishes away, brought in Aunt Ella's delicious pumpkin and mince pies which we couldn't resist.[3]

About 1920, the family bought their first car, a Model T Ford. Ella was the only one who learned how to drive, making her responsible for chauffeuring her sister to all of her church functions and meetings. She also appears to have done much of the cooking. More than anything else, Ella mostly took care of others in the family. First, as her mother became increasingly feeble in the 1920s, Ella cared for her. After Emilie died in 1932, Ella cared for her father until his death at 101 in 1939. In the 1950s, brother Hal and sister Bessie required her care. The 1926 *Hallock Genealogy* described Ella as "a very useful and esteemed member of the household of her parents, a brother and sister."[4]

Daughters of the Revolution and WCTU

In 1919 Bessie joined the newly formed North Fork chapter of the Daughters of the Revolution—a competitor organization to the Daughters of the American Revolution, supposedly with stricter criteria for admission.[5] Keenly interested in genealogy, Bessie qualified via two ancestors—Capt. Zachariah Hallock and Rev. Daniel Youngs—neither of whom actually fought in the Revolution and both of whom signed an oath of loyalty to the king during the war!

The local organizer of the North Fork chapter, soon renamed the Yennicott chapter, was Riverhead's leading reformer Mary Stackpole, also the town's leading voice in the women's suffrage movement. Indeed, at least locally, suffrage was also a cause of the Daughters of the Revolution.

Bessie served on the Yennicott chapter's "most important" committee, charged with organizing Loyal Leagues in the schools to further its "Americanization program."[6] This work fit in with the growing nativist movement that swept through older Protestant communities in the wake of World War I, in response to the waves of immigrants who threatened to overwhelm old stock Americans. The Yennicott chapter's primary target for "Americanization" presumably were the children of the wave of Polish immigrants who came to the North Fork in the previous decades.

Like many other women's organizations of the time, Daughters of the Revolution meetings also served as social events, often with organized entertainment.[7] For instance, in 1920 one local paper reported that Bessie played the piano at a meeting of the Yennicott chapter of the Daughters of the Revolution at Quawk's Nest, the elaborate summer home of Mrs. Stuart Hull Moore in Cutchogue (see fig. 12.2).[8]

For many years Bessie also played an active role in the Woman's Christian Temperance Union (WCTU), serving as the local chapter's longtime president. Like the Americanization program of the Daughters of the Revolution, the temperance movement was also in part a reaction to immigration and a way for old stock Americans to differentiate themselves from the hard drinking Irish, Italian, and Eastern Europeans who came later. There is, however, little record of any accomplishments of the local WCTU chapter and it completely ignored Prohibition-era rum-running in the Hallockville neighborhood and elsewhere on the East End. While the group met regularly and often discussed temperance issues, it appears to have functioned more as a social organization.

Figure 12.2. Bessie in the Homestead dining room in 1923 playing her piano, located next to an east window to give her light to read the music. Above the piano is a print of the great composers that still hangs in that spot and the bust of Beethoven. Bessie Hallock photo. *Source:* Hallockville Museum Farm. Used with permission.

Bessie's Brownie Camera

Bessie acquired a Kodak Brownie around 1918 and used it in the following decades to document life on their farm—a way of life she knew was fast disappearing. She had a good eye, as these images attest. She carefully pasted her photos into albums, sometimes with fanciful titles. Today, these are an important archive for the Hallockville Museum Farm. (See figs. 12.3 and 12.4 for examples.)

David Cory, a prolific author of children's books, used some of Bessie's photos to illustrate his 1935 work *Cowbells and Clover: Down on the Farm in Picture and Story*. Corey captioned the cover view—which actually shows Bessie's brother Hal and sister Ella on a wagon load of hay going toward the Homestead Barn—as "The Boys bringing in the hay" (see fig. 12.4). How sexist!

When the *American Agriculturalist*, then a leading farm magazine, asked readers for photos of triplets, displaying their keen sense of humor the Hallocks sent a photograph of their ewe with triplet lambs, noting that it was the "best this family could furnish." Halsey was in his 80s and his three

Figure 12.3. Ella, Georgia, and Eula with Old Nell, 1912. Bessie Hallock photo. *Source:* Hallockville Museum Farm. Used with permission.

Figure 12.4. Bessie's August 1925 photo showing her brother and sister atop the hay wagon by the barn became the cover photo for *Cowbells and Clover* with the caption "The Boys bringing in the hay." *Source:* Hallockville Museum Farm. Used with permission.

children at home remained unmarried. In 1976, Ella Hallock recalled that these lambs "played follow the leader up the steps, over and down the other steps of the horseblock" (photo at https://hallockville.org/hallocksbook/).⁹

A Golden Wedding Celebration

In 1916, Halsey and Emilie celebrated their golden wedding anniversary. Friends and neighbors gathered to honor their "happy conclusion of fifty years of wedded life." The *County Review* chronicled the party in great detail:

> It is not often that a golden wedding is celebrated, but to have that celebration occur as a surprise was the rather unique experience of Deacon D. Halsey Hallock and his wife, Emilie J. Wells Hallock. Wednesday night of last week, a merry company of relatives gathered in their home at Sound Avenue to remind them that the happy conclusion of fifty years of wedded life,

more than a personal incident, was the occasion for gratitude and joy on the part of all who know and honor them.

It was on the morning of November 15, 1866, that the young couple were married, with Simeon O. Benjamin as best man and Adelia J. Hallock Benjamin, sister of the groom, as bridesmaid. And many a hearty laugh was called forth by the recollections of that early morning wedding and the bridal trip to Ohio, on which the best man and bridesmaid accompanied the bride and groom. And it was the bridesmaid of half a century ago, who with the help of her neighbors, planned the surprise celebration of the golden anniversary of the treasured event.

The guests arrived laden with good things to add reality and zest to the celebration, and all enjoyed a bountiful and toothsome repast. The evening was lived over again in the pleasant and vivid recollections that came from many lips. Music appropriate to the occasion on piano, violin and organ, brightened the passing hours, and old songs that had not been heard for many years awakened tender memories of other days. The groom and best man caught the spirit of the occasion and delighted the company with a song that was popular when they were young. But the feature of the evening occurred when Deacon Hallock very simply and yet with feeling, spoke of the wonderful changes and development he had witnessed in the last fifty years, asserting as his conviction that there had never been a more wonderful period since the years that ushered in the dawn of Christianity, and questioning whether this world would ever behold a so momentous period again.[10]

The article also pointed out that golden wedding anniversaries were not that rare in the family. Halsey's parents, his sister Adelia, and his brother Charles also celebrated their golden anniversaries. The article concluded that in "an age gone mad with speed" it was still possible to discover "that there is a sane, balanced, temperate, unhasting otherworldliness that is rewarded with the most fruitful and satisfying inheritance that this world can give."

After Halsey and Emilie celebrated their 63rd wedding anniversary in 1929, Bessie even wrote a letter and sent a photo to the *American Agriculturalist*, which published an article noting that four others in Halsey's family and three in Emilie's celebrated their golden anniversaries, then quoted

Bessie as saying that "none of these couples, and none of any of the rest of the family were ever users of tobacco or alcohol in any form." It further quotes her saying, "They are just ordinary farm folk trying by precept and example through the home and church to inculcate ideals of sobriety and integrity in their fellow men, including their children and grandchildren."[11] (See fig. 12.5.)

All may not have been quite as idyllic as these accounts portray. Many years later, Halsey and Emilie's always-clear-eyed granddaughter, Lois Young, had some rather different recollections of her grandparents:

Figure 12.5. In 1923 Bessie posed her parents by the sitting room window in their favorite rocking chairs. Emilie is reading the *Farm Journal*, a favorite magazine for rural America, and Halsey is reading *The Outlook*, a leading weekly of news and opinion from 1870 to 1935. Halsey made the Winthrop desk partly visible on left out of scrap lumber. It still rests in the same spot in the Homestead. *Source:* Hallockville Museum Farm. Used with permission.

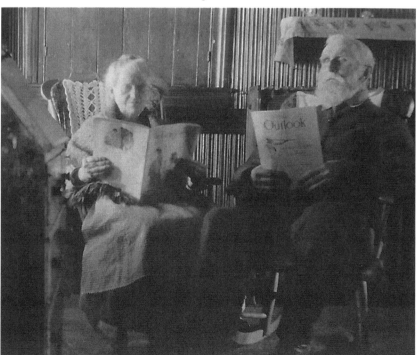

"Grandma always sat in a chair by the window. Grandma had rheumatism so bad [she] had to be dragged around in a chair. Grandpa always sat on the other side. I didn't like to talk to him because he was so deaf. One had to shout in his ear." Lois described her grandmother as rather cross in her old age and recalled her daughters hated combing her hair because it hurt her so much.[12] However, Lois also recalled her grandfather pulling his chair over and sitting next to her grandmother holding hands. "Grandpa was much more sentimental than Grandma."

USS Shenandoah

When the US Navy's pioneer rigid airship, the *USS Shenandoah*, cruised along the shoreline of Long Island Sound in November 1923, Bessie rushed out with her Brownie and took a photo that she sent to the crew of the *Shenandoah*. They sent back a photo taken from the airship showing Hallock Pond and the north end of the farm (see fig. 12.6).

Figure 12.6. Photo that the crew of the *Shenandoah* sent Bessie, showing Carey Camp in the upper right, Hallock Pond just to the left of the gondola, and Hallock farm fields stretching south toward Sound Avenue. *Source:* Hallockville Museum Farm. Used with permission.

Halsey Writes about the Farm

When Halsey was in his late 80s and early 90s and suffering from serious hearing loss and diminishing eyesight, Ella, Bessie, and Hal encouraged him to write down some of his memories.[13] Here, in his own words, are his memories and thoughts about the farm he spent his life tending and preserving:

> Since the later 1700s this place has belonged to families by the name of Hallock and I believe that I am going to be the last as my son is a bachelor and the name has lost out. I can hardly believe that this name will not be here much longer. I would like that somehow a way could be found to have these few acres held in the name of Hallock forever as a mark of esteem and high regard to the many departed families of Hallocks who have long since gone to their eternal home.
>
> This little farm has no equal. It can be said that every prospect pleases replete with opportunity for further development. This farm, which I call home, is one of the oldest farms kept in the Hallock name continuously for nearly 200 years. I take great pleasure in . . . that fact.
>
> I am impelled this morning to a little further expatiate upon the peculiar characteristics of this farm. Directly at the north of the little lake lies a bank of pure sand about 20 feet in height. The south slope is covered with beach grass making a pretty picture from the lake. Then there are two ravines deep and broad, one is naked of verdure and the other covered with wild growth lying upon a bank of clay. Some 60 or 70 feet above the Sound and to the east is, what was formerly a part of the farm, a much greater gully or space filled with solid earth that had a constant spring of fresh water. . . . If the world stands and the artifices of man continue as at present the north shore of this branch of Long Island will be of more value to .the city of N.Y. than it is at the present time. Not for farming, oh no, but for those on pleasure bent.
>
> Perhaps it may be proper to say that I am feeling some pleasure in the fact that I am in possession of the choicest and last bit of the many acres bought by Capt. Zachariah Hallock. I believe that this 60 acres is the very choicest of any of the

whole. It may not be as a farm for cropping but it possesses more possibilities for a pleasant and attractive home for a man of means to build. As I am about to leave it and my children cannot hold it long, I love to think of it as sometime being a gentleman's home I mean just what that word implies.

I have no need to tell you that this is my earthly home. The little place to call mine for a little while to leave as a heritage to my loved ones. I love this pleasant spot both for its antiquity and for its present. If my years could be put back 50 years I would be delighted to use my talents in developing its possibilities—excluding farming altogether, then making of it an Eden for the weary city to rest and recuperate as a summer home rest or a palatial home.

I love to think of what this little spot might become with the use of money, of course, money makes the mare go. This strip of land has a better use than farming. These little oases here and there along the thoroughfare are made more to be sought for a summer rest for city people. . . .

A new day has dawned upon the age-long beauty spot of this region now soon to pass from the name known so long—Hallock. Now would that it might have a little fame and a new name that would honor those who have long since passed away.

I have written this before, but I want to write it once more, ere I pass on there is charm about this place that should make it win in the race for notoriety.

There are few farms so situated as to be used for other purposes than merely raising farm products. I believe farming in the near future looks doubtful. I believe a farm having practical possibilities for beautifying its natural landscape to attract the nature lovers should be used for such purpose.

Many decades after Halsey wrote these words, the creation of the Hallockville Museum Farm and Hallock State Park fulfilled some of his wishes that his farm could be preserved for recreational use and that the Hallock name would endure on the spot. As a nonagenarian, Halsey was surprisingly clear-eyed about the future. The Depression hit the farmers of Sound Avenue hard, with the lack of rainfall for several years compounding the problems caused by low prices. In 1932, the five teachers in the Northville school all accepted voluntary $100 pay cuts "because of farming conditions in the vicinity." The principal, Ada Bergan, stated that the teachers decided to take this action "because of the poor condition in the agricultural region." It was their "small way" of being "of assistance" to the residents of the school district in their time of hardship.

Halsey didn't foresee farming or the way of life he had known as continuing on the North Fork. Even though his family retreated into their past, he envisioned a different Sound Avenue world. Summer residents from the city started showing up in the community during the first decades of the 20th century. Although they didn't build large-scale mansions such as those that popped up on some shorefront areas further east on the North Fork, they did construct numerous small cottages along the shore of Long Island Sound. In many ways, Halsey foresaw his farm and the entire North Fork as the tourist destination that it has become in recent decades.

In 1929, at the age of 91, Halsey wrote a paper for the centennial celebration of the Sound Avenue Church, a gala super attended by 215 persons in the Sound Avenue Hall. He was unable to read the paper himself, leaving that task to his daughter Bessie. Nevertheless, it was still full of his usual wit, humor, and vigorous writing. "One hundred years is a long time," he began. "So says the boy who is looking forward to some great event. But not so does it seem to those who have reached 90 years or more." At another point, he joked that "dear brother Fitch," the minister, was likely to be "making wry faces" because of the length of his talk.[14] He concluded, "Though I am an old man in years, I am young in spirit as you can see." But he couldn't resist adding, "I have never tasted spiritous liquor or used tobacco in any way. Have always worked for prohibition, and if the gainer or loser, judge ye."

Hallock Pond and the Long Island Sound Shore

The Hallocks were fond of their pond—always referring to it simply as the "farm pond"—which sits 71 feet above sea level. It is not spring fed. Instead, it is a "perched pond" sitting well above the water table on a thick layer of impervious clay deposited by the Wisconsin glacier. The clay prevents rainwater from percolating down to the water table far below. Such perched ponds are relatively common on Long Island, with others existing to the east in Mattituck and elsewhere. The pond played an important role on the Hallock family farm—providing water for livestock, ice for the icebox, and a beautiful location for an occasional picnic—as well as a favorite subject for Bessie's photographic eye.

The Hallocks also appreciated the natural beauty of the bluffs, woodland, and beach at the north end of the farm, as the photos attest. In 1912 they even built an observation tower to better take in its beauty.

In 1903 the Boys Club of New York acquired the north end of the former George C. Hallock farm a little west of the Homestead and created Camp William Carey with a mission "to begin to make useful American citizens out of the undisciplined children of foreign immigrants." Most of the immigrants were Italian. About 500 new campers ranging from 8 to 15 years old arrived by bus every other Monday for two-week stays. On quiet days, the Hallocks probably could hear the shouts and laughter of the boys at Carey Camp, as it was generally called. In 1944 the Hallocks sold the north end of their own farm, including most of Hallock Pond, to the camp.

Halsey's Final Years

As Halsey approached his 100th birthday on July 4, 1938, the family began to celebrate his longevity. In an era when average life expectancy ranged from about 40 to 50 years, the last three generations of Hallocks in the Homestead lived to an average age of 87 years, with Halsey making it to 101 and his daughter Ella to 100 years. The family even collected newspaper clippings every time there was a mention of another centenarian anywhere in the country. It was a small collection.

In 1936, the local paper ran an article about his 98th birthday, noting that despite impaired hearing and vision, he was still "remarkably well and is unusually alert, both mentally and physically." He enjoyed a picnic on Moriches Bay a few weeks before and celebrated the day with a family outing at Orient State Park. The article concluded that "along with the years there have developed a dignity and worth of Christian character and a serenity and nobility of spirit."[15]

Halsey always had a sense of humor. Many years later his daughter Ella recalled a conversation between her father and her uncle Addison Wells (Emilie's brother) on the occasion of the latter's 80th birthday in 1929. Uncle Addison said, "It is funny but there aren't many old folks around anymore, in fact I only know of one," to which Halsey, who was then 90 replied, "Well, I don't even know of one."

At age 95, he wrote his niece, Virginia Wines, a birthday greeting with these words:

> Little words of kindness,
> Little deeds of love,
> Make our earth an Eden
> Like to that above.[16]

Like many of the short verses the Hallocks often recited, this is a slightly changed version of the widely published 1845 poem "Little Things" by Julia Abigail Fletcher Carney that Halsey perhaps remembered from his youth.[17]

He cast his 20th and final vote for president in 1936 at 98 years old. Being a good Republican, naturally it went to Alfred Landon. The occasion led him to recall his first vote for president for Abraham Lincoln—"a source of joy ever since." He even recalled the "exciting days" as Lincoln waited for the results. "How the country was racked with anguish from Shore to Shore."[18]

From age 90 on, he surprised and amused his family with a little couplet or verse each birthday. On his 97th birthday, he wrote:

> I have left the pier on my ninety-eight year
> Waving a banner to those in the rear.

At the beginning of his second century, he wrote:

> Through winter's cold and summer's heat
> I am here and hard to beat.

And on July 3, 1939, two days before his 101st birthday:

> I've come to the end of my hundred-first year
> Being thus far on my earthly career.[19]

Halsey's 100th

For Halsey's 100th birthday on July 4th, 1938, the Hallock family went all out—hosting 100 visitors (see fig. 12.7). An article in the local paper dutifully noted that "his family tree stems back through the Hallock, Young and Aldrich families to the first settlers of Southold Town, and through the Halsey family to Thomas Halsey, a first settler of Southampton Town." It

Figure 12.7. Halsey Hallock's 100th birthday, July 4, 1938, featured a cake with 100 candles (hard to see, mostly arranged around the circumference of the cake plate) and 100 guests to celebrate. Bessie Hallock photo. *Source:* Hallockville Museum Farm. Used with permission.

also noted that he lived on a farm bought by his great-grandfather, Zachariah Hallock, in 1780. The paper attributed his long life to his "splendid heredity" and "to his "life long habits of simple living and high thinking," as well as his being an "enthusiastic temperance advocate."

The article noted many of his memories of life. "It is a different world that those memories recall, a world without improved highways, automobiles, radios or electric gadgets, but a world rich in sane living and the things of the spirit: And his joy in recalling it is so real and so abundant that those who listen cannot but share it with him."[20]

Halsey's Death

Even in his 102nd year, Halsey continued to be active. Seventy people attended his 101st birthday on July 4, 1939, including Robert Wells, Herman Hallock, and Georgianna H. Young, ages 93, 82, and 85, respectively. That month, although able to see little, he enjoyed 10 long rides with the family to visit friends old and new. They went to Sag Harbor, Coram, Orient Point, and the dunes in Southampton. Following that ride he wrote, "After many a tack / We're now glad to be back." Then he slipped into an illness of 14 weeks before, as his daughters wrote at the time, on November 13, 1939, "He slipped away to his heavenly home. No more weakness, deafness nor blindness. All infirmities left behind. What a glorious future!" Rev. Wells H. Fitch, known never to even mention the deceased in his funeral sermons, chose this text from Genesis for his remarks: "And thou shalt go to thy fathers in peace; thou shalt be buried in a good old age."

The *Long Island Traveler* said that Halsey was Eastern Suffolk's only centenarian, someone who throughout his "long, full and gracious life . . . was ever considerate, generous and helpful in his relations with his neighbors."[21] The Mattituck *Watchman* described him as "Northville's grand old man . . . a quiet, unassuming man of sterling character who held the respect and esteem of all who knew him."[22] Even the *Brooklyn Daily Eagle* ran a brief article headed "D.H. Hallock, 101, of Pioneer Stock." The article mentioned that he "had been a leader of the choir, a member of the First Grange of Northville and an active member in the Riverhead Town Agricultural Society."[23] Halsey's estate was valued at $20,580 (approximately $500,000 in today's dollars) in real and personal property. He left his farm and most of his personal estate to his three unmarried children, Hal, Bessie, and Ella.

It is amazing to think of the changes that Halsey witnessed during his long life. The railroad didn't arrive on eastern Long Island until he was six, and he probably didn't take his first train ride until he was a teenager. He lived to witness not only the invention of the bicycle, the automobile, and the airplane but also the advent of transatlantic passenger flights. Similarly, the mail service was the fastest means of communication when he was born. The telegraph was not invented until he was six, but by the time he cast that first vote for Lincoln, news of the election results reached him within a day. He also witnessed the invention of the telephone and radio—and if he had attended the 1939 World's Fair, he would have seen the first television. On the farm the only sources of power when he was born were oxen, horses, and human brawn. By the time he died, steam power had come and gone, and the internal combustion engine and electricity provided power for machines, equipment, and domestic conveniences (like indoor plumbing) that were unthinkable a century earlier.

Chapter 13

Last Decades in the Homestead

1939–1979

My house gave out before I did.

—Ella Hallock to Virginia Wines, 1979

In the four decades after the death of Halsey Hallock in 1939, very little had changed in the Hallock Homestead. His three unmarried children Hal, Bessie, and Ella continued to live in the old house, on limited means. They made no significant changes to either the exterior or interior. They purchased no new furniture. They did minimal maintenance. The final exterior painting done in 1940—at a cost of $38 (about $800 today)—gradually faded away.[1] The outbuildings soon fell into decay.

Hal seldom participated in activities outside the Homestead and farm. His name never appeared in the community columns of the local newspaper. He served briefly as an officer of the Village of Sound Avenue in its final days in the late 1920s, but unlike his father, he never took any leadership positions in the church, the Grange, or any other community organization. He had mostly retired from farming by 1925, when still in his 50s, although he kept a few animals for a little longer.

In contrast, sister Bessie led a much more active life, focused mostly on music—both performing and teaching. For over 50 years she served as organist and choir director of the Sound Avenue Church. She often played for special programs, such as the festival she organized in 1948 to celebrate the bicentennial of the 18th-century hymn writer Isaac Watt.[2] She even "presided" at the organ for a few weddings, when the ceremonies started being performed in the church after World War II. Bessie also remained active on numerous church committees and served as the president of the local chapter of the Woman's Christian Temperance Union (WCTU) for 30 years.

Sister Ella appears to have been less involved in things outside the Homestead. She never took any leadership or committee positions in the church, Grange, or WCTU, although she did teach the primary Sunday school class for many years. Ella, as often happened to unmarried youngest daughters in the farm community, spent most of her time taking care of other family members, first her mother, then her father, and then her brother and finally her sister Bessie. As the only one who could drive, she also served as chauffeur for all of them—especially for sister Bessie, who needed a way to get to choir rehearsals, music lessons, and her various activities.

In many ways Bessie and Ella retreated into the past, with a keen interest in history, especially family history. Bessie remained active in the Yennicott chapter of the Daughters of the Revolution as long as her health allowed. She and Ella compiled detailed records of every gravestone in the Jamesport, Aquebogue, and Sound Avenue cemeteries, where most of their ancestors lay buried—recording not only names and dates but also names of parents and other relatives. According to their niece, Lois Young, wherever they went the sisters never missed an opportunity to visit a cemetery—one of their favorite activities. Bessie also wrote two versions of her "Autobiography of an Old House," the first in the 1930s and the second in 1956.[3]

With her deep interest in family history, Bessie prepared this genealogy chart with herself and her siblings in the center (see fig. 13.1). She names all 16 of her great-great-grandparents and 30 out of 32 of her great-great-great-grandparents. But, in the ninth ring out, which included first generation ancestors such as William Hallock, she only managed to fill about half of the 256 spaces. Altogether, she managed to fill in over 275 of her ancestor's names out of a possible 510 over nine generations, and sometimes she managed to go back a few generations further.

In 1949, the Sound Avenue Church honored Bessie for her 50 years of service as organist.[4] For the occasion, she wrote a history of music at the church. However, probably because of the myasthenia gravis that would soon completely take away her ability to speak, a member of the choir read the address. Bessie served as organist for another year, when her illness further weakened her muscles, forcing her to withdraw from church and

Figure 13.1. Genealogy chart prepared by Bessie Hallock. A clearer copy of this image is available at https://hallockville.org/hallocksbook/. *Source:* Collection of the Suffolk County Historical Society.

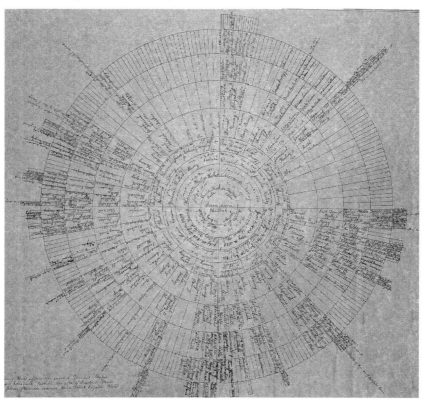

community activities and eventually leaving her only able to communicate by grunting and writing notes.

Paula Corwin, who in 1955 married Lloyd Corwin Jr., a great-grandson of Emilie and Halsey, told this story about visiting the Hallocks:

> "But we always go up there on Sunday afternoons" [Lloyd] explained to his new bride. "They are my father's aunts and uncle."
>
> So, we went. There was always a pattern, a sameness, to it. Everyone had their own chair, grouped around the glowing or unlit parlor stove. Aunt Bessie led the conversations, Uncle

> Hal interjected comments, and Aunt Ella popped up and down to bring visual aids to prove a point, or to give evidence of a correspondence, or to show an interesting stamp from some far-off missionary.
>
> Refreshments were not usually offered. It was of course, right after a traditionally large Sunday dinner, and more food was not necessary. On occasion, oatmeal or sugar cookies would be passed. Aunt Ella always seemed to be more interested in a box of chocolates, which my mother-in-law sometimes brought.[5]

For a while after her diagnosis, Bessie continued to live at home, taken care of by her sister. By 1957, her condition worsened, forcing her to move to a nursing home. During this period, Ella spent much of her time driving back and forth to visit her sister—first in Quogue and later in Greenport. Bessie died at the Westhampton Nursing Home on November 25, 1966, at age 86. Her one-paragraph obituary in the Sound Avenue column of the local paper said that she had been a member of the Sound Avenue Church for 72 years, its organist for 51 years, and president of the local WCTU for 30 years.

Sound Avenue Quilters

After the death of her siblings, Ella became an enthusiastic member of the Sound Avenue Quilters. This group of nine older Sound Avenue women came together in 1965 to hand stitch quilts in the traditional manner. The group met in member's homes, where they set up their quilt frame on the top of four old kitchen chairs provided by Ella Hallock.

According to Estelle Evans, the youngest member, there was no loose gossip about neighbors at the quilting sessions, mostly because of "Cousin" Ella, who was more interested in talking about the news. M. Elma Terry Helms (1903–1986), one of the regulars in the group, offered the following recollections:

> I've read that "quilting bees" are noted for plenty of gossip, but I can say truthfully that we spent a good bit of time learning genealogy. Miss Ella remembered so much of that information

to pass on to us. I, for one, learned about many of my ancestors and how they were related to me. Miss Ella was a great storyteller and she entertained us with wonderful anecdotes she recalled from years back. Those "bees" added up to many, many stitches, and many more happy memories.[6]

Changes in Their World

While the Hallocks quietly lived out their lives in the old Homestead, their Sound Avenue world changed rapidly. After World War II, the pace of urbanization on Long Island accelerated. While this did not directly impact Sound Avenue farmers, raising land values and difficulties of competing in the commodities market gradually forced most of the potato farmers out of business. The remaining growers either consolidated, diversified, or sold to someone in more profitable lines of agriculture such as "agritainment," nursery, sod, or grapes. At the same time, increasing population growth on the North Fork led to much increased traffic on Sound Avenue, making it less desirable to live on the road itself and leading to the abandonment and demolition of many of the old houses that once lined the highway—although new developments located just off of Sound Avenue burgeoned.

As farming declined, descendants of the old families gradually moved away, abandoning many of the old farmhouses. Of the 172 houses that stood along Sound Avenue when the Rural Free Delivery route was established in 1899, only about 40 survived by the start of the 21st century. The church, once the center of the Hallock's community, gradually lost members until forced to merge with the Congregational Church in Jamesport to form First Parish in 1972. First Parish struggled on for another 40 years but continued to shrink until it finally closed the doors and handed over its remaining buildings to the denomination for sale in 2014.

The independent Northville school district lost its autonomy when all of the former local districts in the Town of Riverhead consolidated into a central school district in about 1956. The centralized district closed the four-room building a few years later, supposedly for structural reasons. Meanwhile, the Grange, once the thriving center of social life in the farming community, also gradually faded away. By the 1980s, when it was the last surviving Grange on Long Island, only a few elderly members remained. It ceased to exist in about 1990.

Northville Dock

The first of many threats to Sound Avenue's bucolic splendor occurred in 1956 when Northville Dock Corporation bought up the Long Island Sound frontage of the farm that Emilie Hallock grew up on and several adjacent farms. The company constructed a mile-long pipeline into Long Island Sound and the first two oil storage tanks. By 1986, Northville Dock grew to 21 tanks holding over five million barrels of oil.[7] While the company helped preserve some adjacent farmland and contributed to cultural programs in the town, it also caused several major oil spills.[8]

Fuel Desulfurization

In 1970 a bigger threat emerged at the Northville Dock site in the form of a proposal to rezone 470 acres of farmland along Sound Avenue to construct a $150 million fuel desulphurization plant. Despite assurances from the company that the "installation would not pollute land, air or water" or cause objectionable odors or noise, the proposal met with "unconcealed disbelief" at a community meeting.[9] Nearby residents mobilized to oppose the effort, handing out bumper stickers that read simply "It stinks." At one protest meeting at the Grange Hall, community members hung an oil-stained duck on the front of the lectern, visible only to the audience, not to the speakers from the company. At a Sound Avenue Quilters work session during the controversy about the fuel desulphurization plant, Ella Hallock got up quietly from her seat and walked dramatically around the quilting frame, finally saying, "All I know is that it melts the stockings off your legs."[10] Ultimately, the New York interests withdrew their proposal when it became obvious they would not get approval from the Riverhead town board for the necessary changes in zoning.

Riverhead Harbor Industrial Park

Another threat directly targeted the Hallockville neighborhood. In 1963, Levon Corporation, controlled by George Semerjian of Port Jefferson, purchased 500 acres of farmland and waterfront immediately north of the Hallock Homestead for $1 million.[11] He presented a plan to the Town of Riverhead for a $250 million industrial park and requested that the town rezone the area from agricultural and residential to industrial use, which it quickly did.

The project was to be built around a huge deep-water harbor, hence the name Riverhead Harbor Industrial Park. The artist's rendition showed a half-mile-square harbor surrounded by flat sea-level land covered with dozens of sleek, clean industrial buildings (see fig. 13.2). One ocean-going ship is shown maneuvering in the harbor while another approaches the twin jetties protecting the harbor entrance. Two more large ships are tied up along the shores, immediately behind what is now the Hallockville Museum's old barn. The developers projected completion of the entire project by 1973, with the first berthing facilities to be completed by July 1966.

Levon offered $1,800 to $2,000 per acre for most of the property, depending on whether it included frontage on Long Island Sound. For many of the farm families, this provided a welcome way to pay off mortgages or to exit the potato business, after a series of disastrous years. Ella Hallock, then near 80, was not enthusiastic about selling her historic family farm for this project. However, Irving Downs, a neighbor and second cousin who

Figure 13.2. The developer used this image to promote the Riverhead Harbor Industrial Park proposal that involved dredging a large deep-water harbor in the fields just north of the Hallock Homestead. Sound Avenue is visible in the upper left. *Source:* Collection of the author.

recently retired from farming and wanted to sell, called on "Miss Ella." He argued that, with her property situated right in the middle of the proposed project, if she did not agree to sell her farm, none of the other landowners—most of them farmers who needed the money—would be able to do so. He told Ella that she was "standing in the way of progress" and that this project would be wonderful for the future of Riverhead.[12] In the end, she sold the remaining 39 acres of the farm for $72,426 but retained life rights to live in the Homestead.

The End of the "Sand Mine in Disguise"

Given that most of the property stood 70 to 100 feet above sea level, it was a most unlikely place to build a deep-water harbor. Nevertheless, in 1967 work began on the first of two proposed 550-foot stone jetties, and the company started extracting sand and exporting it to Connecticut—the real reason for the project.[13] Almost immediately, the new jetties caused severe erosion of the cliffs to the east, alarming local property owners and threatening to topple their bluff-top homes into the water. One of the threatened property owners happened to be Otis Pike, the Democratic congressman then representing the East End, who led the opposition to the jetties.

According to Pike, "There has been an almost fraudulent sale of this project to the town board." He charged that "they [Levon] keep calling it an 'industrial park' and it's a sand and gravel operation. That's all it is and that's all it's been. It's much easier to sell a phony industrial park than a real sand operation, so they disguise it. This is exactly what they have done and they've gotten away with it."

For much of the next year, battles raged over approval of permits for the jetties, dredging and a well capable of pumping the 1.5 million gallons of water per day necessary to wash the sand before it could be shipped to Connecticut to build interstate highways. Throughout the battle, Riverhead's town board and its chamber of commerce remained staunch supporters of the project and all the development and jobs it would bring, refusing to concede that it was basically just a big sand mine.[14]

After shutting down the work for a while, the Army Corps of Engineers ultimately approved the permits. The property owners to the east then went to state court. The New York attorney general's office joined the case after determining that homeowners lost "alarming amounts of cliff-top property to the undercutting action of the winter seas." In mid-1971 the court issued an order forcing the developers to tear down the jetties and close off the entrance to the would-be port, effectively ending the project.

Had both the fuel desulfurization project and the Levon projects been completed as planned, Sound Avenue would have had over 1,000 acres of property zoned for heavy industry—right in the middle of some of the town's most beautiful farmland and shorefront.

LILCO's Nuclear Power Plants

In 1973, the defunct sand mining operation sold the entire parcel to the Long Island Lighting Company (LILCO) for approximately $2 million. A year later, after starting construction on its ill-fated Shoreham project, LILCO announced plans for four nuclear power plants on its "Jamesport" property. An article in the *Riverhead News-Review* declared, "Amid concrete bones of Levon Corporation's Jamesport sand mining fiasco, the nuclear age will come to eastern Long Island."[15]

Proponents of nuclear power talked of "electricity too cheap to meter." Executives of the company, who mostly lived on the west end of the island, assumed that the rural people of the North Fork would not be sophisticated enough to mount much of an opposition to such a big and powerful company.

Nevertheless, another huge fight ensued, with battle lines divided in now-familiar ways. On one side were environmentalists and many concerned local citizens; on the other were Riverhead town officials, including supervisor Allen M. Smith, who pressed the familiar argument that the project would create much-needed local jobs and increase the town's tax base.

In January 1975, with Ella approaching 90 and plans proposed for nuclear power plants just north of the Homestead, a local newspaper reporter Ronnie Wacker stopped in to interview her (see fig. 13.3):

> On the property where LILCO plans to build two nuclear power plants lives a reflective lady who has watched the changes on Sound Avenue for 89 years.
>
> "It's saddening in a way," says Ella Hallock of the families, now gone, who were neighbors for 50, and 60 and 70 years. "There's hardly a place along the road that is the same family."
>
> Local history buffs frequently stop by to photograph the farm buildings, the milk shed that used to be a cobbler shop

Figure 13.3. Early in 1975, a reporter for the *Suffolk Times* talked with Ella Hallock about the proposed nuclear power plants and her 210-year-old house. *Suffolk Times*, January 16, 1975. *Source: Times/Review* Newspapers. Used with permission.

across the road, the barn, the four-holer privy, the cut stones that were hauled in sailboats from Connecticut for the footpaths.

Miss Hallock sat awhile with visitors the other day around the large, pot-bellied stove which radiates a circle of warmth in the central room of the house. It has a working furnace but doesn't nearly do the job, she said. Braided rugs took the chill off the linoleum floor and family mementos on the walls recalled generations of Hallocks who have occupied the rooms.

An angular, sprightly woman with sandy grey hair [a wig], Miss Hallock talked of the past with humor and wistfulness.

The youngest of five children, there were four girls and an older brother. She helped with haying, milking the cows, bringing in the corn sheaves, collecting the eggs, all the activities that filled a farm family's life.

She cared for her elderly parents and latter nursed sister Bessie for nine years when a rare ailment, myasthenia gravis, weakened her muscles.

"Sometimes you look back and wonder how you did it all," she mused companionably, "But you know," she said to her visitor, "if it's there to be done, you get the strength somehow to do it."

In recent years she has joined a quilting group in the Northville area, "But," she said with some resignation, "They're dropping off at the top. One woman who is 95 or 96 finds it hard to get to meetings. Another who is 90 isn't coming so often. Frequently we're down to four."

Of these, notes her cousin [Virginia] Wines, "Miss Ella is usually the first to start and the last to quit. She's got lots of enthusiasm."

Which may well be what makes it possible to adjust so gracefully to the changes on Sound Avenue even though they may bring two atomic power plants to the fields where she and her sisters used to run among the daisies and the clover.[16]

In another interview that June, Ella "adopted a philosophical attitude towards the future of Sound Avenue and the family homestead," telling a *New York Times* reporter that she recognized "time does make changes." Ella added, "I love the house and I know we need electricity. So, I am not taking sides either way. I guess I won't have too many years of living next to a nuclear reactor anyway."[17]

A month later, when speaking of the many interviewers and photographers who had visited lately, Ella said, "There is no end to them. Good gracious . . . it's getting to be a joke, every time I turn around. . . . I could live without it, a peaceful life as a peaceful old lady . . . I've been shot at so many times I'll be finished pretty soon."[18]

The controversy over the proposed nuclear plants raged on for five years. Most public figures on the East End eventually opposed the plan, but the Riverhead town board remained strong supporters because of the anticipated tax revenues and job benefits.[19] The anti-nuclear forces got a substantial boost in March 1976 when the Long Island Farm Bureau announced its opposition to LILCO's proposed nuclear plants, citing the danger a leak of radioactivity could threaten local agriculture.[20]

The battle raged on for two more years. Proponents, as the *New York Times* noted in a late 1978 article on the plant, were "strenuously arguing the inevitability of progress and the need for cheap power."[21] Up to that point, the US Nuclear Regulatory Commission (NRC) had never turned down a power company's request for a permit to build a nuclear-powered plant. Not surprisingly, in January 1979, the NRC, gave the company approval for the first of two 1,150-megawatt nuclear plants.

However, opposition, led by the Farm Bureau, continued to grow. By this point, all the other East End towns and the county of Suffolk were united in their opposition to the plant.²² The serious accident that March at the Three Mile Island nuclear power plant near Harrisburg, Pennsylvania, only strengthened the opposition. By coincidence, the movie *The China Syndrome*, about the consequences of such a meltdown, released only three weeks before the accident, helped compound public anxiety.

At the local level, the members of the town board continued to reaffirm their support for the nuclear power plants in Riverhead. Nevertheless, the formal end came the following year, in January 1980, when the state's nuclear siting board, controlled by Governor Carey, denied the application for the two 1,150-megawatt plants.²³

Ella's Years Alone

In her last years in the Homestead, Ella continued to do what she could to take care of the place. Her cousin Virginia Wines often found her edging the walkway to the side door, commenting that whoever lives in that house would need to do the same. Whenever it snowed, she climbed out the second floor back hall window to sweep the drifts off the little flat-roofed connector between the two parts of the house to keep the melting snow from leaking into the sitting room below. She even kept a broom leaning in the corner by the window for just that use. When the daughter of William Hallock, who had lived next door on the site of the museum's Cichanowicz farmhouse, visited from Oklahoma, her husband called Ella "the liveliest Hallock he had ever seen."²⁴

Elma Terry Helms, a Sound Avenue quilter, shared these recollections of visiting her in the Homestead:

> Usually during the holiday season, I would go down to call on Miss Ella; she had received her Christmas cards from near and far. She always had interesting stories to relate concerning each sender, very often amusing. Just sitting near that wonderful parlor stove in a comfortable rocking chair was enough to bring back pleasant memories. . . . After an afternoon visit with Miss Ella, I always came away with a warm and special regard for her. She was my first Sunday School teacher, so from the time I was a little girl, she meant a great deal to me.²⁵

During these years, Ella continued to drive around in her tan Chevy Nova. After so many years of driving, when something went wrong with the car, she almost always identified the problem. A careful driver, she told the author's mother that she always liked it when a traffic light was red—then she knew what she had to do. Fellow quilter Estelle Evans remembered Ella picking her up in the Nova to go to Hattie Aldrich's house, about a mile to the west. "She never got out of second gear! But we didn't say anything about that."[26]

She kept her sense of humor to the end. In 1976, at age 92, she wrote a note to an ailing neighbor Nellie Dunn "to take good care of herself" so there would still be someone around who was older.[27] When Virginia Wines asked her about never having married, Ella responded, "Where there is life, there is hope." Another time, Ella told Wines, "A horse would take you home better than a car." She remained a storyteller, for instance talking about the time her Irish immigrant neighbor, Bridget Gilson (1834–1925), was riding in a wagon with her husband when it upset. According to Ella, Bridget said, "I was glad I didn't have on my split drawers."[28]

Ella moved out of the Homestead in April 1979 because her ancient heating system gave out and the single faucet on her kitchen sink froze. She later told her cousin Virginia Wines, "You know what my problem was? My house gave out before I did." She was in her 95th year and the house was already well over 200 years old.

After Ella moved out, her niece Lois Young was surprised to find the refrigerator in the kitchen pantry not working. She discovered that Ella left it unplugged. Given the temperature in the unheated pantry in the winter, she saw no need to waste electricity by keeping the fridge working!

Ella Arminda Hallock lived for five more years, in a private room at a nursing home in Riverhead. She died there on April 26, 1985, just over a month past her 100th birthday.

Author's Recollections

The author has his own memories of the Hallocks. His grandmother was a first cousin to Bessie, Ella, and Hal. Hence, he always called them Cousin Bessie, Cousin Ella, and Cousin Hal. The "Cousin" title was just part of their name. As a boy in the 1950s, he visited often at the Homestead. The three siblings never invited anyone to a meal, but they always welcomed visitors for good conversation. Bessie and Ella sat in the two chairs on either side of the stove that resided in front of the radiator, both struggling in the winter to keep the sitting room warm. Hal, until his death in 1957 at age 88, sat on a sort of daybed under the two windows on the east wall.

Guests sat in the chairs on either side of the central table. Bessie could not talk because of her illness, so Ella interpreted. Hal remained largely silent, but the conversation was always lively. Ella was also a frequent guest at the Wines house, especially for big holiday meals like Thanksgiving and Easter, but also occasional Sunday after-church dinners.

The author remembers taking his firstborn child, a daughter named Abby, to visit Cousin Ella in 1976 when she was 90. Ella remembered that Abby's parents had ridden across the country on a tandem bicycle and that the birth announcement featured a tandem with an extra seat. In response Ella wrote him a little note afterward: "She'll look so cute upon the seat of a bicycle built for three." Despite all his visits to the Homestead as a boy, teenager, and young man, he never saw the rest of the house until it became a museum.

The author's last recollection of visiting Cousin Ella was about 1983, when she was 98 or 99. By this time, she resided in the nursing home on Harrison Avenue in Riverhead. Her most prized possession—the needlework sampler by her mother showing the family—hung next to her bed (https://hallockville.org/hallocksbook/). As always, the conversation was lively and she shared numerous clippings and quotes from things she was reading.

Other Recollections of Ella

Justine Wells, a Hallockville founder and former Riverhead town historian, wrote the following:

> The tall and slim red-headed young woman was musically talented, playing the violin and singing with a pleasing contralto voice. She had a keen mind and an awareness and memory for genealogy and history, with a willingness to share her interests.
>
> Friendly and hospitable to all, she made newcomers to the community feel welcome. She faced the changes and vicissitudes of life with grace and equanimity that bespoke a well-disciplined character. Highlighting her stories and reminiscences was a marvelous sense of humor that delighted both young and old.
>
> A hardy "pioneer" woman, Miss Ella can be remembered in her 90's, driving her little tan Nova to church or to quilting, shoveling snow from the homestead roof to prevent the inevitable leaks, or up on a chair cleaning the flue of her kitchen chimney.

"She hath done what she could," and what Ella Arminda Hallock did with her life was indeed remarkable![29]

Virginia Wines wrote this about Ella shortly after her death: "Cousin Ella remembered, her sister Bessie remembered, and her father Halsey Hallock remembered. Their memories and their records so willingly shared with visitors preserved a feeling of family, a feeling of community, a sense of history."[30] Estelle Evans, another cousin, recalled, "Whenever it was time to say goodbye, Cousin Ella would stand at the door, or the window if it was cold. That's how I think I'll always remember her—standing in the doorway, waving, and waving goodbye until we were way out of sight."[31]

When still a spry, young 90 years old, Ella recited the following to her cousin Virginia:

> Time which steals our years away
> Shall steal our pleasures too,
> But the memory of the past shall stay
> And half our joys renew.[32]

Chapter 14

Epilogue

Hallockville Museum Farm, Keyspan Project, Hallock State Park

> I would like that somehow a way could be found to have these few acres held in the name of Hallock forever as a mark of esteem and high regard to the many departed families of Hallocks who have long since gone to their eternal home.
>
> —Halsey Hallock

Proposed industrial developments and population growth threatened the very existence of Sound Avenue as the bucolic country road the Hallock family had lived on for so many generations. Riverhead town's first master plan in 1964 anticipated turning Sound Avenue into a four-lane highway. The idea resurfaced in 1973, when a draft of another master plan proposed a four-lane parkway—an idea quickly withdrawn after a barrage of negative comments at the public hearing.

In the 1970s, the nuclear power plants proposed by Long Island Lighting Company (LILCO) put additional pressure on the historic roadway. The company's studies showed that traffic would increase by 6,000 cars per day and that there would be a 20-fold jump at the construction peak. To accommodate this traffic, the company again proposed widening portions of Sound Avenue into a four-lane highway capable of handling 36-ton trucks. Naturally, this incited another firestorm of local opposition. A LILCO land-use consultant claimed that Sound Avenue had "less-than-great scenic value" compared to scenic roads elsewhere—it was "just another road." In response, a *Riverhead News-Review* editorial called the proposal "hogwash," typical of LILCO's haughty attitude that seemed to say "To hell with some of the most beautiful land on Long Island or New York State."[1]

As LILCO promoted its plans to make Sound Avenue a multi-lane highway, the nuclear controversy also focused attention on preserving the rural scenery and historic houses along the rest of Sound Avenue. In the mid-1970s, the Society for the Preservation of Long Island Antiquities (now Preservation Long Island) conducted a historic resource inventory of Sound Avenue, including the Hallock Homestead and other Hallock family farmsteads along the frontage of the LILCO property and filed it with the State Historic Preservation Office.

The Sound Avenue Scenic and Historic Corridor

At the same time, community members started an effort to have the entire length of Sound Avenue declared a historic corridor by both the Town of Riverhead and by the New York State Legislature. The legislation passed both houses and was signed into law in June 1975. The bill did not, however, contain any provisions or funding actually protecting Sound Avenue. Instead, it deferred to and encouraged local town and county governmental bodies to formulate plans for the "preservation, enhancement and interpretation of the historic, scenic, natural and cultural assets of the corridor."[2]

Founding of the Hallockville Museum Farm

LILCO's ill-fated nuclear ambitions did produce one major benefit for the East End—the founding of the Hallockville Museum Farm. A group of concerned local residents began meeting in 1975 to devise a way to save the circa-1765 Hallock Homestead, its deteriorating outbuildings, and six more farmsteads still standing along Sound Avenue that belonged to LILCO. Their idea was to create a living farm museum and a center for traditional crafts. Because all of these farms originally belonged to members of the Hallock family, the museum's founders chose to use the "Hallockville" name given to the area in the late 19th century.

The last of Capt. Zachariah Hallock's descendants, Ella Hallock, then a spry 90 years old, still lived in the old family home under her life tenancy. Vacant for a decade or more, most of the other homes showed signs of their abandonment.

From the beginning, LILCO cooperated with the group trying to get the museum operating, hoping for a modicum of goodwill from the community. Initially, the company allowed Hallockville Inc. to use the Naugles barn and then in 1977 leased the Naugles farmhouse and outbuildings to the fledging museum for 10 years at $1 per year.

Two years later, in 1979, when the single faucet in her kitchen froze, forcing Ella to move to a nursing home, the museum began using the Homestead itself and the surrounding grounds. In 1981, after Ella ceded her life-tenancy rights, LILCO donated the Homestead, the surrounding farm structures, and two and a half acres of land to the museum. That same year, the fledging museum held its first fall festival and its first Christmas open house in the Homestead.

In 1982, much-needed work began on the Homestead Barn, which had fallen into serious disrepair. With the barn completed, work moved to the Homestead itself, including replastering of the west front bedroom and a new roof.[3] At the same time, Hallock descendants formed the Hallock Family Association and began meeting annually at the new museum. In 1984, the Homestead, barn, and other surviving outbuildings were listed on the National Register of Historic Places.

In 1988, Hallockville moved the circa-1840 Hudson-Sydlowski House from its original location a half mile west of the museum campus to serve as its administrative offices (see fig. 14.1).[4] Around the same time, the museum moved the circa-1837 Bethuel E. Hallock House from the south side of Sound Avenue to a location behind the Homestead Barn to use as staff housing.[5] In 1997, using a $100,000 legacy from an early supporter, the museum acquired six more acres along Sound Avenue, including the circa-1930 Cichanowicz farmhouse and the site of the mid-19th-century Isaiah Hallock barn. In 1999 the museum moved the circa-1936 Naugles barn behind the Cichanowicz farmhouse on the exact spot where the Isaiah Hallock barn once stood. In 2003, Hallockville moved Aunt Frances's Washhouse, also known as the Trubisz Little House, from the Trubisz farm next door. The Combs Decoy Shop and the Trubisz Sprout House arrived the same year. Reconstruction or moving of several smaller structures brought the number of buildings on the museum campus to 19.

Figure 14.1. The Hudson-Sydlowski House enroute to the Hallockville Museum. *Riverhead News-Review*, September 15, 1988. Source: *Times/Review* Newspapers. Used with permission.

Preserving the "KeySpan Property"

Gradually, after the demise of LILCO's nuclear ambitions in 1980, forces came together that ultimately resulted in the preservation of the entire property—a remarkable story combining local grassroots efforts and powerful statewide and regional trends. Along the way, many near misses occurred, with the property coming close to being developed several times. Ultimately, however, with inspired leadership from all sides, the needs of an enlightened corporation came together with those of environmental groups, farm organizations, and state and local governmental leaders, resulting in a unique deal that hopefully becomes a model for future preservation efforts.

After New York State rejected LILCO's proposal for the two nuclear plants, the company proposed building an 850-megawatt coal-fueled plant on the site, abandoning the project entirely in 1983 as it ran into increasing difficulties with its Shoreham nuclear plant—less than 20 miles west of Hallockville—that eventually resulted in the closure of that plant and the near-bankruptcy and forced sale of the company. The 500 acres surrounding the Hallockville Museum sat idle, apparently forgotten as underbrush, and even trees, gradually grew up in the areas that Levon's operations disturbed in the 1960s. Farming continued on the roughly 300 acres of agricultural land, with the Kujawaski family on the western half and the Cichanowicz family and others on the eastern half.

Finally, in 1998, after most of LILCO's assets passed to the Long Island Power Authority, the remnants of the company merged with Brooklyn Union Gas to form KeySpan Energy Corporation. As part of this transaction, the surplus Hallockville property came under the control of KeySpan. Soon after taking over custody of the property in 1998, KeySpan CEO Robert B. Catell began to get inquiries from developers, including Donald Trump, who approached him at a charity affair and wanted to build a resort and golf course there. Fortunately, David J. Manning, the company's senior vice president for corporate affairs, who dealt with many environmental issues in the energy industry over the course of his career, offered a different vision. He encouraged Catell to resist pressure from developers, pointing out how unique this property was on an island with supposedly only 10 of 200 miles of coastline accessible to the public.[6]

Rumors of developer interest spread rapidly. North Fork Audubon and virtually every other environmental group in the area, including the North Fork Environmental Council, the Pine Barrens Society, and the League of Conservation Voters, rated preservation of this property high on their priority lists but were unable to find a mechanism to make preservation a reality.[7]

With preparatory steps already in place, including the 1985 designation of Long Island Sound as one of the first estuaries selected in the Environmental Protection Agency's National Estuary Program, the Audubon Society, under the leadership of David Miller, then its Northeast director, launched the first "Listen to the Sound" initiative in 1990.[8] A decade later, the second "Listen to the Sound" report called the KeySpan property "an ideal acquisition, part preserve and part recreation area." Local Audubon chapters identified the KeySpan property as their single highest priority.[9] These recommendations dovetailed nicely with an initiative governor George Pataki announced in his 2000 "State of the State" address to add 10 Long Island Sound access points over the next 10 years, an effort to which he committed $25 million. New York Audubon called the parcel "truly one of the most magnificent open space projects in recent history" and in early 2002 named it "one of the top acquisition priorities" in the state.[10]

KeySpan wanted to help but also needed to meet the fiduciary needs of its shareholders—it could not just give the property away. At the same time, local governments remained concerned over the loss of tax revenue, always their key hot-button issue. The continued high interest from developers added more pressure to get the deal done soon.

Negotiations proved complicated, with Riverhead Town worried about taxes, the company focused on shareholder value, and the state concerned about funding. Agricultural organizations believed that the farmland needed to end up in the hands of farmers. Environmental organizations pushed hard for preservation of the entire parcel. In the end, with New York Audubon playing a critical role, a deal was announced on October 24, 2002. It called for the state to pay $16 million for the property, with $1.5 million going to the town and the Jamesport fire district in a one-time payment in lieu of taxes and the rest going to KeySpan. Hallockville received 20 acres as a gift from KeySpan, and the Long Island Antique Power Association received two acres with the right to purchase three more. About 225 acres of spectacular scenery, including Hallock Pond and a mile of shorefront on Long Island Sound, was to become a new state park. The approximately 300 acres of farmland, stripped of its development rights, would be sold to working farmers with the proceeds used to develop a new state park on the northern part of the property.

The Trust for Public Land (TPL) led by Rose Harvey served as a critical player in the negotiations and also performed an essential service in the execution of the deal. The maze of state rules regulating the sale of public property made it extremely complex, if not impossible, for the state to sell farmland itself. By structuring the deal so that TPL bought the entire parcel, then sold the parkland and an environmental easement on the farmland to the state and the farmland to individual farmers, it avoided the procedural nightmares that made it difficult for the state to do the deal directly.

Needing local expertise, the TPL asked the Peconic Land Trust to design and undertake the actual process of selling farmland to farmers. By early 2004, after much deliberation with the Farm Bureau and other interested parties, the Land Trust devised a plan that divided the farmland into seven parcels ranging in size from 20 to nearly 40 acres. In addition, by prior agreement, an eighth parcel of 69 acres was reserved for the Kujawski family, descendants of Polish immigrants who had farmed parts of the property for nearly a century. The Peconic Land Trust and Farm Bureau also developed a selection process designed to weed out "speculators or hobbyists" and select the most qualified farmers, based on their environmental records, to participate in a lottery. Farmers drawing lucky numbers qualified to buy parcels at a price of $13,000 per acre—the appraised value of similar agricultural parcels—but could use their land only for agricultural purposes, except for the two existing old Hallock family houses that remained standing.

In the spring of 2005, the state announced the creation of a new state park, then called Jamesport State Park and Preserve. The State Parks Department spent the next several years working on elaborate plans for its development. However, the severe state budget shortfalls that ensued following the financial crisis of 2007–08 brought this effort to a halt. Even though the money from the sale of the farmland to farmers had been set aside, the parks department did not feel it appropriate to be opening a new state park at the same time that existing state parks were being temporarily shuttered.

How the Hallock Name Prevailed

Many locals objected to the Jamesport name given to the new park. The Hallocks and their neighbors always considered the area part of the hamlet of Northville or the community of Sound Avenue, never Jamesport. That name, coined by James Tuthill around 1832 when he purchased Miamogue Point and laid out a street grid for an ambitious whaling port, originally referred just to the area today called South Jamesport. After the railroad came through in 1844, the first post office used "Jamesport," although located on Main Road in the area previously called "Old Aquebogue" or "Lower Aquebogue." Then, in the 20th century the name began migrating further north when Carey Camp used a Jamesport post office address and campers arrived at the Jamesport railroad station. Levon Corporation, LILCO, and KeySpan all referred to their property as "Jamesport." They had lots of company. The local papers, as well as town officials, often used the designation, despite protests from old-timers that it was really "Northville."

The author and fellow Hallockville board member John Stefans reached out to parks commissioner Bernadette Castro to change the name of the park, but she chose to keep the Jamesport name. However, when Carol Ash became parks commissioner in 2007 in the Spitzer administration, she was more receptive to a name change. The author, then part of the parks department's team planning the new park, proposed three names, all honoring the Hallock family's long legacy of stewarding that land: "Hallockville State Park," "Hallock Pond State Park," and "Hallock State Park." The parks department ultimately rejected the first two to avoid confusion with the

Hallockville Museum and to not draw too much attention to the pond, which they considered the cleanest body of water in their system. Much to the delight of the community, Ash announced the new name, "Hallock State Park and Preserve," at a public information meeting at Hallockville in 2010.

By happy coincidence, Rose Harvey, head of the TPL at the time of the KeySpan deal that created the new state park, in 2010 became parks commissioner in the new Cuomo administration. Because of her previous involvement, she took a particular interest in the Hallock State Park project. New plans were developed, though much scaled back from the original concept. Soon construction began on a visitor's center and an access roadway. Harvey presided at an opening ceremony for the park on a beautiful summer day in August 2017.

A Final Word

By the third decade of the 21st century, the Sound Avenue world known to the Hallocks has almost totally disappeared. Only three farms remain operated by descendants of the "old families"—one Wells family farm, one Reeve, and one Wines. A few other Puritan descendants still live on the avenue but have long since left farming. The Sound Avenue church, after many years of decline, ceased to exist about 2015 and the building became the home of a new Baptist congregation. The Grange Hall became a Buddhist temple. Most of the old homes are gone too. Sound Avenue itself became a heavily trafficked thoroughfare.

Nevertheless, Sound Avenue remains a special place—what *Newsday* reporter Steve Wick called "my favorite road." The Hallockville Museum Farm, surrounded by protected farmland, endures as a testament to the agrarian way of life that once characterized most of Long Island. The Hallock family name also endures—both in the Hallockville Museum and Hallock State Park and Preserve—just as Halsey Hallock wished a century earlier, with the beauty of the fields the Hallocks worked and the shorefront they treasured all preserved for future generations to enjoy.

Appendix

Table A. Guide to the Hallocks

Information is from Lucius H. Hallock, *A Hallock Genealogy* (1926), and notes added by Bessie Hallock and Virginia Wines to the author's copy. Generation numbers start from Peter as in *Hallock Genealogy*. Bold names in the chart show the line of descent that traces down to the family that lived in the Hallockville Museum Farm's Hallock Homestead.

Table A.1. The Mythical Founder

Peter (dates unknown). According to family legend, Peter was the first to land in Southold in 1640, but no evidence exists that he ever set foot in America.

Wife	Children
[First wife unknown]	**William**
	Abigail
"Widow Howell"	

Table A.2. The Second Generation

William (c. 1610–1684). Born in England, moved to Southold in 1640s. Built house on Hallock Lane near Hallockville soon after 1661.

Wife	Children
Margaret Howell. Married 1640. Born in England, daughter of his father's second wife, the "Widow Howell," by her previous marriage.	Elizabeth (unknown–1719). Married Richard Howell, son of "Widow Howell," Peter's second wife by previous marriage. Mary Martha Sarah Abigail John **Thomas (see below)** Peter William II

Table A.3. The Third Generation

(2) Thomas (1660–1719). Lived in Hallock Lane house.

Wife	Children
Hope Comestock (?–1733). Married c. 1680.	Thomas Richard Anna Patience Hope Benjamin Kingsland **Zerubabel I (see below)** Ichabod

Table A.4. The Fourth Generation
Zerubabel I (1696–1761). Lived in or near Hallock Lane house.

Wife	Children
Esther Osman (1695–1773). Married 1719.	**Zerubabel II (see below)** William Esther John James Daniel Sarah Eunice Joseph Benjamin Y

Table A.5. The Fifth Generation
Zerubabel II (1722–1800). Lived in or near Hallock Lane house.

Wife	Children
Elizabeth Sweezy (1722–1806). Daughter of neighbor, married 1743.	Zerubabel III. No Revolutionary War service. Caleb. No Revolutionary War service, moved to Oneida County. Richard. Served in Revolution, moved to Orange County. Annie. Married Thomas Conklin of Mattituck. **Zachariah I (see below).** No Revolutionary War service. John. Served in the Revolution, moved to Orange County. Ezra. No Revolutionary War service. Mary. Married Timothy Davis of Mattituck.

Table A.6. The Sixth Generation
Zachariah I (1749–1820). Shoemaker and farmer. Acquired Homestead for son Zachariah II in 1801. Also spelled "Zacharias." Known as **Capt. Zachariah** after being commissioned in the state militia in 1790.

Wife	Children
Hannah Young (1754–1823). Married 1771.	Hannah. Married Beriah Brown, lived in Jamesport. Elizabeth (c. 1775–1827). Married Jonathan Howell. **Zachariah II (see below).** Esther (1779–1866). Married Wines Reeve, moved to New York City. Harmony (1770–?). Married [?] Baker, moved to Brooklyn. John (1781–1859). Lived next west of Homestead. Fannie (1787–1804). Died at age 17. Bethuel (1790–1866). Lived next east of Homestead. Sarah (dates unknown). Unmarried, lived with sister Harmony Baker in Brooklyn. Mary (dates unknown). Unmarried, lived with sister Harmony Baker in Brooklyn.

Table A.7. The Seventh Generation
Zachariah II (1776–1854). Moved into Homestead 1801, a year after his marriage. Also known as Zachariah Jr.

Wife	Children
Mary Aldrich (1784–1809), first wife, married 1800.	Hannah (1802–1849). Married Rogers Aldrich, carpenter of Jamesport. Parents of Serepta Aldrich. **Herman W. (see below).** Mary Owen (1807–1823). Died as a teenager. Zachariah III (1809–1864). Also known as Riah, lived in main part of Homestead from marriage to Arletta Young in 1833 until 1845 when he exchanged houses and farms with his brother Herman and moved to West Farm.
Christiana Howell (1785–1860), second wife, married 1810.	No children.

Table A.8. The Eighth Generation
Herman W. (1804–1881). Moved from West Farm back to Homestead in 1845.

Wife	Children
Arminda Young (1811–1882). Married 1828.	[unnamed] (1829–1829). Died as an infant. Charles (1831–1831). Died as an infant. Mary Christiana (1832–1835). Died at age three. Charles H. (1833–1907). Moved to Smithtown and then back to Sound Avenue. Daniel Y. (1836–1926). Moved to York, Pennsylvania. **David Halsey (see below).** Adelia J. (1841–1929). Married Simeon Benjamin 1858. Known as Delia. Hannah J. (1850–1908). Married Marshall Dedrick in 1880, moved to Kansas and then Illinois. Known as Jennie.

Table A.9. The Ninth and Tenth Generations
David Halsey (1838–1939). Known as **Halsey**.

Wife	Children
Marietta A. Terry (1841–1865). Married 1860.	[Unnamed] (1865–1865). Died at birth.
Emilie J. Wells (1847–1932). Married in 1866.	**Halsey W. "Hal"** (1869–1957). Never married, lived entire life in Homestead. Eula (1871–1968). Married Charles Wells in 1891. They bought south half of Hallock farm in 1906. Georgia (1875–1916). Married Henry F. "Harry" Cowin in 1897. **Bessie Leona** (1880–1966). Never married, lived in Homestead. **Ella Arminda** (1885–1985). Never married, last to live in Homestead until she moved out in 1979 at age 95.

Table A.10. Other Hallock Relatives Mentioned (Generation Numbers in Parentheses)

---

(8) Caleb Hallock (1823–1899), grandson of Capt. Zachariah, son of John, lived three farms west of the Homestead.

(8) Daniel W. "Wells" Hallock (1820–1897), grandson of Capt. Zachariah, son of John, lived two farms west of the Homestead.

(8) Isaiah Hallock (1812–1882), grandson of Capt. Zachariah, son of John, lived next west of Homestead on site of the Hallockville Museum's Cichanowicz House.

(8) John Franklin Hallock (1806–1887), grandson of Capt. Zachariah, through his son John. Lived next east of the Homestead.

(8) Joseph Newton Hallock (1832–1913), grandson of Capt. Zachariah's brother Daniel, second cousin of Herman. Grew up in Franklinville. Principal of both Franklinville and Northville academies. Editor of *Christian at Work*.

(9) Eugene Hallock (1838–1904), great-grandson of Capt. Zachariah through his son Bethuel. Lived three farms east of Homestead.

(9) George C. Hallock (1842–1927), son of Isaiah, great-grandson of Capt. Zachariah through his son John. Lived four farms west of Homestead.

(9) George Wilson Hallock (1834–1907), son of Zachariah III, great-grandson of Capt. Zachariah through his son Zachariah II. Moved to Smithtown.

(9) Henry L. Hallock (1846–1900), son of Zachariah III, great-grandson of Capt. Zachariah through his son Zachariah II. Lived on West Farm.

(9) Herman H. Hallock (1837–1942), son of Halsey's brother Charles, great-grandson of Capt. Zachariah through Zachariah II.

(9) John Hallock (1832–1904), great-grandson of Capt. Zachariah, lived next east of Homestead.

(9) "Aunt" Frances (Young) Hallock (1837–1906), wife of John, lived next east of Homestead. Called "Aunt" as a Sunday school teacher.

(9) Lucius H. Hallock (1853–1933), great-grandson of Capt. Zachariah's brother Daniel, third cousin of Halsey. Grew up in Franklinville, attended

Northville Church during Civil War years, moved to Orient with father in 1874, author of *Hallock Genealogy*.

(9) Samuel Tuthill (1839–1924), great-grandson of Capt. Zachariah, grandson of John Hallock by daughter Joanna who married Jehiel Tuthill, lived about a mile west of the Homestead. Generally called Sammy.

(10) Henry A. Hallock (1877–1968), son Henry L., great-great-grandson of Capt. Zachariah. Lived on West Farm.

(10) Minnie Hallock (1866–1955), daughter of Halsey's brother Daniel, great-great-granddaughter of Capt. Zachariah. Lived with Hallocks in the Homestead in 1930s.

Notes

Introduction

1. VW, *Album VII*. The Virginia Wines albums are in the collection of the Hallockville Museum Farm. Some are available online, https://liu.access.preservica.com/index.php?name=SO_39ec8f82-55a8-4c98-806f-806b446d46ce.
2. DHH, *My Memories*, ed. Lois Young (Hallockville Museum Farm, 2001).
3. Estelle Evans, *Receipts and Reminiscences of the Hallock Family & Friends* (Hallockville Museum Farm, 1987).
4. Steve Wick, *Newsday*, June 30, 1985.
5. Barbara Shea, *Newsday*, October 26, 2001.
6. Bill Bleyer, *Newsday*, May 12, 2002.
7. *Riverhead News-Review*, November 20, 1998.
8. Richard Wines, "Northville" (1958), in VW, *Album VII*, collection of HMF.

Chapter 1

1. William A. Hallock, "Hallock Ancestry," American Tract Society, 1866, inside cover.
2. For a general discussion of the Puritan migration and its impact, see David Hackett Fischer, *Albion's Seed* (Oxford: Oxford University Press, 1989), esp. 16, 17, 31.
3. For more on the early founders of Southold Town, see Warren Hall, *Pagans, Puritans, Patriots of Yesterday's Southold* (Cutchogue-New Suffolk Historical Council, 1975), 14–28.
4. See John Michael Vlach, *Barns* (New York: W. W. Norton, 2003), 16–17.
5. Fischer, *Albion's Seed*, 64–66.
6. James L. Evans, "Nawth Fawk Tawk" (master's thesis, SUNY Geneseo, 1967; revised 2017).

7. For a discussion of Puritan child naming ways, see Fisher, *Albion's Seed*, 90–97.

8. Evans, "Nawth Fawk Tawk," 1.

9. For more on variants on the family name and its origins, see LHH, *A Hallock Genealogy* (1926; repr. 1975), 12–13.

10. William A. Hallock, "A Brief Sketch of the Hallock Ancestry in the United States," American Tract Society, New York, 1866. A version updated by Jacob N. Imandt was published in 1929 and reprinted by The Morgan Press, West Long Branch, NJ, in 1940.

11. Charles Hallock, *The Hallock-Holyoke Pedigree and Collateral Branches in the United States: Being a Revision of the Hallock Ancestry of 1866* (Amherst, MA: Carpenter and Morehouse, 1906).

12. Hallock, "Hallock Ancestry," inside cover, 390.

13. LHH, *A Hallock Genealogy*, 12–13, 532–33; Rev. Epher Whitaker, *History of Southold, LI: Its First Century* (Southold, NY, 1881), 30; Charles E. Craven, *History of Mattituck, LI, New York* (1906), 73n.

14. Southold Town Records, printed by Towns of Southold and Riverhead, 1882, vol. 1, 3.

15. Southold Town Records, 1:122, 218, 222, 224, 226, 242, 316.

16. See Fisher, *Albion's Seed*, 30, 131. In the 17th century, literacy rates were higher in East Anglia than other parts of England.

17. Abstracts of Wills, Surrogate's Office, City of New York, 1665–1801 (New York Surrogate's Court: 1893–1913), Liber 3–4, 128–29. VW copy in "Hallock Land" folder.

18. Craven, *History of Mattituck*, 113.

19. Craven, 86–88.

20. Craven, 102–3.

21. Craven, 96–102; Whitaker, *History of Southold*, 313–18; Orville B. Ackerly, "Celebration of the 100th Anniversary . . . of the Town of Riverhead" (1892), in *Seeking the Past: Writings from 1832–1905 Relating to the History of the Town of Riverhead*, ed. Tom Twomey (New York: New Market Press, 2004), 121.

22. Aquebogue Church Records, Transcription, in VW *Album XVI*.

23. Craven, *History of Mattituck*, 95–113.

24. Aquebogue Church Records, Transcription, in VW *Album XVI*. Herman and Arminda's son Daniel joined the Northville Church in 1852, as did George Wilson Hallock, his cousin, and the son of Zachariah III. Halsey and his first wife joined in 1863.

25. Much of the material in this section first appeared in two articles by the author and his wife Nancy Gilbert, "Slavery in Riverhead," published in the *News-Review* in 2007. Starting in 2018, the author, along with Amy Folk, Steve Wick, and Sandi Brewster-Walker, has been part of the North Fork Project, documenting

the history of slavery on the North Fork. Much of that research is available at https://www.forgettingtorememberproject.org.

26. Hallock, "Hallock Ancestry," inside back cover.

27. The author, as part of his research for the North Fork Project, estimates that approximately 550 enslaved lived on the North Fork during the nearly two centuries before the institution of slavery was abolished by New York State.

28. William Pelletreau, ed., *Abstract of Wills on File in the Surrogate's office, City of New York* (New York: New York Historical Society, 1893–1913), Liber 23, 73.

29. Will of Zerubabel Hallock II, 1785, VW typescript of original.

30. Frederic Gregory Mather, *The Refugees of 1776 from Long Island to Connecticut* (Baltimore: Genealogical Publishing, 1972; repr.), 1058. The original was published in 1913. They signed in Brookhaven during June, July, and August 1775.

31. Mather, 994–96, 1008–09.

32. Craven, *History of Mattituck*, 144; E. M. Ruttember and L. H. Clark, *History of Orange County* (Philadelphia: Everts and Peck, 1881), 677; LHH, *Hallock Genealogy*, 415, 732–42; Mather, *Refugees of 1776*, 282, 413, 750.

33. LHH, *Hallock Genealogy*, 201. He may not have moved until after 1795. A Bessie Hallock note in her copy of the *Hallock Genealogy* cites his purchase of an item at the general store in Franklinville (now Laurel) in 1790, and his oldest son, who died in 1795 at age fourteen, is buried in Mattituck; *Hallock Genealogy*, 554, states that he lived in Mattituck, but it also mentions that a daughter, Mary, who died at age sixteen in 1798, is buried in Baiting Hollow.

34. Hallock deeds, VW typescript, in Hallockville Museum Farm. MSS in collection of SCHS.

35. Hallock deeds, March 30, 1870, and April 1, 1783.

36. See Richard A. Wines, "Defense of the Eagle: New Discoveries about This Coast Guard Legend," HMF, 2018.

37. Samuel Terry Hudson, "An Account of the Battles at Penny's Landing and Luce's Landing, June 1814," *Riverhead News*, August 5, 1924; repr. HMF.

38. BLH, "Old House"; Hallock family diaries record participation in the fishing company.

39. Attributed to the Northville correspondent of the *Riverhead News*, repr. *South Side Signal*, January 7, 1882.

40. Samuel Terry Hudson, "An Account of the Battles at Penny's Landing and Luce's Landing, June 1814" (1899), *Riverhead News*, August 5, 1924; repr. HMF, 1990.

41. BLH, "Old House."

42. Graves are in the Aquebogue cemetery.

43. DHH, *My Memories*, 23. Cited that she lost three children. We don't know the year of the third.

Chapter 2

1. Demolished in 1999.
2. VW *Album XVIII*.
3. DHH, *My Memories*, 25.
4. *County Review*, June 30, 1938, 1.
5. *County Review*, 27.
6. Transcription of newspaper clipping, 1937, VW *Album XIV*.
7. Melinda Corwin, Diary, VW *Album VIII*.
8. DHH, *My Memories*, 13.
9. The first two-story house on Sound Avenue was built by Capt. Abraham Luce in 1780, VW *Album XII*, but most other houses remained story-and-a-half Capes in the 1840s.
10. VW *Album VIII*; Riverhead Town Bicentennial Committee, *Riverhead Bicentennial Album* (Riverhead, NY: Town of Riverhead, 1976), 70.
11. Composition by David Halsey Hallock, 1854, typescript in VW *Album VIII*.
12. Henry Wilson Young, clippings from the *Sentinel* (Kansas), of which he was the editor, 1921–1925, VW *Album VIII*.
13. DHH, "Composition," 1854, MS, collection of HMF.
14. Adelia Benjamin, "A Short Paper on Looking Backward" (1917), typescript in VW *Album VI*.
15. The teacher may have lived at home or received room and board in the community. However, the low pay still raises questions as to how someone could have lived on that amount. One answer is that life was much simpler. Most expenses we take for granted today—electronics, cars, healthcare, travel—basically did not exist then. One or two changes of clothes would have lasted a year. However, it would have required saving the entire salary for 15 years to buy a 30-acre farm at then-current prices on Sound Avenue. The teacher may also have worked other jobs when not teaching. Teacher pay in the Northville district appears to have been typical but was likely even below that of farm laborers, who according to 1850 United States Census averaged $11.50 per month in New York with board and $15.40 without board. See United States Census, *Statistical View of the United States: Being a Compendium of the Seventh Census* (Washington, DC: 1854), 164.
16. Subsequent reports do not break out this statistic.
17. DHH, *My Memories*, 28–29. DHH spells the name "Salsburg." Salburg followed a trajectory common to other early Jewish immigrants to Long Island, from itinerant peddler to successful merchant. See Brad Kolodny, *The Jews of Long Island: 1705–1918* (Albany: State University of New York Press, 2022).
18. Thomas M. Stark, *Riverhead: The Halcyon Years 1861–1919* (Huntington, NY: Maple Hill Press, 2005), 13.
19. Census returns differ on Pope's place of birth, and he never clearly explained his origins—even to his own children.

20. The 1850 census lists Thomas Pope (age 9) living in Riverhead with Mary Knowles (age 56) and James Pope (age 26). Mary (Thomas's grandmother) was born in England. James (Thomas's uncle) was also born in England; Thomas, in Canada. See also DHH, *My Memories*, 24.

21. Note with Thomas Pope, letters, 1898–1931, MSS, collection of HMF. Typescripts of letters are also in VW *Album XIV*.

22. BLH, "Old House."

23. DHH, *My Memories*, 24–25. Thomas Pope, letters.

24. Thomas Pope, letter, July 10, 1921.

25. The gold fields were not actually at Pikes Peak, which is about 85 miles south.

26. Pope, letter, March 24, 1898.

27. DHH, Diary, 1855, partial years to 1859, occasional entries to 1890. This diary exists in two transcripts. One, prepared by Virginia Wines, is dated 1972 with an indication that Ella Hallock owned the original, part in VW *Album XIV*. Lois Young prepared another transcript, collection of HMF.

28. DHH, *My Memories*, 23.

29. BLH, "Old House."

30. DHH, Diary, September 3, 1855.

31. Arminda Hallock to Halsey and Adelia Hallock, February 19, 1956, MSS in collection of HMF.

32. Pope, letter, July 10, 1921.

33. *Corrector* (Sag Harbor), June 20, 1857, 1.

34. Two of Capt. Zachariah's daughters, Harmony and Esther, moved to Brooklyn and New York City with their husbands. Esther married Wines Reeve of Mattituck. Their granddaughter, Cora Reeve Jones, also lived in the city but had a summer home in Jamesport (Bessie Hallock note in author's copy of *Hallock Genealogy*, 284). She was a concert pianist and could have facilitated Daniel's musical education, as well as Bessie's a generation later.

35. DHH, *My Memories*, 19–20.

36. Healthline, "The Worst Outbreaks in US History," updated May 10, 2023, https://www.healthline.com/health/worst-disease-outbreaks-history#scarlet-fever.

37. Bessie Hallock, Sound Avenue Cemetery Records, Virginia Wines typescript, collection of SCHS.

38. Aquebogue Cemetery Records.

39. Adelaide Hallock to Marietta Terry, April 20, 1857, typescript at HMF.

40. BLH, "Old House."

41. If accurate, the church wedding is unusual, as most weddings took place in the bride's house at that time.

42. DHH, *My Memories*, 23.

43. DHH, 17.

44. Zachariah Hallock, Account Book, 1771–1817, MSS, collection of SCHS; James Fanning Store Account Book, MSS, collection of SCHS.

45. "Inventory of the Personal Property of Zacharias Hallock Deceased, to Be Kept by His Executors," June 10, 1820, MSS in collection of SCHS.
46. DHH, *My Memories*, 14–16.
47. James Y. Downs, Church Records, VW *Album IV*.
48. DHH, *My Memories*, 17.
49. *Sag-Harbor Express*, September 13, 1860, 1.
50. DHH, *My Memories*, 14–16.
51. George F. Hummel, *Heritage* (New York: Frederick A. Stokes: 1935), 5.

Chapter 3

1. Estelle Evans, conversation with author, 2010.
2. Richard Albertson, Diary, 1860–1863, typescript in VW *Album XIX*.
3. BLH, "Old House."
4. DHH, *My Memories*, 19–20. Several members of the Skidmore family lived about half a mile west of the Franklinville Academy. An account of the 50th anniversary celebration of the other couple in the 1860 double wedding, George H. and Nannie Tuthill, appeared in *County Review*, November 25, 1910, 1. They were the author's great-great-grandparents.
5. Letter from A. Adelaide Hallock to Marietta Terry, April 20, 1857, typescript in VW *Album XIV*. LLH, *A Hallock Genealogy*, gives her name as Adeline A. Hallock. Her full name may have been Adeline Adelaide Hallock.
6. BLH, "History of Our House" and "Old House."
7. Melinda Corwin, Diary, typescript in VW *Album XII*.
8. *Sag-Harbor Express*, May 30, 1861, 2.
9. *Sag-Harbor Express*, June 26, 1862, 2; Harrison Hunt and Bill Bleyer, *Long Island and the Civil War* (Charleston, SC: History Press, 2015), 23.
10. Leslie T. Wells, Legal Records, VW *Album X*.
11. Newspaper clipping (1929), Mary Downs, scrapbook in author's collection.
12. ST, Diary, March 19, 1863.
13. ST, Diary, July 15, 1863.
14. *Brooklyn Daily Eagle*, July 15, 1863, 2; Hunt and Bleyer, *Long Island and the Civil War*, 105–6.
15. Arthur Channing Downs Jr., ed., *Riverhead Town Records, 1792–1886* (Huntington, NY: *Long Islander*, 1967), 443–44.
16. *Riverhead Town Records*, 449–50, quoted in fn.450.
17. These statistics are based on an analysis of the number of young men in the 1860 census compared to a list of Riverheaders who served in the war in Georgette Lane Case, "We Will Not Forget: Riverhead's Civil War Soldiers & Sailors," Riverhead Town Historian, 2011.
18. DHH, *My Memories*, 20.

19. New York, Civil War Muster Roll Abstracts, 1861–1900.

20. *New York Times*, September 2, 1863.

21. According to Lois Young, granddaughter of Halsey Hallock and great-grandniece of Daniel, he was "a bit of a dreamer [and] probably went off to the Civil War for that reason." Conversation with the author, January 18, 2006.

22. It is not clear if this was included or was in addition to the $400 sign-up bonus offered by the federal government.

23. There are 14 letters to his parents and his brother Halsey dating from March 7, 1864, through August 14, 1865, typescripts by Lois Young, collection of HMF.

24. Obituary, *County Review*, December 16, 1926, 18.

25. March 4, 1865, letter is dated at Hatcher's Run.

26. April 17, 1865.

27. According to Lois Young, Elisha Wells's granddaughter.

28. Lois Young conversations with author, July 8, July 22, and September 9, 2004. See also Richard Wines, "Why Is the Flagpole So Tall," *News-Review*, January 13, 2005.

29. Civil War letters of Elisha Wells, June 17, 1864, and December 26, 1864, VW *Album V*.

30. James H. Tuthill to Arminda Hallock, November 17, 1864, and February 10, 1865, typescripts, collection of HMF.

31. Civil War Documents Collection, Riverhead Town Historian.

32. Riverhead Town Records, 193, 565.

33. New York State Archives, Civil War Muster Roll Abstracts, 1861–1900.

34. Muster Roll Abstracts, US Register of Deaths of Volunteers, 1861–1865. Bartels's gravestone in Poplar Grove National Cemetery, Petersburg, Virginia, indicates the rank of lieutenant, but no record exists of such a promotion.

35. DHH, *My Memories*, 20.

36. DHH, 20–21.

Chapter 4

1. DHH, *My Memories*, 20.

2. Emilie's mother, Betsey Youngs was the daughter of John Youngs, a brother of Deacon Daniel Youngs and son of Rev. Daniel Youngs, Arminda Hallock's father (the Youngs family dropped the "s" in the mid-19th century).

3. Collection of HMF.

4. "The Seminary Bell," July 2, 1862, typescript in VW *Album X*.

5. G. A. Gaston Jacquemin-de-Zouval to Emilie J. Wells, July 27, 1865, typescript in VW *Album XIV*.

6. DHH, Diary, 1872.

7. DHH, *My Memories*, 20.

8. From a notebook kept by Bessie Hallock, private collection of a Hallock relative.

9. In 2019, the Hallockville Museum received a donation from the Marie Wells Remer estate that included three samples of dress material belonging to Emilie Jane Wells saved by one of her nieces. A note with the material indicated that the gray-blue one, presumably the traveling dress mentioned above, was bought in 1865. Another sample was a golden-brown material with an accompanying note describing it as the wedding dress.

10. Much of this account is based on Halsey's recollections many years later. DHH, *My Memories*, 21.

11. DHH, 3, 21.

12. Matilda E. Platt (1827–1904) was a daughter of Arminda's sister Jemimah, who married Gen. David Williamson and lived in the house still standing in Jamesport opposite the head of South Jamesport Avenue. Matilda married Gilbert Platt. The couple moved to Brooklyn by 1860.

13. Robert Holder, "The Beginnings of Buffalo Industry," 12, http://bechsed.nylearns.org/pdf/low/The%20Beginning%20of%20Buffalo%20Industry.pdf.

14. Emilie and her daughters treasured these artifacts, part of a private collection featured in the Hallockville Museum's 2003 special exhibit *Emilie Jane: Keepsakes of a Lifetime*.

15. Years later, Ella Hallock remembered that while her parents still lived in the west side, Emilie was embarrassed sometimes to have to walk past the windows in Herman and Arminda's side of the house when they had company to get to the shared outhouse.

16. BLH, "Old House."

17. DHH, Diary, 1884.

18. Bessie's account is strangely silent as to when the kitchen shed addition was added. She says that her brother Hal could barely remember when this happened, since he was born in 1869, which puts the date probably around 1873 or a little later. It is framed in such a way that it must have been built after the ceiling was raised on the adjacent dinning/sitting room.

19. Probably the east windows were also recycled nine-over-six colonial era ones too, but we know these were later replaced in the 1920s.

20. DHH, Diary, March 14, 1873.

21. Thomas M. Stark, *Riverhead: The Halcyon Years 1861–1919* (Huntington, NY: Maple Hill Press, 2005), 23.

22. *Sag-Harbor Express*, February 25, 1875, 3.

23. Natalie Fitzgerald, "American Missionary Association (1846–1999)," Blackpast, September 8, 2018, https://www.blackpast.org/african-american-history/american-missionary-association-1846-1999/.

24. Unfortunately, none of Hannah's letters have survived. But there are a few allusions in BLH, "Old House."

25. Information provided by Daniel Dedrick. The 1870 census shows the couple living with her parents, John (a tailor) and Mary Rockwell in New Hudson, New York.

26. Hannah and Marshall lived for a decade or so in Kansas and then moved to Chicago. We know that Hannah visited one more time, in Bessie's account: "In 1890 the walls of my frame echoed to the shouts of Jennie's three small children for Jennie visited the old home once more before going to live in Berwyn, Ill." She also attended a family reunion in York, Pennsylvania in 1898.

27. Will of Herman W. Hallock, 1881, MSS, collection of SCHS.

28. BLH, "Old House."

29. Stark, *Riverhead*, 13.

30. The infant Herman Hallock Dedrick died August 17, 1882, at age eight months, according to his gravestone in Belle Plaine, Kansas.

31. DHH, *My Memories*, 25.

Chapter 5

1. *Brooklyn Daily Eagle*, Thursday, December 1, 1881.

2. *Long Island Traveler*, June 20, 1878, 2.

3. *Sag-Harbor Express*, August 30, 1860, 2.

4. Melinda Corwin, Diary, VW *Album XII*.

5. DHH, Church Centennial Talk (1929), VW *Album IX*.

6. Lucius H. Hallock to DHH, March 19, 1933, MSS, collection of HMF. Lucius Hallock (1853–1933) grew up on Herrick's Lane, and his father was a brother of Joseph N. Hallock, the liberal principal of the Northville Academy.

7. Lucius H. Hallock to DHH, March 19, 1933.

8. Unattributed newspaper article, c. 1899, Ida Young's Scrapbook, 16, SCHS, copy in VW *Album XIV*. Although George M. Cohan did not write "Johnny Get Your Gun," also known as "Over There," until 1917, the phrase had been much used as a recruiting slogan in the Civil War. The article "Great Christian Endeavor Horse Race" stated that even the minister, the good Rev. Fishburn, who had initially preached against the racing, decided to mute his opposition after recalling an incident involving one of his predecessors.

9. *Long Island Traveler*, March 12, 1874, 3; *Long Islander*, June 9, 1865. See also ST Diary, May 28, 1865; James Y. Downs, Church Records, VW *Album IV*.

10. Also see James Y. Downs Book, in VW *Album X*.

11. Melinda Corwin, Diary, VW *Album XII*.

12. ST Diary, March 27, 1871.

13. DHH Diary, January 15, 1872; *Sag-Harbor Express*, January 4, 1872, 2.

14. *Sag-Harbor Express*, January 18, 1872, 2.

15. As recalled many years later by Clarence B. Wardle, a former Northville resident.

16. ST Diary, February 28 and March 3, 1873.

17. Northville Church and Parish Book, 1860–1876, collection of HMF.

18. ST Diary, contains numerous entries pertaining to Wright and the problems in the church during the year 1877.

19. Record of the Northville Congregational Church (1861–1901), collection of HMF.

20. Record of the Northville Congregational Church.

21. Most meetings of the church or parish had about 18 members in attendance. Parish Records of the Congregational Society of Northville, 1875–1903, collection of HMF.

22. ST Diary, May 5, 1877.

23. *Brooklyn Daily Eagle*, May 17, 1877, 2.

24. DHH Diary.

25. *Brooklyn Daily Eagle*, May 16, 1877, 2.

26. *Brooklyn Daily Eagle*, May 17, 1877, 2.

27. In one story about the 1814 battle near the museum, the *Eagle* managed to get 18 facts wrong, including who won the battle. *Brooklyn Daily Eagle*, February 28, 1898.

28. DHH Diary.

29. ST Diary, October 17, 1878.

30. *Brooklyn Daily Eagle*, May 17, 1877, 2.

31. ST Diary, May 23, 1877.

32. *Brooklyn Daily Eagle*, July 8, 1877.

33. *New York Herald*, July 6, 1877.

34. *New York Herald*, July 11, 1877, 4.

35. An article in the *Eagle* at the time indicates it may have been the other minister who punched Wright.

36. *Riverhead Weekly News*, October 22, 1878. Clipping in VW *Album IX*; also in *Album XII*.

37. *Brooklyn Daily Eagle*, October 22, 1878; *Long Island Traveler*, October 24, 1878.

38. Parish Records of the Northville Society 1875–1903, 6, collection of HMF. The church's records have some gaps, possibly the result of later attempts to bury evidence of the conflict.

39. *Long Island Traveler*, April 25, 1878, 2, repr. from the Sag Harbor *Corrector*. This cryptic article from the *Corrector* that April reported Caleb and "Jacob" Hallock suing the Northville Church for libel. Jacob Hallock is a mystery, as no person of that name appears in the *Hallock Genealogy* or in the federal manuscript census for the North Fork in the 1860s and 1870s. Probably this was Isaiah Hallock, Caleb's brother and another of Tuthill's uncles. The same clipping is in VW *Album X*, hand dated May 1877, but without specifying the paper, which was likely the *Riverhead News*, and may be a reprint in 1977 of an article a century earlier.

40. The original article has been lost, but a subsequent defense of the magazine stated these facts. *Christian at Work*, repr. in *Sag-Harbor Express*, June 13, 1878.

41. *Long Island Traveler*, June 20, 1878, 2. A cryptic article appeared in the *Brooklyn Daily Eagle*, April 1879, about a lawsuit from a "Mr. Hallock" against the editor of the *Christian at Work* with many of the same details.

42. *Sag-Harbor Express*, October 26, 1882, 2.

43. Clarence Russell Comes, "Riverhead's Versatile Building," *Long Island Forum*, December 1953, in VW *Album X*, claimed that the church was burned down in the early days of the Civil War by "Copperheads," Southern sympathizers. The timing is wrong, but the sympathies may be correct.

44. *Brooklyn Daily Eagle*, December 1, 1881, 2.

45. *New York Times*, May 16, 1877, 5.

46. *New York Times*, May 16, 1877, 8.

47. Parish Records of the Northville Society 1875–1903, 5, collection of HMF.

48. *Brooklyn Daily Eagle*, February 7, 1879.

49. *Riverhead Weekly News*, November 19, 1878, in VW *Album X*.

50. Recollection of Elsie Anna Wells, in VW *Album VI*.

51. *Brooklyn Daily Eagle*, December 11, 1884, 4, and December 12, 4. George Mitchell Terry lived in the house just west of the Sound Avenue Church that later became the author's childhood home.

52. *Brooklyn Daily Eagle*, December 11, 1884.

53. *Long Island Traveler*, December 12, 1884, 4; *New York Times*, December 5, 1884, 5; December 6, 1884, 5.

54. Recollections of Elsie Anna Wells who later lived in Deacon Terry's house, VW *Album VI*.

55. *Brooklyn Daily Eagle*, December 30, 1884, 2, 4. The *Eagle* ran two stories about the scandal on the same day!

56. *Corrector*, December 27, 1884, 2.

57. ST Diary, December 25, 1884.

58. *South Side Signal* (Babylon, NY), January 3, 1885, 3.

59. *New York Times*, December 30, 1884, 5.

60. ST Diary, December 29, 1884.

61. *Brooklyn Daily Eagle*, December 30, 1884.

62. ST Diary, December 29, 1884.

63. *Brooklyn Daily Eagle*, December 30, 1884, 2; *New York Times*, December 30, 1884, 3.

64. *Brooklyn Daily Eagle*, January 4, 1885.

65. Record of the Northville Congregational Church (1861–1901), January 20, 1885, collection of HMF.

66. *Brooklyn Daily Eagle*, February 9, 1885, 4.

67. *Long Island Traveler*, December 19, 1884, 4.

68. *Brooklyn Daily Eagle*, February 25, 1885, 4.

69. *Brooklyn Daily Eagle*, March 2, 1885, 4.

70. *Long Island Traveler*, February 5, 1886, 7; February 12, 1886, 3.

71. *Long Island Traveler*, February 2, 1887, 2.

72. For example, see *Long Island Traveler*, July 20, 1883, 2; *Suffolk Weekly Times*, July 19, 1884, 2; and September 23, 1882, 3.

73. *Suffolk County News*, November 8, 1895, 2.

74. *Suffolk County News*, December 6, 1895, 1.

75. *Brooklyn Daily Eagle*, December 3, 1895.

76. The manuscript returns for the 1860 census do not indicate addresses or hamlets of individuals. However, most of the Northville names are grouped into two sections. The author has endeavored to separate non-Northville names that occasionally appeared mixed together.

77. *Riverhead News*, September 3, 1904, in VW *Album X*.

78. DHH, VW *Album X*.

79. Record Book of the Sound Avenue Congregational Church, collection of HMF.

Chapter 6

1. Autograph Album, "Bessie L. Hallock, Northville, LI, December 25th (a gift from Nina) 1886, 6 years old," typescript by Lois Young, collection of HMF. Nina was the daughter of Halsey's sister Adelia, who had married Sound Avenue farmer Simeon Benjamin. She would later marry Henry A. Hallock (1877–1968), son of Halsey and Adelia's first cousin Henry L. Hallock (1846–1900)—and thus Nina's second cousin. The quote from Halsey refers to *Ecclesiastes* 12:1: "Remember now thy Creator in the days of thy youth, while the evil days come not, nor the years draw nigh, when thou shalt say, I have no pleasure in them."

2. Trustees report, quoted in *Riverhead Bicentennial Album* (Riverhead, 1976), 70.

3. The joint graduation program with the District 10 school survives in the Hallock papers. Copy in VW *Album VIII*.

4. Ronnie Wacker, "Atomic Plants to Overshadow Historic Hallock Farm," *Suffolk Times*, January 16, 1975, 2; VW conversation with Ella, 1972, VW *Album VIII*.

5. *South Side Signal*, June 5, 1897, 3.

6. VW *Album XIV*.

7. Ronnie Wacker, "Atomic Plants."

8. *County Review*, October 20, 1905, 4; *South Side Signal*, December 19, 1891, 2.

9. ST Diary.

10. Jen Carlson, "Flashback: NYC Earthquake of 1884," *Gothamist*, January 21, 2010, https://gothamist.com/news/flashback-nyc-earthquake-of-1884.

11. "Quotes from Miss Ella," July 1976, VW *Album XIV*.
12. According to Bessie, this was installed "in Ella's memory."
13. DHH, *My Memories*, 16.
14. DHH and E. J. Hallock to Charles S. Wells, 1906 deed, MSS, collection of SCHS.
15. *County Review*, January 11, 1918, 7; January 10, 1919, 6; Deed, MSS, collection of SCHS.
16. The electric service came from Mattituck in 1926 and only extended as far west as the Carey Camp Road. The rest of Sound Avenue did not receive service until the following year.
17. DHH Diary, collection of HMF.
18. Minutes of Busy Workers Society of Northville, VW *Album III* and *Album IX*.
19. *Long Island Traveler*, April 15, 1887, 3. No copy of the cookbook can be located, but numerous recipes from it appear in Estelle Evans, *Receipts and Reminiscenses of the Hallock Family & Friends* (Riverhead, NY: Hallockville Museum Farm, 1987).
20. Minute Books, Northville Academy, collection of HMF.
21. *County Review*, September 3, 1925, 3; October 30, 1930, 7. Record books of all of the various organizations connected to the Sound Avenue Congregational Church are part of a large collection of material donated to HMF by First Parish Church (formerly the Sound Avenue Church) as it was winding down its affairs in 2008 to 2013.
22. Rev. S. H. Doyle, "Christian Endeavor," *County Review*, February 2, 1906, 6.
23. *County Review*, October 20, 1905, 8; May 31, 1912, 4; January 10, 1913, 4.
24. *County Review*, February 16, 1912, 3.
25. *County Review*, December 29, 1916, 1.
26. BLH, "Old House."
27. *County Review*, March 22, 1907, 8; April 5, 1907, 4; June 28, 1907, 4; September 30, 1910.
28. *County Review*, June 5, 1914, 5.
29. *County Review*, March 2, 1906, 4.
30. *County Review*, June 28, 1907, 4; Record Book, Sound Avenue Literary Society, 1905–1912, collection of HMF.
31. *County Review*, April 3, 1914, 6.
32. Wacker, "Atomic Plants," 2; Ella A. Hallock, "The Account of Saturday, November 28, 1914, Is the Tale That I Now Relate," repr. in *Hallockville Happenings*, November 1998.
33. Ella's mother, Emilie, was visiting her ill daughter Georgia "at the home of Harry" Corwin, her husband.
34. *County Review*, April 30, 1920, 11.
35. Obituary in the *Hallockville Happenings*, VW *Album XIV*.

36. DHH Diary. This entry was probably written by Ella. She and her sister apparently continued to use their father's diary.

Chapter 7

1. Lois Young, a granddaughter of Halsey Hallock, quoted this to the author in a conversation in 2005.
2. Richard Wines, "The Nineteenth Century Agricultural Transition in an Eastern Long Island Community," *Agricultural History* 55 (1981): 50–63.
3. DHH, *My Memories*, 1–3.
4. Interview with Ella Hallock, 1982, Oral History Collection, HMF.
5. The 1860 census reported crop production from the previous year, Halsey's map showed 1860 data.
6. DHH, *My Memories*, 6.
7. DHH, 4.
8. See Richard Wines, *Fertilizer in America: From Waste Recycling to Resource Exploitation* (Philadelphia: Temple University Press, 1985), 33–53.
9. *American Agriculturist* 23 (1864), 173.
10. Clarence H. Danhof, *Change in Agriculture: The Northern United States, 1820–1870* (Cambridge, MA: Harvard University Press: 1969), 230–32.
11. John Horace Wells, "Farm Implements and Machinery," *Riverhead News*, March 30, 1917.
12. Wells, "Farm Implements." The John H. Manny reapers and mowers cost $135.
13. John T. Downs, Farming Notes, VW *Album IV*.
14. John T. Downs, notes for *Riverhead News* articles, 3, VW *Album IV*.
15. Richard Wines, "The Nineteenth Century Agricultural Transition in an Eastern Long Island Community," *Agricultural History* 55 (1981): 61.
16. *Long Island Traveler*, May 2, 1890, VW *Album VIII*.
17. Southold *Traveler*, June 24 and July 29, 1892. Potato leafhoppers are a serious threat to potatoes.
18. Wines, "Agricultural Transition," 62.
19. Horace J. Wells, "Potato Culture Old and New," *L I Forum*, February 1965.
20. Samuel Tuthill, "Paper Presented at the Fiftieth Anniversary Celebration of the Riverhead Town Agricultural Society, Live Stock and Fencing," VW *Album VIII*.
21. *Long-Islander*, October 7, 1893, 2.
22. *County Review*, September 15, 1911, 5.
23. *County Review*, May 21, 1915, 6.
24. BLH, "Old House."
25. *Long Island Traveler*, June 27, 1878.

26. Transcriptions of 1901 newspaper clippings, VW *Album XIV.*

27. Years later, Ella Hallock recalled that "Grandma Arminda always washed in the west part of the shop. The women called it the washhouse but the men wanted it called the shop. There was a fireplace and the water was heated in a really big iron pot. I remember a pounder barrel that was used for washing. A big barrel that had a handle to pound the clothes." "Quotes from Miss Ella," September 1980, VW *Album XIV.*

28. Halsey's diary mentions that they converted the cider mill to a wood house in 1855—after his grandfather's death.

29. "Peter Tumbledown" comes from a cartoon series that appeared in the *Farm Journal* in the 1930s.

30. "Quotes from Miss Ella," October 1978 and September 1980, VW *Album XIV.*

31. Henry Pope, born on the Isle of Wight, is listed on the farm in the 1850 census. Tommy apparently came later. After brief service at the beginning of the Civil War, Henry moved to Buffalo, where he worked as a coachman according to the 1870 census.

32. John Horace Wells, "Written by John Horace Wells in 1894," typescript in VW *Album VIII*; Paper presented [at Farmers' Club?] on "The Farm's Evolution," *Riverhead News*, March 30, 1917, 1; *Portrait and Biographical Record*, 212.

33. In 1881, the Hallock diaries indicate that "Uncle Clarence" worked on the farm—Emilie's younger brother Clarence, who would have been 20 and renting a farm in Smithtown at the time of the 1900 census.

34. A surprising number of the Bohemian immigrant couples are named Joseph and Josephine. However, a search of the census data for subsequent decades turns just one probable couple—Joseph and Josephina Hübel. They immigrated from Bohemia as newlyweds in 1884. They did not have children at the time, the first of their two children was born two years later. By 1900, they settled in a Bohemian enclave on East 74th street in the Upper East Side of Manhattan where Joseph was enumerated as a cigar maker—apparently a specialty among Bohemian immigrants. Different census years show different birth dates, but most likely they were in their mid-20s when they lived as newlyweds in the Homestead room always after referred to as the "Bohemian Room." The 1910 census indicates they still spoke "Bohemian," now referred to as Czech.

35. As told to Virginia Wines, VW *Album XIV.*

36. DHH Diary.

Chapter 8

1. Nathaniel S. Prime, *A History of Long Island, From its First Settlement by Europeans to the Year 1845*, excerpted in *Seeking the Past: Writings from 1832–1005*

Relating to the History of the Town of Riverhead, ed. Tom Twomey (New York: New Market Press, 2004), 17.

2. *Sag-Harbor Express*, August 23, 1860, 2.

3. J. Chace, *Map of Suffolk County, L.I., N.Y. from Actual Surveys* (Philadelphia: John Douglass, 1858). For an excerpt of the Chace map, see https://hallockville.org/hallocksbook/.

4. F. W. Beers, *Atlas of Long Island* (New York: Beers, Comstock & Cline, 1873).

5. Richard M. Bayles, *Sketches of Suffolk County: Historical and Descriptive* (1874).

6. George Miller, "History of the Town of Riverhead," repr. Twomey, ed., *Seeking the Past*, 27.

7. Richard M. Bayles, *Long Island Handbook* (1885), excerpted in VW *Album VII*.

8. Osborne Shaw, "Obituary of Richard M. Bayles," *Patchogue Advance*, November 7, 1930.

9. Richard M. Bayles, "Riverhead," repr. Twomey, ed., *Seeking the Past*, 46.

10. *Brooklyn Daily Eagle*, February 7, 1879, 2.

11. Based on a statistical analysis of Bessie Hallock's Sound Avenue Cemetery Records. In the years before 1859, 70 percent of the burials were under 20 years old, possibly because this was a new cemetery, with older adults tending to be buried in the Aquebogue cemetery.

12. *Sag-Harbor Express*, March 18, 1869, 2.

13. Northville Academy Book (collection of HMF) has a list of shareholders.

14. Record Book of Northville Academy, collection of HMF. The bell was made by Hedges, Free & Co., a Cincinnati foundry that also made iron "plantation bells" as a sideline for "the Southern market." The 1938 hurricane blew the bell tower off the building. The bell rested in the building's coal bin until rescued by the Hallockville Museum, where it is now exhibited in a special kiosk.

15. *Suffolk Weekly Times,* August 22, 1861; VW *Album X*.

16. "Northville Academy Handbook" (1862), collection of HMF.

17. E. A. Bell, "The Northville Academy," *Traveler-Watchman*, October 10, 1846, in VW *Album X*.

18. *Suffolk Weekly Times*, August 22, 1861.

19. *Riverhead Bicentennial Album*, 56.

20. *Riverhead News*, September 3, 1904, in VW *Album X*.

21. James Y. Downs list, in VW *Album X*.

22. Benjamin D. Price, "Catalogue of Architectural Plans for Churches and Parsonages," Philadelphia: Board of Church Extension, Methodist Episcopal Church, 1889.

23. VW *Album X*.

24. 1904 clipping, in VW *Album X*.

25. The architect listed on the plans is J. Shaw from Jamaica, LI—probably Joseph Shaw. The only other buildings by him on record are a few two-story shop and home combinations in Brooklyn. The asymmetric twin towers had plenty of European antecedents but may have owed their immediate heritage to Richard Upjohn's 1844 design for the Church of the Pilgrims in Brooklyn.

26. *Brooklyn Daily Eagle*, June 18, 1904, 1.

27. John T. Downs, Journal, in VW *Album VIII*. This building now belongs to the author and his wife who use it as a garden ornament.

28. Henry Wilson Young, clippings from the *Coquiville Valley Sentinel* (Oregon) of which he was the editor, dated 1921 through 1925, VW *Album VIII*. Young (1847–1927) grew up on a farm adjacent to the location of the new District 10 school. He attended the old school as a boy, then taught there for a year in 1873 after returning from a trip to South America. Most of his subsequent career was as a newspaper editor, first in Illinois for seven years, then in Kansas where he served briefly as a state senator, and finally in two small towns in Oregon where he died in 1927.

29. As told by the author's uncle, Willard Downs.

30. *County Review*, July 27, 1917, 1.

31. *County Review*, November 10, 1927, 3.

32. John T. Downs, Notes, and Leslie T. Wells, article, typescripts in VW *Album VIII*.

33. *Republican Watchman*, March 27, 1886, in VW *Album VIII*.

34. DHH Diary, in VW *Album VIII*.

35. Lois Young, granddaughter of Halsey Hallock, said that Sound Avenue was always a different sort of place. "They loved to play cards in Aquebogue. Sound Avenue was much more sanctimonious—on the surface." Conversation with Lois Young, July 8, 2004.

36. *Long-Islander*, January 14, 1899, 1; *Suffolk County News*, January 13, 1899, 3, and March 31, 1899, 1; *East Hampton Star*, January 13, 1899; *South Side Signal*, January 14, 1899, 3.

37. *Suffolk County News*, April 7, 1899, 1.

38. *Riverhead News*, September 3, 1904.

39. Fullerton photographed the intersection of Phillips Lane and Sound Avenue. The image is part of the Harry T. Tuthill Fullerton Collection of the Suffolk County Historical Society, https://createsend.com/t/d-E09221B03A2E56E1.

40. U.S. Post Office, "Postal History: Rural Free Delivery," https://about.usps.com/who/profile/history/rural-free-delivery.html.

41. *East Hampton Star*, May 19, 1899, 4.

42. VW *Album XII*; also see Thomas M. Stark, *Riverhead: The Halcyon Years 1861–1919* (Riverhead, NY: Maple Hill Press, 2005), 65.

43. Leslie T. Wells, Notes, in VW *Album VIII*.

44. *Suffolk County News*, October 6, 1899, 1.

45. John H. Hagen, "The Iron Pier," *County Review*, October 1, 1941, in VW *Album XIII*.

46. *County Review*, March 24, 1905.

47. Leslie T. Wells, Notes and DHH Diary, in VW *Album VIII*.

48. "Hallock Notes and Quotes from Hallock Account Books," in VW *Album XIV*.

49. *County Review*, February 11, 1926, 4.

50. *County Review*, April 28, 1927, 9. The Hallock Homestead received electric power a year earlier than the rest of Sound Avenue as the result of a line that ran from Mattituck to service Carey Camp.

51. June 1928 clipping, probably from *Riverhead News*, in scrapbook of Ella Wells, in VW *Album V*.

52. Stark, *Riverhead*, 118–20.

53. The manuscript census did not provide street addresses or identify which hamlet people lived in. Sometimes the census taker skipped around between communities, with some households in Jamesport or Aquebogue intermingled with Northville returns. The author has done his best to remove these, but it is impossible to be precise about the boundaries.

54. *Long Island Traveler*, July 8, 1892.

55. Paul Hoffman, Tony Trubisz, Irene Robinson, Willard Downs, Edward Sydlowski, Nancy Gilbert, Celia Naugles, Henry Tractenberg, the Helen Sawicki family, and many others contributed to the "Polish Immigrant Farmers" exhibit at Hallockville in 2006 that is the basis for this section. Much of the information is from interviews with surviving family members.

56. Based on 2008 interviews with Anthony Trubisz, his aunts Irene Trubisz Robinson and Teresa Trubisz Zimnowski, and his mother's friend Bertha Rudnicki, who came after World War II from the same place in Poland as Anthony's grandfather.

57. DHH Diary, 1927.

58. *County Review*, September 23, 1910.

59. *County Review*, February 11, 1921, 10.

60. *County Review*, April 8, 1921, 1.

61. *County Review*, December 9, 1921, 1.

62. *Brooklyn Daily Eagle*, November 20, 1923.

63. It is difficult to precisely locate families geographically on the 1920 Federal Census manuscripts. However, of the approximately 400 residents that can definitely be placed in the new village of Sound Avenue, 57 percent were from Poland or Russia, Galicia, and Lithuania.

64. Arthur Channing Downs Jr. "Riverhead's Only Incorporated Village," *Long Island Forum*, January 1968, 11; February 1968, 32.

65. New York State Archives, "The Greatest Reform School in the World: A Guide to the Records of the New York House of Refuge" (1989).

66. *Long-Islander*, August 20, 1869, 2,

67. *Long-Islander*, February 22, 1869.

68. *Sag-Harbor Express*, November 3, 1881, 2; *Long-Islander*, November 4, 1881, 3. He received four months off for good behavior but was subsequently arrested for another robbery in Smithtown and sentenced to 10 years, of which he served eight and a half years before his final discharge in 1891. New York (State) Department of State, Discharges of Convicts by Commutation of Sentences, 1883–1913, series A0604, vol. 7. New York State Archives, Albany, New York.

69. ST Diary, January 6, 1868. Sammy Tuthill's father-in-law was Salem Wells, who lived next door in one of the oldest houses still standing on Sound Avenue. The boy was probably one of the many young boys and girls sent to the community by the House of Refuge on Randall's Island.

70. ST Diary, March 31, 1881.

71. *Long Island Traveler*, December 4, 1873, 4.

72. *Sag-Harbor Express*, March 4, 1886, 2; October 28, 1866, 2.

73. *County Review*, March 2, 1906, 4.

74. For general background, see Frank Cavioli, "People, Places, and the Ku Klux Klan on Long Island," *Long Island Forum* (August 1986): 159–67. For the Flanders and Jamesport meetings, see *County Review*, September 14, 1923; October 23, 1923; and December 14, 1923. Recently, Klan paraphernalia was discovered in the attic of one of the stalwarts of the Jamesport Congregational Church.

75. The 1820 census lists one female slave under 14 and another 14–26 in Luce's household, as well as a free Black male 14–26. The age of the young slave girl corresponds with Chloe—about one year old. The older female slave and the free Black male could be Chloe's mother and father.

76. For more on Tate, see *County Review*, January 18, 1940, 4.

77. ST Diary.

78. "Brooklyn's Call to Home Seekers," *Brooklyn Daily Eagle* (*Eagle Library*, no. 136, February 1908), 18–19.

Chapter 9

1. David Hackett Fischer, *Albion's Seed* (Oxford: Oxford University Press: 1989), 87–97.

2. VW *Album III*.

3. DHH, *My Memories*, 18.

4. Thomas Pope, letters, 1898–1931, MSS, collection of HMF. Born in 1843, "Addie" Angelina Adelaide Hallock, the daughter of Jacob and Laura Hallock, lived a little east of the Homestead Hallocks in West Mattituck, and was 14—two years younger than Pope. Typescripts of letters are also in VW *Album XIV*.

5. DHH, *My Memories*, 20.

6. ST Diary, November 13–14, 1866.

7. Henrietta Terry Wells, Diaries, 1883–1884, private collection, partial typescript in VW *Album III*.
8. *Brooklyn Daily Eagle*, May 14, 1883, 4.
9. *Long Island Traveler*, April 6, 1883, 1.
10. *South Side Signal*, April 28, 1883, 2; Sag Harbor *Corrector*, May 5, 1883, 3.
11. See Thomas M. Stark, *Riverhead: The Halcyon Years 1861–1919* (Huntington, NY: Maple Hill Press, 2005), 102–3.
12. ST Diary, December 26, 1883.
13. Jim Evans, "Nawth Fawk Tawk," master's thesis, SUNY Geneseo, 1967, rev. 2017), 13–14.
14. ST Diary, November 13, 1866.
15. *Long Island Traveler*, October 15, 1886, 2. The term "callithumpian" harkens back to 18th-century groups that disrupted parliament or elections in Great Britain, but in 19th-century America it mostly referred to boisterous groups that used crude noisemakers such as pots, pans, tin horns, or cow bells to celebrate New Year's parades or other such events.
16. *County Review*, December 15, 1916, 6.

Chapter 10

1. DHH Diary, 28; his memory may have been confused, as Melinda Corwin recorded in her diary that General Training Day was September 20, 1838; VW *Album VIII*.
2. Estelle Evans, *Receipts and Reminiscenses of the Hallock Family & Friends* (Hallockville Museum Farm, 1987), 54. Also see "Quotes from Miss Ella," February 1977, VW *Album XIV*. "Mr. Dimon" was probably Frank Dimon, who rebuilt the Jamesport Manor in the 1870s. John Franklin Hallock's hill is now part of Hallock State Park, just to the east of the upper parking area. The "next hill to the northwest" is on the north end of the Halsey Hallock farm and is called Jacob's Hill on USGS surveys.
3. VW *Album XIV*.
4. *Charters and General Laws of the Colony 119*, Records of the Governor and Company of the Massachusetts Bay (Boston: T. B. Waite and Co., 1814), 366.
5. Sag Harbor *Corrector*, December 18, 1850, 3; December 21, 1850, 3.
6. *Sag-Harbor Express*, December 29, 1870, 2.
7. ST Diary, 1884.
8. Recollection of Eula's daughter Lois Young as told to the author. Oranges were not widely available at the time.
9. *Long Island Traveler*, January 9, 1879, 2.
10. Corwin, Diary, March 2, 1844.
11. Noah Youngs, Day Book, typescript, VW *Album III*.

12. Mary Downs, Scrapbook, author's collection.
13. Evans, *Receipts and Reminiscenses*, 51.
14. Mary Downs records, quoted in Evans, *Receipts and Reminiscenses*, 94.
15. Conversation with author. Anthony is the grandson of Kazimierz Trubisz, who bought the farm from the Hallocks in 1918.
16. New England Historical Society, "Puritan Easter, or The Devil's Holiday," https://www.newenglandhistoricalsociety.com/puritan-easter-devils-holiday/.
17. *Long Island Traveler*, April 29, 1881, 2.
18. *Long Island Traveler*, March 30, 1888, 1.
19. ST Diary.
20. ST Diary. Not clear who this was.
21. *Riverhead Weekly News*, December 20, 1886, VW *Album X*.
22. Evans, *Receipts and Reminiscenses*, 27.
23. Noah Youngs, Day Book, excerpt in VW *Album VI*.
24. Elsie Anna Wells, notes, in VW *Album VI*. She lived just to the west of the Sound Avenue Church in the house previously owned by George Mitchell Terry.
25. Henrietta Terry Wells, Diary, August 1883.
26. August 22, 1900. Richard Wines, "Northville," 4, VW *Album VII*.
27. Leslie T. Wells, Notes, VW *Album VIII*.
28. The record books of the Sound Avenue Grange are in the collection of the Hallockville Museum Farm.
29. VW *Album IX*.
30. *Brooklyn Daily Eagle*, July 27, 1899, 7.
31. Unattributed newspaper article, c. 1899, Ida Young's Scrapbook, 16, collection of SCHS, copy in VW *Album XIV*.
32. *Brooklyn Daily Eagle*, August 5, 1899, 2.
33. Conversation with Lois Young, July 8, 2004.

Chapter 11

1. Hallockville Museum Farm, 1987, rev. ed. 2000. In typically modest manner, Estelle Evans's name does not appear on the title page except as a member of the Cookbook Committee.
2. Account Book of James Fanning's store in Aquebogue, 1794–1807, collection of SCHS.
3. See also Richard Wines, "Receipts and Reminiscenses of the Hallock Family and Friends (A New Introduction)," 2021, https://hallockville.org/cookbook/.
4. Cuyler B. Tuthill, "Recollections of Jamesport," *Long Island Forum*, May 1965, 101.
5. Evans, *Receipts and Reminiscenses*, 110–11. Quoted from great-grandma (Henrietta) Harmony Haines, a farmer's daughter born in Southold around 1845.

6. David Hackett Fisher, *Albion's Seed* (Oxford: Oxford University Press, 1989), 136.
7. Evans, *Receipts and Reminiscenses*, 117.
8. Evans, 108. Eva Gordon Slaterbeck (1871–1966), who grew up in Peconic.
9. Daniel Hallock to Halsey Hallock, Fort McHenry, March 7, 1864.
10. Evans, *Receipts and Reminiscenses*, 76.
11. Estelle Evans's recollection, as related to the author.
12. Evans, *Receipts and Reminiscenses*, 96.
13. Molasses cookies have become a signature item for cooking sessions on the woodstove in the Homestead kitchen.
14. John T. Downs, Notes, MSS, 124. Private collection.
15. Evans, *Receipts and Reminiscenses*, 82.
16. DHH, *My Memories*, 12–13.
17. DHH, 7.
18. Estelle Evans, "Time Was." VW *Album III*.
19. Evans, *Receipts and Reminiscenses*, 51, 112; Henrietta Terry Wells, Diary, 1883, excerpts in VW *Album III*.
20. Melinda Corwin, Diary, VW *Album XII*.
21. Thomas Pope, letter, quoted in Evans, *Receipts and Reminiscenses*, 46.
22. Evans, 46.
23. Evans, 47, 50.
24. Henry W. Young, 1906; in Evans, *Receipts and Reminiscenses*, 44.
25. Evans, 43. Benjamin was the granddaughter of Herman Hallock's brother Zachariah III.
26. Minutes of the Busy Workers Society of Northville, photocopy in VW *Album III* and *Album IX*.
27. Henry W. Young, 1906; in Evans, *Receipts and Reminiscenses*, 35. Henry W. Young was the great-grandson of Rufus Youngs (1748–1828), Capt. Zachariah Hallock's brother-in-law.
28. Evans, *Receipts and Reminiscenses*, 39.
29. Evans, 39.
30. Thomas Pope, letter; quoted in Evans, *Receipts and Reminiscenses*, 46.
31. In the 19th century, apples and pears were often dried. John T. Downs recalled his mother, who was born in 1807, doing this. Evans, *Receipts and Reminiscenses*, 91.
32. Evans, 86.
33. L. H. Bailey, *Standard Encyclopedia of Horticulture*, vol. 3 (New York: Macmillan, 1930), 3246.
34. Henrietta Terry Wells, Diary, 1883, VW *Album III*.
35. ST Diary.
36. Evans, *Receipts and Reminiscenses*, 22–23.
37. Evans, 24.

38. Thomas Pope to DHH, March 24, 1898; quoted in Evans, 46.
39. John T. Downs, Notes, MSS, 124. Private collection.
40. ST Diary, 121.
41. Evans, *Receipts and Reminiscenses*, 62.
42. Evans, 84.
43. Evans, 88.
44. Evans, 116.
45. Evans, 125. Laura Terry Downs (1815–1894) was actually the great-grandmother of Laura Downs (1898–1997).
46. Evans, 42.
47. Cuyler B. Tuthill, "Recollections of Jamesport," *Long Island Forum*, May 1965, 101.
48. See, for instance, Ola Powell, *Successful Canning and Preserving* (J. B. Lippincott: 1917).
49. Evans, *Receipts and Reminiscenses*, 79–80.
50. United States Department of Agriculture, "Home Canning of Fruits and Vegetables," *Farmers' Bulletin 1211*, 1921.

Chapter 12

1. Estelle Evans, *Receipts and Reminiscenses of the Hallock Family & Friends* (Hallockville Museum Farm, 1987), 10. Lillian Hallock Sirrine was a granddaughter of Halsey's brother Charles Hallock.
2. Evans, 10. "In an Eighteenth Century Drawing Room" became a popular hit in 1939, recorded by a number of bands including Guy Lombardo, but was based on a Mozart piano concerto. "Little Old Lady" was a 1936 Hoagy Carmichael hit.
3. Evans, 10.
4. LHH, *Hallock Genealogy*, 267.
5. *County Review*, June 20, July 18, and July 25, 1919. The Daughters of the Revolution, organized in 1890 and disbanded in 1983, was a competitor to the Daughters of the American Revolution and appears to have been especially strong on Long Island. The papers of the DR are at the SCHS.
6. *County Review*, November 28, 1919, 1.
7. *County Review*, November 10, 1922, 3.
8. *County Review*, September 17, 1920, 1.
9. "Quotes from Miss Ella," October 1978, VW *Album XIV*.
10. *County Review*, November 24, 1916, 1.
11. E. R. Eastman, ed., *American Agriculturist*, to Bessie L. Hallock, May 26, 1930, MSS, collection of HMF. An undated clipping from the *Agriculturist* is also attached to the letter.
12. As told to the author.

13. Written by David Halsey Hallock between 1925 and 1937. One of his nieces, Lois Young, edited, organized, and transcribed these writings. This selection appeared in "25th Anniversary Commemorative Journal," Hallockville Museum Farm, 2000. Other selections appear in DHH, *My Memories*.

14. "D. Halsey Hallock, Paper for Century Celebration at Northville," [probably printed in *Riverhead News*] 1929, VW *Album X*.

15. Unidentified clipping, July 9, 1936, VW *Album X*.

16. MSS in VW *Album XIV*. Halsey slightly changed (or perhaps misremembered) the last line, which originally read "Like the Heaven above."

17. The last verse of the Julia Carney 1845 poem "Little Things" reads: "Little deeds of kindness / Little words of love / Make our earth happy / Like the Heaven above."

18. DHH, "Recollections," 2.

19. DHH, "Recollections," 6.

20. Evans, *Receipts and Reminiscenses*, 54.

21. *Long Island Traveler*, November 16, 1939, 1.

22. *County Review*, November 30, 1939, 18; *Watchman*, November 16, 1939, 1.

23. *Brooklyn Daily Eagle*, November 15, 1939, 13.

Chapter 13

1. Handwritten note in Lois Young's typescript of DHH Diary.

2. *County Review*, November 25, 1948, 10.

3. BLH, "Old House." The handwritten first version, attributed to the 1930s, is in VW *Album XIV*.

4. *County Review*, September 15, 1949, 5.

5. Estelle Evans, *Receipts and Reminiscenses of the Hallock Family & Friends* (Hallockville Museum Farm, 1987), 11.

6. Evans, 12.

7. "Northville Dock," *Newsday*, March 24, 1986.

8. "Northville Dock Leak," *Traveler-Watchman*, May 17, 1990.

9. *Traveler-Watchman*, February 26, 1970, 1.

10. As told to the author by Estelle Evans, one of the members of the group.

11. *Sunday Review*, November 10, 1963.

12. Story told in the author's family.

13. *Riverhead News-Review*, October 12, 1967.

14. *Riverhead News-Review*, February 26, 1970; March 5, 1970.

15. *Riverhead News-Review*, July 4, 1974.

16. Ronnie Wacker, "Atomic Plants to Overshadow Historic Hallock Farm," *Suffolk Times*, January 16, 1975, 2.

17. *New York Times*, June 22, 1975.

18. Quote from Ella, April 1975, VW *Album XIV*.
19. *Long Island Weekly, New York Times*, November 12, 1978.
20. *Suffolk County Agricultural News*, clipping at Riverhead Town Historian, n.d.; *Traveler-Watchman*, April 29, 1976.
21. *New York Times*, November 12, 1978.
22. *Riverhead News Review*, January 4, 1979; March 3, 1980.
23. *Newsday*, January 30, 1980.
24. "Quotes from Miss Ella," September 1980, VW *Album XIV*.
25. Evans, *Receipts and Reminiscenses*, 12.
26. Estelle Evans, conversation with the author, January 2, 2019.
27. Quotes from Cousin Ella, VW *Album XIV*.
28. VW *Album VII*.
29. Evans, *Receipts and Reminiscenses*, 8. A slightly shorter version appeared as an obituary in *Hallockville Happenings*, 1985.
30. Evans, *Receipts and Reminiscenses*, 11.
31. *Weekender*, October 7, 1982, 2; clipping in VW *Album XIV*.
32. Recited July 1975. Ella attributed the quote to the mother of a friend, but it is actually from Thomas More (1477–1535), the English humanist and statesman, slightly altered.

Chapter 14

1. Clippings, some undated, in VW *Album XIV*.
2. New York State, *Laws of 1975*, chap. 640. Originally S-5814 and A-8189.
3. *Hallockville Happenings*, Spring 1983.
4. *Riverhead News-Review*, September 15, 1988. Donated to Hallockville by Jack and Peter Van de Wetering.
5. Donated by Robert Entenmann, heir to the Entenmann bakery fortune, who acquired the property as part of his horse farm.
6. Robert B. Catell and Kenny Moore, *The CEO and the Monk: One Company's Journey to Profit and Purpose* (Hoboken, NJ: Wiley, 2004), 78–79. The actual shoreline is approximately 1,600 miles and considerably more is open to the public.
7. *Audubon (New York) Advocate*, Winter 2003.
8. *Listen to the Sound 2000: A Citizen's Agenda for the Long Island Sound*, National Audubon Society, Save the Sound and Regional Plan Association.
9. *Listen to the Sound 2000*, 41.
10. *Riverhead News-Review*, January 17, 2002.

Bibliography

Austin, Barbara, editor. *Journey Through Time: The Riverhead Bicentennial 1792–1992.* Riverhead, NY: Riverhead Bicentennial Commission, 1992.
Bayles, R. M. *History of Suffolk County, New York with Illustrations, Portraits and Sketches of Prominent Families and Individuals.* New York: W. W. Munsell & Co., 1882. Riverhead selection repr. in Twomey, *Seeking the Past*, 34–80.
Beers, F. W. *Atlas of Long Island, New York.* New York: Beers, Comstock & Cline, 1873.
Bendroth, Margaret. *The Last Puritans: Mainline Protestants and the Power of the Past.* Durham: University of North Carolina Press, 2015.
"Brooklyn's Call to Home Seekers." *Brooklyn Daily Eagle (Eagle Library)* 136, February 1908.
Case, Georgette Lane. *We Will Not Forget: Riverhead's Civil War Soldiers & Sailors.* Town of Riverhead, NY, 2011.
Case, J. Wickham. Southold Town Records. Towns of Southold and Riverhead, 1882.
Catell, Robert B., and Kenny Moore. *The CEO and the Monk: One Company's Journey to Profit and Purpose.* Hoboken, NJ: Wiley, 2004.
Cavioli, Frank. "People, Places, and the Ku Klux Klan on Long Island." *Long Island Forum*, August 1986, 159–67.
Chace, J. *Map of Suffolk County, L.I., N.Y.: From Actual Surveys.* Philadelphia: John Douglass, 1858.
Craven, Rev. Charles E. *History of Mattituck, Long Island, N.Y.* Mattituck, NY: 1906.
Downs, Arthur Channing Jr., editor. *Riverhead Town Records, 1792–1886.* Huntington, NY: *Long Islander*, 1967.
———. "Riverhead's Only Incorporated Village." *Long Island Forum*, January 1968, 11–34.
Evans, Estelle. *Receipts and Reminiscenses of the Hallock Family & Friends.* Riverhead, NY: Hallockville Museum Farm, 1987.
Evans, James. "Nawth Fawk Tawk." Master's thesis, SUNY Geneseo, 1967. Revised 2017.
Fischer, David Hackett. *Albion's Seed.* Oxford: Oxford University Press, 1989.

Hallock, Bessie L. Sound Avenue Cemetery Records. Virginia Wines typescript, Suffolk County Historical Society.

———. "Autobiography of an Old House." 1956. Typescript in VW *Album XIV*. A manuscript of an older version called "History of Our House" is also in VW *Album XIV*.

Hallock, Charles. *The Hallock-Holyoke Pedigree and Collateral Branches in the United States: Being a Revision of the Hallock Ancestry of 1866*. Amherst, MA: Carpenter & Morehouse, 1906.

Hallock, David Halsey. Diaries, 1855–1890. Typescripts of MSS by Lois Young and Virginia Wines. Collection of Hallockville Museum Farm. Typescripts labeled "Items Taken from Hallock Diaries," probably excerpted by Ella Hallock. Some of the later entries in the diaries are likely by daughters Bessie and Ella.

———. *My Memories*, edited by Lois Young. Riverhead, NY: Hallockville Museum Farm, 2001.

Hallock, Lucius H. *A Hallock Genealogy*. 1926; repr. 1975. The author's copy has notes that Virginia Wines copied from Ella and Bessie Hallock's book, as well as additional notes of her own.

Hallock, William A. "A Brief Sketch of the Hallock Ancestry in the United States." New York: American Tract Society, 1866. Updated by Jacob N. Imandt in 1929; repr. West Long Branch, NJ: Morgan Press, 1940.

Hallock, Zachariah. Account Book. 1771–1819. MSS. Suffolk County Historical Society.

Hallockville Museum Farm. Oral History Collection; 92 tapes recorded from 1972 through 2002. Available at New York Heritage Digital Collections. https://nyheritage.org/organizations/hallockville-museum-farm. Includes two interviews with Ella Hallock, as well as recordings of other family members and neighbors, including descendants of Polish immigrants.

Henrietta, James A. *The Evolution of American Society, 1700–1815*. Lexington, MA: D. C. Heath, 1973.

Hummel, George F. *Heritage*. New York: Frederick A. Stokes, 1935.

Hunt, Harrison, and Bill Bleyer. *Long Island and the Civil War: Queens, Nassau and Suffolk Counties During the War Between the States*. Charleston, SC: History Press, 2015.

Hyde, E. Belcher. *Atlas of Suffolk County, Long Island, New York*. New York: E. Belcher Hyde, 1909.

Kolodny, Brad. *The Jews of Long Island: 1705–1918*. Albany: State University of New York Press, 2022.

Mather, Frederic Gregory. *The Refugees of 1776 from Long Island to Connecticut*. Baltimore: Genealogical Publishing, 1972. Original published in 1913.

New York State Archives. "The Greatest Reform School in the World: A Guide to the Records of the New York House of Refuge." 1989.

Portrait and Biographical Record of Suffolk County, Long Island, New York. New York: Chapman, 1880.
Price, Benjamin D. "Catalogue of Architectural Plans for Churches and Parsonages." Philadelphia: Board of Church Extension, Methodist Episcopal Church, 1889.
Prime, Nathaniel S. *A History of Long Island: From its First Settlement by Europeans to the Year 1845, with Special Reference to its Ecclesiastical Concerns*. New York: Robert Carter, 1845.
Riverhead Town Bicentennial Committee. *Riverhead Bicentennial Album*. Riverhead, NY: 1976.
Stark, Thomas M. *Riverhead: The Halcyon Years 1861–1919*. Huntington, NY: Maple Hill Press, 2005.
Talmage, Nathaniel A. "The Growth of Agriculture in Riverhead Town." Riverhead, NY: 1977.
Terry, Henrietta. Diary, 1883–1884. Typescript. VW *Album II*.
Tuthill, Samuel. Diaries, 1863–1890. Typescript of MSS. VW *Album XII*.
Twomey, Tom, editor. *Seeking the Past: Writings from 1832–1905 Relating to the History of the Town of Riverhead*. New York: Newmarket Press, 2004.
Vlach, John Michael. *Barns*. New York: W. W. Norton, 2003
Whitaker, Rev. Epher. *History of Southold, L.I., Its First Century*. Southold, NY: 1881.
Wick, Steve. *Heaven and Earth: The Last Farmers of the North Fork*. New York: St. Martin's Press, 1996.
Wines, Richard A. *Defense of the Eagle: New Discoveries about This Coast Guard Legend*. Hallockville Museum Farm, 2018.
———. *Fertilizer in America: From Waste Recycling to Resource Exploitation*. Philadelphia: Temple University Press, 1985.
———. "The Nineteenth Century Agricultural Transition in an Eastern Long Island Community." *Agricultural History* 55 (1981): 50–63.
Wines, Virginia. *Albums I–XXXIII*, MSS. Hallockville Museum Farm. The albums are large loose-leaf binders in which Wines inserted photos, clippings, manuscripts, her typewritten transcripts of manuscripts, and other material relevant to the history of the town of Riverhead. Vols. are arranged in two series, along Sound Avenue and Main Road, according to where the subject lived. No page numbers. Some of these volumes are available online at Perservica, Long Island University's Palmer School of Library and Information Science. https://liu.access.preservica.com/index.php?name=SO_39ec8f82-55a8-4c98-806f-806b446d46ce.
———. *Pioneers of Riverhead Town*. Riverhead, NY: Suffolk County Historical Society, 1981.
———. "West from the Canoe Place: A Study of the First and Second Aquebogue Divisions." Riverhead, NY: Suffolk County Historical Society, 1975.

Index

abolitionism and opposition to, 55–57, 85, 102, 179, 182
additional material, 8
African Americans. *See* persons of color
agricultural revolution, 129–30
Agricultural Society. *See* Riverhead Town Agricultural Society
Albertson, Richard, 47, 294n2
alcoholic beverages, 234–35
Aldrich, Hattie, 226, 231
Aldrich, Jacob, 19
Aldrich, Mary. *See* Hallock, Mary Aldrich
Aldrich, Rogers, 42
Aldrich, Serepta, 39, 42, 47, 284
American Agriculturalist, 244, 246, 311n11
American Missionary Association, 80
American Revolution, 19–21, 129, 226, 242, 283
Americanization, 119, 242–43
anniversaries, golden, 206, 246
anti-slavery movement, 50. *See also* abolitionism
apples, 131, 231, 233
Aquebogue, 2–3, 16–17, 36, 109, 124–25, 140, 166, 222, 279, 305n35
Aquebogue church (Old Steeple), 41, 189, 191; founding of 17–18; schism in 1829, 25–27
Aquebogue Dividend, First, 14–15
Aquebogue, Old. *See* Jamesport

Articles of Association, 19
Ash, Carol, 279–80
asparagus, 183, 229–30, 236–37
Audubon societies, 277–78
Aunt Frances's Washhouse, 119, 275

Backowsky, Mike, 140–41
Baiting Hollow and Roanoke Telephone Company, 115
barn raisings, 213–14
barn. *See* Homestead Barn
barns: color of, 183; Dutch style, 10; English style, 10, 141–42
Bartels, Erich, 63–64
Baxter Academy of Music, 72
Bayles, Richard M., 154
Beebe, Nancy "Nannie," 55
Benjamin, Adelia Hallock (sister of Halsey), xv, 28, 35, 39, 44–45, 55, 70–72, 124–25, 246, 285
Benjamin, Albert, 213
Benjamin, Florence, 229
Benjamin, Mrs. Halsey, 195
Benjamin, Lorenia, 70
Benjamin, Maria "Libby," 70
Benjamin, Nina "Nannie," 105, 213, 300n1
Benjamin, Simeon (founder of Elmira College), 70–71
Benjamin, Simeon O. (Halsey Hallock's brother-in-law), 47, 70–72, 102
Benjamin, William, 177

Bergan, Ada, 251
berries, 230
Bethuel E. Hallock House, 11
bicycle riding, 101
birthdays, 30, 213
Blacks, 80, 102. *See also* persons of color
Bleyer, Bill, 56
Blizzard of 1888, 112
Bohemian immigrants, 147
Bohemian Room, 147, 303n34
Bradbury, William, 48
Brady, Charles, 127
bread, 234
Brister (enslaved by William Hallock II), 18
Brister (enslaved by Rev. Daniel Youngs), 19. *See also* Youngs, Brister
Brooklyn, 42–43, 45, 63, 70, 96, 74, 155, 177, 180, 192, 214, 284
Brooklyn Daily Eagle, 90–92, 298n27
Brown & Jackson store, 79, 193
Brown, Nelly (wife of Sherwood Tuthill), 190
Brown, Reuben, 19–21
Brown, Richard, 19
butter, 79, 130

cakes, 197, 209, 225, 233–35, 254; wedding, 194–95, 233
cakewalks, 179
camp meeting. *See* Jamesport, Methodist Camp Meeting
Camp William Carey. *See* Carey Camp
canning, 236–37
Cape Cod houses, 10–11, 32–33
Carey Camp, 252
cars, 116–17, 144, 242
Case, Henry, 167
Castro, Bernadette, 297
Catell, Robert B., 277
cattle, 130, 138, 140, 225
cauliflower, 136, 139, 210, 250, 216
cedar, eastern red, 140
cheese, 222
cemeteries and cemetery records, 258
cherries, 231

Chevrolet, Louis, 169–70
chicken houses, 55, 144–46, 149
chickens, 130, 132, 149, 210, 221, 226, 228, 234, 238, 240
chicken, pressed, 195, 209, 227
child labor, 177
Christian at Work, 45, 94–95, 286
Christian Endeavor. *See* Young People's Society of Christian Endeavor
Christmas, celebration of or lack thereof, 10, 43, 196, 203–206
church meetings, 42–43
churches. *See* Aquebogue church, Jamesport church, Mattituck church, Riverhead church, Sound Avenue church
Cichanowicz family, 174–75, 240, 277
Cichanowicz farmhouse, 57, 175, 268, 275, 286
Cichanowicz, Konstanty and Adela, 171–72, 174–75
Cichanowicz, Frank, 114
cider, 48–49, 198, 231, 234–35
cider press (or mill) 40, 134, 144, 303n28
cisterns, 113, 142, 149, 153
Civil War, 53–65, 69–70; draft, 57, 59; few local volunteers for, 58–59; opposition to, 57–58; post-war reconstruction, 80; substitutes, 63–64; town borrowing for substitutes, 63. *See also* Hallock, Daniel
clams, 228–29
colored persons. *See* persons of color
Combs Decoy Shop, 275
Comestock, Hope, 282
Conklin, David, 72
Conklin, Meta, 126
conservatism, cultural, 12, 29, 85, 102, 157, 183, 203, 204, 206
cookies, molasses, 225, 240
Copperheads, 57–58, 86, 180, 299n43. *See also* Democrats
cordwood. *See* wood
corn, 131–36, 140, 222–24

corn crib, 145–46
Corwin, Elizabeth Hallock, 13
Corwin, Fanny (wife of Daniel Tuthill), 188
Corwin, Fennimore, 109
Corwin, Frank, 169
Corwin, Halsey, 109, 125
Corwin, Henry F. "Harry," 74, 108–109, 124, 143
Corwin, Isaiah Seymore, 205
Corwin, Jabez, 177, 204, 212
Corwin, Lloyd, 109, 125
Corwin, Lloyd, Jr., 259
Corwin, Melinda (wife of Jabez Corwin), 31, 55, 86–87, 102, 188, 202, 204–205, 207, 231
Corwin, Nathan, 157
Corwin, Paula, 259
Cory, David, *Cowbells and Clover*, 244–45
courtship, 185–88
Craven, Charles, 14, 17
Crescent Duck Farm, 109
Cultivator, The, 134
cultivator, bicycle, 136–37

D. Y. Hallock & Sons, 110
Daughters of the Revolution, 242–43, 311n5
Dedrick, Herman Hallock, 82
Dedrick, John, 80–81
Dedrick, Marshall P., 80–81
Democratic party, 57–58, 95, 102, 125, 179, 264
Depression, Great, 173, 175, 250
desk, 241, 247
dialect. *See* language
Dimon, Frank, 202, 308n2
disease, 46–47, 59, 61, 155
Doroski, John B., 114
Downs, Allison O., 97, 196; Terry-Downs scandal, 97–101
Downs, Clara (wife of Allison O. Downs), 97–101
Downs, Daniel Y., 152–53
Downs, Ella (Wells), 233–34

Downs, Elma, 236–37
Downs, George, 46
Downs, Irving, 263–64
Downs, James Y., 49, 84
Downs, John T., 176, 230–31
Downs, L. Leland, 198
Downs, Laura, 234
Downs, Liela, 100–101
Downs, Manly W., 97–98
Downs, Mary Wells (wife of L. Leland Downs), 198–99, 209–10, 213, 232–33, 235
Downs, Nathaniel, 46, 100
Downs, Rachel, 100
draft. *See* Civil War, draft
Dunn, Nellie, 269
Duryea, Ernest and Grace, 107

Eagle (revenue cutter), 23
earthquake, 112
East Anglia, influence of, 9–13
Easter, 44, 210–12
electrical service, 116, 168–69
Elmira Female College, 70–71
entertainment, 165, 212–19
Episcopal church, Episcopalianism, 211
Evans, Estelle, 113, 165, 196, 209, 224, 260, 271, 309n1; *Receipts and Reminiscenses*, xvi, 221, 223–25, 229–32, 235, 238
Evans, James, "Nawth Fawk Tawk," 11–13, 197
Evans, Evan, 24
excursions, 110–11, 190, 192–93, 213, 214–15

fair. *See* Suffolk County Fair
Fanning, Edward and Alma, 47
Fanning, Elbert A., 161–62
Fanning, James, store of, 222
Fanny (person of color), 37
farm equipment, 132, 140–41
farm help, 147–48, 171, 173, 177–79
farm, map of. *See* Hallock farm map
Farmers Club. *See* Riverhead Town Agricultural Society

farming practices, 129–38, 140–46, 148–49
farmyard, 144–47
fast days, 41, 206–207
fences, 138–39
fertilizer, 132–33, 156, 165
fiddle music, 212–13
fish, as fertilizer, 23, 129–31, 156; as food, 229
Fishburn, M. H., 218
Fishel store, 38, 78–79
Fishel, Andrew, 38
Fishel, Arthur, 82
Fishel, Edwin, 82
Fishel, Gilbert, 82
Fishel, Jonas, 38, 82
fishing for fertilizer, 23, 129–30
fishing company, 23, 130, 291n38
Fitch, Wells H., 255
foodways, 221–28
Fourth of July, 30, 43, 201–202
Franklinville (Laurel), 20–21, 47, 57, 205, 286, 291n33
Franklinville Academy, 39, 44–46, 53–55, 68, 107, 157, 223
Freedmen's Aid Society (or Commission), 80, 179, 182
Freedman's Relief Association, National, 80
Friendship, NY, 71, 79–80
frugality, 148–49
fruits, 229–31
Fuel Desulfurization Plant, 262
Fullerton, Hal B., 166

Gajeski, Florence Zaweski, 210
games, 12, 120, 165, 208, 218
garage, 144
General Training Day, 30, 201, 308n1
German immigrants, 63, 147
Gilson, Bridget, 269
Ginna (enslaved by Zerubabel Hallock II), 18
gold rush. *See* Pikes Peak gold rush
Grange Hall. *See* Sound Avenue Hall

Grange, Sound Avenue, 78, 174, 213, 215–18, 255, 261
Great Awakening, First, 16–18
Great Awakening, Second, 49
Great Migration (African-American), 182–83
Greenport, 30, 48, 177, 191, 201
Griffing, Lizzie, 98
Griffith, Rev. T. H., 101–103
guano, 132

Hallett mill, 77–78
Hallock Family Association, 275
Hallock family: dominance in community, 154–55; genealogies about, 13–14; roots of, 13–14, 254; standard of living, 78–79
Hallock farm, 249–51; 1820 map, 22; Halsey's 1859 map, 130; map in late 19th century, 135. *See also* farmyard, farm equipment, farm help, farming practices, sustainability
Hallock Farmstead, map of, 146
Hallock Homestead, 263–64, 281, 284; early history of, 11, 22; first west wing, 31–32, 55; kitchen 77–78, 113, 115, 296n18; life in, 105–27; photos of, 6, 114; raising the roof of, 32; renovations and improvements, 32, 55, 75–78, 112–16, 257; second west wing, 55, 65, 82, 113–15
Hallock name, 250
Hallock Pond, 134, 140, 248, 249, 251–52
Hallock State Park and Preserve, 16, 21–22, 139–40, 250, 308n2; creation of, 250, 277–79; name of, 279–80
Hallock, Adelia J. *See* Benjamin, Adelia Hallock
Hallock, Amanda (Wells) (wife of Daniel Hallock), 47, 186–87, 191
Hallock, Angelina Adelaide, 54
Hallock, Annie, 283

Hallock, Arletta (wife of Zachariah Hallock III), 31–33
Hallock, Arminda Young (wife of Herman Hallock), 19, 25–26, 29–30, 33, 37–39, 44, 70, 72, 81–82, 130, 144, 147, 205–206, 233, 285; photo of, 25
Hallock, Benjamin Laurens, 15–16, 230
Hallock, Bessie Leona (daughter of Halsey), xv, 75, 105, 201, 215, 248, 251, 266, 281, 285; "Autobiography of an Old House," 31–33, 42–43, 45, 81–82, 116; cemetery records, 258; church organist and choir director, 169, 206, 257–58; education of, 106–107; final years, 242, 257–60; genealogy chart, 258–59; lack of marriage, 125–27; music, 107, 119–22, 172, 243, 257; as music teacher, 240–41; photos by, 2, 6, 12, 21, 108, 115, 117, 121, 137, 139, 145–46, 227–28, 239, 244–45, 247, 254; photos of, 75, 111, 126, 243; social life, 119–22
Hallock, Bethuel, 22, 172, 284
Hallock, Bethuel E. (son of Bethuel Hallock), house of, 275
Hallock, Caleb (son of John Hallock), 26, 31, 94–95, 171, 181–82, 285; destruction of liberty pole, 57
Hallock, Caleb (son of Zerubabel Hallock II), 20, 283
Hallock, Christiana Howell (2nd wife of Zachariah Hallock II), 23, 30, 55, 284
Hallock, Charles (1st son of Herman Hallock), 27, 285
Hallock, Charles H. (2nd son of Herman Hallock, brother of Halsey Hallock), 27, 31, 32, 39, 43–44, 102, 110, 152–53, 246, 285
Hallock, Daniel (brother of Zachariah Hallock I), 20, 26
Hallock, Daniel W. "Wells" (son of John Hallock), 26, 171, 285

Hallock, Daniel Y. (Halsey Hallock's brother), 27, 31, 45, 130, 133–34, 157, 186–87, 191, 285; Civil War service and letters, 59–61, 224, 295n28; music, 48, 83; photos of, 59, 145; temperance movement, 49
Hallock, David Halsey. See Hallock, Halsey
Hallock, Edna (wife of George C. Hallock), 97
Hallock, Ekford, 188
Hallock, Elizabeth (Howell) (wife Zerubabel Hallock II), 17–19
Hallock, Ella Arminda (daughter of Halsey), 7, 75, 130, 169, 201–202, 215, 225, 232–33, 252, 285; driving, 116, 240, 242, 258; education of, 106–107; final years in Homestead, 257–61, 263–71, 275; lack of marriage, 125–27; music, 107, 121; photos of, 21, 75, 111, 121, 126, 244–45; poem "The Account of Saturday," 122–25; recollections of, xv, 240–42, 268–71; social life, 119–21
Hallock, Ella Jane, 229
Hallock, Ella May, 231
Hallock, Ellen B., 158
Hallock, Emilie (Wells) (wife of Halsey Hallock), 19, 117, 248, 285; at Northville Academy, 157–58; marriage, 68–71, 296n9; photos of, 71, 108, 111, 247; poems of, 72, 105
Hallock, Esther (wife of Wines Reeve), 284, 293n34
Hallock, Esther (wife of Zerubabel Hallock I), 16, 18, 283
Hallock, Eugene, 58, 91, 94–95, 213, 219, 286
Hallock, Eula (wife of Charles Wells), 62, 74–75, 81, 111, 118, 206, 233, 285
Hallock, Ezra, 19–20, 283
Hallock, Frances, "Aunt" (wife of John Hallock), 106, 118–19, 158, 286

Hallock, George C., 58, 97, 229, 286
Hallock, George Wilson, 31, 156–57, 164, 286
Hallock, Georgia (wife of Henry F. Cowin), 74–75, 107–108, 111, 118, 285
Hallock, Hal. *See* Hallock, Halsey W.
Hallock, Halsey, 8, 9, 19, 26, 105, 191, 191, 207, 213, 215, 219, 222–23, 226, 285; birth, 28–30, 231; childhood, 30–31, 201; dealing with scandals, 83–88, 90–92, 94, 97, 102–103; death of, 254–55; desk of, 241, 247; diary, 40–50, 187, 204, 207, 213, 215, 228, 293n27, 316; education, 33–36, 43–45, 106; family life, 72–79, 81–82; farming practices, 129–38, 140–141, 143–44, 148–49; final years, 252–54; first marriage, 53–55, 187, 187; honeymoon trip, 70–72, 80; loss of first wife, 64–65; "My Memories," 312n13; name, 30; photos of, 46, 71, 109–11, 137, 228, 239, 247, 254; poems, 72–73, 105, 239, 252–53; remembrances of, 240–42; retirement and old age, 230–55; school composition, 34–35; second marriage, 86–70; visions of future for farm, 249–51, 273; vote for Lincoln, 50, 53; wedding anniversaries, 245–47; youth, 37–40
Hallock, Halsey W. "Hal" (son of Halsey and Emilie Hallock), 8, 72–73, 81, 107, 111, 141, 172, 176, 225, 257, 260, 285; photos of, 139, 239–40, 245
Hallock, Hannah Young (wife of Zachariah I), 221–22, 284
Hallock, Hannah (wife of Rogers Aldrich, Herman's sister), 42
Hallock, Hannah J. (wife of Marshall Dedrick, Halsey's sister), 28, 38, 44, 71–72, 80–82, 101, 285, 297n26
Hallock, Harmony, 284, 293n34
Hallock, Harold, 240
Hallock, Henry A., 287
Hallock, Henry Lewis, 164, 167, 179, 286
Hallock, Herman H. (son of Charles Hallock), 167, 213–14, 254, 286
Hallock, Herman W. (father of Halsey Hallock), 19, 23–26, 31–34, 44, 47, 70, 72, 78, 81, 85–86, 133, 144, 147, 206, 229, 284–85; marriage and children, 24–28, 205; photo of, 25
Hallock, Isaiah, 26, 57, 84, 87, 94–95, 171, 205, 212, 286, 298n39
Hallock, Jacob, 298n39
Hallock, James (brother of Zerubabel Hallock II), 17
Hallock, Johana (wife of John Hallock), 26
Hallock, John (son of Zachariah Hallock I), 22, 26, 284
Hallock, John (son of John Franklin Hallock), 156, 158, 286
Hallock, John (son of Zerubabel Hallock II), 20, 283
Hallock, John Franklin, 26, 177, 202, 286
Hallock, John Morse, 156, 172, 182, 218–19
Hallock, Joseph Newton, 44–45, 49, 68, 154, 157, 286
Hallock, Laura (wife of Charles Hallock), 43, 47
Hallock, Lucius H., 14, 86, 286; *Hallock Genealogy*, 146, 281, 297n6
Hallock, Mabel, 126
Hallock, Marietta (Terry) (1st wife of Halsey Hallock), 45, 53–55, 59, 64; photo of, 46; death of, 64–65, 67, 285
Hallock, Mary Cristina (daughter of Herman Hallock), 27, 32, 285
Hallock, Mary (daughter of Zerubabel Hallock I), 283
Hallock, Mary Aldrich (1st wife of Zachariah Hallock II), 22–23, 284
Hallock, Mary Owen, 284

Hallock, Matilda Keziah, 31
Hallock, Minnie, cover photo caption, n.p., 287
Hallock, Olive, 126
Hallock, Peter (mythological founder), 9, 13–14, 281
Hallock, Peter (second cousin of Zerubabel Hallock II), 17
Hallock, Richard, 20, 283, 291n33
Hallock, Thomas, 15, 282
Hallock, William A, "A Brief Sketch of the Hallock Ancestry," 13
Hallock, William I (son of Peter Hallock), 14–15, 281–82; land of, 15–16
Hallock, William II (son of William Hallock I), 18, 282
Hallock, Zachariah I (Capt.), 18–19, 21, 23–24, 42, 48, 79, 135, 144, 153, 226, 254, 283–84; account book, 48, 224; farming practices, 129–30; inventory after death, 49, 129, 222, 227, 235; land purchases, 20–23, 172; map of purchases, 22
Hallock, Zachariah II, 18, 22–24, 26, 30–32, 34, 49–50, 133, 235, 284
Hallock, Zachariah III, 8, 26, 30–33, 63, 85, 156, 204
Hallock, Zachariah IV, 156
Hallock, Zerubabel I, 15–18, 282–83
Hallock, Zerubabel II, 15–16, 18–20, 47, 283–84
Hallock, Zerubabel III, 20, 157, 283
Hallockville Museum Farm, 5, 133, 137, 143, 146, 171, 175, 196, 215, 234, 236, 227, 247, 281, 304n14; founding of, 250, 274–76
Hallockville name, 22–23, 153
Hallockville neighborhood, 1820 map, 22
Halsey, Jerusha, 30
Halsey, Mary, 30
Halsey, Stephen, 30
Halsey, Thomas, 30, 253
Halsey. *See* Hallock, Halsey
Harris, Thomas, 57, 179, 207

Harvey, Rose, 278, 280
Hawkins, Irene (Wells), 241
Hawkins, Jedediah, 72
hay, 131, 133–36, 142, 205
hay rake, 136
heating, central, 116
hedgerows, 139, 236
Helms, M. Elma Terry, 260–61, 268
Hicks, William, 179–80
high school. *See* Riverhead High School
holidays. *See* Christmas, Easter, Fourth of July
Homestead Barn, 10; changes to 141–43; photo of, 12
Homestead. *See* Hallock Homestead
house exchange, 31–32
House of Refuge, New York City, 177–79
Howell, Chauncy, 103
Howell, Christiana. *See* Hallock, Christiana
Howell, Elizabeth A., 121, 126
Howell, Jonathan, 19
Howell, Margaret, 282
Howell, Richard, 15–17, 20, 281–82
Howell, W. H., Mr. and Mrs., 121
Howell, "Widow," 281–82
Hübel, Joseph and Josephina, 147, 303n34
Hudson, Charles, 156
Hudson, Samuel, 157
Hudson, Samuel Terry, 136–37, 157, 173, 215. *See also* cultivator, bicycle
Hudson-Sydlowski House, 33, 137, 157, 173, 215, 275–76
Humel, George Frederick, *Heritage*, 50–51
Hunt, Harrison, 56
hunting, 222

ice skating, 43
icehouse, 145
Independence Day. *See* Fourth of July
Indian pudding, 223–25
infare, 43, 196–97

inheritance practices. *See under* Puritan roots
Irish immigrants, 102, 141, 156, 171, 177, 269
Irishman's jack knife, story of, 113
Iron Pier, 111, 143, 167–68, 215

Jacob's Hill, 170, 308n2
Jacquemin-de-Zouval, G. A. Gaston, 69
Jamesport (James Port), 3, 31, 42, 110–11, 131–32, 156, 191, 202, 235, 265
Jamesport church, 16, 191
Jamesport Meeting House. *See* Jamesport church
Jamesport Methodist Camp Meeting, 110–11, 192–93
Jell-O, 209–10
Jessup, Ruth (wife of Noah Youngs), 186, 235
jetties, 264–65
Jewish immigrants, 37–38
Jones, Cora Reeve, 293n34
Jones, William Sidney, 164
July 4. *See* Fourth of July

Kemp, Robert "Father," 191
KeySpan Energy Corporation, 277–78
KeySpan property, 276–78
kitchen. *See* Hallock Homestead, kitchen
Klu Klux Klan, 181
Kujawaski family, 277

Ladies Mutual Benefit Society, 117, 121
lambs, 222, 241, 244–45
language, local dialect, 11–13
Lang, Henry, 179
lard, 234
Larkin Club, 213
laundry, 144, 303n27
Laurel. *See* Franklinville
lawsuits, 91, 93–95, 99–100, 299n41

Lee, Frederick, 24
Levon Corporation, 262–65
liberty poles, 56, 103
LILCO. *See* Long Island Lighting Company
Lincoln, Abraham: election of 1864, 58, 85; vote for, 19, 38, 50, 53, 58, 103, 253
Listen to the Sound, 277
Literary Society. *See* Sound Avenue Literary Society
Long Island Farm Bureau, 278
Long Island Lighting Company (LILCO), 265–68, 273–77
Long Island Rail Road, 31, 43, 133–34, 152, 156, 255, 279
Long Island Sound, 20, 111, 130, 167, 174, 262–63, 277–78
Luce boys, 218
Luce, Almina (wife of Caleb Hallock), 181–82
Luce, Abraham (Capt.), 292n9
Luce, Abraham (Rev.), 19, 177, 181–82
Luce, Chloe, 181–82
Luce, Eleazer, 19
Luce, Hallock, 56, 99
Luce, John T., 37, 177
Luce, Lulu, 121
Luce, Sarah E., 183; drawing of church, 56
Luce's Landing, 23, 167
Lyceum Club of Sound Avenue, 112

Manning, David J., 277
manure, 129–31, 149, 205
marriage, frequent remarriage, 23. *See also* weddings
Mattituck, 1, 15, 42, 147, 169, 191, 216, 222
Mattituck church, 16–17
Mattituck Creek, 30, 111, 158, 202
McDermott, William L., 140, 167, 219
meat, 225–28, 238

mechanization, farm, 140–41
meeting houses. *See* Aquebogue church, Jamesport church, Mattituck church
menhaden fishing, 23, 129
Miles, Zachariah, 177
militia, 19, 21, 23–24, 30, 201, 284
mills, 77, 222, 235
molasses, 222–23, 225, 230, 235, 240; cookies, 225, 310n13
Moore, Stuart Hull, Mrs., 243
Morell, George, 140
Morell, William, 140
Mosley, Fred, 161
music, 12, 182, 212, 232, 246; in Hallock family, 45, 48, 72. *See also* Hallock, Bessie; Hallock, Daniel

names used in book, 8
naming conventions, 12
National Freedman's Relief Association, 80
nativism, 142
Naugles barn, 10, 171, 275
Naugles, George (father), 141–41, 171
Naugles, George (son), 174–75
Negroes. *See* persons of color
New England, connections with, 10–11, 15, 17, 41, 48, 156, 185, 203, 207, 223, 229
New Haven, CT, 23–24, 62, 196
New York City, 31, 38, 45, 48, 63, 98, 110, 132, 172, 174, 177, 180, 192, 284, 293n34; market for produce, 43, 133–34, 139, 156
New York Times, sensationalism in, 96–97
Niagara Falls, 72
Nois, Innocence, 179
North Fork dialect. *See* language
Northville. *See* Sound Avenue (community)
Northville (name), 2
Northville Academy, 97, 107, 68, 134, 154, 157–59; bell of, 304n14

Northville church. *See* Sound Avenue Church
Northville Dock Corporation, 262
Northville schools. *See* schools
nuclear power plants, proposed, 265–68, 276–77

orchards, 231
Old Folks Concerts, 191
Old Landing Club, 216
Old Nell, 148, 244
organs, 48, 78. *See also* Sound Avenue church, organ
Orient Point, 191
Osman, Esther, 283
outhouse, 144, 149, 296n15
oysters, 78, 165, 213, 229, 236

Paris Exposition (1889), 137
parties, 180, 196–98, 201, 206–13, 241
Pataki, George, 277
Peconic Bay, 43, 111, 130, 191, 213, 228, 235
Peconic Land Trust, 278
peddlers, 38, 79, 82, 292n17
Perkins store, 79
Perkins, J. Henry, 63
persons of color, 37, 80, 102, 147–48, 171, 177–83, 212, 215
Peter Tumbledown's Outfit, 145–46
Philadelphia Centennial Exposition (1876), 79, 81, 138, 179
pier. *See* Iron Pier
pies, 123–24, 173, 229–33, 238, 242
pightle, 11–12
pigs, 149, 207, 221–22, 224, 232, 234, 238; importance of, 149, 226
Pike, Otis, 264
Pikes Peak gold rush, 39, 293n25
Platt, Matilda, 70, 296n12
plumbing, indoor, 116, 169
Polish immigrants, 140–41, 147, 170–76, 210, 215, 242, 316
pond. *See* Hallock Pond

Pope, Henry, 40, 147, 303n31
Pope, Thomas "Tommy," 8, 38–40, 45, 147, 187, 228, 233
porches, 116, 121, 169
post office, 151
potato beetle, 136
potato cellar, 131, 142–43
potatoes, 131, 133–36, 139, 142–43, 149, 171, 224–25, 238, 261
Potter, Rev., 87
Practical Cook Book, 118, 230–31
Price, Benjamin D., 159
Prime, Nathaniel, *History of Long Island*, 151
Prohibition, 174–75
puddings, 230–31, 234
Puritan roots, cultural impact of, 6, 9–13, 16, 83–85, 142, 161, 165, 185, 201–203, 202, 210–11, 217, 289n2, 305n35; inheritance practices (expectation to provide farms to sons), 16, 20–22, 24–25, 30, 44, 48, 55
Puritans, 14–15; great migration of, 9; meeting houses, 16–17

Quakers, 16
quilts and quilting, 148. *See also* Sound Avenue Quilters

race, stock car (1909), 169–70
racing, horse, 218–19
racism, 177–82, 207, 212
railroad. *See* Long Island Rail Road
reapers 132–33, 136–37, 165, 302n12
Receipts and Reminiscenses. See Evans, Estelle
recycling, 148–49
Reeve, Allen, 46
Reeve, Charles, 39–40
Reeve, D. W., 179, 205
Reeve, Isaac, 178
Reeve, John R., 175–76
Reeve, Keziah (wife of Noah Youngs), 186

religion, 9–10, 12, 16–17, 37–38, 41, 51, 161, 173, 181, 212
Remer, Marie Wells, 241, 296n9
Republican party, 53, 58, 63, 125, 253
revivals, 17, 41, 49, 87, 97–98, 192
Revolutionary War. *See* American Revolution
RFD. *See* rural free delivery
Riverhead (downtown), 26, 42–43, 48, 77–78, 82, 92, 107, 132, 134, 148, 166, 169, 180–81, 189–95, 198, 207–208, 222, 232, 269
Riverhead (town), 2–3, 15–16, 18, 23, 140–42, 154, 160, 168–69, 175–77, 182, 242; in Civil War, 53, 57, 58–61; town board of, 261–62, 264–65, 267–68, 274, 278
Riverhead church, 185, 204
Riverhead Harbor Industrial Park, 262–65
Riverhead High School. *See under* schools
Riverhead Savings Bank, 183
Riverhead Town Agricultural Society, 134, 136–38, 164–66, 173, 209, 213, 255
Riverhead Union School. *See under* schools
RLHA club, 120
Romanowsky, Alex, 171
roof, raising the, 32–33
rum-running, 174–75, 243
runaways, 178
rural free delivery (RFD) route, 1–2, 166–67

Salburg, Solomon, 37–38
Sam porridge, 222, 224
Sammy. *See* Tuthill, Samuel
samp, 222–24, 238
sand mining, 264–65
sarsaparilla, 235–36
sausage, 221, 226, 236
Saxton, Brewster Hampton, 96–97

scandals: District 10 school, 97–98; Terry-Downs, 98–101; Wright, 88–97
scarlet fever, 46–47, 54
schools: books, 36–37; budgets, 36–37; District 10, 34, 36, 68, 161–62; District 10 scandal, 97–98; District 11, 33–37, 39, 106–107, 156, 162; Northville elementary (after 1911), 250, 261; Northville Union School, first building (1911) 162–64; Northville Union School, second building (1916), 164; Riverhead High School, 107; Riverhead Union School, 107; teacher salaries, 292n15
seafood, 228–30
seasonal cooking, 237–38
self-sufficiency. *See* sustainability
Semerjian, George, 262
serenades, 99, 197–98
sewing machine, 78
sex, lack of premarital, 186
Sharper's Hill, 191
Shaw, Joseph, 305n25
Shea, Barbara, 4
sheep, 18, 130, 139–40, 143, 222, 225, 234, 239, 241. *See also* lambs
Shenandoah, USS, 248
shoemaker shop, 21, 144, 237
Shoreham nuclear plant, 265, 276
Silas (fiddler), 212
Sing Sing prison, 179
singing schools, 43, 48
Sirrine, Lillian Hallock, 240
Skidmore, George H., 160, 164
slavery, 18–19, 50, 85, 177, 290n25, 291n27
sleigh riding, 116, 165, 195, 213
Smith, Allen M., 265
Smithtown, NY, 43–44, 81, 147, 156, 286, 303n33
smokehouse, 144, 146, 149, 226–27, 231
soap, 113

Society for the Preservation of Long Island Antiquities (Preservation Long Island), 274
Sons of Temperance, 118
Sound Avenue (community) (Northville), 1, 274; cultural conservatism, 1, 4, 11–13, 26, 50–51, 102–103, 151; descriptions, 3–4, 83, 96, 151–54, 158, 176; divisive nature of, 83, 95–96, 175; final years, 280; homogeneity of, 5, 102, 170–71, 176; industrial development in, 262–68, 273–74; litigiousness of, 93, 95, 97–99; map of, 3; mobility, 155–56; modernity, 157, 183; name of, 2–3, 166–67, 280; population and demographics, 102, 126–27, 154, 170–71; prosperity, 151–52, 156, 176, 183; scandals, 88–101
Sound Avenue (incorporated village), 2, 175–76
Sound Avenue (road): descriptions, 3–4; history, 1, 25–27; name 1–2; threats to, 273–74
Sound Avenue Cemetery, 304n11
Sound Avenue (Northville) church, 41, 44, 68, 185, 206, 211–12, 251; attempt to burn, 86–87; burned, 90–92, 100; Civil War troubles, 57, 85; first building (1831), 26–27; first building, drawing of, 56; final years, 280; fourth building (1904), 160–61, 305n25; melodeon controversy, 83–84, 103; organ smashing, 85–86, 95–96, 103; origins, 16–18, 25–27, 102; organs, 97, 120, 159, 161, 169; revivals, 41, 49, 87, 97–98; rewriting history, 100, 103; scandals, 88–101; second building (1859), 84–85, 157, 213; second building, drawing of, 56; third building (1881), 159–60
Sound Avenue Grange. *See* Grange

Sound Avenue Hall (Grange Hall), 26–27, 85, 126, 134, 163, 165, 262, 280
Sound Avenue Literary Society, 107, 122, 181
Sound Avenue Quilters, 260–62, 267
Sound Avenue Scenic and Historic Corridor, 274
Sound, Long Island. *See* Long Island Sound
Southold (hamlet), 54, 59, 156, 187, 190–91, 262
Southold (town), 2, 33, 45, 59, 114, 102, 253, 281–82; early history, 9–10, 13–16, 18, 289n3
Southold cemetery, 65, 69
Southold Savings Bank, 183
Spencer, Herbert, 179
Stackpole, Mary, 242
standard of living, 78–79
Steeple Church. *See* Aquebogue church
Stefans, John, 279
stoves, 35, 76–77, 115–16, 123, 144, 149, 185, 217, 233–35, 259, 266, 268–69
Straight College (New Orleans), 80
strawberries, 231–33; festival, 232; shortcake, 232–33
Success (name), 2, 151–52
suet, 234
Suffolk County Agricultural Society, 134
Suffolk County Fair, 110, 134, 138, 140
Suffolk County Temperance Society, 190
sugar, 222–23, 225
Sunday school, 119, 203–204, 206, 213, 218, 258, 268, 286
sustainability, 148–49, 221
Sweezy, Elizabeth, 283
Sweezy, Richard, 17, 19–20
Sydlowski, John, 173, 240

Talladega College (Alabama), 80
Talmage, Henry R., 168, 216

telephone service, 115, 168, 170
temperance movement, 48–50; 97–98, 118–19, 134, 157, 175, 234–35, 238, 243, 247, 254, 258; conventions, 98, 190; meetings, 41, 47, 49, 88, 164, 190, 201, 212–13
tenant house, 146, 148
tennis club, 112
Terry, Charles (brother of Marietta Hallock), 59
Terry, Daniel C., 207, 208
Terry, Edward "Eddie," 147
Terry, Elizabeth "Lizzie" (wife of Leslie Terry), 209
Terry, Frances, 198
Terry, George Mitchell, 207, 212, 299n51; as head trustee in Wright affair, 90, 93–94; Terry-Downs scandal, 97–101
Terry, George Mitchell, Mrs., 99–100
Terry, Henrietta (wife of Herbert T. Wells), 118, 188, 208, 209, 214, 225, 227–28, 232, 234; courtship and marriage of, 188–99; photo of, 184; wedding dress, 183–84
Terry, King Hiram Jesse, 54
Terry, Leslie, 188
Terry, Marietta A. (Halsey Hallock's first wife). *See* Hallock, Marietta
Terry, Mary Hallock Luce, 225
Thanksgiving, 41, 44, 201, 203, 206–10, 227–28, 270
That (person of color), 37
Thompson, Jack, 147
threshing barn, 142–43
threshing machines, 136–37
tobacco, 178; abstinence from, 50, 247, 251
tractors, 140–41, 239–40
Trubisz family, 210, 240, 277
Trubisz Little House, 119, 275
Trubisz Sprout House, 275
Trubisz, Anthony, 210
Trubisz, Charles, 172, 174
Trump, Donald, 277
Trust for Public Land, 278

Index | 331

Trykoski, John and Annie, 172–73
turkeys, 207–10, 222, 227–28
Tuthill, Cuyler B., 223, 235–36
Tuthill, Daniel, 188
Tuthill, Eliza, 187, 198, 205, 207–208
Tuthill, Epher, 118
Tuthill, George H., 46, 54
Tuthill, James (founder of Jamesport), 31
Tuthill, James Harvey (Riverhead lawyer), 58
Tuthill, James Henry (nephew of Arminda Hallock), 62–63
Tuthill, Nathan, 72
Tuthill, Olin P., 217
Tuthill, Polly, 31
Tuthill, Samuel "Sammy," 8, 87, 90–92, 94, 97, 99, 137–38, 140, 154, 177, 179–80, 183, 187, 190, 197–98, 201, 205, 207–208, 210, 212–13, 232, 287
Tuthill, Sherwood, 190, 206
Tyte, Arthur M., 182

Union School. *See under* schools, Riverhead Union School and Northville Union School

Vail Music Hall, 191
Vail store, 79, 225
Van de Wetering, Jack and Peter, 313n4
Van Tuyl store, 78
vegetables, 82, 93, 149, 209, 229, 236–38
vote, 253; for (or against) Lincoln, 6, 38, 50, 53, 58, 85, 103, 182, 255; women's right to, 124–25, 176; against alcohol, 175

Wacker, Ronnie, interview of Ella Hallock, 265–66
War of 1812, local battle, 23–24
Wardle, Clarence B., 213, 297n15
Warner, Charles H., 168
washhouse, 55, 113, 144, 303n27

WCTU. *See* Woman's Christian Temperance Union
weddings, 43, 45, 47, 69–71, 74, 99, 108, 120, 174, 185–98, 201, 205, 208–209, 233, 245–46, 258, 293n41
Wells, Addison, 107, 152, 252
Wells, Amanda (wife of Daniel Hallock). *See* Hallock, Amanda
Wells, Benjamin F., 58
Wells, Betsy, 68, 117
Wells, Caleb, 205
Wells, Charles (Halsey Hallock's son-in-law), 62, 74, 108, 113–15, 135, 218–19
Wells, Clarence, 147
Wells, Elisha, 179; Civil War service, 61–62
Wells, Eliza. *See* Tuthill, Eliza
Wells, Ella Estelle, 199
Wells, Elsie Anna, 299n50, 299n54, 309n24
Wells, Emilie J. (wife of Halsey Hallock). *See* Hallock, Emilie J.
Wells, Henrietta. *See* Terry, Henrietta
Wells, Herbert, 100, 118, 183, 188–99, 214, 226, 234
Wells, Horace J., 137, 140, 147
Wells, James H., 92, 208
Wells, John Horace, 136, 170, 193, 197
Wells, John O., 84
Wells, John H., 178
Wells, Joseph, 208
Wells, Joshua, 43, 136
Wells, Joshua Minor, 68, 197
Wells, Justine, 270–71
Wells, Laura. *See* Hallock, Laura
Wells, Leslie Terry, 166, 199
Wells, Mary Hallock. *See* Downs, Mary
Wells, Salem, 187, 212, 307n69
Wells, William, 15
West Farm, 24–25, 31–32, 34, 284
Westhampton Beach, 192
wheat, 82, 131, 134–36, 222

Whitaker, Epher, 14, 54
Wick, Steve, 3
Williams, John and Viola, 148
Williamson, David, 296
Williamson, James Harvey, 207
Wines, Abigail, 270
Wines, Richard, 4, 7, 53, 116, 212, 238, 269–70, 291n27, 294n4, 299n51, 305n27
Wines, Virginia, 127, 252, 257, 268–69, 271, 281; *Albums*, xv–xvi, 289n1, 317
Withall, Mary, 179
Whitman, Walt, 65
Woman's Christian Temperance Union (WCTU), 118–19, 175, 243, 258
Women's Home Missionary Union, 118
women's organizations, 117–22
women's suffrage, 119, 125, 242
wood (cordwood), 34, 82, 139–40, 145, 204–205, 208
woodhouse, 144–46
Woodhull, John A., 70
World War I, 127
Wright, Henry Newman, 88–98, 103, 159

Yale College, 45, 68, 157
yellow journalism, 91, 96–97
York, PA, 109–10, 133, 156, 285, 297n26
Young Ladies' Busy Workers Society, 118, 230
Young People's Society of Christian Endeavor (YPSCE), 107, 119–20, 213, 218–19
Young, Charles, Mr. & Mrs., 122
Young, Henry Wilson, 34, 162, 229–30, 305n28, 310n27
Young, James, 19
Young, Lois (Wells), xvi, 62, 108, 219, 240, 247, 269, 295n27, 305n
Young, Nicholas, 42
Youngs, Albert, 31
Youngs, Arminda. *See* Hallock, Arminda
Youngs, Brister and Zipporah (born enslaved), 19, 177
Youngs, Brister, Jr. (son of enslaved), 177
Youngs, Christopher (vicar of Southwold England), 14
Youngs, Daniel (deacon), 19, 25
Youngs, Daniel (minister of Aquebogue church), 18–19, 25
Youngs, Hannah (wife of Zachariah Hallock I). *See* Hallock, Hannah
Youngs, John (first minister of Southold), 10, 14–15
Youngs, John (grandfather of Emilie Hallock), 295n2
Youngs, John (grandson of enslaved), 177
Youngs, Noah, 186, 204, 213
Youngs, Phillis (daughter-in-law of enslaved), 177
Youngs, Polly, 31
Youngs, Rufus, 230
YPSCE. *See* Young People's Society of Christian Endeavor